Women and Religious Traditions

Women and Religious Traditions

Edited by

Leona M. Anderson
and Pamela Dickey Young

OXFORD
UNIVERSITY PRESS

1904 ❖ 2004

100 YEARS OF
CANADIAN PUBLISHING

OXFORD
UNIVERSITY PRESS

70 Wynford Drive, Don Mills, Ontario M3C 1J9
www.oup.com/ca

Oxford University Press is a department of the University of Oxford.
It furthers the University's objective of excellence in research, scholarship,
and education by publishing worldwide in

Oxford New York

Auckland Bangkok Buenos Aires Cape Town Chennai
Dar es Salaam Delhi Hong Kong Istanbul Karachi Kolkata
Kuala Lumpur Madrid Melbourne Mexico City Mumbai Nairobi
São Paulo Shanghai Taipei Tokyo Toronto

Oxford is a trade mark of Oxford University Press
in the UK and in certain other countries

Published in Canada
by Oxford University Press

National Library of Canada Cataloguing in Publication Data

Women and religious traditions / edited by Leona M. Anderson and Pamela Dickey Young.

Includes bibliographical references and index.
ISBN 0-19-541754-2

1. Women and religion.   2. Women—religious aspects.
I. Anderson, Leona M., 1951–   II. Young, Pamela Dickey, 1955–

Cover Design: Brett J. Miller
Cover Image: Jed & Kaoru Share / Getty Images

1 2 3 4 - 07 06 05 04
This book is printed on permanent (acid-free) paper ∞.
Printed in Canada

CONTENTS

CONTRIBUTORS

Leona M. Anderson is Professor in the Department of Religious Studies at the University of Regina where she teaches Hinduism. Her research interests include Sanskrit literature, classical and popular Hinduism, Hindu ritual, and iconography. Her publications include *The Vasantotsava: Indian Spring Festival, Texts and Contexts* (New Delhi: 1993/4) and *The Ganesh Festival* (51 mins. colour video (VHS) documentary, 1999). Dr Anderson received her Ph.D. in Religious Studies from McMaster University and she studied Sanskrit at the Deccan College, Pune.

L. Clarke is Assistant Professor of the History of Religion and Islam at the Department of Religion, Concordia University, Montréal. Among her recent publications are: 'Hijáb According to the Hadíth: Text and Interpretation' in *Veiling and Dress Codes in the Diaspora Muslim Women's Voices* (Scholars' Press, 2002); 'The Rise and Fall of Esoterism (taqiyah) in Shiite Islam' in *Mystical Thought in Islam: New Research in Historiography, Law, Sufism and Philosophy in Honor of Hermann Landolt* (London: B. Tauris & Ismaili Institute of London, 2002); and 'The Universe Alive: Nature in the Masnaví of Jalál al-Dín Rúmí' in *Thinking about the Environment: Our Debt to the Classical and Medieval Past* edited by T. Robinson (Lanham, MD: Rowman & Littlefield, 2002).

Monique Dumais, professor in theology and ethics at the Université du Québec à Rimouski is the author of *Les droits des femme* (1992), *Femmes et pauvreté* (1998), *Choisir la confiance* (2001) published by Médiaspaul, Montréal. In 1976, she was a co-founder of the collective L'autre Parole.

Jacoba Kuikman is Department Head and Associate Professor of Religious Studies at Campion College at the University of Regina. She is currently working on a manuscript on Jewish-Christian relations in the first century. Her work focuses on women's studies, women in Judaism, fundamentalism, and the Holocaust.

Dawn Martin-Hill is Mohawk, Wolf Clan from and currently living at Six Nations of the Grand River. She is a mother of four children ages four to twenty. She holds a Ph.D. in cultural anthropology and is one of the original founders and currently Academic Director of the Indigenous Studies Program at McMaster University. Dawn's research interests include: Indigenous knowledge and Aboriginal women, decolonization of women and Indigenous Medicine and philosophy in contemporary practices. Central to her research interests is the establishment of Indigenous Knowledge as an intellectual discipline for Aboriginal scholars. Dawn is the recipient of the Canada US Fulbright Award, Niagara Chapter of Native Women's 'Achievement Award', and Recognition Award by the Aboriginal Community of Hamilton. Her research has been sponsored by Social Science and Humanities Research Council, Canada Arts Council, Assembly of First Nations, Aboriginal Healing Foundation, and National Aboriginal Health Organization.

Eva K. Neumaier has published extensively in academic journals and is the author of several books, her latest being *The All-Creating Sovereign Mind, the Motherly Buddha. A Translation of the Kun-byed rgyal-po'I mdo*. She taught at the Ludwig Maximilian University of Munich, the University of Calgary, the University of North Carolina, Chapel Hill, and the University of Alberta from where she recently retired. Her areas of specialization include Tibetan Buddhism, folk religion and history, as well as women in Buddhism.

Lee D. Rainey teaches Chinese studies at Memorial University of Newfoundland. Her research focuses on classical Chinese philosophy and she has written articles on the concept of '*qi*', the Confucian philosophy of music, and the hidden language of the women of Hunan.

Pamela Dickey Young is Professor and Head of the Department of Religious Studies at Queen's University, Kingston, Ontario. Her most recent book is *Recreating the Church: Communities of Eros* (Trinity Press International, 2000). Her current research focuses on sexuality in the Christian tradition.

INTRODUCTION

Leona M. Anderson and Pamela Dickey Young

Many years ago, upon discovering how underrepresented women are in texts for the study of religious traditions, we decided to begin developing and teaching courses in Women and Religion. In the usual portrayals of religion, we found, women are notable by their absence. *Women and Religious Traditions* seeks to remedy that. It has grown out of our experience in teaching, and is intended to be a resource for instruction in both World Religions, and Women and Religion.

This book is divided into chapters that each explore an important religious tradition. Each could be used separately as an introduction to the issues concerning women and their roles within the tradition discussed. In addition, we have included two thought-provoking case studies to encourage and foster discussion of specific situations. We hope that *Women and Religious Traditions* will provide an introduction to the subject that will furnish the reader with enough background and direction to encourage further work on women in religious traditions.

Having said that, it is not self-evident how *religion* ought to be defined. Even the scholarly construction of specific religious traditions is a particularly westernized idea. It grows out of a Christian-informed imperialistic view that often classifies religions in categories that best fit Christianity and only more tenuously fit other traditions. Despite this, there is much usefulness in examining religious traditions and how women are perceived and treated within the structure of those traditions.

Winston L. King (1987, 1995: 285) says that 'Religion is the organization of life around the depth dimensions of experience—varied in form, completeness and clarity in accordance with the environing culture'. The notion of 'depth dimension' is useful here; it allows us to focus our attention on the way 'religious' people conceive of and organize the totality of their world such that these conceptions and organizations provide structure for understanding and responding to the universe. Religions attempt to deal especially with the most puzzling of human questions and predicaments, including issues such as the existence of evil or the inevitability of death, and provide a means to deal with these concerns. Religions provide symbol systems—that is, particular ways to understand and portray what is thought to be Ultimate. Frequently there is a central symbol or symbols—for example, god(s) or goddess(es) or both, nirvana, and the Dao. Religion also often employs myths, poetry, or metaphor, rather than direct description, to evoke the ultimate quality of what it is attempting to embody. Sometimes these symbols, myths, and metaphors are found in sacred texts, sometimes they are passed on through oral traditions. Religion regularly uses rituals as a means to bring the participant into contact with whatever is conceived as Ultimate and to hold at bay the chaotic forces of the universe. Often, religions identify sacred places or endow certain objects with sanctity. Historically, religion has been communal; but in the modern western world, at least, people tend more and more to individualize belief and practice in order to deal with this 'depth dimension'.

King also draws attention to the notion of the 'environing culture'. It is important to understand the vast diversity of forms taken by even a single religious tradition over time, in various geographical settings and even in specific individual and/or communal contexts. No 'religion' or religious tradition is a monolith. It is helpful here also if we make a distinction between the 'official' way that religious traditions present themselves and the host of 'unofficial' forms that traditions take. While the 'official' form often dominantly or exclusively presents males in positions of action and authority, there may well be other faces or presentations that understand women as important actors or authority figures.

Religions often include bodies of mythology. Myth here is understood to function as a vehicle to convey meaning about the world, about our place within the world, and about a particular conception of the Ultimate. Mythology, however, is a complex and polysemic system of constructing meaning, and individual myths are continuously reconfigured in response to changing circumstances. We are not, in this volume, engaged in the quest for the 'authentic' version of any particular myth. On the contrary, we are interested in the way myths have privileged male experience in the past, and how, in the present, they are being rewritten to include female experience.

The category 'women' is not itself an uncontested one. In feminist work there has historically been a distinction drawn between biological sex (male–female) and gender. The latter, gender, is understood to reflect social constructions of ways to act properly based on one's given maleness or femaleness. For many years now, feminist theory has argued that the gender roles that men and women are assigned to play out in their lives are malleable; they are constructed and hence can be reconstructed in other ways. Recently some scholars have begun to argue that not only gender roles, but also sex itself is socially constructed. The fact that we tend to separate males from females as a sorting device and on that basis build whole societies is itself a construction rather than a necessity (Delphy 2001). Of course there are different reproductive roles—but why has so much rested on the difference (even opposition) of those roles, rather than on other biological categories such as eye colour, age, and the like?

In many, perhaps most, religious traditions, sex and gender have been seen as basically synonymous. One is ascribed a certain gender role on the basis of an essentialized view of one's biological sex. Thus one's biological sex becomes the marker for assigning particular gendered religious and moral roles and expectations. Within many religious traditions in the contemporary world there has been some movement on the front of the reconstruction of gender roles, as, for example, the ordination of women in most Protestant Christian churches and in liberal Judaism. Despite this, there has been virtually no recognition of how most religious traditions rely on and employ the supposed 'bedrock' of biological sex to provide categories and concepts on which much doctrine, practice, and belief is based. Nor has there been much recognition of the implications thereof. Thus the whole notion of 'sex' remains highly bifurcated as male and female, and treated as a 'given', whether as a mandate from god or as a general presupposition about the universe. In addition to bifurcation and ossification of the roles, rights, and privileges of men and women, this essentialized stance also influences how religious symbols are seen and interpreted: the 'maleness' of the god of western monotheistic traditions, for example, or the interactions of the gods and goddesses of Hinduism. This leaves unexamined how 'sex' itself is socially constructed and imbued with meaning and cultural import.

In *Women and Religious Traditions*, given the current discussions on sex and gender, we do not assume that the category 'women' is necessarily constructed on a bedrock of biological essentialism. Rather, we use the category of 'women' as a way to pinpoint certain issues in the study of religion that are often neglected. We focus on certain ways of seeing 'women' as a category and explore the implications of religious systems that treat men and women differently. We note that typically men have been ranked higher than women in a variety of ways. We read various religious traditions through the category 'women' to discover and highlight features of these religions that have often been ignored. At the same time, we acknowledge that the term *women* is multivalent and context dependent, and that one cannot speak to or for *all* women.

We assume that patriarchy is evident in many historical times and places and that religious traditions have, for the most part, been permeated by social systems (and have sometimes permeated social systems) with views that not only exalt maleness over femaleness but also mete out societal and religious privileges (for example, wealth, power, and influence) on the basis of male privilege. Patriarchal systems are social systems that elevate males and those roles attached to maleness, over females. Patriarchal systems are those that, to greater or lesser degree, render women's voices and experiences inconsequential and invisible. Patriarchy is not the only form of privilege, however, and is often intertwined with other sorts of privilege that exalt some people and diminish others on the basis of race, class, and sexual orientation.

Due to Rosemary Radford Ruether's (1972) astute analysis of 'dualisms' within Christianity, feminist critics of religion from a very early stage noted the parallel between the way in which the male over female dualism informed the dualism of mind/soul over body/nature in many religious traditions. Thus, feminist analysis of sex and gender within religious traditions began as an analysis of the dualisms that connected men to god (or the Ultimate) as well as to mind and spirit, and women to body and nature. In looking at religious traditions from a feminist perspective, one often is struck by the tendency of religions to view men as closer to whatever is considered important, and women as closer to that which is of lesser value. In Hinduism, for example, men are sometimes considered better equipped for the religious quest, while women are best suited for worldly tasks such as producing children and maintaining the household. In religions such as Christianity and Judaism, men are sometimes conceptualized as closer to God by reason of their masculinity, while women are somewhat removed from God by reason of their femininity. Indeed, many religious traditions view women, and issues associated with women, as problematic. Women are rendered variously as temptresses, deceivers, weak, ignorant, or simply distractions. As such, they are to be controlled, secluded, and sometimes shunned.

We do not think that there is any single convincing explanation for patriarchal privilege. There is no one simple answer to the question of why this privilege arose. In this book we will not attend to the question of why. There are a number of scholarly works that deal with this question, and the jury is still out. Rather, we will attend more to the 'how' of patriarchy—how it has functioned in various religious traditions.

We have asked each author to take a feminist approach to her material, by which we mean that each approaches the material with questions of whether and how a particular tradition (or traditions) has sorted people into gender and sex categories and what that has meant for women in terms of status, roles, power, and so on. Within each tradition there are women who are themselves suspicious of how women have been treated. There are also women who do not see that suspicion as important and who are content to remain within their own tradition without questioning the status and roles of women. The authors have tried to portray this spectrum, taking seriously the integrity of the tradition under discussion and exploring its inner diversities. In *Women and Religious Traditions* we use the term *feminist* broadly to include women in a wide variety of positions that recognize and seek to change the fact that women have been systemically seen and portrayed as inferior to men. We examine some of the ways in which these portrayals of women have had social, political, economic, and religious consequences.

It is important to recognize in this context that feminist methodologies are multiple. Though feminists have in common their concern for the position and status of women, they do not necessarily agree on the manner in which these concerns should be understood or addressed. Feminist methodologies tend to focus on issues of power and the way in which power manifests itself in a given social context, privileging some members and disenfranchising others. They are also attentive to differences and the manner in which differences (be they gender, race, economic, or other forms of difference) are constructed. Feminist methodologies encourage us to question these matters. Students interested in feminist methodology might consult the *Dictionary of Feminist Theories* by Letty Russell and J. Shannon Clarkson, eds (1996). There are also several journals that publish current materials in feminist studies, including the *Journal of Feminist Studies in Religion*.

In *Women and Religious Traditions* we are not exhaustive by any means in our choice of traditions, but we chose those that most often appear in religion courses in North American universities and colleges. The decision to place them in a roughly historical order reflects the manner in which courses on Women and Religion are often taught. Each chapter of the book is organized to deal with several specific topics:

1. History and status of women: Contributors were asked to make some general observations about the history of the tradition and the status and roles of women within it.
2. Texts, rituals, and interpretations: Each chapter contains some information about texts and rituals as they reflect and affect the status of women, though for text-based traditions this information is greater than for traditions that are ritual-based. Our questions in this section include those of interpretation and authority: how are women depicted in the texts and the interpretive tradition; who is considered to be an authoritative interpreter; how does this influence women in the tradition; do women accept these interpretations; and do they interpret their roles differently from the way men interpret them?
3. Symbols and gender: Each chapter addresses the symbols within a

particular religious tradition, and the manner in which symbols are gendered or interpreted in relation to gender. Several of the chapters comment, in this context, on the role of goddess or goddesses within the tradition and of central female figures. They also comment on the ways in which these figures function as symbols and describe various strategies devised by women in these traditions for retrieving and reconceiving these figures so that they can empower women.

4. Sexuality: Each chapter addresses issue of how sexuality is configured and the implications of so doing. Some chapters speak to the question of rituals related to women's sexuality, as, for example, rituals celebrating the birth of females or celebrating first menstruation, first sexual experience, and menopause. Other chapters examine the manner in which heterosexual relationships and same-sex relationships between women are being configured in various religious traditions.

5. Social change: Contributors were asked to explore how the particular tradition they were writing about might promote social change in the status of women.

    a) Official and unofficial roles of women: Questions here include whether women play roles that are not necessarily privileged as 'central' but which make for interesting reinterpretations. Are there lifestyle alternatives for women and, if so, what are they? In this context, several chapters explore the opposition between 'domestic' and 'public' spaces and comment on the impact this distinction has on the religious lives of women. Other chapters comment on the propensity of various traditions to elevate women who support their men and act as guardians of family piety.

    b) Backlash: Each chapter comments on the degree to which there has been backlash against women or whether fundamentalisms have affected women in the tradition. As noted in the Christianity chapter, Letty Russell comments in this regard: "backlash is a powerful counterassault on the rights of women of all colors, men of color, gay, lesbian and bisexual persons, working-class persons, poor persons and other less powerful groups both in the US and abroad" (Russell 1996: 477). Backlash is a topic that has been articulated particularly in the case of the western traditions of Judaism, Christianity, and Islam, but it is also evidenced in some of the other traditions examined in this text.

c) Unique features: Our assumption throughout this volume is that each religious tradition is unique and must be understood as such, and so we asked contributors to describe how these particular features affect women.

REFERENCES

Delphy, Christine. 2001. 'Rethinking Sex and Gender'. *Feminism in the Study of Religion: A Reader.* Ed. Darlene Juschka. New York: Continuum. 411–23.

King, Winston L. 1987, 1995. 'Religion'. *Encyclopedia of Religion.* vol. 12. New York: Macmillan: 282–92.

Ruether, Rosemary Radford. 1972. *Liberation Theology: Human Hope Confronts Christian History and American Power.* New York: Paulist.

Russell, Letty. 1996. 'Practicing Hospitality in a Time of Backlash'. *Theology Today* 52: 476–84.

Russell, Letty M., and J. Shannon Clarkson, eds. 1996. *Dictionary of Feminist Theologies.* Louisville: Westminster John Knox.

CHAPTER 1

≈

WOMEN IN HINDU TRADITIONS

Leona M. Anderson

INTRODUCTION AND OVERVIEW

As almost every textbook on Hinduism will tell you, the term *Hindu* is a modern Western one originating from an older term that described the people living along the Indus River, in the northwest part of the Indian subcontinent. Because Hinduism originated as a geographic designation, there is a lot of confusion as to what exactly it means to be a Hindu. One characteristic of Hinduism is clear, however: it is diverse, and this diversity extends to the status of women within the Hindu fold.

Hinduism is often presented as a total way of life, and within that life there are a multitude of images, ideas, rituals, and traditions. There is no one founder and no one book but many texts that are believed to contain revelation. Hinduism is the most ancient of the living religions, having reached a high state of development from at least 1500 BCE, and it has survived the missionary drive of other religions. Many gods and goddesses populate this tradition and this plurality of deities has made Hinduism more tolerant and accepting of other, non-Hindu beliefs of deity.

Woman's roles in Hinduism differ depending on a number of factors, including region, caste, occupation, and education, so that it is virtually impossible to present an image of woman that is coherent and self-contained. One must, therefore, speak to the question of women in India in a pluralistic fashion, recognizing that there are a number of concerns and clusters of concerns that are relevant. The following chapter seeks to address a select number of these concerns, but it is by no means exhaustive.

BASIC CONCEPTS

The Hindu vision of the world is cyclical, an ever-repeating cycle of births and deaths known as *samsara*, which has no beginning and which repeats itself over long periods of time. The present age is the last stage of the development of the world. Political strife, war, poverty, inflation, and the like characterize this age. Finally, after several more eons, the world will become so degenerate that it will be destroyed and the cycle will repeat itself. Humans undergo a sequence of births and deaths that parallel that of the world. Samsara refers to the cyclical pattern of birth and death undergone by individuals as well as that undergone by the world. In one of the most sacred texts of Hinduism, the *Bhagavad Gītā,* the movement from death to rebirth has been compared to a change of clothing:

> Just as a person casts off worn garments and puts on others that are new, even so does the embodied soul cast off worn out bodies and take on others that are new. (2.22) (Mascaro 1968: 50)

Samsara is not haphazard, but governed by the law of action and reaction, cause and effect, also known as the law of *karma* (literally, action). The doctrine of karma is a doctrine of consequences. As a moral law, it means that every action, every thought, has a result. There are no shortcuts. Individuals are responsible for their actions, not just in one lifetime but over a series of many lifetimes. Our position in this life is determined by our past actions and our current actions will determine our subsequent births. The goal is, first, to attain a better birth by performing morally good actions, and second, to attain *mokṣa* which means release from the cycle of birth and death. Thus, the *Bṛhadāranyaka Upaniṣad* states:

> According as one acts, according as one conducts oneself, so does one become. The doer of good becomes good. The doer of evil becomes evil. (4.3.35–8) (Vyas 1987: 81)

The Paths

There are three paths that serve as general guidelines for the attainment of mokṣa in Hinduism: the path of knowledge, the path of action, and the path of devotion. These paths are not exclusive; a combination of them is common in religious practice. Nor are these paths the only means available to reach the final goal.

The path of knowledge emerges out of the earliest of Hindu texts, the Vedas, especially the Upaniṣads. The basic idea is that knowledge, not just ordinary, discursive knowledge, but intuitive knowledge of truth, will effect *mokṣa.* An important concept in this path is *Brahman,* which is equated with *prāṇa* (breath, life). Brahman permeates the world as salt permeates water (*Chāndogya Upaniṣad* 6.13; Hume: 248). A second term of note is *Ātman,* the individual's innermost self or soul or the universal self. Ascetic discipline assists in the process of detaching oneself from the pursuits of the world and from an interest in one's individual existence.

The religious quest in the Upaniṣads involves realizing the fundamental identity of Brahman and Ātman—the realization that one's essential self transcends individuality, limitation, decay, and death. The realization of this truth wins the disciple liberation or mokṣa. Although there are a few women acknowledged as authorities, this path restricted rather than liberated women. Woman came to be associated with *māyā* or the world of appearance, equated with the physical world of multiplicity and thus opposed to the spiritual realm of unity. The goal of the path of knowledge is to transcend māyā.

The second path is the path of action. The emphasis on this path is *dharma,* which is often understood as action in accordance with certain social and ritual standards. The details of these standards have been gradually worked out from the Brāhmaṇas (*c.* 500 BCE) through the later texts including the Dharmaśāstras (law books). This latter is a large body of teachings on various social and ritual responsibilities. There is also according to this path the notion that one should act selflessly.

The rules of dharma encompass rules of caste behaviour. Caste is a complicated system of social stratification. One way to look at it is as a set of occupational categories, though this is more an ideal than a reality. Each caste in modern India encompasses a large range of occupations and social statuses. A typical formulation of caste has it that there are four castes, including the *Brahmins,* whose duties are purely religious. Brahmins are mandated to study and teach. They are the custodians of all knowledge that the Veda—a large corpus of literature considered to contain revelation—implies and as such they are held in high esteem. The second caste is the *Kṣatriya* or warrior caste, whose primary duty is the protection of their subjects. At the head of this caste stands the king. The third caste is the *Vaiśya*. This caste includes merchants, bankers, and landowners. They have the moral responsibility of wealth. Finally there are the *Śūdras,* or labourers, whose duties are service to the other three castes. Within this system there are a seemingly infinite number of subdivisions. Outside of this system, there are a large number of people who typically perform menial tasks and are referred to as outcastes or, as Mahatma Gandhi called them, the Harijans (people of god).

In addition to caste, there are also laid out certain stages of life or *āśramas.* These include student, householder (who is devoted to marriage and the production of children), forest-dweller, and renouncer. The latter two stages involve removing oneself from the world and ultimately becoming a wandering renouncer, living on alms alone, abandoning one's caste identity and all of one's possessions.

The impact of these two systems of stratification on the position and status of women is significant. Both situate women within clear structural boundaries and assign to them clear roles. The caste system, as described above, accords the Brahmin a high status. Overall, this system can be described as *brahmanic patriarchy,* a term which emphasizes that both brahmanism and patriarchy are key features that must be taken into consideration when analyzing the position of women in India (Chakravarty 1993: 580 in Omvedt: 187). Women's dharma was to be chaste, loyal, and subservient, especially to their husbands, but their essential nature was one of disturbing, uncontrolled sexuality and it needed to be controlled by men who were their protectors and guardians (Omvedt: 187). This control included bans on widow remarriage, seclusion of women in the household, and assigning to women the religious duty of devotion to their husbands as gods (Omvedt: 187). Further, there was a kind of caste-patriarchal bargain: high-caste women accepted a life of subordination and seclusion in exchange for a share in the status and wealth of their husbands (Omvedt: 187). Evidence of the continuing pervasiveness of brahmanic authority is to be found in a 4 October 2002 decision of the Supreme Court in Delhi, which stated that non-Brahmins can also perform religious ceremonies and work as temple priests, but only if they are well-versed in relevant rituals (Bhatnagar 2002).

The āśrama system assigned a high value to the second stage of life, especially for women. Women fulfilled their spiritual destiny through marriage and they were mandated to treat their husbands as gods. Women came to be identified with the domestic realm and the protection of that realm, and widows, because they no longer contributed to the domestic sphere, were treated with contempt. At the same time that women were increasingly excluded from the public realm they were assigned the role of guardian of tradition. Women were generally excluded from the last stage of the āśrama system, renunciation, because they were not permitted to travel alone. And more often than not, they were refused entry to ascetic religious orders.

The final path is the path of *bhakti* (devotion). Emphasis in this path is the development of a strong personal attachment to a personal deity. Worship, love, and devotion are key concepts, though the relationship between deity and devotee tends not to be a relationship of equals. This path encourages a 'feminine' mode of religiosity, including surrender and subservience to the deity. Male and female devotees alike are encouraged to relate to male deities as would female devotees. The cultivation of worship, love, and devotion contributes positively to the pantheon of gods and goddesses that populate the Hindu imagination. The multiplicity of goddesses who are worshipped in this context provides us with insight into the conception of the feminine in Hindu culture. The goddess is identified with the physical world, nature, orderliness, and intensity. The earth, for example, is depicted as a goddess, as is the Indian subcontinent. From the seventh to the twelfth centuries CE, various devotional movements gained in prominence and more religious options became open to women, who began to frequent temples, lead devotional groups, and compose songs. A significant number of female devotees became acknowledged as saints.

During the colonial period and in response to the European presence in India, the Vedic tradition and brahmanism were reinterpreted. Many institutions, including *sati* (widow-burning) and child marriage, came under attack as the reformers of the nineteenth and twentieth centuries, responding to the European critique of Hinduism, sought to rid it of elements they believed did not represent its core. As this core came to be further defined, it became clear that patriarchy and brahmanism were to play a major role. The sanctity of marriage, bans on widow remarriage, and the authority of husbands in the home all came to be seen as central to Hinduism. As Omvedt argues in her review of Uma Chakravarty's book *Rewriting History:*

> A new brahmanism was being constructed, which saw brahmans as the elite representatives of a broader 'Hindu community' whose characteristics included the extension of the devoted wife, the pativrata to all castes. (Omvedt 2000)

Women emerged as freedom fighters and supporters of the cause for independence. Independence was achieved in 1947, and article 15 of the Indian constitution prohibits discrimination against any citizen on the grounds of religion, race, caste, sex, or place of birth. Despite this prohibition, the status of women remains below that of men. One could well argue that nationalism alongside colonialism reified the idea of the Hindu woman who guards the inner sanctum of Hindu culture. Both the nationalist and the colonialist agenda resonate with traditional patriarchal control of women. The current rise in popularity of Hindu fundamentalist movements has resulted in an even more rigid interpretation of the roles of male and female.

Today, there are numerous important Hindu women in the spotlight, and researchers focusing on women's issues, including religion, are on the increase. The status of women in India today is complex and multifaceted; caste, region, class, and relative wealth all contribute to this complexity. Further, the experience of Hindu women cannot easily be homologized to the Western experience, especially to Western feminism. As Suma Chitnis argues, feminist anger in the West is in part tied to the hypocrisy of a culture that stresses the value of equality and individual freedom, but nevertheless denies social and legislative equality to women. This concept of equality does not have much relation to the highly stratified society of India (Chitnis cited in Humes: 145). Today's Hindu women are active in their attempts to reformulate tradition in the context of modernity and change. There are numerous centres and institutes that focus on women's issues, including for example, the Centre for Women's Development Studies in New Delhi, a research centre that works towards the realization of women's equality and development in all spheres of life. The press *Kali for Women* is important to mention in this regard because it primarily publishes primarily current feminist material. Though efforts on this front are ongoing, the status of women in India remains largely below that of men.

TEXTS AND INTERPRETATIONS

In Hinduism, several texts are considered sacred. However, unlike many other religions, no one text is considered authoritative. Rather, there is a large corpus of literature known as the Vedas, which are considered to contain revelation. There are, further, a number of other books that have been composed from very early times through to modernity that are relevant to our study and are considered, to one degree or another, sacred. In this huge body of literature, we find a large amount of material pertaining to the role of women and to the feminine aspects of Hinduism, but this material is penned, of course, by patriarchal hands. Hindu texts are excellent sources on the status of women in particular times and at particular places in the tradition, as viewed through male eyes. Though there are many texts in Hinduism, the focus here is the Veda (and its component parts), the law books, and the Epics.

Veda and the Vedic Age
The earliest texts in Hinduism are known as the Vedas and they are said to be composed by the Āryans, a group of Indo-European-speaking peoples who appear in the subcontinent about 1500 BCE. *Veda* means 'knowledge' and these texts are considered to be repositories of all knowledge. The Vedas are often divided into three categories: the hymn books, the earliest of which is the Ṛg *Veda*; the Brāhmaṇas, or priestly manuals; and the Upaniṣads and Āraṇyakas, which are more philosophical. The first category contains hymns of praise to various deities, the majority of which are male and include, for example, the warrior god, Indra; the god of fire, Agni; and the intoxicating god, Soma. The Brāhmaṇas are almost completely preoccupied with sacrifice and tell us much about the details, history, and symbolic significance of this practice. The Brāhmaṇas reflect a stabilization of culture; priests dominate and a pattern of elaborate sacrifice emerges. The Upaniṣads and Āraṇyakas are usually dated at around the sixth century BCE and reflect a period of questioning of the efficacy of sacrificial ritual and a critique of the status quo.

Vedic religion is life affirming, and religious rituals focused on achieving the basic goals of life: progeny, prosperity, longevity, and preservation. Sacrifices were performed for good crops and for progeny, among other goals. Women played a crucial role by producing children and maintaining family life. A primary player in this tradition is the householder and his wife, who are required to perform certain sacrificial ceremonies throughout their lifetimes. The *Śatapatha Brāhmaṇa (SB)* and the *Taittirīya Brāhmaṇa (TB)* make this necessity perfectly clear: 'a ritual without a wife is not a ritual' (*TB* 2.2.2.6; see also *SB* 1.3.1.12). Some scholars suggest that women during this period enjoyed a certain amount of freedom and were esteemed in the religious milieu of the Vedas.[1] Katherine Young, for example, calls attention to the role of women as necessary partners in sacrifice as well as to her essential role in bearing children (1999: 60f.). Even in this era, however, it is clear that the role of husband and father was dominant.

The sacrificer's wife plays an important cooperative role in the rituals, but she may not participate if she is sonless. The *Aitareya Brāhmaṇa* states that one's wife should be looked on as one's mother insofar as through her one is reborn again in the form of one's son (vii.13). Also in the *Aitareya Brāhmaṇa,* we read: 'A wife is a comrade, a daughter a misery, and a son a light in the highest heaven.' Commenting on the role of the sacrificer's wife, Stephanie W. Jamison (1996: 53) writes, 'One of the wife's most important roles is that of injecting sexuality into the perfect, ordered world of the ritual. One of the abiding concerns of all Vedic rituals, no matter what else they are directed toward, is fertility, the increase of prosperity through the generation of offspring and cattle, and the assurance of good pasturage and crops through abundant rain.' Here then, fertility and food are of abiding concern. The texts make so many overlapping connections between wives, food, sex (fertility), and hospitality that it is difficult to summarize their implications.

Female imagery, especially goddess imagery, is not dominant in the Vedic texts although it has been argued that the great goddesses of later Hinduism are found, in seed form, in the Vedas. There are goddesses, to be sure, but they tend to be minor deities. The imagery of the cow is also frequent, and goddesses are often likened to cows or mothers of cows that yield milk for the benefit of the world, blessings being bestowed through her udder. Womb imagery is also common, and the four corners of the fire pan found in sacrificial ritual are said to be shaped like nipples (*SB* VI.5.2.16–19). There is also agricultural symbolism as, for example, the plowing and planting of crops, which is related to female fecundity.

A central myth of the Brāhmaṇas is that of Prajāpati exhausting himself in creating the world, and a primary aim of the sacrifice is to restore or reinvigorate Prajāpati. Later on, this theme is found with respect to goddesses such as Durgā and Kālī, who receive blood offerings that restore the vital, creative power that becomes exhausted when they create.

Another important myth in the Brāhmaṇas is the eternal struggle between the gods (*devas*) and the demons (*asuras*). In this context, the goddess Vāc (intelligible speech) plays a significant role. In the *Śatapatha Brāhmaṇa*, the gods purchase the Soma from the demons with Vāc. In this same text, Vāc is equated with the earth but tries to escape the gods by hiding in the sap of the plants and the trees (IV.6.9.16). There are hints also that it is through Vāc, or in pairing with her, that Prajāpati creates. Speech is the intermediary between humans and gods and this intermediary function is especially evident when the gods offer Vāc up in sacrifice. It is also clear that Vāc's actions have eternally paradigmatic effects when it comes to women. That is, women are the way they are because in the beginning Vāc did this or that. One myth of Vāc's creation is thus:

> Both the gods and asuras were born of Prajāpati. The gods inherited mind, sacrifice (*yajña*) and heaven and the asuras inherited speech (Vāc) and the earth. The sacrifice, thinking that he could lure Vāc into the camp of the gods because she was a woman, beckoned to her but she disdained him. So it is, we are told, that a woman, when beckoned, at first disdains man. He tried again and Vāc just nodded 'no.' When he tried a third time, Vāc said 'come to me'. Thereupon the gods warned him that women are alluring, and advised him to make her come to him. Finally Vāc approached him and when she did, the gods enveloped her completely in fire, making her into an offering of the gods. So it was that the asuras were deprived of speech. (*SB* IV.6.9.16)

Vāc also has the capacity to create havoc when she is upset. Sometimes she turns into a lioness and is only calmed when she is promised all offerings (*SB* III.5.1.13–22).

Another goddess who is fairly significant in this context is Nirṛti. The devas and the asuras are separated into opposing camps; the devas have access to the sacrifice, and the asuras do not but they are constantly trying to get a share. Nirṛti is allied with the asuras, or at least she is clearly seen as a being that seeks to have a share of the sacrifice and to disrupt it. She represents all those things that sacrifice seeks to avoid or insure against, including death, sickness, chaos, and injury. She embodies, as it were, the asuras and those forces that would destroy or diminish the beneficial effects of the sacrifice.

Upaniṣads

The Upaniṣads are basically philosophical texts that emphasize the relationship between student and teacher. Most of the teachers are men, but there are women, such as Gargi, who appear as authoritative in these texts. The Upaniṣads privilege the idea of renouncing the world and tend to place a lower priority on worldly concerns such as long life, progeny, and so on.

Because the Upaniṣads emphasize renunciation, an ideal that is usually unavailable to women for various reasons, the status of women tended to decline from that of the earlier period where they played a role in the sacrifice. The world of impermanence came to be identified as an obstacle to the attainment of mokṣa and, at the same time, the world became increasingly associated with women. By association, women came to be considered a source of bondage. There are Upaniṣads dedicated exclusively to the goddess, including, for example, the *Devī Upaniṣad*. In these texts the gods glorify the goddess and seek refuge in her. However, these texts appear much later in the tradition, from the ninth century onwards.

If women were central to the family-oriented religion of the early Veda, their situation soon changed. The importance of producing sons grew and women became silent and invisible in all but those rituals aimed at producing pregnancy. Women were gradually restricted in their public participation in religion at the same time that their roles in the domestic realm became rigidly controlled. Institutions such as child marriage, purdah (veiling and seclusion of women), and the prohibition of widow remarriage crept into the tradition, and the study of the Veda fell almost exclusively to males. In the context of their domestic duties, women were encouraged to develop a capacity for sacrifice. Scholars such as Katherine Young argue that self-sacrifice is essentially a feminine mode of religion in Hinduism (1999: 75), a mode related to female subservience and male dominance.

The Laws of Manu

Regulations governing morality in Hinduism tend to be context specific and dependent, for example, on caste, stage of life, region, custom, and tradition. However, the legal tradition as represented in texts known as the Dharmaśāstras, or law books, is notable for its influence on the status of women. In particular, *The Laws of Manu* is a pivotal text for the subordination and mistreatment of women in Hinduism. There are few texts so prolifically quoted and profoundly implicated when it comes to the position of women. The authority of *The Laws of Manu* was entrenched by the British during the colonial period[2] and it is a contested point. For example, when a statue of Manu was being installed in the Rajasthan high court, protestors burned copies of his text (Kishwar 2000: 3). It is difficult to know whether Manu reflects practice contemporary to him or not. Though it is most likely that Manu writes about how he would have people behave ideally, many of his prescriptions when it comes to women are found elsewhere in the tradition, including in the Epics and other literary works. According to Manu, women are subordinate to their fathers, brothers, and husbands. Manu does not hesitate to subordinate women. He says:

Her father protects (her) in childhood, her husband protects (her) in youth, and her sons protect (her) in old age; a woman is never fit for independence. (ix.3)

Manu mandates women to worship their husbands as if they were gods and he declares that marriage is the supreme mode of female religious fulfillment. Also in Manu we find the seemingly universal notion that women are dangerous (ix 13, 17), and he warns women that disloyalty would bring them all sorts of harm, including being born into the womb of a jackal and tormented by disease for these sins (ix 29–30). Though Manu's authority is contested, a key source of female power is through their husbands and sons (see, for example, Bannerji: 195).

The Epics

There are two major epics in the Hindu tradition, the *Mahābhārata* and the *Rāmāyaṇa*, the first compiled from 400 to 200 BCE and the second from 300 BCE to 300 CE. These texts are narrative in format and subject to numerous versions. As well as relating a basic or frame story, each contains material pertinent to the status of women. Female imagery in these texts tends to be associated with pilgrimage spots including temples, rivers, and lakes. There are no independent great goddesses, and the goddesses that do appear are subject to male authority. Two figures of interest for our study are Draupadī from the *Mahābhārata,* and Sītā from the *Rāmāyaṇa.* Draupadī is a dramatic, rebellious personality, while Sītā never rebels.

The Mahābhārata and Draupadī

The frame story of the *Mahābhārata* revolves around a conflict between two branches of one family, the endearing Pāṇḍava brothers and their followers, and their not-so-endearing cousins, the Kauravas. Draupadī is the beautiful and intelligent wife of the five Pāṇḍava brothers and an interesting figure from the perspective of women. She was won in an archery contest by Arjuna, and afterwards became known as Pañchalī, the wife to all five brothers. To facilitate her marriage to multiple partners, Draupadī is said to have spent one year with each husband.

When Yuddhiṣṭhira, the eldest of the Pāṇḍavas, loses Draupadī in a game of dice, she challenges the assembly. Duryodhana, the winner of the bet, insists that Draupadī is indeed his to do with as he pleases and orders that she be publically disrobed. Furious at this insult to her honour, Draupadī loosens her coiffed hair and vows that she will not knot it again until she has washed it in Duryodhana's blood. As she is disrobed, the more her sari is pulled away the longer it becomes. Draupadī is thus a figure who takes issue with the forces of patriarchy and male power. In a modern story of Draupadī written by

Mahāveta Devī, Draupadī is depicted as a Naxal figure named Dopdi. The text focuses on resistance to hegemonic powers.

A word here must be added on the *Bhagavad Gītā,* or the Song of the Lord, which is included in the *Māhābhārata* but also appears as a separate text of great importance to Hinduism. The *Gītā* is a text that takes up issues of war and power, and hence it is not surprising that the male voice is overwhelmingly dominant. The *Gītā* is almost entirely bereft of the female voice.

The Rāmāyaṇa and Sītā

One of the most pervasive role models for women in the Hindu epics is Sītā, the devoted wife of Rāma and also, in many circles, the ideal women. Sītā is one of the most difficult of the Hindu goddesses/women to portray. She is the heroine of the *Rāmāyaṇa* and the personification of wifely fidelity and purity. Hindu women strive to live up to her example. Brides are commonly blessed with the words 'be like Sītā'. Sītā has no particular identity of her own; she is so completely submissive to her husband, Rāma, that she gives up her very life to protect his honour. Indeed, Sītā refuses independence, refuses to accept life on any other terms than prescribed to her by her position as wife of Rāma, to whom she owes blind obedience. The story of the *Rāmāyaṇa* can be summarized as follows (Shastri):

> Rāma, the eldest son of the king of Ayodhya Daśaratha, wins Sītā in an archery contest. Rāma is forced into exile in the forest, accompanied by Sītā and his brother Lakṣmana. While in the forest, Rāma is lured away by a demon in the form of a golden deer. At Sītā's request, Rāma chases after the deer, and while he is away, the demon Rāvaṇa abducts her. Aided by Sugrīva, the monkey king, his minister, Hanuman, and the monkey army, Rāma besieges Laṅka, defeats Rāvaṇa's armies, kills Rāvaṇa, and brings Sītā back. Upon her rescue, Rāma makes the following surprising statement:
>
> > Lovely One, the ten regions are at thy disposal; I can have nothing more to do with thee! What man of honour would give reign to his passion so far as to permit himself to take back a woman who has dwelt in the house of another? Thou hast been taken into Rāvaṇa's lap and he has cast lustful glances on thee; how can I reclaim thee, I who boast of belonging to an illustrious House? (Chapter 117, 335–6)
>
> Sītā is shocked, but she recovers quickly and retorts:
>
> > Why dost thou address such words to me, O Hero, as a common man addresses an ordinary woman? I swear to thee, O Long-armed Warrior,

that my conduct is worthy of thy respect! If my limbs came into contact
with another's, it was against my will, O Lord, and not through any inclination on my part. (Chapter 118, 336)

She then orders that a funeral pyre be built and throws herself into the
flames. The gods rescue her and she emerges unscathed. Rāma is
crowned king but continues to be plagued by jealous thoughts of Sītā,
and the inhabitants of Ayodhya doubt the purity of Sītā's character
because she lived in the house of another man. Sītā becomes pregnant
and is banished to the forest, where she gives birth to two sons, Lava
and Kuśa.

When Sītā returns to the kingdom with her sons some 15 years
later, she declares her chastity before the assembly that requests the
earth to swallow her up as proof of her purity. Rāma admits that she is
virtuous and begs to be forgiven for abandoning her. The earth breaks
open, and swallows Sītā up.

Throughout all of these ordeals, Sītā retains her composure and
character. Her love for Rāma does not waver, even after she is rejected
by him. She says:

So I, thus well-equipped and of the top rank, well versed in all the
aspects of dharma, O revered one, can I ever be expected to disrespect
my lord when husband is the god for all the women. (Chapter 119,
338–9)

For some, Sītā is such a clear construction of Hindu patriarchy, and Rāma
is such a blatantly typical example of the patriarchal ideal that it is difficult to
imagine why she is so beloved in India. As Linda Hess in 'Rejecting Sītā' puts it:

The specificity of the husband–wife relationship, the relentless reminders of
the husband's superiority, the horrifying abuse inherent in the model of the
husband-lord and the worshipful wife who lives only to guard her purity and
surrender to his will, the sacralizing of the whole arrangement by making the
perpetrator an incarnation of God . . . . (Hess 1999: 8)

Sītā is thus identified as a pure and innocent virtuous woman and an ideal
wife, an image exploited to serve the patriarchal brahmanic system. Her ideal
status links her quite clearly to suffering, and sends the message that a good
Hindu woman should obey her husband without question, even when he subjects her to abuse. Response to this ideal has been mixed. Nabaneeta Dev Sen
rejects Sītā, saying that there is little women in the Epics can do other than get

abducted or rescued, pawned or molested or humiliated in some way or other (1998: 18). Others try to subvert Sītā. Bina Agarwal's 1985 poem begins: 'Sītā speak your side of the story, / We know the other side too well' (quoted in Hess: 17).

At the same time, because the Sītā myth focuses on the subservience of women, it also functions as a vehicle to articulate certain concerns of women (Sen 1998: 18). Women's folk traditions use the myth of Sītā to interpret and give voice to certain day-to-day experiences and problems and to critique more traditional ways of viewing both the Sītā story and the lot of women, especially in rural areas. Here Sītā tends to be portrayed as the one who patiently bears injustice, the typical suffering wife; she is a sorrowful figure, the victim of loneliness and injustice. Major themes here revolve around the most intense moments of insecurity or physical risk in women's lives: Sītā's birth, wedding, abduction, pregnancy, abandonment, and childbearing. Women complain about neglect and the denial of their rights, not about hard work or poverty. This voice of disenchantment and criticism is one that only women can share with Sītā, or Sītā with women.

As Anne Murphy and Shana Sippy tell us, the *Rāmāyaṇa* is a living text, told and retold in ritual and performance traditions not just in India but throughout the world (2000: 17). Here Sītā is a symbol of the oppression of women but also the epitome of female power. Sītā's ordeal by fire is in many ways the defining moment in Sītā's life and in her relationship with her husband. It is here that she proves her strength and her virtue. It is here that she emerges as a powerful Śaktī (Murphy and Sippy 2000: 20).

One might also cite the Lakshmi Mukti program in Maharashtra, which emphasizes that husbands who keep their wives economically dependent and powerless in the family cannot hope to get a fair deal with government. This campaign tried to empower women with land rights, arguing that the curse of Sītā stayed with them (Kishwar 1997b: 26). Kishwar tells us that the purpose of the Lakshmi Mukti program was to see that no modern-day Sītā would ever have to suffer the fate of Rāma's Sītā because she had nothing to call her own. By transferring land to their wives, village men were paying off 'a long overdue debt' to Sītā (Kishwar 1997b: 27).

SYMBOLS

One of Hinduism's most appealing characteristics is its richness in female symbolism. The ubiquity of female imagery is evidenced, for example, in the multitude of goddesses that populate Hindu texts and Hindu ritual practice. There are probably as many goddesses in Hinduism as there are gods, though this is not always the way in which Hinduism is presented. To be sure, there

are a significant number of male deities, but these male deities do not dominate the female deities—at least not entirely. The goddesses are intriguing to
the student of Hinduism for a number of reasons. First, their sheer number is
staggering; the traditions of Judaism, Islam, Christianity, and even Buddhism
pale in comparison. No other living religious tradition displays such an
ancient, continuous diverse history of goddess worship. Second, the goddesses
of Hinduism offer an interesting counterpoint to other traditions that are
goddess-challenged. Because much of the work on goddesses in the Western
world focuses on the past as a central source of meaning, the goddesses of
Hinduism are important as contemporary examples of 'living' goddess traditions. Finally, the goddesses are noticeably diverse and complex, and each one
is unique, and this tends to put to rest the myth of the one-dimensional mother
goddess. It is important to note at the outset that though goddesses are venerated by literally millions of Hindus, male and female, there is no necessary
parallel between the status of women and that of female divinities in
Hinduism, though many would like this to be so. What these figures do point
out is how the female personality at the divine level and the distribution of
power in that realm is formulated, and this does not generally correspond to
the human level.

It is interesting to note also that Hindu India continues to produce and
worship female figures. Still, the goddesses in even the earliest of texts are
patriarchal attempts to describe desired behaviour or envisioned roles of
women in various capacities. Hindu goddesses are conceptualized not from the
vantage point of women but rather from a predominantly male perspective.

One recurring paradigm would have us accept that there are two types of
goddesses, or one goddess with two sides: goddesses who nourish and protect,
and goddesses who are fearful and destructive.[3] In the first category we find
goddesses whose primary modus is to create and nurture life. These goddesses
respond to prayers for safe childbirth, sons, and prosperity. These nurturing
and auspicious goddesses are almost always controlled by male gods or shel-
tered by them as, for example, by marriage. These goddesses are safe and
domesticated, protective and nurturing, and their powers are adjudicated by
social and cultural norms. High-ranking goddesses are mothers, cows, and the
providers of sustenance.

Śrī-Lakṣmī, the consort of Viṣṇu, for example, is associated with riches and
abundance at the family and state level. She is a goddess of fertility and purity,
a model wife and obedient servant of her husband. She is often depicted as
devoutly and eternally massaging Viṣṇu's feet while he sleeps at the end of the
cosmic cycle of creation. Another example of this type of goddess is Sītā, mentioned above, the exemplary wife of Rāma in the *Rāmāyaṇa*, who is willing to
sacrifice everything, including herself.

In opposition to these goddesses, there are goddesses who are ambivalent, dangerous, and sometimes erotic. Goddesses of this latter type devour one's essence, play non-feminine, martial roles, and are called upon in times of crisis such as epidemics, warfare, and famine. These threatening figures are generally unmarried, but if they are married they dominate their consorts. These goddesses are often conceived as sexually threatening figures and they are exemplified as killers of their demon lovers or goddesses who dance on their lovers' corpses. Durgā, for example, beheads the demon Mahiṣa, and Kālī dances uncontrollably on Śiva's corpse (Kinsley 1986: 116f.). Chinnamastā is another example of a goddess of this type. Chinnamastā is depicted as headless, feeding herself and others with her lifeblood as she stands on top of a copulating couple. In fulfilling her role as sustainer and maintainer of life, she has exhausted and destroyed herself. According to David Kinsley, goddesses of this type are often tamed by marriage:

> A central point of the South Indian myths about Durgā and Mahiṣa is that any sexual association with the goddess is dangerous and that before her sexuality can be rendered safe she must be dominated by, made subservient to, defeated by, or humiliated by a male. (Kinsley 1986: 115)

To subdue Kālī on the battlefield, Śiva takes the form of an infant, and Kālī picks him up and nurses him. When this fails to soothe him, she dances until he becomes delighted and calm.

O'Flaherty argues further that the Hindu female cannot be simultaneously erotic and maternal (O'Flaherty 1973: 102, 111) and Madhu Kishwar notes that Indian men are trained to fear the wrath of non-consort goddess figures and revere consort goddesses. Further, she says, similarly a woman who rises above being sexually accessible, consort of none, nor in search of a consort, tends to command tremendous awe and reverence (Kishwar 1997c: 25).

The goddess emphasizes symbiosis, the interconnections that nurture life and sustain it, and as such she is a powerful force that inhabits and permeates all things. In Hinduism, the goddess is envisioned sometimes as the entire cosmos, a great all-encompassing, living being. She is present everywhere, from the gods to each blade of grass. At dissolution she is said to withdraw the world into her womb and then to exist as the seed of the universe—until the next creation, when she grows and blossoms forth. As a spider weaves its web, the goddess creates the universe out of her own body. The mountains are her bones, rivers her veins, trees her body hair, the sun and moon her eyes. Thus, the goddess connects all spheres of reality. She is a mediator, and devotion to her focuses on the improvement of life in this world. She is a great healer with the cooling effect of healing waters. She is nourishment, the food of the earth, and no one is denied her blessings. The immanence of the goddess is rooted in everyday subsistence—and this is one basis for the feminist position.

EARLY GODDESSES

Compared to the Indus Valley civilization and the later traditions of Hinduism, the early Vedas contain surprisingly few goddesses, and those that do appear play comparatively minor roles, though there are certain parallels between the goddesses in the early Vedic literature and later goddesses, including Śrī, Sārasvatī, and Vāc. Early Vedic religion is dominated by male deities such as the warrior god, Indra, and the god of fire, Agni. The goddesses of the Vedas are often associated with the human and natural world and as such they evidence its complexity and orderliness. In this context, we can cite Pṛthvī, the goddess of the earth; Usas, the dawn; Rātrī, the night; Nirṛti, decay and corruption; Sārasvatī, the river; Vāc, speech; and Śrī, prosperity.

Śaktism

Both Śaktism and Tantra arose during the sixth century CE. Śaktī refers to female power, the creative force of the universe, and the energizing power behind all male deities. In Śaktā traditions, the female principle is regarded as the supreme deity and the life-giving power of the universe. Although individual Śaktis are generally categorized according to association with either Śiva or Viṣṇu, they do not seem to be helped or hindered by their presence or lack thereof. Śaktis have a propensity to violence, but their battles are both necessary and worthy of praise. On more than one occasion, Śaktī rescues a god who has been overcome by a demon. Though she is the recipient of worship, she is also greatly feared (see Kinsley 1986: 124–5). Without his Śaktī, who is known as Pārvatī, Śiva is powerless and inert. Further, there are a number of Śaktī texts, including Śaktī purāṇas, which contain information on Śaktī worship, including pūjā, donations, meditations, and pilgrimages to Śaktā Pīṭhas (sacred sites).

Saundaryalaharī

The *Saundaryalaharī*, a text composed *c.* 1000 CE, conceives of the universe as animated and controlled by feminine power. In it, we find an example of the notion that Śiva can act only when he is united with Śaktī. On his own, he is unable to stir (v. 1). The goddess is supreme and the text describes her in detail starting with her diadem and down through the separate parts of her body, ending with her feet and a prayer that the poet may drink the water in which they are bathed. Here too, the universe is said to be created by her from a speck of dust, but Śiva shatters it and uses it to dust himself as with ashes (v. 2). From the closing and opening of her eyes the earth is dissolved and created (v. 24).

Yoni

A pervasive feminine symbol in Hindu ritual and mythology is the yoni, or female genital organ. Śiva's penis or liṅga and the goddess's vagina are common motifs in Hindu temples and in Hindu iconography. The yoni symbolizes female creativity, the power of life-giving force. Typically the yoni is depicted as smallish against the backdrop of the usually huge liṅga.

One of the most important goddess temples is at Kamakhya, which is revered as the most potent of all Śaktī sites. It is unique in that it enshrines no image of the goddess. In a corner of a cave within the temple, there is a block of stone with a yoni imprinted on it. The yoni is moistened by water dripping from a spring within the cave, and devotees touch it and leave offerings of flowers and leaves upon it. Once a year, during the goddess' menses, the temple is closed for three days; on the fourth day, the doors are opened and pilgrims are allowed in. It is said that during those three days, the spring water that keeps the yoni moist turns a pale red colour. Priests wipe the yoni clean, and the cloths they use are prized by pilgrims who believe them to have great powers.

SEXUALITY

The varieties of Hindu views on sexuality can only be understood within the cultural context of India, especially in the case of kinship and marriage structures. The control of women's sexuality in Hinduism, as in other traditions, is intimately linked to notions of purity, virginity, and sexual loyalty. 'Women are not to have any independent sexuality outside of the context of marriage' (Bannerji: 197). The practice of child-marriage underscores their lack of control over their own sexuality. The chaste wife, on the other hand, should be attractive and always ready for her husband's pleasure (Bannerji: 198).

It is also the case that notions of sexual liberation that originate in the West cannot be easily transplanted on Indian soil, where community takes precedence over individuality. Despite this, there are certain features of Hinduism that might be understood to challenge traditional gender roles.

Androgynes

One such feature, not uncommon in Hindu mythology and iconography, is the androgyne. The most common androgyne is the Ardhanārīśvara, or the lord (iśvara) who is half woman. This image is usually understood in relationship to the deity Śiva and his Śaktī, or female power. The image is ancient; extant examples date from the middle of the first century CE (Goldberg: 26). The figure is easily identified: its right half is male and the left half is female. Like androgynous images elsewhere, the Ardhanārīśvara expresses male attitudes toward females. It is a male construction, and Śaktī functions here as wife, the active energy behind the male deity Śiva. The male side is dominant; for example, when he chants the Veda, she smiles (Goldberg: 99). We have little data on how this figure is perceived by women (Goldberg: 133).

Androgynes are sometimes understood as symbols of equality and balance. Philosophically, Ardhanārīśvara can be understood as representing the eternal unity of male and female principles, the non-duality of Śiva and Śaktī. The image functions as a devotional device to aid worshippers (Goldberg: 11) who seek self-realization of their inner male and female principles. At the same time, the image often distorts the male–female relationship (O'Flaherty 1973: 284). They are male images, not female images. In an interesting comment in this regard, O'Flaherty says:

> Most ancient Indian androgynes are primarily male—men who can have babies as women do . . . on the other hand, it does not happen that some woman or goddess suddenly finds herself endowed with a phallus, or, to her surprise and ours, becomes able to produce children all by herself. (O'Flaherty 1980: 29)

O'Flaherty suggests that androgynes are often associated with fears of loss of power and virility:

> . . . all these myths lend themselves to the psychological interpretation that a man transformed into a women is a man suffering from impotence. (O'Flaherty 1973: 308)

Gender Ambiguity

In the tantric tradition in particular, individuals are perceived as composed of both male and female principles. The primary deity in Tantra, Śiva, is envisioned as both male (Śiva) and female (Śaktī), and most of the male gods in Hinduism are conceptualized as incomplete without their feminine counterpart, their Śaktī. In Hindu mythology transformations of male deities into females is not uncommon. For example, Viṣṇu transforms himself into the beautiful woman Mohinī in order to win back the nectar of immortality (amṛta) from the demons who have stolen it, and Kṛṣṇa takes on a female form to destroy a demon. In some Hindu myths a male deity takes on a female form specifically to experience sexual relations with another man, and at the Jagannatha temple in Orissa Balabhadra, the ascetic elder brother of the deity Jagannatha, is homosexually seduced by a transvestite (Nanda: 22). Male transvestitism among the sākhibhāva (worshippers of Viṣṇu) seems to be the norm and sometimes devotees imitate female behaviour simulating Rādhā (Kṛṣṇa's lover) in order to worship Kṛṣṇa. These latter sometimes simulate menstruation, they also may engage in sexual acts with men as acts of devotion, and some devotees even castrate themselves in order to more nearly approximate a female identification with Rādhā (Bullough 1976: 267–8, Kakar 1981, and Spratt 1966: 315 in Nanda: 21). In other tantric sects, religious exercises involve a male devotee simulating a woman in order to realize the woman in himself and to transcend his own self. On the other hand, we note that homosexuality was condemned in the ancient law books including *The Laws of Manu*. This latter text tells us that two men who engage in anal sex lose their caste (xi.68), other law books say that they are reborn impotent.

Hijras

An interesting case of gender ambiguity is the hijras. The term *hijra* refers to a community whose cultural identity is reflected in their renunciation of male sexuality. Hindu culture defines this community as neither men nor women. We may also refer to them as the combined man/woman or an institutionalized third gender (Nanda: 20). Generally hijras dress as women and use the female gender to refer to themselves. They live in households in various districts throughout India.

Many hijras identify themselves with Śiva, himself a somewhat ambiguous figure in the realm of sexuality. Hijras will also identify themselves as wives of Kṛṣṇa, but the experienced gender identity of many of them is as women (Nanda: xix). Some hijras are born hermaphrodites and some undergo an emasculation operation, but it is not at all clear how many hijras comply with either of these conditions. Nanda demonstrates in her study of this community that most members of this community join voluntarily (xx).

Hijras worship at all mother goddess temples and Śiva temples, their major object of devotion is Bahuchara Mata, a version of the Indian mother goddess whose main temple is near Ahmedabad in Gujarat. Every hijra household has a small shrine dedicated to Bahuchara Mata and ideally each should visit her temple. It is in the name of this goddess that hijras shower blessings of fertility and prosperity on newborns and married couples. In Bahuchara's temple, hijras act as temple servants of the mother and bless followers (Nanda: 24). The origin of her worship is as follows:

> Bahachura was a pretty, young maiden in a party of travelers passing through the forest in Gujarat. The party was attacked, and, fearing that they would outrage her modesty, Bahuchara drew her dagger and cut off her breast, offering it to the outlaws in place of her virtues. This act, and her ensuing death, led to Bahuchara's deification and the practice of self-mutilation and sexual

abstinence by her devotees to secure her favor. Bahu is also specially worshipped by childless women in the hope of bearing a child. (summarized
from Nanda: 25)

Emasculation is the major source of ritual power of the hijras (Nanda: 24). It is
the source of their uniqueness and the most authentic way of identifying oneself
as a hijra. Emasculation links the hijras to the two most powerful deities in
Hinduism, Śiva and the mother goddess. It is emasculation that sanctions the
hijras' ritual role as performers at marriages and births (Nanda: 24).

Hijras call into question the basic social categories of gender on which
Indian society is built. This makes them objects of fear, abuse, ridicule, and
sometimes pity. But they are also conceptualized as special, sacred beings who
have achieved their status through ritual transformation (Nanda: 23). While
the west attempts to resolve sexual contradictions and ambiguities by denial or
segregation, Hinduism appears content to allow opposites to confront each
other without resolution and even to grant them a measure of power (Nanda:
23).

Fire

A word here about Deepa Mehta's 1998 film *Fire* seems in order. This film
depicts a friendship and sexual relationship between two middle-class women,
Rādhā and Sītā, married to two brothers in an extended family. The title of
the film itself is evocative in the Hindu context. While it is true that Sītā (whose
name was changed to Nītā in the Hindi version) is not the only role model
for Hindu women, she is a powerful one. The film is about the rejection of the
traditional mould of marriage for women and the same-sex relationship that
these two women, Rādhā and Sītā develop. The film sparked a controversy in
India and was interpreted by some as an all-out attack upon Hindu values. It
was banned in Delhi and Mumbai after violent demonstrations (Naim: 955).
Critics argued that it presented India as homophobic; that its Canadian director, Deepa Mehta, relied heavily upon a Western perception of the plight of
Indian women; and that the film demeaned and caricatured the Hindu family
life. The film's defenders argued that lesbian love was not uncommon in Indian
literature and tradition, but its critics maintained that the film suggested that
same-sex relationships among women are most likely to arise only when they
are treated badly by men (Kishwar 1998: 7) or that female homoeroticism is
'caused' by a denial of women's natural heterosexual desires—that is, a sexually denied heterosexual female becomes a lesbian. Few reviewers considered
the issue in terms of the human condition—that homosexuals, male and
female, could be as helpless and normal in their desire and orientation as any
so-called 'normal' heterosexual. Perhaps that is why at least one lesbian activist

group in Delhi, called 'Ekangi', is reported to have stayed away from taking a public position on the film (Naim: 957).

SOCIAL CHANGE

Just as the roles of women are diverse in the Indian subcontinent, so too are the forces of change. It is not possible to enumerate all of them, but the following sections describe a few.

Bhakti

The bhakti tradition swept the subcontinent from the seventh to the twelfth century CE emphasizing individual and personal spirituality. At its best, bhakti cuts across caste, class, and gender lines and removes many of the barriers of ritual and religious practice established previously. Women in the bhakti tradition become recognized as spiritual leaders and models of devotion. Though it is true that this movement is rooted in brahmanic patriarchy, there is evidence that among certain groups women's religiosity did, in fact, challenge existing norms. This path is not woman-centred, but many women came to be recognized as great devotees, including Mīrabai in the sixteenth century CE (see sidebar), and Andal in the ninth century CE (see sidebar).

Mīrabai (1498–1546)
Leona M. Anderson

Mīrabai is a famous poet-saint of North India. She was born at the height of the bhakti movement and is often cited for breaking some of the barriers of gender. She was the only daughter of a Rajput chieftain in what is today known as Rajashthan. Her mother died when she was a child and she spent much of her childhood in her grandfather's house. Upon the death of her grandfather, her uncle arranged her marriage, but Mīrabai, we are told, took no interest in her earthly spouse, since she believed herself to be married to Lord Kṛṣṇa. When her husband died, Mīrabai was said to have been abused by her conservative male relatives who locked her in her room and tried to poison her. During this time, she became increasingly detached from the world. She began to frequent the temple and converse with the sadhus. Eventually, Mīrabai settled in Vrindavan, and, shortly before her death, she moved to Dwarka.

Mīrabai claims the freedom to worship Kṛṣṇa as her husband. Her songs express her intense love for Kṛṣṇa, which is compared to the love a wife has for her husband. Her poetry focuses on the longing of the individual to merge with the universal, the wife to merge with her husband. She passionately describes the madness of her love and the pain of separation. She borrows many of the traditional clichés of Indian love poetry that express deep, personal emotions. She writes in 'The Wild Woman of the Forests':

> The wild woman of the forests
> Discovered the sweet plums by tasting,
> And brought them to her Lord—
> She who was neither cultured nor lovely,
> She who was filthy in disarrayed clothes,
> She of the lowest castes.
> But the Lord, seeing her heart,
> Took the ruined plums from her hand.
> She saw no difference between low and high,
> Wanting only the milk of his presence.
> Illiterate, she never studied the Teachings—
> A single turn of the chariot's wheel
> Brought her to Knowledge.
> Now she is bound to the Storm Bodied One.
> By gold cords of Love, and wanders his woods.
> Servant Mira says:
> Whoever can love like this will be saved.
> My Master lifts all that is fallen,
> And from the beginning I have been the handmaiden
> Herding cows by his side
>
> (Trans. Jane Hirshfield)

Antal
Michelle Folk

The ninth-century CE Alvar named Antal is the leading female saint of the Śrīvaiṣṇava movement. Her poems, the *'Tiruppavai'*, or 'Sacred Vow of Pavai', and the *'Nacciyar Tirumoli'*, or 'Sacred Song of the Lady', are included in the *Four Thousand Verses of the Alvars*, a text referred to as the *Tamil Veda*.

The Alvars, or 'those who dive deep into the divine', were a group of Vaiṣṇava poet-saints who lived in Tamilnadu in South India during the seventh to tenth centuries CE. The Alvars are believed to be incarnations of the attributes and/or companions of the deity Viṣṇu. Antal is the only female belonging to the Alvar tradition. As such, she is believed to be the incarnation of the goddess Bhūdevī, or Earth, the second consort of Viṣṇu and receives worship accordingly at the temple in her hometown of Śrīvilliputtar. The Antal temple there, built in the thirteenth century CE, houses a manifestation of Viṣṇu, flanked by Antal as his consort, on his right, and the eagle Garuda, the vehicle of Viṣṇu, on his left in its inner sanctum sanctorum.

Antal's poetry focuses on Kṛṣṇa (Dehejia: 4). Sexual longing and union, as expressed in the symbolism of the *gopīs,* or cowherd women, are the means whereby she articulates her religious experience as she visualizes herself as a gopī engaging in dalliances with Kṛṣṇa, using sexual imagery as the metaphor and means to ultimate realization.

It is also interesting to note that the strengthening of brahmanic and patri-archal structures that typified the colonial period and tended to exclude women from the religious sphere contrasts with the present day, when many women are accepted as spiritual leaders (Omvedt 2000: 190).

Manushi

The media is a powerful instrument for social change and the journal *Manushi* has played a prominent role since its inception in 1978 in addressing issues that pertain to women and social change. *Manushi* regularly publishes material relevant to the position of women in Hinduism. According to its mandate, '*Manushi* sees itself as playing a catalytic role towards making our society more just and humane'. In the first issue of *Manushi* in 1978 we read:

> Why *Manushi? Manushi* hopes to provide a medium for women to 'speak out', to raise questions in their own minds, to generate a widespread debate, and move towards a shared understanding—for a common struggle. *Manushi* wants to bring women's organizations and activists in touch with each other, reach women everywhere who want to break out of their passivity and isola-tion, enquire into and re-evaluate the historical experience of women all over the world, counter the systematic distortion of the life, situation and image of women, and trivialization of women's issues carried on by mass-media.

Manushi's editor and founder, Madhu Kishwar, lives in Delhi and is a well-known activist and the author of several books and articles.

Women Priests

Although many changes have taken place in Hindu worship, the priesthood is traditionally a male domain and resistant to change. However, challenges to the male monopoly of the priesthood have existed since at least 1976. Today, schools in different locations teach women to perform rites of worship and marriage, read religious texts, and conduct various types of sacrifice (Manjul 1997: 38). In 1976 in Maharashtra there were only a small number of women trainees, but this number gradually grew, and from 1976 to 1999, more than 7,000 women priests from all castes have graduated (*Women Priests* 2002). Women now train other women. There has been resistance, especially from male priests who resented the competition and argued that Hinduism did not confer upon women the right to perform rituals. Female priests receive a fee, though sometimes not as much as their male counterparts, and they use the income to supplement the family income (Manjul 1997: 39). There are a growing number of women priests in India today and they are gaining steadily in their popularity amongst clients. As one client puts it, 'Women priests do not take shortcuts while performing rituals' ('Women Priests' 2002).

Powerful and Public Women

Given the status of women in Hindu India, it is striking to note that many high-profile remarkable women, especially in the political realm, have periodically dominated the political scene. Indira Gandhi, Jayalalitha, and others come to mind immediately. One explanation for their success is that they possess female power or Śaktī parallel to that of numerous unattached goddesses in villages throughout India. Village myths tell us of ordinary human women who were cheated into marrying untouchables or raped by a local villain, or killed or buried by cruel brothers. Out of such desecrations they rose in fury, and grew in stature to become figures that spanned heaven and earth, with powers of destruction that terrified the village into submission, sacrifice, and worship (Kishwar 1999: 3). Theirs are not myths of descent or avatara, but of ascent from the human into divine form (Ramanujan 1992: 20). 'These non-consort goddesses represent the other side of the beneficent mother, who punishes, afflicting people with plague and pox, and when propitiated, heals the afflicted. They are deities of crisis; they preside over famine, plague, death and madness' (Kishwar 1999: 10). In a 1999 article in *Manushi*, Madhu Kishwar equates modern Indian female politicians, including Mamta Banerjee, Jayalalitha, Mayawati, and Sonia Gandhi, with Durgā (Kishwar 1999: 8–10). Kishwar argues that Indian males, who have difficulty accepting the authority of women as wives, have no difficulty in accepting their mothers as authority figures to whom unconditional deference and respect is shown (Kishwar: 7). Such a family upbringing for most Indian men, combined with the tradition of goddess worship, provides a good training ground for men to be psychologically subservient to strong women who assume charge of the family and act as matriarchs.

Another explanation for the powerful position of certain women in India is simply that they inherit their positions from their husbands. In such circumstances, however, one wonders why male heirs do not inherit, especially when males are so preferred to females. Dipankar Gupta argues that it is easier for a female to gain power after the death of a king or powerful male political figure because sons, unlike daughters or wives, are compared to their fathers. Because women are not supposed to have any attributes relevant to the public sphere, they are not measured for their abilities in that sphere. A female heir does not threaten the male order, but makes it possible to revere the departed male hero, unhindered by comparison. Later, women can and do become leaders in their own right, but their initial ascendance stems from the fact they had charismatic fathers or husbands, as in the case of Indira Gandhi. Thus, Gupta maintains, only when women are considered to have no worthwhile qualities of their own, can they be elevated as pure symbols (Gupta 2001).

While neither of these arguments is particularly convincing in and of itself, both rely on an appeal, at some level, to constructions of power and the manner in which these constructions are accorded religious sanction.

Women's Devotional Songs

Women's folk songs illustrate the perpetual articulation and reinterpretation of women's social and religious roles within oral traditions (Gold 1996: 13). Women sing devotional folk songs about the gods (Śiva, Kṛṣṇa, Sītā, Rādhā) and about their experiences (their husbands, their children, and so on). Some of these songs have women complaining about the habits, behaviour, and character of their husbands. Gold notes that many of these songs depict husband-and-wife exchanges and construct a fictional intimacy that strongly contradicts anything visible or permissible in public; or they reflect on the culturally enforced distance between spouses, and attempt in various ways to mend this state of affairs (16). These songs give voice to women's grievances and subvert the image of women as compliant participants in their oppression. These songs seem to illustrate Himani Bannerji's point that 'women make their idea of god their criticism of man's world' (202).

WOMEN'S OFFICIAL AND UNOFFICIAL ROLES

While male space is public space, women's space in Hinduism tends to be the domestic sphere. In this context, we might speak also of the dichotomy of the spiritual and the material. Women's roles tend to fall into the latter and are often constructed with reference to dharma, or duty that is specific to women. The term most frequently found in this respect is *strīdharma* (literally, the dharma of women). A woman's dharma is to be dependent; she is to sacrifice everything for the well-being and protection of her family and her community, and she is to do so with an attitude of devotion. This is not to say that women in India do not function in public nor that they do not seek mokṣa as a religious goal. Rather, Hindu women often spend most of their time in religiously sanctioned domestic tasks, and they are seen as upholding dharma as a religious goal more often than they are seen as public figures seeking, by any of the traditional means, voice in cultural change or a path to mokṣa.

The role of women has been further complicated in the colonial and post-colonial era. Victorian British gender ideology, based on the 'natural' division of society into male and female spheres, was imposed on Indian public society (Chatterjee 1993: 35–157). Male and female categories became racialized, and private and public domains were altered. Outside in the world, imitation of and adaptation to Western norms was a necessity; but at home, they were tantamount to annihilation of one's very identity (Chatterjee: 121). Women became invested with the duty of preserving the inner sanctity of national culture. It is this dichotomy of the public/private sphere or material/spiritual sphere that is at the heart of the independence movement. 'In demarcating a political position in opposition to colonial rule, Indian nationalists took up the woman's question as a problem of Indian tradition' (119). 'The Anglo-Indian strategy of using women's subordination in India as a handy stick with which to beat back Indian demands for political equality had converted the "woman-question" into a battleground over the political rights of Indians' (Chatterjee 1993: 45). The result was a convenient explanation both for continuing to see women as guardians of conservative traditional Hinduism and for excluding women from public institutions.

Wives and Mothers

Women in Hindu India have been dominantly identified as wives and mothers. In a very immediate way, a Hindu woman is defined by her relationships and in particular by the male upon whom, at any particular moment in her life, she is dependent. The duties of women (their strīdharma) are many, but most involve service to others, especially their husbands and children.

The role of wife is primary, and marriage is arguably the single most important life cycle ritual for women. The ideal wife, the wife who exhibits total devotion to her husband, is known as a pativrata (literally, one who has taken a vow to her husband). One of the most popular pativratas in Hindu mythology is Sāvitrī. Her story is as follows:

> King Aśvapati had no children and when he became old he took a vow and the goddess Sāvitrī appeared before him and granted him a boon. Aśvapati asked for a child. In due course, a female child was born and Aśvapati named

her Sāvitrī in honour of the goddess. The child grew up and eventually the time came for her to be married. Sāvitrī chose Satyavana, a prince cursed to die in a year. When, after the year had expired, Yama, the god of death, came to take him away, Sāvitrī would not let him go and pleaded with Yama to revive him. Sāvitrī's virtue and devotion to her husband eventually won back his life. (*Mahābhārata*: 803f.)

The pativrata vows to protect and serve her husband as if he were a god and to provide him with children (especially sons). Though there are many variations on this theme, generally women are seen as the responsibility of men and their primary roles are to produce sons and facilitate their husbands' salvation through domestic and ritual chores. By surrendering to her husband, by obliterating her own wishes, the ideal wife (especially the upper-caste wife) enhances the qualities of her husband and gains salvation for him and for herself (Omvedt 2000: 188). Manu, for example, makes it clear that

A virtuous wife should constantly serve her husband like a god, even if he behaves badly, freely indulges his lust, and is devoid of any good qualities. Apart [from their husbands], women cannot sacrifice or undertake a vow or fast; it is because a wife obeys her husband that she is exalted in heaven. (115)

Hindu marriages tend to be arranged marriages, not 'love' marriages, and it is uncommon for a woman to remain unmarried in Hindu India. Unmarried women are considered unfortunate creatures and this state reflects badly upon herself and her family. As an unmarried woman, she belongs to no recognized social category (see, for example, Phillimore 1991: 331). Thus, women who do not follow the conventions of conduct that mandate marriage are often deemed dangerous.

Indian women's strategies for building a stable family life are varied, but the foremost concerns are those relating to their children. Women can demand obedience, love, and service from their children in a manner that they cannot from their husbands. As mothers, women are culturally revered. The popularity and power of mother figures such as Ānandamayī Mā (see sidebar) and Ma Nirmālā Devī, who command huge followings among men, demonstrate this cultural reverence (Kishwar 1997c: 25). As Himani Bannerji remarks:

It is not surprising that women frequently try to use the ideology of motherhood to their own advantage. As she is only sexual 'for', rather than 'in' herself, motherhood becomes a woman's preferred vocation in which a physicality of a direct but different sort with young children gives her some satisfaction and keeps the husband at bay within socially approved sanctions. (198–9)

Ānandamayī Mā (1896–1982)
Leona M. Anderson

Up until her death in 1982, Ānandamayī is said to have possessed extraordinarily powerful divine intoxication and the ability to heal, perform miracles, and have prescience. Her body is said to have undergone various
transformations in evidence of her divinity. These spontaneous outbursts
of religious sentiment are common identifying marks of divinity and
include such manifestations as sweating, crying, and hair standing on end.
For example, the sound of religious chanting sometimes rendered her body
stiff; sometimes caused it to lengthen or shrink and contort. She is said
to have taken on the appearance of various goddesses, and is attributed
with the power to heal by touch alone. Ānandamayī was married at an
early age, but when her husband tried to touch her on their wedding night,
he received an electric shock that threw him across the room. He became
her devotee and lived a celibate life thereafter. Ānandamayī did not have
any formal religious training, nor was she initiated by a guru. She travelled
ceaselessly and established a network of ashrams throughout India.
Ānandamayī's international centre is located in Kandhal, where accommo-
dation is available for her devotees.

As you love your own body, so regard everyone as equal to your own body.
When the Supreme Experience supervenes, everyone's service is revealed as
one's own service. Call it a bird, an insect, an animal or a man, call it by any
name you please, one serves one's own Self in every one of them.[1]

[1.] Ānandamayī Mā. *Ananda Varta Quarterly* I/60. <http://www.cosmicharmony.com/Sp/
AnandMM/Mataji.htm#Sublime>

Amrita Basu and Ritu Menon tell us that in India, woman as mother represents the nation or motherland, man as father represents the state. Patriarchal
control is exercised by the paternalistic male rulers of the state who offer protection to its women and children on the assumption that they cannot protect
themselves. The price of this protection is control over women's sexuality (Basu
and Menon 1998 in Goldberg: 169, note 2). If we look closely at the Ārya
Samaj movement in the nineteenth and twentieth centuries, we find that
despite this movement's espousal of women's education and stress on the role

of education in preventing exploitation of women, women were educated to be suitable wives and good Hindu mothers for the newly educated men (Kishwar 1989: 98).

Vratas or Vrats

Austerities known as *vrats,* or vows, play an important role in structuring the religious practice of many Hindu women. The observance of vrats produces good fortune and happiness for the continued sustenance of their families. Sometimes, vows are taken when an obstacle arises, but they are also taken for the safety and security of others and for personal and communal reasons. A single woman might take a vow for a good husband; a married women (as a pativrata), for the welfare and protection of her husband and family; and a widowed women for the continued protection of her family and departed husband. In practice, vrats most often involve a regimen of fasting. Their observance often includes the narration of a legend tracing the origin of the vrat, the devotion to it, and how it is to be performed. The observance of vrats has been linked to ideals of wifeliness; vrat rituals tend to demarcate domestic space as women's space and give this space a religious orientation in the promotion of prosperity and fertility within the household. Vrats are, then, attempts to realize in their day-to-day lives what patriarchy requires of women (Bannerji: 199). At the same time vrats are highly individualistic and they function in the lives of Hindu women in more than one way. Women observe vrats, as Pearson shows, as social events that have elements of religiosity, but they also afford an opportunity for women to interact with other women in the preparation of food, art, and in discourse (Pearson 1996: 200f.).

A popular vow among Indian women in the north is to the goddess Santoshi Mā, a deity popularized in Vijay Sharma's 1975 film *Jai Santoshi Mā* (Hail Santoshi Mā). The film is about the efficacy of making a vow to the goddess Santoshi Mā. After the film's release, the popularity of this vrat and of Santoshi Mā literally swept across North India, where it remains immensely popular.

Widows

There are roughly 30 to 50 million widows in India today and their fate is relatively bleak; this is especially true for those who are uneducated and unprovided for by their husbands or relatives. Traditionally, widows are prohibited from remarriage, from wearing coloured saris (white clothing is prescribed), and from wearing jewellery. Until Independence in 1947, they were mandated to shave their heads. They are often considered to be a burden to the family. Though there is no authoritative religious scripture to support this treatment of widows, often they are shunned by those who believe that widows are somehow responsible for their husband's demise and that their dharma was not strong enough to ensure their husbands' longevity.[4] High-caste widows seem more susceptible to restrictions than low-caste widows (Chen 2002). Many widows relocate to pilgrimage centres, especially Vrindavan, which is sometimes referred to as the City of Widows, and there, they rename themselves *dasi* (servant). The Indian government provides less-fortunate widows a small pension, but most women report that it is difficult to collect.

There are a number of training centres for widows in India today, including Aamar Bari (meaning, My Home) in Vrindavan, which opened in 1998 (Coulter 2002). Organizations such as SEWA (Self-Employed Women's Organization) in Ahmedabad have recently introduced a scheme whereby a woman can insure against her husband's death.

In a report on the 1994 Bangalore Conference on Indian Widows, Marty Chen examines the status of Indian widows and tells us that, although the Hindu Succession Act of 1969 made women eligible to inherit equally with men, widows are still deprived of their legal rights. The inheritance rights of the majority of Indian rural widows are governed by actual practice, and practice can differ from village to village, even in the same region and among the same caste, and conflicts often arise.

Many Indian women are unwilling to remarry after a divorce or widowhood, especially if they have children, because of the risks involved particularly to their relationship with their children (Kishwar 1997c: 24). Mahatma Gandhi believed that a real Hindu widow was a treasure, a gift to humanity (Kishwar 1997c: 25). He further described her as one who had learned to find happiness in suffering, and had accepted suffering as sacred humanity. Not all widows in India are treated badly. Many remain at home and are treated with respect. However, the number of widows that do not receive this treatment is alarming.

Sisters and Brothers: Rakṣabandhana

One of the most popular festivals in North India is the festival of Rakṣabandhana, observed in July or August. *Rakṣa* means protection and *bandhana* means tie or bond. Together, they refer to a bond that unites male and female, most usually brothers and sisters. The ritual is a simple one: sisters place a dot of kumkum on the foreheads of their brothers and then tie a thread around on their brothers' wrists. The thread symbolizes a bond between them: the sister seeks prosperity and good fortune for her brother, and, once accepted, the brother ensures his protection of his sister. Usually brothers offer a gift in return, and it is believed that the thread they wear protects them from all evil. The Hindu mythological story relating to this festival tells us that when the gods suffered a terrible defeat at the hands of the demons and Indra lost his kingdom, Indrānī, his consort, prepared a charm and tied a thread around Indra's wrist. Indra easily defeated the demons by virtue of this thread and won back his kingdom.

Asceticism, Celibacy, and Nakedness

Sexual abstinence in India not only is commonly believed to bestow extraordinary power on human beings, it is also one of the paths to liberation. Indian mythology is replete with stories of sages who practise such extreme asceticism that Indra's throne in the heavens starts shaking. In these cases, the gods usually send some exceedingly attractive nymph to distract the ascetic from his meditation. The message is clear: women impede asceticism (*Śiva Saṁhita* 5.3, Bahadur 1981: 52 in Goldberg: 137).

Asceticism in India is a dominantly male pursuit (Sethi: 13). As a consequence, women who renounce the world are treated with ambiguity at best and mistrust and antagonism at worst. The female renouncer is dangerous because she is not bound to a male; she is outside the pale of social norms. As Sethi puts it:

> By being wedded to a heavenly consort, the renouncer is like a prostitute, the eternal bride . . . who lives her religious life outside male control. In seeking union with God, she is also similar to the widow who displays loyalty to her marital ties even beyond the life of her husband. Her self-denying and ascetic lifestyle is similar to the widow (6). However such autonomy and agency was available only in relation to God. It is highly improbable that this had any significant impact on transforming gender relations among the laity. (14)

Further, the ascetic life is often symbolized by nakedness, and because of the strong social prohibition against nakedness for women, female renouncers are rare. Despite this, there have always been female sādhus (sādhvīs) who have been treated with a great deal of respect. Examples include Madhavi, Sulabha in the Māhābhārata (Van Buitenen 1978, III: 404–5, 410–11; Sorensen 1904: 657); Vedavatī in the *Rāmāyaṇa* (Shastri 1952: v. 3, 420–2); and older female renouncers such as Śabarī and Svayaṁprabhā in the *Rāmāyaṇa* (v. 2,154–8, v. 2, 295–7). There is also evidence, as Rāmaswamy notes in her 1997 work, for the existence of nunneries and nuns in South India. Many of the most revered women in Hindu religious history opted out of sexual relations altogether, as, for example, Mīrabai, Akka Mahādevī (who walked naked), and Lal Ded, all of whom came to be treated as virtual goddesses.

Today, women account for a small percentage of the sādhu (renouncer) population of India. Some sects refuse admission to women, fearing their corrupting influence on the celibates; others, such as the Juna Akhara, are mixed, and a few are all-female. To live the life of the female sādhu (sādhvī) is one of the few ways women can escape the oppressive life of widowhood, and so it is not surprising that a large number of female renouncers take up this life after their husband's death.

FUNDAMENTALISM

Hindu fundamentalism is a political movement, and the relevant political parties are the BJP (Bhāratīya Janatā Party), the RSS (Rāshtrīya Swayaṁsevak Sangh), and the VHP (Viśva Hindā Pariṣad). Together, they make up the *sangh parivar.* In addition there is a range of organizations, institutions, and temple networks from which these parties draw their support. Their ideology is known as Hindutva, and their agenda is to transform India into a Hindu state.

Backlash
An obvious example of backlash is to be found in what is sometimes described as Hindu fundamentalism. However, it is important to note that Hindu fundamentalism is distinct from fundamentalism in Christianity and Islam. Hinduism is a tradition of diversity evidenced by its great many sacred texts, personalities, deities, and paths to the attainment of liberation. Belief in a particular god is not even necessary in some sects of Hinduism. Hence, Hindu fundamentalism is not based on the claim of one true god, one true path to salvation, or a literal reading of sacred text. Indeed, one might argue that Hinduism is one of the most disorganized of religious traditions, and this characteristic makes religious and political solidarity difficult to attain.

An important feature of Hindu fundamentalism is its rejection of the West. Hindus of this persuasion see themselves as defending their tradition against the onslaught of Western colonialism and Western imperialism, against those Western traditions that claim an exclusive belief system and impose that belief system on others. Hindu fundamentalists are not missionaries and do not seek to convert others to their beliefs. Nor do they seek the creation of a Hindu state that prohibits the practice of other religions. The charge of intolerance is often used to discredit this movement, but its intolerance is not comparable to that exhibited periodically by Western religions. What Hindu fundamentalists do seek is to restore what they see as essential to the grandeur of the Hindu tradition, as understood in their particular way.

The impact of this ideology on women is significant. Basically Hindu fundamentalists seek to return women to traditional roles within the family (Robinson: 188). RSS and BJP literature is replete with images of Hindu mother and consort goddesses such as Sītā and Sāvitrī, which invoke the notion of the good Hindu woman who is chaste, subservient to the needs of her family, devout, and pure. The fundamentalist position seems to be that, though women and men are equal, there are essential differences between them (Robinson: 188). As Ratna Kapur and Brenda Crossman remark in *Women and Hindutva*:

> But what is this position to which women are to be returned? The BJP has stated that 'men and women are equal but they are not the same'. Since women are not the same as men, they are not to be treated the same as men. Accordingly, the BJP's policies emphasize the ways in which women are different from men, and in so doing reinforce sexist stereotypes that have contributed to women's inequality. For example, the BJP support policies that emphasize women's roles as mothers and wives (maternal health care), while rejecting policies that go too far beyond these traditional roles for women (compensation for housework). (1994: 42–3)

Hindu women are attracted to fundamentalism because it affirms their roles as mothers, wives, and daughters, and this is the cornerstone of the BJP's position. This movement is appealing to women who support Hindu fundamentalist movements also because it does not reject popular Hindu traditions (Robinson: 196)

There are numerous organizations and roles for women internal to the various fundamentalist political parties, including, for example, the female wing of the RSS, designed to promote 'virtues' such as physical courage and strength and devotional attachment to the ideals of Hindu womanhood. Like the RSS, the women's wing is given physical, intellectual, and spiritual training. Both the BJP and VHP also have special women's organizations. These spaces and roles offered to women in the sangh parivar affirm their social importance, though decision making in the sangh is dominantly male. Women's traditional roles in the family—as mothers, wives, and daughters—are here supported and celebrated (Robinson: 199). Much attention is paid to female members of parliament belonging to the VHP, including Uma Bharati. Female renouncers such as Rithambara also play an important role in the fundamentalist agenda. In keeping with the notion that the holy women are identified as goddesses and referred to as *matajis* (respected mothers; Erndl: 94), several modern female renouncers promote particular political agendas as embodiments of Śakti.

On the devotional front, a primary image is the eight-armed Durgā, a female warrior who presides primarily over women. Important also is the female image of Mother India, an icon that visualizes the country as a great goddess. The Motherland as goddess was important during the independence movement and it continues to provide inspiration, focusing attention on the importance of mothering and reproduction. The image of the Motherland is also that of the reified woman (Sarkar: 51) and it is not without violent over-tones. In this regard, we note Tanika Sarkar's statement that 'the woman in this vision of Hindutva conceives and nurtures her sons as instruments of revenge; she gives birth to masculine violence; the space for this violence is reserved for men. . . .' (284)

Hindu fundamentalism represents a challenge to women's rights as well as to their individuality. Because women in these movements base their platform upon supporting women's traditional roles in family and home (Robinson: 189), they therefore must disagree with the women's movement in India and see it as contrary, selfish, and Western (non-Hindu).

UNIQUE FEATURES

Several features of Hinduism are unique. The following sections focus on four: the manner in which the Indian subcontinent is sacralized by the goddess in the Śaktī Pīṭhas; the practice of satī, or widow burning; and the worship of Durgā and Kālī, both representing a living tradition of the worship of the feminine in the form of the goddess.

The Śaktī Pīṭhas

The Śaktī Pīṭhas are sites in the Indian subcontinent that are believed to be sacralized by the goddess. One myth of the origin of these holy sites is as follows:

> Satī was the daughter of Dakṣa Prajāpati and the consort of Śiva. Dakṣa decided to perform a great sacrifice and he invited all of the gods except Śiva. Satī was insulted by this slight on her husband and attended the sacrifice. She rebuked her father and threw herself into the sacrificial fire. When Śiva dis-covered what had happened, he became enraged and rushed to the sacrifice. Finding the corpse of Satī, he hoisted it over his shoulder and began to dance the Tandava dance, signalling the end of the world. Fearing the worst, Viṣṇu took his cakra and hacked off the corpse of Satī from Śiva's shoulder. The pieces of her body fell to earth and were scattered all over India. (paraphrased from Kinsley 1986: 37–8)

Each place where a piece of Satī's body fell to earth is considered sacred. The number of such sites varies, depending on the source, from 18 to 51. At many of these locations, temples have been erected to indicate the part of the goddess' body that fell there: her breasts, hair, tongue, arms, eyes, feet, brains, nose, lips, chin, and vagina, among others.

Satī

The term *satī* means 'good woman' and it refers to a woman who serves her husband in every way. This term also refers to a woman who immolates herself on the funeral pyre of her husband. The practice of satī is sometimes understood with reference to the above myth of Satī, the consort of Śiva. Sometimes, we are referred to the immolation of Sītā, the wife of Rāma. Chilling images of Sītā's fire ordeal show her smiling serenely as the blaze engulfs her. In more modern times our attention is directed to what are commonly referred to as dowry deaths—where women are set ablaze when their saris 'accidentally' catch fire from contact with a kerosene stove (Courtright 1993: 29).

The British banned satī in 1829 and they were supported in this endeavour by eminent thinkers including Raja Ram Mohan Roy, who argued that this practice was not intrinsic to Hinduism. Modern Indian laws on the subject include the Commission of Satī (Prevention) Act, 1987, which problematically equates satī to suicide and clearly speaks of it as a voluntary act on the part of women.

One of the most famous satīs of recent times is the case of Roop Kanwar in Rajasthan (see, for example, Oldenberg). More recently in 2002 in Madhya Pradesh, the widow Kuttu Bai committed satī. Shrines are built for the worship and glorification of women who have committed satī and some of these shrines are very popular. In the context of the religious life, Courtright has observed that wifely and ascetic duties are sometimes combined in the lives of the *jivit satīmātās* (living satīs) (Courtright 1995: 11). These living satīs are women who declared their intention to commit satī at their husband's pyre, but were prevented by their kinsmen for fear of criminal prosecution. Instead they follow a life of extreme asceticism. While the renouncers or ascetics are believed to be able to transcend sensory perceptions by the heat of their meditation, the satīmātās are kept alive by the heat of their pativrata dharma. Their detachment from the world led Harlan to comment that 'the living satīmātā remains in this world but is no longer of it' (see Courtright 1995: 12).

Whatever the case, the practice of immolating women is deeply troubling, especially from a feminist perspective. John Stratton Hawley (1993: 176) says that feminist treatments of satī are reluctant to reduce it to its lowest common denominator—misogyny—and dismiss it. The subject is difficult and women differ on how to evaluate it. He notes further that 'By thinking about this common, complex object, feminists speak not only to the world but to each other. While they push back the boundaries of external ignorance, they also establish boundaries that divide and clarify their own group' (Hawley: 1993: 176). In this way satī points to both the crudeness and the subtlety with which patriarchal mystification can operate (Hawley 1993: 176).

Durgā

Durgā, the great heroine and warrior queen, is without question one of the most impressive goddesses and also the most popular deities of the Hindu pantheon. Durgā rides a lion into battle and uses her beauty to seduce her victims into a fatal confrontation. Durgā is unmarried and possesses dangerous power. In her most important role, she slays buffalo demon Mahiṣa (Kinsley 1986: 95f.).

The story of Durgā first appears in the sixth-century text, the *Devīmāhātmya,* which tells the story of the genesis of Durgā and her slaying of Mahiṣa. The myth can be summarized as follows:

> The demon Mahiṣa is granted a boon that he will be invincible to all opponents except a woman, and he becomes intoxicated with pride, and challenges and defeats Indra in battle. He then takes over heaven and begins harassing the devotees of the gods. Angry and frustrated at their defeat and inability to avenge themselves, the gods gather and emit their collective energies, out of which emerges a beautiful woman who possesses the multiple characteristics of the gods. She wields eight different weapons, each representing one of the male deities, and she is given a lion as her mode of transportation.
>
> Because Durgā is unprotected by a male deity, Mahiṣa assumes that she is helpless. Durgā challenges Mahiṣa to battle. Ultimately, he transmutes into a buffalo and Durgā decapitates him. On the battlefield, Durgā creates female helpers from herself, most notably Kālī and a group of ferocious goddesses called Matṛkās, or mothers. These goddesses are manifestations of Durgā's fury and they are wild, fierce, and bloodthirsty. (Coburn 1991 and Tewari 1988)

The creation of the goddess occurs as a direct result of a cosmic crisis that the male deities are unable to rectify. The situation calls for a female warrior. As such, Durgā violates the model of the Hindu woman. She is not submissive, she is not subordinated to a male deity, she does not participate in household duties, and her greatest talent lies in what is traditionally held to be a male function: fighting in battle. As an independent warrior, she can stand against any male on the battlefield. Unlike the usual female, Durgā does not lend her power or śaktī to a male consort but rather takes power from the male gods and uses it in her own heroic pursuits. By giving Durgā their inner strength and heat, the gods also surrender any power they have to control her. Although she is created by male gods and does their bidding, she fights without direct male support against male demons, and she always wins. And Durgā does not create male helpers, but female ones.

Durgā's relationship to Mahiṣa has some sexual overtones, though later Sanskrit texts downplay this element or omit it altogether, perhaps because she is the consort of Śiva.

Once the demon has been slain and world order has been restored, Durgā says that she is 'quick to hearken to the pleas of her devotees and that she may be petitioned in times of distress to help those who worship her' (Kandiah 1990: 23). Thus, she becomes a personal saviour as well as a cosmic one.

One of the most important festivals in the Hindu calendar is the autumnal festival of Durgā Pūjā, during which the story of her defeat of the buffalo demon Mahiṣa is recited. The festival lasts for nine days, commemorating the battle, and the tenth day marks Mahiṣa's final defeat. The central image of the festival is Durgā slaying the buffalo demon. She is generally depicted having many arms, each of which bears a weapon, standing on her lion and plunging her trident into the chest of Mahiṣa. Clearly the imagery promotes Durgā's central role as ferocious warrior and maintainer of the cosmic order (Tewari 1988).

The festival coincides with the autumn harvest in North India, and Durgā is considered to be the underlying force of the fertility of the earth. During the worship, the priest anoints the icon of Durgā with water from auspicious sources, including the major holy rivers of India. He also anoints her with agricultural products such as sugar-cane juice and sesame oil, and offers her certain soils that are associated with fertility. Animal sacrifice is a common feature of Durgā worship. Blood replenishes her powers and reinvigorates her.

Durgā is also worshipped in a domestic capacity as the wife of Śiva and the mother of several divine children. Durgā takes on the role of a returning daughter during her festival, and many devotional songs are written to welcome her home or to bid her farewell. These particular songs make no mention of her roles as warrior or cosmic saviour. Instead, she is identified with Pārvatī, the wife of Śiva, and as the daughter of Himālaya and Menā (Coburn 1991). During Durgā Pūjā, it is customary for daughters to return to their home villages, and their arrival is the cause of much celebration. At the end of Durgā Pūjā, the image of the goddess is removed by a truck or other conveyance and carried away for immersion in a local river. Many women gather around the image to bid it farewell and it is not uncommon to see them actually weeping as the goddess, their 'daughter', leaves to return to her husband's home (Coburn 1991: 153).

The various roles of Durgā remain distinctive and autonomous and do not readily blend into each other. Her ability to slay the powerful forces of evil does not seem to give her any authority over her husband, Śiva. Nor here is Durgā best known for her exploits on the battlefield. On the contrary, her position within the household as consort of Śiva does not seem to differ significantly from that of her female devotees. Still, Durgā is more powerful than the majority of goddesses in the Hindu pantheon and serves as a reminder of that potential energy and ability within female deities. Hindu women can draw strength from her, but there is 'no inherent, invariable relationship between powerful goddesses and the advocacy of women's empowerment' (Pinchman: 191).

Kālī

Kālī is one of the most interesting and popular goddesses in Hinduism. Kālī is strong, independent, ruthlessly violent, a threat to men and women alike. She is free and she is fierce. She is attractive because she embodies awesome raw power. For many Western women, Kālī represents the embodiment of the strength that lies unrealized in women generally. However, this is not necessarily the way she is viewed in India, and it is easy to lose sight of the fact that she, like the other goddesses in the Hindu pantheon, is the product of patriarchal thought.

Kālī's official genesis in the textual tradition is located in the *Devīmahātmya,* which we noted above with respect to Durgā. In the *Devīmahātmya,* Kālī emerges from the forehead of the warrior queen Durgā. Her appearance is terrifying: simultaneously horrifying and mesmerizing. Devotional images depict her as black in colour with a bright and gaudily painted red lolling tongue, red eyes, and wearing a very long necklace of human heads. She also wears a girdle of human arms and two dead bodies as earrings. She has three eyes and her hair hangs loose. In two of her four arms she wields a sword and the head of the demon she has just slain. With the other two, she motions her followers to fear not, and she confers boons. Sometimes she wears a tiger skin, but generally she is naked save for her girdle of human arms. She stands on the body of a figure, sometimes identified as Śiva. Her Śaktī, her female power, energizes the entire world, but she prefers to dwell in the cremation grounds where dissolution is the order of the day.

This image is rich and interpretations of it are many. The goddess's dark hue is often cited as representing depth and infinity, as, for example, the void of space, the fathomless depths of the dark vortex, the depth of the ocean. Black, in its absence of colour, is here understood to transcend all colours. 'Just as all colors disappear in black, so all names and forms disappear in her' (*Mahanirvana Tantra* 13.5 in Avalon 1972: 295). Her black colour also indicates the unknown and the unknowable, reminding us of our fear of the dark. Kālī's nakedness is a challenge and counterpoint to Hindu notions of nakedness. It represents a pure, untouched state, a state of innocence. But Kālī is a naked killer, strong and hot, unafraid of her body and uninhibited by ordinary rules of human society. Without the illusion of clothes to cover her up and protect her, she shows us exactly what and who she is. She challenges us, provokes us to confront ourselves directly.

Her dishevelled hair forms a curtain of illusion. Her red lolling tongue dramatically depicts the fact that she consumes all creatures. She tastes the flavours of the world, so to speak, and finds them intoxicating. Her sword cuts through ignorance, ego, and illusion; the severed head indicates the sum total of conscious knowledge, marking the separation of intellect, reason, and ordinary thought from true wisdom; the waistband of human arms represent work that hands and arms perform in the world and reminds us that all deeds produce karma and that the binding effects of this karma can be overcome—severed, as it were, by Kālī. She blesses her worshippers by cutting them free from karmic bondage (Kinsley 1997: 89).

In contrast to Śiva's sweet expression, plump body, and ash-white complexion, Kālī's emaciated limbs, angular gestures, and fierce grimace convey a wild intensity. Her loose hair, skull garland, and tiger wrap whip around her body as she stomps and claps to the rhythm of the dance. Kālī's boon is the boon of freedom. She teaches us to confront suffering, pain, our own inevitable decay and death. Kālī laughs mockingly at us when we ignore, deny, or try to explain away these facts of our existence. Kālī is the great swallower, though unlike the swallowing habits of deities like Gaṇeśa, her swallowing is depicted as terrible. She tastes and enjoys the world, and she is indiscriminate in her enjoyment of its flavours. She is all-devouring Time, the one who swallows the living and keeps their skulls around her neck, symbolic of her action, as trophies of battle or trophies of the ultimate victory of death over life.

There are numerous temples and images of Kālī throughout the subcontinent, but she is most popular in Bengal. Animal sacrifice is an indispensable part of Kālī worship, and goats, sheep, and buffalo are commonly sacrificed at Kālī temples (Banerji 1992: 175). One of the most famous saints of Bengal, Rāmakṛṣṇa (1836–86), devoted his life to the worship of Kālī, composing numerous poems in her praise. His predecessor Ramprasad Sen (1718–75) is also of note as a great devotee of Kālī. Ramprasad composed some of the most popular devotional songs performed in her worship.

Kālī's human and maternal qualities continue to define the goddess for most of her devotees to this day. Kālī's devotees form a particularly intimate and loving bond with her, but the devotee never forgets Kālī's demonic, frightening aspects or distorts Kālī's nature and the truths she reveals. Ramprasad Sen mentions these characteristics of Kālī repeatedly in his songs but is never put-off or repelled by them. Kālī may be frightening, mad, and a forgetful mistress of a world spinning out of control, but she is, after all, the Mother. As such, she must be accepted by her children. In the following the poet, Ramprasad Sen has to beg and cajole her to get what he wants. He often insults her, calling her stony-hearted and more. The relationship between deity and devotee here is a very personal one:

Can there be compassion in the heart of one who is the daughter of a
  mountain?
If she is not unkind, can She kick her husband in the chest?
Thou art called 'compassionate' in the world; but there is no trace of
  compassion in Thee, O Mother!
Thou wearest a necklace of heads cutting them off from mothers' sons
The more I cry 'Mother, Mother', the more Thou turnest deaf ears to my
  cries.
Prasada is used to suffering Thy kicks; yet he utters 'Durgā,' Durgā.

(Ramprasad 1966: 141)

It is also interesting to note that in Bengal, where Kālī is most popular, there
is a tradition of female saints, some of whom are regarded as the embodiment
of Kālī. One such teacher is Śrī Ānandamayī Mā (1896–1982), the blissful
mother (see sidebar, page 28).

NOTES

1. In this early period women may in fact have participated in Vedic rituals, There is some evi-
    dence that they were permitted to discourse on sacred texts (Young 1999: 62) and perform
    sacrifices (Altekar: 198f.).
2. It was Sir Jones who first translated *The Laws of Manu* and after having translated it, Manu
    became authoritative, perpetuating the notion that the British were simply enforcing tradi-
    tional Hindu law (Kishwar: 2000).
3. See, for example, O'Flaherty who delineates these two types as goddesses of the breast and
    goddesses of the tooth.
4. In some cases a widow could escape this contamination by performing satī or ritual immo-
    lation which represents the final and the most perfect act of self-effacement and fulfillment
    of her duties and religious pursuit. Through satī a woman could achieve her greatest
    honour within orthodox Hinduism.

REFERENCES

Ānandamayī Mā. *Ananda Varta Quarterly.* I/60. Online. <http://www.cosmicharmony.com/Sp/
  AnandMM/Mataji.htm#Sublime>
Avalon, Arthur, trans. 1972. *Tantra of the Great Liberation* (Mahanirvana Tantra). New York:
  Dover Publications.
Altekar, Anant Sadashir. 1983. *The Position of Women in Hindu Civilization from Prehistoric Times
  to the Present Day.* Delhi: Motilal Banarsidass.
Bahadur Srisa Chandra Vasu, Rai, trans. 1981. *Śiva Samhitā.* Delhi: Satguru Publications.

Banerji, Sures Chandra. 1992. *Tantra in Bengal: A Study of Its Origin, Development and Influence*. New Delhi: Manohar Publications.

Bannerji, Himani. 2001. *Inventing Subjects: Studies in Hegemony, Patriarchy and Colonialism*. London: Anthem Press.

Bhatnagar, Rakesh. 2002. 'Anyone Can be a Temple Priest'. *The Times of India* (New Delhi): 5 Oct: 1.

Chakravarty, Uma. 1998. *Rewriting History: The Life and Times of Pandita Ramabai*. New Delhi: Kali for Women Press.

Chatterjee, Partha. 1993. *The Nation and Its Fragments: Colonial and Post Colonial Histories*. Princeton: Princeton University Press.

Chen, Marty. 2002. *Empowering Widows in Development*. Online. 13 Oct. <http://www.oneworld.org/empoweringwidows/10countries/india.html>

Coburn, Thomas B. 1991. *Encountering the Goddess: A Translation of the Devi-Mahatmya and a Study of Its Interpretation*. Albany, New York: State University of New York Press.

Coulter, Diana. 2002. 'In India's Town of Widows, a Home for the Forgotten'. *Christian Science Monitor* 10 July: 8.

Courtright, Paul B. 1993. 'Iconographies of Satī'. *Satī: The Blessing and the Curse. The Burning of Wives in India*. Ed. John Stratton Hawley. New York: Oxford University Press: 27–53.

Dehejia, Vidya. 1990. *Antal and Her Path of Love: Poems of a Woman Saint from South India*. Albany: SUNY Press.

Devi, Mahasweta. 1997. *Breast Stories*. Trans. Gayatri Spivak. Calcutta: Seagull.

Devīmāhātmya. The Glorification of the Great Goddess. 1963. Ed. and trans. Vasudeva S. Agrawala. Banaras: All-India Kashiraj Trust.

Eggeling, Julius, trans. 1966. *The Śatapatha-Brāhmaṇa*. 5 vols. Delhi: Motilal Banarsidass.

Erndl, Kathleen M. 2000. 'Is *Shakti* Empowering for Women? Reflections on Feminism and the Hindu Goddess'. *Is the Goddess a Feminist?: The Politics of South Asian Goddesses*. Eds Alf Hiltebeitle and Kathleen M. Erndl. New York: New York University Press: 91–103.

Gold, Anne Grodzins. 1996. 'Khyal: Changing Yearnings in Rajasthani Women's Songs'. *Manushi* 95: 13–21.

Goldberg, Ellen. 2002. *The Lord Who Is Half Woman: Ardhanārīśvara in Indian and Feminist Perspective*. Albany, NY: SUNY Press.

Gupta, Dipankar. 2001. *Mistaken Modernity: India Between Worlds*. Second impression. New Delhi: HarperCollins Publishers India.

Hawley, John Stratton. 1993. 'Afterword: The Mysteries and Communities of Satī'. *Satī: The Blessing and the Curse. The Burning of Wives in India*. Ed. John Stratton Hawley. New York: Oxford University Press: 175–86.

Hess, Linda. 1999. 'Rejecting Sītā: Indian Responses to the Ideal Man's Cruel Treatment of his Ideal Wife'. *Journal of the American Academy of Religion* 67: 1–32.

Hirshfield, Jane, ed. 1994. *Women in Praise of the Sacred: Forty-three Centuries of Spiritual Poetry by Women*. New York: HarperCollins Publishers.

Hudson, Dennis. 1995-6. 'Antal's Desire'. *Journal of Vaisnava Studies* 4.1: 37–76.

Hume, Robert Ernest, trans. 1996. *The Thirteen Principal Upanishads.* Second ed., rev. New York: Oxford University Press.

Humes, Cynthia Ann. 2000. 'Is the *Devi Mahatmya* a Feminist Scripture?' *Is the Goddess a Feminist?: The Politics of South Asian Goddesses.* Eds Alf Hiltebeitle and Kathleen M. Erndl. New York: New York University Press: 123–50.

Jai Santoshi Mā. 1975. Dir. Vijay Sharma. Bombay and Guttenberg, NJ: Worldwide Entertainment Group.

Jamison, Stephanie W. 1996. *Sacrificed Wife/Sacrificers Wife: Women, Ritual and Hospitality in Ancient India.* New York: Oxford University Press.

Kandiah, M. 1990. *Śrī Durgā Devī Temple of Tellippalai.* Delhi: Sri Satguru Publications.

Kapur, Ratna, and Brenda Crossman. 1994. 'Women and Hindutva'. *Women Against Fundamentalisms* 5: 42–3.

Keith, Arthur B., trans. 1996. *Rigveda Brāhmaṇas: The Aitareya and Kausitaki Brāhmaṇas of the Rigveda.* Delhi: Motilal Banarsidass.

Kinsley, David R. 1986. *Hindu Goddesses: Visions of the Divine Feminine on the Hindu Religious Tradition.* Berkeley: University of California Press.

———. 1997. *Tantric Visions of the Divine Feminine: The Ten Mahāvidyās.* Berkeley: University of California Press.

Kishwar, Madhu. 1989. 'The Daughters of Aryavarta'. *Women in Colonial India: Essays on Survival, Work and the State.* Ed. J. Krishanmurti. London: Oxford India Paperbacks.

———. 1997a. 'Yes to Sītā, No to Ram! The Continuing Popularity of Sītā in India'. *Manushi* 98: 20–31.

———. 1997b. 'Freeing Sītās From Bondage'. *Manushi* 98: 26–7.

———. 1997c. 'Women, Sex and Marriage'. *Manushi* 99: 23–6.

———. 1998. 'Native Outpourings of a Self-Hating Indian: Deepa Mehta's *Fire*'. *Manushi* 109: 3–14.

———. 1999. 'Indian Politics: Encourages Durgās, Snubs Women'. *Manushi* 111: 5–9.

———. 2000. 'From Manusmriti to Madhusmriti'. *Manushi* 117: 3–8.

Kurtz, Stanley. 1992. *All the Mothers Are One: Hindu India and the Cultural Reshaping of Psychoanalysis.* New York: Columbia University Press.

The Laws of Manu. 1975. Trans. G. Buhler. Delhi: Motilal Banarsidass.

Manjul, V.L. 1997. 'The Hitherto Forbidden Realm'. *Manushi* 99: 38–9.

Mahābhārata. 1834–9. 5 vols. (Calcutta edition).

Mascaro, Juan, trans. 1968. *The Bhagavad Gītā.* Middlesex, England: Penguin Books.

Murphy, Anne, and Shana Sippy. 2000. ' Sītā in the City: The Rāmāyaṇa's Heroine in New York'. *Manushi* 117: 17–23.

Naim, C.M. 1999. 'A Dissent on Fire'. *Economic and Political Weekly* 17–30 April: 955–7.

Nanda, Serena. 1999. *The Hijras of India: Neither Man nor Woman.* 2nd edn. Belmont, CA: Wadsworth Publishing Company.

O'Flaherty, Wendy Doniger. 1973. *Asceticism and Eroticism in the Mythology of Śiva*. London, New York: Oxford University Press.

————. 1980. *Women, Androgynes and Other Mythical Beasts*. Chicago: University of Chicago Press.

Oldenburg, Veena Talwar. 1993. 'The Roop Kanwar Case: Feminist Response'. *Sati: The Blessing and the Curse*. Ed. John Stratton Hawley. New York: Oxford University Press: 101–30.

Omvedt, Gail. 2000. 'Towards a Theory of Brahmanic Patriarchy'. *Economic and Political Weekly* 22 Jan. Online. 14 Sept. 2003 <http://www.epw.org.in/showArticles.php?root=2000&leaf=01&filename=2832&filetype=html>

Pearson, Anne Mackenzie. 1996. *Because It Gives Me Peace of Mind: Ritual Fasts in the Religious Lives of Hindu Women*. McGill Studies in the History of Religions. Albany: SUNY Press.

Phillimore, Peter. 1991. 'Unmarried Women of the Dhaulu Dhar: Celibacy and Social Control in Northwest India'. *Journal of Anthropological Research* 47(3): 331–50.

Pinchman, Tracy. 2000. 'Is the Hindu Goddess Tradition a Good Resource for Western Feminism?' *Is the Goddess a Feminist?: The Politics of South Asian Goddesses*. Eds Alf Hiltebeitle and Kathleen M. Erndl. New York: New York University Press: 187–202.

Rāmanujan, A.K. 1992. 'Who Needs Folklore'. *Manushi* 69: 2–16.

Ramaswamy, Vijaya. 1997. *Walking Naked: Women, Society and Spirituality in South India*. Shimla: Indian Institute of Advanced Study.

Robinson, Catherine A. 1999. *Tradition and Liberation: The Hindu Tradition in the Indian Women's Movement*. New York: St. Martin's Press.

Sarkar, Tanika. 2001. *Hindu Wife, Hindu Nation: Community, Religion and Cultural Nationalism*. New Delhi: Permanent Black.

Sen, Nabaneeta Dev. 1998. 'When Women Retell the *Rāmāyaṇa*'. *Manushi* 108: 18–27.

Sethi, Manisha. 2000. 'Caught in the Wheel: Women and Salvation in Indian Religions'. *Manushi* 119: 13–17.

Shahani, Roshan G., and Shoba V. Ghosh. 2000. 'Indian Feminist Criticism: In Search of New Paradigms'. *Economic and Political Weekly* 28 Oct: Online. <http:// www.epw.org.in/showArticles.php?root=2000&leaf=01&filename=2832&filetype=html>

Shastri, H.P., trans. 1952. *The Rāmāyaṇa of Valmiki*. London: Shanti Sadan.

Sharma, Arvind, and Katherine K.Young, eds. 1999. *Feminism and World Religions*. Albany, NY: SUNY Press.

Sharma, Kṛṣṇa. 1995. 'Interviews with Women, Interviewed by S. Anitha, Manisha, Vasudha and Taritha'. *Women and the Hindu Right: A Collection of Essays*. Eds T. Sarkar and V. Butalia. New Delhi: Kālī for Women Press.

Sinha, Jadunath, trans. 1966. *Rāma Prasada's Devotional Songs: The Cult of Shakti*. Calcutta: Calcutta Sinha Publishing House.

Subramanian, V.K., trans. 1986. *Saundaryalahari*. New Delhi: Motilal Banarsidass.

Taittirīya Brāhmaṇa. 2 vols. 1967–9. Poona: Ānandāśrama Sanskrit Series,.

Tewari, Naren. 1998. *The Mother Goddess Vaishno Devi*. New Delhi: Lancer International.

Van Buitenen, J.A.B., trans. 1978. *The Mahābhārata*. Chicago: University of Chicago Press.

Vyas, R.T. 1987. *Bṛhadranyaka Upanisad: A Critical Study*. Baroda: Sadhana Press.

'Women Priests for the Jet Age'. *The Times of India*. June 2002. Online. <http://timesofindia.indi-atimes.com/cms.dll/html/uncomp/articleshow?art_id=13804983>

Young, Katherine. 1999. *Feminism and World Religions*. Ed. Arvind Sharma. Albany, NY: State University of New York Press.

FURTHER READING

Hiltebeitle, Alf, and Kathleen M. Erndl, eds. *Is the Goddess a Feminist?: The Politics of South Asian Goddesses*. New York: New York University Press, 2000.

Jeffery, Patricia, and Amrita Basu, eds. *Appropriating Gender: Women's Activism and Politicized Religion in South Asia*. NY: Routledge, 1997.

Kinsley, David. *Hindu Goddesses: Visions of the Divine Feminine on the Hindu Religious Tradition*. Berkeley: University of California Press, 1986.

McDermott, Rachel Fell and Jeffrey J. Kripal, eds. *Encountering Kali: In the Margins, at the Center, in the West*. Berkeley: University of California Press, 2003

Robinson, Catherine A. *Tradition and Liberation: The Hindu Tradition in the Indian Women's Movement*. New York: St Martin's Press, 1999.

CHAPTER 2

～

WOMEN IN JUDAISM

Jacoba Kuikman

INTRODUCTION AND OVERVIEW

Judaism is one of the oldest civilizations originating in the ancient East. The earliest stages of the history of the Jewish people are recorded in a collection of narratives in the Hebrew Bible from its beginnings up to the time of Ezra, possibly as late as 400 BCE.

The Second Temple period spans a time frame dating from about 515 BCE when the Temple, destroyed by the Babylonians in 586 BCE, was rebuilt, until 70 CE when the Romans destroyed it again. This event heralds the beginning of the Rabbinic period during which the Rabbis collected and put into writing the vast amount of interpretation of the Biblical texts circulating orally. For almost 2,000 years normative Judaism would revolve around the study of what came to be known as the Talmud, an exclusively male endeavour.

Without a homeland, Jews suffered extensively at the hands of Christian Europe during this period. Murdered, expelled, and ghettoized Jews survived in part through strict sex-role differentiation with women in the private sphere of the home and men active in the synagogue and study hall. The Enlightenment of the seventeenth and eighteenth centuries allowed Jews entrance to the modern world as citizens, and many Jews assimilated into society. However, the liberal German Reform movement sought to restructure religious practice and worship to resemble the dominant Christian milieu. This marks the beginning of what might be called the modern period, which saw the slaughter of some six million Jews at the hands of Nazi Germany between 1938 and 1945 and the birth of the State of Israel in 1948.

HISTORY AND STATUS OF WOMEN

A brief overview of some of the pivotal biblical events that span some 1,000 years will provide a framework for a discussion of the foundational elements for Judaism and the place of women within that religion.

The Biblical Period

Genesis tells us that Abraham, who migrated from Ur of the Chaldees to Canaan (Gen. 11:31), made a covenant with God to whom he gave his sole allegiance in the form of observance of laws concerning the individual and the community. In return God promised Abraham and his descendents the Land. Abraham and his wife, Sarah, had a son named Isaac. As a test of Abraham's faith, God commanded him to sacrifice Isaac. This archetypal story in the history of Judaism tells us that God stays Abraham's hand, thus fulfilling the promise that Abraham will have descendants. Isaac's son Jacob, later named Israel, had 12 sons whose descendants would come to be known as the 12 tribes of Israel. Not only is his daughter, Dinah, given short shrift in the Bible, but also the narrative relates that she was raped and infers that this was a consequence of inappropriate, independent behaviour on her part. In addition to the patriarchs of Genesis, Abraham, Isaac, and Jacob, the matriarchs among the women in Genesis, Sarah, Rebekah, Leah, and Rachel, function as role models in Judaism

A famine brought Jacob and his family to Egypt, where for many years thereafter the Israelites lived in slavery. The textual evidence has it that Moses, with considerable help from his older sister Miriam, led the Israelites out of Egypt, thus liberating them from slavery. This liberation event, the so-called Exodus, occurred around the year 1280 BCE. The gift and reception of the Ten Commandments at Mount Sinai was followed by a long period of wandering in the desert.

Living among the Canaanites in the 'promised land', the Israelites found themselves powerfully distracted by Canaanite culture and religion. Military leaders who earned the title of judge, including Deborah, were chosen to fuse together a struggling and often divided people. Around 1020 BCE Saul was chosen as the first king of Israel. David, a poet and author of many of the Psalms, is considered to be Israel's second and greatest king, a messiah and model for the future messiah. Establishing Jerusalem as the capital city, he built a sanctuary to God/El there. David's son, Solomon, built the first temple through heavy taxation and forced labour, resulting in the eventual secession of 10 of the 12 tribes. The 10 tribes in the north came to be known collectively as the Kingdom of Israel, while the tribes of Judah and Benjamin, which remained in Jerusalem, were known as the Kingdom of Judah. Conquest of Israel by the Assyrians in 722 BCE resulted in the dispersal of the 10 tribes, and today they are known as the 10 lost tribes of Israel.

This roughly marks the beginning of the Prophets who inveighed against idolatry and social injustice but who also comforted God's 'suffering servant', especially following the destruction of the Temple in 586 BCE by the Babylonians and the exile into Babylon of most of Judah. The Jews exiled in

Babylon nevertheless flourished, and in the absence of the Temple, initiated other forms of prayer and worship. Permitted to return to Jerusalem in 538 BCE after Cyrus conquered Babylonia, the Jews rebuilt the temple, completing it by 515 BCE. About 100 years later, two leaders of the Babylonian Jewish community, Ezra and Nehemiah, urged the Jews in Jerusalem to adopt an uncompromising loyalty to the one God and to the laws. Conversion to Judaism was now discouraged since converts were likely to bring their foreign gods with them. This despite the fact that much earlier, Ruth the Moabite, a convert to Israel, had served as ancestor to the great King David.

The women of the Hebrew Bible are not uniformly represented. Although not mentioned as frequently as men and although often not named, they are presented variously as subjects of historical events in both the private and public domain. While the Hebrew Bible is an androcentric text it is not difficult to find role models for contemporary Jewish women; Lot's wife, Yael, Dina, Tamar, Ruth and Naomi, and Judith from the apocryphal literature are examples.

Second Temple Judaism

With the advent of Hellenism, as epitomized by Alexander the Great in the fourth century BCE, the Jews in Jerusalem found themselves once again living under foreign rule. Some Jews embraced elements of Greek culture, and the biblical books were translated into Greek. Under King Antiochus IV Epiphanes, however, Greek religion was forced upon the Jews upon pain of death, a situation that ended with the Maccabean revolt and the reclaiming of the Temple in 164 BCE. Until the Roman conquest in 63 BCE, Israel was an independent kingdom centring on the Temple Cult in Jerusalem under the leadership of the Hasmonean kings.

The next 100 years, up to the destruction of the Second Temple by the Romans in 70 CE, saw the rise of various groups of Jews, including the wealthy and elitist Sadducees; the Pharisees, or sages, who sought to apply the Torah to everyday life and created a body of material known as the Oral Torah; and the Essenes, an ascetic and apocalyptic group whom we know through the Dead Sea Scrolls. The synagogue, whose origins may go back as far as Ezra, was promoted by the Pharisees as an institution of worship alongside the Temple. To what extent women were active in the synagogue as leaders is largely unknown from textual material, but some scholars have provided evidence from Greek and Latin inscriptions that tell us of women bearing various titles such 'head', 'leader', 'elder', and 'mother of the synagogue' as well as 'priestess'. This material suggests that some Jewish women did assume leadership positions in the ancient synagogue (Broote 1982). With the destruction of the Temple, the Pharisee tradition became the foundation for rabbinic Judaism, which in turn has defined Jewish practice in every sphere of life for the past 2,000 years.

Rabbinic Judaism

The Oral Torah, eventually codified in the Mishnah, is the product of pharisaic interpretation of the laws and teachings of the Torah. It also contains meticulous descriptions of the manner in which the laws were to be implemented. The Mishnah and Talmud both name a few women, and they also refer to women generically when they speak of women's legal status in the public and private realm. Largely within this literature, women are seen as 'other', as essentially different from men who constitute the norm. The actual experience and lives of historical women are not evident in these texts.

The Middle Ages

The middle ages in Jewish history span from the time of the completion of the Babylonian Talmud, somewhere between 500 to 600 CE to the sixteenth century when Jews were restricted to ghettos in Western Europe. Jewish communities during this period were diverse. There were large thriving populations of Jews in regions dominated by Muslims, and more insecure, often persecuted, communities in Christian Europe. Despite this diversity, all were governed by the laws of the Talmud, which relegated women primarily to the domestic sphere. The primary sources of information about women in the Middle Ages come from the hands of men seeking solutions to legal problems. This *responsa* literature reveals the discontent and frustration experienced by women in connection with issues such as marriage, divorce, and the inheritance of property. The ban on polygamy by Rabbi Gershon among Ashkenazi Jews in the tenth century was a first but significant change in status for Jewish European women.

Literature from women themselves from this time that might tell us some things about how they negotiated their social and religious status is either nonexistent or unrecoverable. One later exception is the autobiography of Glückel of Hameln, Germany (1645–1724), a mother of 12 children. Relatively highly educated for her time, Glückel is upheld in traditional Judaism as a model of piety for her acts of loving kindness. Her memoir offers important information about Jewish women of her time and in her region.

Jewish women in Western Europe enjoyed a higher standard of living and were more active in family economic affairs than Jewish women living in Islamic centres (Baskin 1991: 102). The few religiously educated women of the time, however, remained on the periphery of male-centred Judaism. Jewish women in England seem to have enjoyed greater freedom, particularly in the economic life of Jewish communities. But on the whole, the expectations of

Jewish women in the Middle Ages can be summarized in a prayer from medieval Northern Europe recorded by parents on the occasion of their daughter's birth: 'May she sew, spin, weave and be brought up to a life of good deeds' (cited in Baskin: 94).

The French revolution in 1749 and the Enlightenment generally initiated emancipation for European Jews, especially those in France and Germany, if they were willing to give up their traditional religious practices and beliefs and their sense of being a 'nation'. Efforts to harmonize Jewish tradition and the desire to participate fully in society and to gain civic equality led in nineteenth-century Germany to the formation of a liberal movement known as Reform. Reform Judaism, in its many manifestations, generally regarded modern ethics and historical biblical scholarship as correctives to the religious tradition based on the Bible and the Talmud. It represented an effort to keep modern Jews within Judaism. Fearing too great a compromise with modernity, more traditional rabbis founded the Conservative movement in Germany. Conservative Judaism sought to retain *halacha,* or Jewish law, as well as the traditional texts, although these were regarded as relevant to a modern context and not as static and immutable. What might be called Neo-Orthodoxy was a kind of reactionary form of Judaism in that it retained the *halachic* core of Judaism. It was possible and necessary for Jews within this movement to embrace Western culture only to the extent that it did not impact negatively on religious observance. In Western Europe, Germany formed the heart of the various Reform movements in Judaism. Conservatism flourished here also, since it allowed full assimilation while retaining some measure of Jewish thought and practice. Eastern European Jewry remained largely Orthodox in the traditional rabbinic sense and would be almost completely decimated by German Nazism.

Assimilation into the modern society of highly educated and sophisticated Western German Jews and even baptism did not spare Jews from the horrors of the Holocaust. Zionism, a largely modern and secular movement, emerged in the nineteenth century as a response to persistent anti-Semitism in France, despite the so-called emancipation of Jews at this time. In Europe, the secularization of Judaism did not concretely affect the influence of Jewish laws on women. German Jewish immigrants to North America brought their different denominational movements with them. Some two million Eastern European Jews fled Russia and immigrated mainly to the United States. North American developments both before and after the Holocaust are complex and beyond the scope of this chapter. An important American phenomenon, however, was the emergence of Reconstructionism in the 1930s. This movement began as a kind of philosophy focusing on Judaism as an evolving religious civilization. It was not based on any notion of revelation but, rather, on perceived human needs.

Various forms of Jewish feminism during the 1960s in the United States agitated for full inclusion in the Jewish religious community, specifically equal participation in synagogue services. While some feminists now argue that the basic problem is theological (Plaskow 1983), others call for justice and change in Jewish law to end both segregated worship and discrimination in the area of divorce (Ozick 1983). These demands eventually led the seminary of the Reform movement to ordain the first woman rabbi in 1972. The Conservative movement elected to include women in the *minyan* (the quorum of 10 men required for public prayer in Orthodoxy). The Reconstructionist movement ordained its first female rabbi in 1974 and gave women equality in all of its rituals. The American Havurah movement, which in the past couple of decades has gained in popularity in major centres in Canada, is a traditional and egalitarian movement that has included women in every aspect of ritual and has experimented with inclusive language.

As one leading feminist scholar notes, however, women rabbis have often encountered prejudice and discrimination when searching for rabbinic positions (Heschel 1983: xvii). And much of the liturgy is still riddled with sexism. For orthodox, traditional women, the gains of feminism are even slower. These Jewish women long to practise their Judaism within a classic Jewish framework. One of the major issues here is segregated worship and the nature and height of the *mechitzah*, the separation between men and women in communal prayer. Fortunately there is dialogue among women in disparate Jewish situations. A case in point is Canada, where leading Jewish feminists of various religious persuasions are in dialogue.

TEXTS AND INTERPRETATIONS

The number of texts compiled throughout Jewish history is nothing less than astounding. Aside from the Hebrew Bible and the Talmud, there exist vast bodies of *Midrashim* (stories that interpret the Torah), classic commentaries on the Torah, various mystical texts (the best known of which is the *Zohar*), responsa literature from the Middle Ages, the *Shulchan Aruch* (a compilation of Jewish law), the *Siddur* (prayer book), and the Passover *Haggadah*. The major texts are the Hebrew Bible, which is commonly referred to as the Torah (although, strictly speaking, the Torah comprises the five books of Moses, or the Pentateuch), and the Jerusalem and Babylonian Talmuds, the latter of which is the better known.

The Torah is the foundation for the whole body of halacha, or Jewish law. According to traditional Judaism, laws codified in the biblical texts are authoritative and, by and large, the basis for the later rabbinic development of law. Because rabbinic decrees are related to biblical laws, these decrees are also given ultimate authority. Traditional Jews read these texts as atemporal and ahistorical. That is, prohibitions are not considered contextually but are read as valid for all Jews in all times and places. Modern Jewish historians and biblical scholars, however, assert that texts containing certain legal material concerning women, for example, have emerged out of specific cultural contexts. Jewish feminists question the authority of these texts in today's world, notwithstanding the abiding importance of Torah in traditional Jewish religious life. Torah is revelation: God, creator of the universe, is understood to have here made himself known in history. The study of Torah and its adjunct literature has been a central, indeed the holiest, enterprise in religious Judaism.

Yet, as women know, the Hebrew Scriptures are deeply patriarchal. Biblical texts and later interpretations of them, as found in rabbinic literature for example, are products of societies in which women's perspectives and experiences were inconsequential and invisible. Biblical texts and interpretations of them reflect male experiences of war, government, or the Temple Cult. The Bible is a product of a creative, dynamic tension between biblical traditions and the experience of the redactors who interpreted these traditions in order to make them relevant in new and different contexts. That is, the biblical texts and subsequent interpretations are contextual and contingent upon a particular time and place, and a world view that was deeply androcentric and male-dominated. These texts preserve male authority. Critical biblical scholarship, however, has recently drawn upon other tools, such as social scientific analysis, to understand gender in the biblical period. It is possible to regard religion as only one expression of the Israelite experience when one understands ancient Israel as a social entity. When one includes other resources in the study of gender and the biblical world, such as the results of archaeology, our knowledge of the people of the time extends beyond the content of the biblical text (Meyers: 6–23).

The Hebrew Bible presents a diversity of images of women, reflecting the viewpoints of different authors and different socio-cultural contexts. Biblical images of women are found in a plurality of writings, legal, didactic, historical, and prophetic, spanning close to a millennium in their dates of composition (from the twelfth century BCE to the third century BCE). These varied images, however, contain some common themes such as those of wife and mother. Perhaps the epitomic biblical text exemplifying the good wife and mother is *Eishet Chayil,* 'What a rare find is a capable wife' (Proverbs 31:10–31).

Biblical images of women are presented variously, and certain women such as Sarah or Deborah are held up in the tradition as role models for women of today. Sarah is the ideal model of wife and mother. One biblical story that is fundamental for Jewish women is the story of the rape of Dinah, one of Jacob's 13 children. Though the 12 sons come to be known as the founders of the 12 tribes of Israel, Dinah is almost completely forgotten. There are countless other examples that prove the androcentric nature of the biblical texts. Jephtha's daughter, not named, is sacrificed for male ideals, and, unlike Isaac, her life is not saved. When God gives the Torah to Moses at Mount Sinai, one of the central events moulding Jewish identity, Moses warns the people: 'Be ready on the third day; do not go near a woman' (Exodus 19:15). The issue is ritual impurity: according to Leviticus 15:16–18, an emission of semen makes the male and his female partner unfit to approach the sacred. But, as Judith Plaskow points out, Moses does not say, 'Men and women do not go near each other' (Plaskow 1990: 25). At a key moment in Jewish history, the giving of the Torah at Mount Sinai, women are invisible in the text even though, as part of the people of Israel, they must have been present at Sinai. Many women experience themselves as excluded and invisible during the annual reading of this text at the festival of Shavuot, or Pentecost. Jewish feminists must reclaim these stories by representing as 'visible the presence, experience, and deeds of women erased in traditional sources' (28). Otherwise the Torah will continue to be a partial record of Jewish experience. 'Modern historiography assumes . . . that the original "revelation" . . . is not sufficient, that there are enormous gaps both in tradition and in the scriptural record' (35).

Feminist historiography, therefore, involves reaching behind the text to recover knowledge about how women actually lived during the biblical period. This process involves retrieving women's experiences in texts, events, and processes that were suppressed, neglected, or erased by both the sources and the redactors and which never became part of Jewish group memory. We are left with the task of adding them to the records. This approach 'challenges and relativizes those memories that have survived' (Plaskow 1990: 35). Feminist historiography incorporates 'women's history as part of the living memory of the Jewish people' (36). The recovery of women's history is not transformative for Judaism, however, 'until it becomes part of the community's collective memory' (36). Accepting the 'Torah behind the Torah' would affirm that Judaism has always been 'richer, more complex, and more diverse than either "normative" sources or most branches of modern Judaism would admit' (51). Many, if not most, of the halachic rulings concerning women are rooted in rabbinic literature comprising five major works: the *Mishnah;* the *Tosefta,* a companion volume to the Mishnah; the Talmud of the Land of Israel (the *Yerushalmi);* the Talmud of Babylonia (the *Bavli);* and a body of Midrash. Jewish tradition accords the same status and authority to this literature as it does to Torah. The tradition teaches that God gave this literature to Moses at Mount Sinai and that it was passed on orally until the time it was written down.

The Mishnah is a six-volume code of law that makes up the foundation of the Talmud. It includes all legal developments since the time of the Torah and it was circulated orally for perhaps hundreds of years before it was put into writing around the year 200 CE by the *Tannaim,* or rabbis. In the generations that followed, the rabbis studied and debated these laws, seeking to understand their underlying legal rationales and to apply these laws to new contexts. Debates were recorded in the form of questions and answers and included all opposing positions and opinions. This literature together with the Mishnah came to be known as the Talmud, which means, literally, 'the teachings' (Hauptman: 184–5). Academies in Babylonia and Israel appended material unique to their own contexts; hence there is a Babylonian Talmud and a Talmud of the Land of Israel, the former the better known. The Talmuds are the texts most frequently cited with respect to laws pertaining to women.

Historians acknowledge that rabbinic literature was the sages'/rabbis' means of making the Torah more meaningful in their own day, especially after the destruction of the Second Temple in Jerusalem in 70 CE. Originally this was a fluid process by which laws in the written Torah could be expanded or modified to meet differing contexts and circumstances. Some scholars insist that in its time the Talmud was a progressive document in its views of women. For example, a Jewish woman could not be married without her consent. Her marriage document was a legally binding contract and a guarantee that her husband would support her. She was entitled to a monetary settlement in the case of divorce. Thus marriage, as envisioned by the rabbis, was not simply the acquisition of a wife but the guarantee of a woman's emotional, social, and sexual satisfaction. The last 'truly revolutionary' ruling for women was the Edict of Rabbenu Gershom in 1000 CE, forbidding polygamy to the Jews of the Western world (Adler: 16). Since this Edict, the Talmud has ceased to evolve to meet the changing needs of women; it has become a static document, and, according to traditional Judaism, God's word and will for all time. It need not be so. In the classical tradition, a law can be modified depending on the consensus of the Jewish community. Therefore, the many laws and customs in the Talmud that deny women independent legal status and equal participation in ritual, prayer, and study as well as those that discriminate against women in marriage and divorce should, in theory, be open to change. Indeed, for some scholars, changing certain laws is a matter of justice (Ozick: 123). One prominent feminist Jewish scholar, however, questions whether Jewish law, as such, is compatible with Jewish feminism at all (Plaskow 1990: 65).

The purpose of various Jewish observances is to infuse life with religious meaning and to cultivate a sense of ethics. The laws concerning these observances fall into two categories that are both positive and negative, each of which is further divided into time-bound and non-time-bound commandments (Hauptman: 190). None of this is in itself problematical. The difficulty for Jewish women is that many of the commandments in the Talmud concerning women are rooted in traditional sex-role differentiation that limits women's roles to the home and family life. Therefore Jewish law exempts women from certain positive time-bound commandments because of their family obligations. For example, a woman is not required to pray communally three times a day. She is therefore not counted in a minyan and she is not allowed to say *Kaddish,* the prayer recited daily during the year of mourning in the context of a minyan, even for a deceased parent. However women are bound by all of the negative commandments, such as the prohibitions against theft, adultery, or murder. Because the conditions for most Jewish women have changed dramatically since these laws were first enacted, halachic change concerning the time-bound commandments for women seems both inevitable and just.

In traditional, Orthodox Judaism, women are still denied the privilege of being called up to read a portion from the Torah in the liturgy. Yet, there is no legal argument supporting this practice. Historically what was at stake was the 'dignity of the congregation' (Megillah 23a in Hauptman: 192). Other commandments such as fulfilling dietary laws and lighting the Sabbath candles on Friday night, which were not legally binding on women, eventually fell almost exclusively to women as caretakers of the home. The 'cumulative effect of these exemptions and shifts of responsibility' was to exclude women from public performance in the synagogue and to turn the academies and synagogues over to men. Communal study and prayer, which constitute the heart and soul of religious Judaism, were, and still are in those circles committed to Jewish law, off-limits in terms of woman's religious experiences (Hauptman: 192–3). One solution to this exclusion of women in traditional congregations is segregated study and worship, and separate women's celebrations. But this solution is still based on the principle of Jewish law that women are Other and must thus be kept apart from men.

A passage that has generated female fury and scorn is the blessing recited by traditional male Jews every morning: 'Blessed be God, King of the universe, for not making me a woman.' For many Jewish women these words suggest that women are inferior and that this inferiority is divinely mandated. Other interpretations of this prayer are possible, however. One scholar observes that in the Tosefta, Rabbi Judah remarks that the blessing is an expression of male gratitude that they are in the privileged position of fulfilling more of the divine commandments than women. In this case the blessing is interpreted as merely a reflection of the social world of the time, which relegated women to the home. If understood in this historical context, the words of the blessing, we are told, 'lose most of their sting' (Hauptman: 196).

Some stories in the Talmud describe women's extraordinary religious knowledge. Perhaps the best known of these women is Bruriah, wife of Rabbi Meir, a sage who contributed extensively to the composition of the Mishnah.

Her male contemporaries respected her, and her views are cited throughout the Talmud. Unlike her husband, who is cited hundreds of times, Bruriah is not mentioned once in the Mishnah. It has been suggested that Bruriah is a rabbinic creation, and that she appears for certain literary purposes. Is she a token woman signifying that women *are* allowed to study Torah or is her function to reinforce the rabbinic injunction that women should *not* study Torah? Whatever the rabbis' original intentions, by the Middle Ages, Bruriah represented 'the folly of permitting women access to sacred learning' (Romney Wegner: 76). The eleventh-century biblical commentator Rashi records that Bruriah's overconfidence led her to be seduced by a student and she subsequently committed suicide. The message here is that women who abandon their assigned roles in traditional religion and culture will experience tragedy. Rachel, the wife of Rabbi Akiba, is an exemplary role model as a woman whose sole purpose in life is to be supportive of her husband's endeavours. According to the Talmud, Rachel lived alone and in poverty for 12 years, enabling the intellectually gifted Akiba to study.

While there are also several Talmudic accounts of individual saintly women and their great compassion for the poor, the Talmud does not hesitate to ascribe less than positive attributes to women in general. A dominant motif here is that women are not only different from men but also inferior to them, especially in terms of their 'physical attributes, their cognitive and affective faculties, and their standards of morality' (Romney Wegner: 77). There are myriad stories that describe women 'as excessively talkative, sharp-tongued, arrogant and outspoken'. Among women's uglier traits are 'cruelty, jealousy, vengefulness and their mean treatment' of each other. 'Women also appear to be superstitious, suspected of being witches, desirous of luxury, and quick to anger' (Hauptman: 205). With respect to these texts, it is necessary to point out that the view of an individual rabbi should not be projected onto the rabbis generally (Hauptman: 197). Nevertheless, it may be argued that these oppressive texts are indicative of general misogynistic rabbinic attitudes of the time. In summary, the Talmud presents a composite image of women with both desirable characteristics as well as negative ones. Positive rabbinic opinions of women, however, are dependent upon women's acceptance of their roles as restricted to the home and family, and this, in turn, reflects the social conditions of the time.

Just as important as the legal sources of the Talmud are the haggadic sources: sections 'that record the rabbi's opinions on a variety of subjects, legends about biblical characters, and stories about contemporary rabbis and their families', some more or less historically true but with 'legendary elements'. These materials are included in the Talmud because of their ethical intent and because they reflect the efforts of the rabbis to educate their readers through stories about characters with whom they 'could identify' (Hauptman: 197). When Dinah, for example, ventured outside of her home and was raped (Gen. 34:1), her family became embroiled in war and deception. For the rabbis this confirmed that a woman's place was in the home. Haggadah, like the legal material of the Talmud, is not uniform in its opinions on women. But on the whole, the Rabbinic haggadic tradition views the role of woman as wife and mother. Not surprisingly, the theme of barrenness as the worst possible disaster for women runs throughout haggadah as well as the Bible.

SYMBOLS AND GENDER

Symbols perhaps even more than rituals and beliefs are windows to understanding a religious tradition. Almost any object and even persons can serve as symbols if they are used to represent something else. Eve, for example, is synonymous with 'temptress' and represents fallenness in the Western mind. Symbols are ambiguous depending on who interprets them. Thus Eve can also be interpreted as consciously exercising her free will in the service of change.

Eve and the Garden of Eden
The traditional Jewish views of men and women, their status, roles, and sexuality, are derived from the Creation narratives in the book of Genesis:

> And God said, 'Let us make man in our image, after our likeness. They shall rule the fish of the sea, the birds of the sky, the cattle, the whole earth, and all the creeping things that creep on the earth.' And God created man in His image, in the image of God He created him; male and female He created them. (Gen. 1:26–27)

> The Lord God said, 'It is not good for man to be alone; I will make a fitting helper for him . . . So the Lord God cast a deep sleep upon the man; and while he slept, He took one of his ribs and closed up the flesh at that spot. And the Lord God fashioned the rib that He had taken from the man into a woman; and He brought her to the man. Then the man said, 'This one at last is bone of my bones and flesh of my flesh. This one shall be called Woman, for from man was she taken. (Gen. 2:18; 21–3)

These two excerpts seem to present us with two contradictory passages concerning the creation of Adam and Eve. The first account tells of the simultaneous creation of male and female, each in God's image. The second contains the well-known rib story in which Adam 'gives birth' to Eve via his rib. Rabbinic commentators, uncomfortable with two contradictory accounts of creation, fashioned a Midrash that enabled the two stories to be read as one continuous text. Genesis Rabbah, part of a rabbinic Midrash collection, describes the creation of a primordial, bisexual humanoid (Gen. 1), which was subsequently split into two separate male and female beings (Gen. 2).

> R. Jeremiah b. Leazar said: When the Holy One, blessed be He, created Adam, He created him a hermaphrodite, for it is said, *Male and female created He them and called their name Adam* (Gen. v, 2). R. Samuel b. Nahman said: When the Lord created Adam He created him double-faced, then He split him and made him of two backs, one back on this side and one back on the other side. To this it is objected: But it is written, *And He took one of his ribs,* etc. (Gen. ii, 21). (Genesis Rabbah VIII: 1)

The text implies that a hermaphrodite is not merely an androgynous being, but two bodies, male and female, joined together. In Genesis 2, the two sides of the androgyne are separated into two separate beings. The fact that the Hebrew word for rib, *tzela*, can also mean side, adds support to this Midrash. But this tradition is immediately countered in the Midrash with the rib account in Genesis 2. This objection led to the normative interpretation of rabbinic literature that woman was created second and subordinate to Adam. Rabbinic literature retained the notion that man and woman were created simultaneously and equally in the image of God as a minority position.

Another attempt to account for the existence of two contradictory creation stories appears in a Midrash of around the eleventh century, the 'Alphabet of Ben Sira'. Here Adam's wife in the first account of creation (his first wife) was Lilith, who, because she was created equal, demanded to be treated equally. When such treatment is denied her, she flies away to the Red Sea where she joins a host of demons and gives birth to hundreds of other demons every day. The tradition of Lilith as demon is as old as the account in Isaiah 34:14 where Lilith resides in a desolate wasteland in the company of owls, ravens, jackals, wildcats, hyenas, and goat-demons. But her demonic roots lie in ancient Sumerian mythology in which she is listed as one of the four vampire demons. A Babylonian terra-cotta relief (*c.* 2000 BCE) shows a nude and beautiful goddess of the beasts with wings and owl feet. She stands on two reclining lions and is flanked by owls (Patai: 221–2, plate 31). She is identified as Lilith.

Medieval Jewish mystics and the rabbis described Lilith as a seductress who returned to the Garden of Eden disguised as the Serpent who seduces Eve. She continued her career by seducing men who sleep alone, and she caused them to have impure, spontaneous, nocturnal emissions. The rabbinic message to women appears to have been a warning not to behave like Lilith lest they become demons like Lilith. Simultaneously, the rabbis and the mystics demonized almost any kind of female behaviour that was independent and assertive.

Modern Jewish feminists, attracted precisely to Lilith's rejection of male authority, have begun to reclaim her as a positive symbol and heroine for Jewish women. Rejecting the patriarchal nature of the Midrash, women are rewriting the story to include the powerful idea of sisterhood, and the strong friendship between Lilith and Eve (Plaskow 1979: 206–7; see also Cantor 1983: 40–50). Eve, too, needs reclamation by women. She is, after all, the one who initiated change in the Garden of Eden. Perhaps the prohibition against eating from the tree of the knowledge of good and evil (Gen. 2:17) existed to be disobeyed. Eve, like Lilith, refused to submit to male authority and became a seeker of knowledge, a tester of limits. She is a conscious actor in the story and chooses knowledge without consulting Adam. Thus, embedded in Jewish tradition are several possible interpretations of the Garden of Eden story. What is absent is a monolithic interpretation of Eve's action as constituting a fall from grace similar to that found in Christianity. The accusation of 'original sin' brought about by Eve/woman is absent from the text. This is a later interpretation from authors with different theologies such as St Augustine. The text reveals that man and woman share responsibility for the alteration of their status and roles (Meyers: 72ff.).

God and Goddess

Jewish tradition recognizes that equating the symbol of God as male with God is idolatrous. At the same time, the images of God that predominate in the Scriptures and other Jewish texts are those of Father and King. Almost every action of Jewish life is preceded by a blessing of God as Lord and King of the earth. Major litanies on the holiest days of the Jewish calendar repeat the epithet 'Our Father, our King'. Traditional Jews use exclusively masculine pronouns for God even though most would contend that God transcends sexuality. The problem, however, is that the concept of a theistic, personal God in a covenant relationship with the Jewish people is at the 'living heart of the Jewish symbol system' (Gross 1983: 236). It is impossible to engage a personal Ultimate without the use of masculine and/or feminine imagery. A turn to a non-personal Ultimate would require relinquishing the notion of the covenant relationship and the commandments to be adhered to. Therefore, anthropomorphisms, as inaccurate as they are in speaking of God, are inevitable (Gross 1983: 237). To pray to a God-She, then, should be equally possible, though also equally incomplete, to praying to a God-He.

The obstinate refusal to accept this argument is located in the nature of those who have created God language, especially those religious, spiritual Jews who have shaped the contours of normative, traditional religious Judaism.

Because of its androcentric nature, women have felt alienated from the Jewish tradition, excluded as they are from its meaningful elements. The first step for the transformation of this tradition might simply be the experience of addressing God as She. The pronouns, whether masculine or feminine or both, might then develop into richer images of God, whether gleaned from within the Jewish tradition itself or from other religious sources. Some feminist scholars regard movement in this direction as feminizing a male model, and they argue that it is ultimately ineffectual in addressing the theological problem of the deeply imbedded belief in the maleness of God.

Resources for female imagery of God exist within the history of Jewish tradition, although they are preserved by and located in patriarchal contexts. For example, the rabbis usually speak of God and his *Shekhinah*, the feminine indwelling presence of God. In the context of the Exodus story God reveals God's self to Moses as *Ehyeh-Asher-Ehyeh* ('I am who I am', or, literally, 'I am who I will be'). Even though this name is gender neutral, God is celebrated as the Lord of War in Exodus 15 and his power is regarded as the privilege of maleness. The few images of God as Mother, as, for example, in Isaiah 42:14; 66:13, or elsewhere in the Bible as wet nurse and midwife, are overshadowed by the predominance of male imagery.

Plaskow points out that the making of the one male God was a long process in the course of ancient Israel's dissociation from the polytheistic Near East. Correlated with this process was a concern with gender and the exclusion of women from public religious life (1990: 125). The gradual development and employment of male God language in Israel coincided with the gradual marginalization of women within the religious realm. Symbols here 'are not simply *models of* a community's sense of ultimate reality. They also shape the world in which we live, functioning as *models for* human behavior and the social order' (Plaskow 1990: 126). Male images of God serve both to describe the divine nature and to support a social system that allocates power and authority to men. 'When God is pictured as male in a community that understands "man" to have been created in God's image, it only makes sense that maleness functions as the norm of Jewish humanity. When maleness becomes normative, women are necessarily Other, excluded from Torah and subordinated in the community of Israel. And when women are Other, it seems only fitting and appropriate to speak of God in language drawn from the male norm' (Plaskow 1990: 127). Evident here is a powerful circular argument. Further to this problem with the male image of God is that it has ceased to function as a symbol and has become an idol instead. The result is that what is worshipped is maleness instead of God.

Plaskow's analysis goes farther. Images of divine authority, while diverse, are replete with images of God's power and dominance. God, holy king of his chosen Israel, is represented as a holy warrior who approves of the slaughter of foreign peoples and the treatment of women as booty and spoils of war (Num. 31:17–18, 32–5). Images such as God as holy king and warrior deny human power and authority and encourage human passivity. They 'fail to acknowledge or evoke from us the energy and empowerment' required to struggle against the very oppression and evil generated by such images (Plaskow 1990: 132–4).

Nature provides a host of images for God that not only resonate with our experience but also nurture responsibility for our wounded environment. In Alice Walker's *The Color Purple*, Celie, a poor, black, abused woman, discovers another face of God in conversation with her lover Shug, a face aside from the 'trifling' and 'lowdown' one familiar to her. Shug knows all too well the white, male God found in church. Celie learns from Shug that God is also found within nature, in the colour purple and not over or outside of it. As Shug puts it: God would be 'pissed off' if we did not notice the colour of flowers. Celie writes in her diary:

> She [Shug] say, My first step from the old white man was trees. Then air. Then birds. Then other people. But one day when I was sitting quiet and feeling like a motherless child, which I was, it come to me: that feeling of being part of everything, not separate at all. I knew that if I cut a tree my arm would bleed. (cited in Plaskow 1990: 145)

The white male God is displaced first with trees, then air, and only then with other people. Symbols for God from nature cross religious boundaries, nurturing friendships and solidarity with other women in a time when the world is in crisis. Traditional Judaism is ambivalent about nature, however. Anything that looks like the veneration of nature was and continues to be associated with goddess worship in ancient Israel, a phenomenon that was carefully erased by the biblical writers. Early Hebrew popular religion includes the names of three goddesses worshipped by the ancient Israelites: Asherah, Astarte, and the Queen of Heaven (who was probably identical with Anath) (Patai: 34–53). Asherah, the earliest of these and likely the consort of YHWH, was represented as a tree or as a nude woman. For example, Saul Olyan contends that the goddess Asherah was the consort of Yahweh and not of Baal on the grounds that Asherah was El's main consort in Canaanite religion and that the biblical writers identify Yahweh with El (Olyan: xiv). Introduced to the Solomonic Temple by King Rehoboam, the son of Solomon, in or about 928 BCE, Asherah's statue remained there for 236 of the 370 years that the Temple stood in Jerusalem. Worship of Asherah was opposed from time to time only by a few prophetic voices (Patai: 50, 52). It is significant that the Hebrew people clung to Asherah as the loving, mother-consort of YHWH-El for six centuries. Perhaps the nature-oriented worship of her tree cult was an expression of resistance to the increased vigour of the abstract Yahwist monotheism to which Asherah eventually fell victim.

Proverbs 8:30 tells us that Wisdom (that is, Torah) was active in creation together with God. In Proverbs 3:18, Wisdom is depicted as *etz chaim*, the Tree of Life to those who hold fast to her. Asherah may be the model for portraying Wisdom as a tree in this passage. The tree metaphor found with reference to the majesty of Wisdom in Sirach 24:12–21 would support this possibility. Here Wisdom is patterned in luscious, rich images of fertility and fecundity. She is the all-nourishing Tree-Mother who invites us to: 'Come to me, you who desire me, and eat your fill of my fruits' (see Kuikman 2000; Wolfson 1: 123 n.1) Female images of Torah or Wisdom in rabbinic literature are more metaphorical in nature and include the images of Torah as daughter of God or the King, as bride of Israel, God, or Moses and as the mother where the father is God (Wolfson 3: 125, n. 12).

The strong prophetic condemnation of goddess worship in ancient Israel attests to its tenacity in the tradition. This condemnation, however, is not to say that Israel was responsible for the death of the goddess, as some Christian feminists have claimed. The accusation that Jews killed the goddess is an echo of the earlier charge of deicide, that Jews are Christ killers. Feminist Jewish scholars and others have condemned assertions that Judaism introduced patriarchy and violence into the world (Heschel 1990; von Kellenbach 1994). Overlooked has been the evidence of the introduction of patriarchy in other parts of the world. Moreover, the notion that early matriarchal, goddess cultures represented an ideal, peaceful, and harmonious time is wishful thinking, given the fact that this is unverifiable and also that goddess-oriented societies today, such as India, do not necessarily promote equality and justice for women. Also overlooked or neglected is the history of the ancient nascent nation of Israel as a small struggling nation in the context of much larger Canaanite patriarchal cultures. What is disturbing here is the (perhaps unwitting) resurfacing in some Christian feminist writings of the old assertion of the superiority of Christianity. Jewish feminist rejection of the patriarchal nature of traditional Judaism is an internal critique, and Jewish feminists resent being placed in a position of defending what they believe needs to be challenged in traditional Judaism.

Feminist Jews who are not comfortable with goddess imagery have a host of non-gendered names for God upon which to draw from biblical and other sources: God as lover or friend; companion or co-creator; fountain, source, wellspring, or ground of all being (Plaskow 1990: 161–5). Metaphors from the Psalms furnish us with rock and refuge. The Jewish mystical tradition has provided the image of God as *Makom*, literally 'place', a sacred place. To imagine God solely as male is simply not necessary, even in traditional Judaism.

SEXUALITY

The traditional, Orthodox view of sexuality is rooted in rabbinic concerns for family unity, including the production of children and future generations. Sexuality is regarded positively as the God-given means by which to propagate the human race. Sexuality must be controlled and mastered, however, in order to render it holy. Within the context of marriage, sexuality is 'an expression of the noblest human creative impulse' (Kaufman: 124). Unlike many other religious traditions, the Orthodox view asserts that Jewish texts are sensitive to female sexuality. The Talmud (Baba Metzi'a: 84a) teaches that women have a greater sex drive than men (Biale: 122). But the rabbis' perceptions of women's sexuality also included the idea, based on her internal anatomy as opposed to the male's external erection, that women were passive. They tell us that despite her strong sexual drives, a woman is 'temperamentally inhibited in initiating sex' (Biale: 125). Therefore it is the man's responsibility to initiate sex when he knows his wife desires it (Biale: 126). Male sexuality, on the other hand, is regarded by the rabbis as active, in danger of 'running wild', and in need of restraint through the restrictions of marriage such as the obligation to procreate (Biale: 122).

The tension women experience between sexual desire on the one hand and passivity on the other was interpreted by the rabbis as part of the curse of Eve which all women have inherited. While the first part of the curse according to Genesis 3:16 is the pain of childbirth, the second reads: 'Your desire shall be for your husband, and he shall rule over you'. What this passage means, precisely, is not at all clear. Medieval biblical commentators present varied interpretations of Eve's desire and Adam's rule. Generally, though, women are seen as caught in a bind between sexual desire and servility. 'Whether because she cannot initiate sex, or because she "pays" for her sexual desire with total obedience, the woman's curse is bound up with her sexuality' (Biale: 125).

Traditional scholars sometimes posit positive views of sexuality within Judaism, comparing them with the more negative attitudes of classical Christianity in which sexuality and original sin are regarded as products of Eve's sin (see, for example, Kaufman: 123). The Talmudic literature is ambiguous, however, regarding the positive nature of sexuality. The rabbis state: 'Let us be thankful to our forefathers, for if they had not sinned we would not have come into this world' (Avodah Zarah: 5a cited in Biale: 121). It appears that some of the sages' views on sexuality do not differ all that much from those in other Western religious traditions. The rabbis saw sexuality as potentially dangerous and therefore in need of regulation (Biale: 121). As well as restricting sexual expression to marriage, confinement of sexuality is achieved through the laws of *niddah*, a Hebrew term referring to a woman who is ostracized, excluded, or separated. The laws of niddah are directed to women regarding sexual contact during and after menstruation. These prescriptions are based on Leviticus 15:19, 'When a woman has a flow of blood where blood flows from her body, she shall be a *niddah* for seven days; whoever touches her shall be unclean until evening'. Two additional texts, Lev. 18:19 and Lev. 20:18, explicitly forbid sexual relations during menstruation. During the biblical period, a woman would be separated from engaging in sexual relations with her husband for seven days and she would be niddah until she immersed herself in a *mikvah*, or ritual bath. When the task of examining the bloodstains shifted from a rabbi to women themselves, the rabbis imposed an extra seven days of seclusion to ensure the woman was free of bleeding.

The laws of *tumah,* or ritual impurity, and *taharah,* or ritual purity, are complex and include cases of contamination in addition to those in the niddah, such as contact with leprosy and seminal discharge. The ultimate source of tumah is the corpse. The purpose of these laws was to prevent impure persons from entering the Temple where the divine Presence resided (see Lev.:11–15). Since the destruction of the Second Temple in 70 CE these laws no longer serve a purpose and, except for the laws of niddah, are today inoperative. Since the laws of niddah are included in the biblical sexual prohibitions, they were retained, especially after the Second Temple was destroyed and religious observance shifted from the public, cultic sphere to that of family life (Biale: 147–8).

Contemporary justification for the laws of family purity includes the idea that mutual love and devotion can be expressed in ways other than physical. The separation, we are told, can be a time of 'intimacy of the spirit', a break from mechanical, monotonous sex. Monthly separation, further, is said to increase desire for sexual expression. There is a kind of revival in the practice of family purity laws among some Jewish women in that it affirms their independence and rejects the treatment of women as sex objects (Kaufman: 145–51). Some Jewish feminists adhere to family purity laws because of their symbolic value. Tumah signifies an end of a cycle, a dying when the rich, potentially life-giving menstrual blood leaves the body. Taharah is the return to potential life in the womb. Menstruation is a nexus point. It is both an end of life and a beginning of something new (Adler 1976: 66).

Other feminist scholars have raised several issues regarding the laws of niddah. A recurring question is why menstruation was the only form of impurity that remained after the destruction of the Second Temple. Tumah practised only in the context of menstruation suggests a sense of stigma or taboo based on male fear of women's sexuality and menstrual blood (Cantor 1995: 138; Koltun 1976: 69). That the rabbis extended the period of women's impurity from seven days to fourteen would seem to raise certain suspicions in this regard despite all protestations that tumah is not regarded as pollution, as it was in other ancient religious societies.

Scholars generally agree that the rabbis are disgusted by female functions in the Talmudic tractate, Niddah. There is also fear of female sexual power, especially the fear of being overwhelmed by it. Thus the creation of a system in which men did not have to deal with women's sexuality for half of each month was in their own interest (Cantor 1995: 138). However, as one scholar observes, the tuman/taharah symbolic system is, at least, inclusive of women. Adler asks why one should reject it just because the later generations of rabbis 'projected their repugnance for women upon it' (1976: 71).

Homosexuality

The only permissible sexual relationship within traditional Judaism is a married, heterosexual one. Homosexual relations between men are explicitly forbidden in Lev. 18:22 as an abomination. Since procreation is one of the major purposes of sexual relations in Jewish law, it is prohibited on these grounds. (While there is no prohibition against lesbianism in the biblical texts, the tradition includes it under the practices of Egypt and Canaan prohibited to the Israelites in verse three of Lev. 18.) The Talmud contains only two minor references to lesbianism, and both describe it as a form of licentiousness. Lesbianism here is not legally punishable, perhaps because no semen is spilled. One might conclude from this evidence that lesbianism scarcely existed during rabbinic times. Alternatively, one might just as easily observe that rabbinic material reflects, almost solely, men's experience and that the experiences of women were simply excluded.

Jewish lesbians encounter marginalization and homophobia both within and outside of the Jewish community. Most Jewish communities and congregations, feeling challenged and threatened, have tended to respond with silence and denial to lesbians who are brave enough to make themselves known. The 1982 publication of *Nice Jewish Girls: A Lesbian Anthology* forced Jewish communities at least to acknowledge the existence of same-sex relationships within Judaism. There are signs of hope in that more progressive congregations, out of a sense of justice, understand the gifts lesbians and community can offer each other. The Havurah movement in North America is, to a great extent, understanding and appreciative of lesbian involvement in the Jewish community. While it is important that individuals deal with and overcome homophobia within the Jewish community, Jewish texts and tradition are the ultimate source of discrimination against Jewish lesbians.

These texts and the tradition have never been monolithic. There has always, throughout the history of Judaism, been a kind of unity within diversity. I believe that a feminist transformation of Judaism, and specifically a 'lesbian transformation of Judaism' (Alpert 1997: 13), rests on changing definitions of Judaism and recognition of the richness of diversity.

SOCIAL CHANGE

Judaism has embedded within it the seeds for social action in a world laden with all forms of injustice: sexism, classism, capitalism, and racism. Yet the transformation of unjust structures has generally been left to the 'dirty work of politics', which has been unhelpfully severed from the realm of spirituality (Plaskow 1990: 213). Unlike traditional Christianity, Judaism has always been infused with the notion that fidelity to halacha and rootedness in the world go hand in hand, although the latter has not usually been translated into political terms (Plaskow: 214). It is here that Jewish tradition and concrete feminist concerns for social justice converge most strongly.

The foundation for building a climate of peace and justice is rooted in the writings of the prophets, who criticized worship without the practice of social justice for those most in need, the orphan and the widow, and the poor.

> Is not this the fast that I choose: to loose the bonds of injustice, to undo the thongs of the yoke, to let the oppressed go free, and to break every yoke? Is it not to share your bread with the hungry, and bring the homeless poor into your house; when you see the naked, to cover them, and not to hide yourself from your own kin? (Isaiah 58:6–7)

The prophetic critique of empty religion devoid of social justice undermines observance of Jewish law for its own sake. Yet it is the intention of the law to infuse the world with justice. For example, even earlier than the prophets, there is the command to 'love the stranger, for you were once strangers in the land of Egypt' (Exodus 22:21). The Jewish tradition of *t'shuvah*, repentance (literally, turning around in a different direction) contains the possibility of change at an individual level and social and communal level.

The rabbinic and mystical concept of *Tikkun Olam* (literally, 'mending the world') has many layers of meaning and has not always been applied politically. But it has its roots in the mystical experiences and visions of the prophets. Though never fully endorsed by the rabbis because of its intense speculation on the nature of God, mysticism has nevertheless persisted in Judaism; the idea of Tikkun Olam has ensured that Jewish mysticism has remained profoundly connected to the world and its problems. Isaac Luria (1534–72) sought to explain the demise of the great Jewish community in Spain in 1492 through the concept of Tikkun as well as two others: *Tzimtzum* and *Shevirat Ha Kelim*. The mystical concept of creation, as Luria envisioned it, required *tzimtzum*, or the withdrawal of God from the universe, leaving room for the act of creation. Miscalculation of God's own power resulted in *shevirat ha kelim*, or breaking of the vessels intended to hold the divine light. As a result evil was released in the world and the *Shekhinah*, God's feminine indwelling presence in the world, was now in exile. The sparks of God were scattered and God's internal unity was disrupted. Tikkun Olam in Lurianic understanding meant 'gathering the sparks' and returning them to the Shekhinah, the channel to God, and thus restoring God as well as the world. Originally the means of restoration involved intense devotion to God and adherence to the commandments. Later transformations of Jewish mysticism through Hasidism and the activism of the nineteenth century added a more political dimension to the notion of Tikkun, as is evident today in the liberal and progressive magazine *Tikkun*.

Jewish women have implemented the various justice traditions within Judaism in some unique ways. Tikkun Olam for Jewish women begins as a corrective to the hierarchical nature of leadership in most synagogues and Jewish social institutions, as well as to the various religious structures that exclude women. But the repair and transformation of Judaism is extended to the larger process of transforming political and economic structures of domination. Concerns for halachic change and fuller inclusivity for women in the religious realm have been extended to include justice concerns for all women, everywhere, thus linking the spiritual and the political.

Women in Black, for example, is a network of women committed to peace and justice around the world. Women usually dress in black and demonstrate in non-violent vigils wherever a certain context of injustice demands opposition. The movement began in Israel in 1988 with Israeli and Palestinian women and their supporters protesting the Israeli occupation of the West Bank and Gaza. Another such group is *Bat Shalom*, a feminist organization of Israeli women working together with Palestinian women's groups toward peaceful cooperation between Israelis and Palestinians.

Jewish *kashrut*, or dietary laws, have traditionally reflected a concern for the welfare of animals and a sense of the sanctity of the basic necessity of eating. Feminist Jews and others concerned about the growing poverty in the world are suggesting that eating 'low on the food chain' to preserve more grain might lead to vegetarianism. The inhumane raising of animals for food and the diseases linked with beef production would support this. Kashrut might be extended to prohibiting foods produced with pesticides and herbicides as well as foods containing hormones (Plaskow 1990: 236). Many foods are the product of exploitative labour practices exported for Western consumption.

Placing these products on the forbidden foods list might result in a boycott and create a greater awareness of the economic and social conditions of peoples from developing countries and how the West is implicated in these conditions.

The minor holiday of *Tu Bishvat*, the new year of trees, might be made into a 'major environmental holy day emphasizing the interconnectedness and relational character of all life in the world' (see Ellen Bernstein in Plaskow 1990: 237). Observance of such a day would help to undercut the dualism that pits inferior matter and nature against the superior realm of spirit and the divine. Recognition of the divine within, rather than outside of, nature might nurture respect for the trees to which we, as physical beings dependent on oxygen, owe our existence. Besides providing us with that oxygen, trees remove carbon dioxide from the environment. The continued buildup of carbon dioxide in the ecosphere over the past few decades through increasing carbon emissions and the rapidly diminishing forests around the globe have led to growing concerns about global warming. Recognizing the tree as sacred would not rule out an 'I–Thou relationship'—to quote Martin Buber—with trees. The 1995 Israeli film *Under the Domim Tree*, which tells the story of teenage Holocaust survivors who attend a youth-camp/boarding school in Israel in the early 1950s, illustrates a poignant example of a human relationship with a tree. The most sought-after place for solitude and healing is under the domim tree, which is almost always 'occupied'. These survivors' experience of sacred place is consistent with mystical Judaism, in which a non-gendered name for God is the Hebrew word *Makom*, literally, Place.

Celebration of Tu Bishvat as a sacred day for trees within the Jewish calendar could connect with a larger esoteric philosophy common to many cultures and mythologies, that of the 'Tree of Life', or Cosmic Tree. Often regarded as an all-nourishing Mother, the Cosmic Tree occurs in many myths active in the creation of the world. She is axis mundi: she stands in the centre of the world, continuing to nourish it. She embodies the Divine in the cycles of rebirth, continual creation, and never-ending life. Not surprisingly, the ancient Hebrew goddess Asherah was often lovingly imaged as a tree. We find ourselves also returning to that image of Torah as Tree of Life in Proverbs 3:18.

Ritualizing concerns for the environment is another way of bringing together the spiritual and the political. In the case of Tu Bishvat, the spiritual realm might well be a means to sustain us in the long haul of messy political struggles concerning clear-cutting and of efforts to create sustainable lifestyles.

WOMEN'S OFFICIAL AND UNOFFICIAL ROLES

The complementary positions that women and men were assigned in the private and public spheres of traditional Jewish life are rooted in the ancient texts, particularly the Hebrew Bible. The survival of the ancient Israelites depended on childbearing. The four Matriarchs of the Bible—Sarah, Rebecca, Rachel and Lea—are regarded as models to be emulated especially in the realm of motherhood. To be fertile was a blessing, while barrenness was a misfortune at best and a disaster at worst. When Ruth, the convert to Israel, was betrothed to Boaz, she was blessed with the wish that she be 'like Rachel and Leah, who together built up the house of Israel' (Ruth 4:11). Ruth proves fertile and gives birth to a son, Obed, grandfather of King David, forerunner of the future Messiah. Sarah is exemplary in traditional Judaism in that she embodies the Jewish ideal of modesty. Sarah's spirituality is evidenced by her fervent completion of all of her household tasks including hospitality (Kaufman: 48–9). Sarah is one of the first women in the Bible to work quietly and subtly behind the scenes to help bring about redemption of the world, to bring the world to a state intended by God. One traditional interpretation of Sarah's banishment of Hagar's son Ishmael (Gen. 21) is that she was more spiritually astute than her husband, Abraham, and therefore was able to see Ishmael's 'corruption' (Aiken: 47). Here, Isaac, not Ishmael, was Israel's hope for the future. The traditional ideal of modesty and the notion that women live on a higher spiritual plain than men are recurrent themes that justify placing restrictions on them and limiting their roles to the private sphere. Indeed, Sarah is to be protected as one would an 'invaluable pearl' (Ghatan: 65).

Some traditional Jewish women regard motherhood as the essence of womanhood, an opening to the world of the spirit. Motherhood is also deeply connected to the future, as was the case with Sarah's treatment of Hagar and Ishmael (for example, Frankiel: 6). The fact that the tradition attributes prophecy, the ability to see the future, to six other biblical women, attests to the importance of these women as role models. Their exercise of power in the realm of the household (Frankiel: 6) reinforces the notion in the Jewish tradition that men and women have different but complementary roles. Notable exceptions to this general rule include Deborah, prophetess and judge in the public domain (Judges 3–16) and Huldah the prophetess (2 Chronicles 35:22–8).

Aside from a few female heroes who are exceptions to the male-centred textual tradition, there are female figures that might be referred to as negative role models in the rabbinical tradition. Yael, for example, who is mentioned in connection with Deborah, kills Sisera, a general of the Canaanite army at war with Israel. The fleeing Sisera seeks 'refuge' in the tent of Yael only to be killed by her when she hammered a tent peg through his skull. The assassination is described elsewhere as 'aggressively phallic' (Levine in Niditch 1989: 46).

Other female figures such as Judith function as a kind of 'feminine unconventional' in subversive literature that aroused a cry of protest around the fifth century BCE, when Ezra and Nehemiah, having returned to Jerusalem from

Babylonian exile, sought to restrict the liberties of Israelite women and impose hardships on them by denouncing intermarriages with the Canaanite foreigners (LaCocque 1990: 1–6). These figures 'use the most controversial resources of their femininity' to become God's instruments (LaCocque 1990: 2). The story of Judith is found in the Septuagint, the Greek versions of the Hebrew Bible. In a later retelling of the Assyrian conquest of Israel, Holofernes commander of the Assyrian army and enemy of Israel, is seduced and then beheaded by Judith while he is 'dead drunk' (Judith 13, New Revised Standard Version). Not surprisingly, rabbis did not canonize (recognize as authoritative scripture) the book of Judith.

In the Middle Ages the greatest Jewish women were considered those who exercised their special status in the context of family life, in the bearing and raising of children. It is in the private sphere that women have 'left an indelible mark on Jewish history'. The few women who exercised influence in the public domain did so 'in response to the needs of the nation' and largely against their own will (Kaufman: 73). One such woman is the German Glückel of Hameln (1645–1724), who wrote her memoirs giving us valuable glimpses of the lives of women during this time. Like other medieval Jewish women whose lives have been recorded, Glückel was of a higher social class than the majority of women of the time. Highly educated for this period she also was a 'warm, good mother' who had 12 children. Her moral directives centred on acts of loving kindness and living out traditional Judaism (Kaufman: 96).

The roles of women in Judaism vary depending on culture and location. Sephardi Jewish women's lives,[1] for example, were determined first by Muslim control of Spain and, after 1492, by Christendom. Jewish women, like Muslim women, were largely limited to the home. Under Christian pressure to either convert to Christianity or be expelled from the country in the late fifteenth century, many Jews lived as underground Jews at great risk to their lives, always under threat from the Inquisition. Jewish women played an important role in keeping certain observances alive, especially those related to the Sabbath and the dietary laws.

Peculiar to Central and Eastern European Jewish women was the recitation of *tkhines*, prayers written in the colloquial Yiddish[2] rather than in Hebrew, the language of public ritual and scholarship from which women were excluded. Tkhines constituted a form of popular devotional religious literature largely written by men. An examination of these prayers reveals that ordinary unlearned Jewish women did have rich religious lives around biological events such as menstruation, pregnancy, and childbirth as well as various domestic duties. Although excluded from communal worship, women had recourse to developing individual spirituality within the context of the home (Weissler 1991: 159–81).

A study of the contemporary experience of elderly, pious Kurdish and other Middle-Eastern Jewish women living in Jerusalem reveals modern expression of sacralizing the female domestic domain. This is a shift away from the study of female symbols and the official roles of women as described by men, in which women are treated as objects, to the study of the lives of women as actually lived (Starr Sered 1992: 7). Functioning within the male-oriented, normative and religious system, they have used this very system to develop 'an alternative scale of measuring value and worth'. In the female domains of family and kitchen, caring for neighbours, giving to charity, and tending to tombs of family and saints, these women have 'a great deal of power and autonomy' (Starr Sered: 4, 139). By creating a tradition within the normative tradition of study of religious texts and participation in public worship, these women have established their own rich religious world of meaning and control.

The twentieth-century experience of North American Jewish women (and men) confirms the reality that scholarly study and communal worship is not, and need not be regarded as the 'essence' of Judaism (Umansky 1991: 285). (Both Umansky and Sered, above, appeal to Carol Gilligan's study on gender and moral development, *In a Different Voice*.) Many immigrant women to the United States and to Canada had been strongly influenced by the German Reform movement, where ethics was considered more important than study and prayer (Umansky: 284). Early in the twentieth century these women began to form volunteer, altruistic social, educational, and philanthropic organizations within both non-sectarian and Jewish contexts.

As society opened up to women in most spheres of life, some women sought rabbinic ordination. In 1972 the Reform movement ordained for the first time a woman, Sally Preisand. One of the first Canadian congregations to hire a female rabbi, Elyse Goldstein, was Holy Blossom Temple in Toronto. The Reconstructionist Rabbinical College in Philadelphia began to accept openly gay and lesbian candidates for ordination in 1984. Today, Rebecca Alpert, one of the first women to be ordained there, works openly as a lesbian rabbi to those Jews who have been relegated to or who have chosen to live on the margins of the Jewish religious establishment. She finds being on the margins a particular vantage point from which to view reality in general and the Jewish and Reconstructionist world in particular, as well as the larger world, joining others at the margins: women of colour, other lesbians, Muslim women, and the working classes (Alpert 2001: 174–7). The freedom of the margins allows her, she maintains, to promote, as a rabbi, abortion rights and opposition to the death penalty, and work with interfaith groups for peace and justice around the world (178–9). Furthermore, she has been welcomed by the 'unaffiliated', approximately one-half of the American Jewish community that does not officially belong to the community through membership in a synagogue. Many of these unaffiliated Jews are themselves marginalized—as singles, gays or lesbians, or poor—by, more often than not, strongly family-oriented and middle-class Jewish communities (179).

Those on the margins have created many new rituals, for example, cere-monies for 'coming out' and gay marriage. Most Jewish rituals such as birth, puberty, and mourning rituals are male-created and many of them are reserved for males. There are new rituals celebrating female persons, including baby-naming ceremonies for girls, rituals connected with menstruation, and *Bat Mitzvah* (puberty, coming of age) ceremonies (Adelman 1990). Jewish women have reclaimed ritual immersion *(mikveh)*, a ritual traditionally prescribed for ritual impurity after menstruation or childbirth. Mikveh ceremonies are now performed as healing ceremonies, especially for victims of rape or other traumas (Broner 1999: 133–48). The *Rosh Chodesh* celebration that marks each month's new moon has evolved into a woman's holiday (Broner: 170–80). The *Haggadah,* or 'the Telling', at the annual Passover Seder meal has been retold over and over again as seen through Jewish feminist lenses (Broner 1993; 1999: 76–104). The Exodus, the Festival of Freedom, is a time of 'crossing borders' by naming women such as Miriam and rewriting them back into the *Haggadah* (Broner 1982: 234–44). Perhaps and hopefully, the frequent crossing of borders in Jewish women's rituals will entice the centre to find ways to accom-modate and incorporate into the mainstream of organized Jewish religious life those on the margins and their new and innovative texts.

BACKLASH

Efforts to bring about change almost always meets with resistance from those determined to maintain the religious status quo. Pushing the boundaries of tra-ditional Judaism to allow for greater inclusivity for women often raises suspi-cions that feminists have sold out their Jewishness or opted for something that can no longer be called Judaism. There is also the fear that Jewish feminists are a threat to the traditional nuclear family, the mainstay of Judaism. Jewish fem-inism in the 1960s began to explore ways to transform the Jewish religious community so that women might become full members. Some women sought to change Jewish laws concerning divorce and segregated seating in synagogues as well as to include women in the minyan, or the quorum of 10 required for communal worship. Liberal sectors of the Jewish community made institutional changes that allowed for the ordination of women. In 1972 the Reform move-ment in the United States ordained its first woman. Opposition to the gains made in these areas and to the ordination of women has come not just from Jewish men but from some Jewish women as well. A leading feminist scholar notes that the Jewish feminist movement is experiencing a 'retrenchment' as it tries to take stock of past successes and attempts to respond to its opponents (Heschel 1983: xvii).

The main objection to Jewish feminisms and Jewish spiritualities is an alleged connection to goddess worship, and the charge that these movements represent a return to paganism. For some feminists, experimentation with God language using female metaphors is necessary to broaden the range of images of God. Even though female imagery rings of goddess worship for some, others who engage in such experimentation may have no inclination toward goddess veneration. Substituting 'Queen of the Universe' for 'King of the Universe' in a *berakha,* or blessing, for example, may not be a successful image for everyone. One well-known traditional scholar who would call herself a feminist writes:

> The answer stuns with its crudity. It is preposterous. What? Millennia after the cleansing purity of Abraham's vision of the One Creator, a return to Astarte, Hera, Juno, Venus, and all their proliferating sisterhood? Sex goddesses, fertility goddesses, mother goddesses? The sacrifices brought to these were often enough human. This is the new vision intended to 'restore dignity' to Jewish women? A resurrection of every ancient idolatry the Jewish idea came into the world to drive out, so as to begin again with a purifying clarity? The answer slanders and sullies monotheism . . . Without an uncompromising monotheism, there can be no Jewish way . . . Not for nothing does a Jew fervently recite, morning and evening, 'Hear O Israel, the Lord our God is One", in order to reaffirm daily the monotheistic principle'. (Ozick 1983: 121)

The underlying angst and false assumptions (such as human sacrifice to goddesses) are clear. One of the issues raised in the above reaction to female God imagery is the nature of monotheism. If monotheism is understood as the worship of only one image of God, a male one, then it is not monotheism but monolatry. Any one image for God is only a partial picture of the divine totality (Plaskow 1990: 151).

Even though female imagery of the divine need not imply goddess worship, there are precedents in the history of Judaism for such worship. The history of ancient Israel is one of separation from their surrounding cultures, the most well known of which are the Canaanites and their many deities. Biblical editors portray Canaanite religion as idolatrous, and in tension with the exclusive worship of Yahweh, who, in the biblical tradition, unlike the Canaanite deities, had no sexual partner. But in the long journey towards monotheism, the high Canaanite father god, El, whose consort was Asherah, was conflated with Yahweh. It was not easy for the majority of Israelites to relinquish other deities such as Asherah. Therefore the tension between

Israelite monotheism and Canaanite polytheism is a dialectic within Israel itself. The prophetic invective against ancient worship is similar to the New Testament contempt for the Pharisees; each condemns the older religion in the process of defining itself. It is prudent to remember the ancient roots of Judaism without demonizing and caricaturing it, just as Christians would do well to remember their origins. Christian treatment of Judaism should function as a warning to Jews of the 'danger of unthinking contempt for another tradition' (Plaskow 1990: 149).

UNIQUE FEATURES OF JUDAISM
AS THEY IMPACT ON WOMEN

Women within Judaism are able to function as Jews in many ways, inside or outside of the religious tradition, or on the margins. A Jewish woman may find her Jewish vocation as an Orthodox Jew, as a liberal in Conservative or Reform Judaism, or in the Renewal Movement which combines elements of orthodoxy with New Age insights. She may be a committed, passionate Jew and also an atheist. There is no body of theology in Judaism to which one must adhere to be a Jew. Judaism is not only a religion, but also a civilization and a nation. A Jew is one born from a Jewish mother. Thus there is an ethnic, but not a racial dimension to Jewish identity. Conversion to Judaism is possible but difficult. A Jew by choice is considered to be fully Jewish in the State of Israel if he or she converts through orthodox channels.

Women who live within the *halachic* framework of Judaism and who accept the presuppositions of Jewish life and law do not see themselves as oppressed but as living within a world structured and ordered by God's will. They may regard themselves as liberated from the obligation to pray three times a day, and they are satisfied and nurtured by their three positive *mitzvoth,* or commandments: lighting the Sabbath candles, ritual immersion, and separation of the *challah* (Sabbath bread) dough.

Women committed to the Jewish religious tradition but dissatisfied with the exclusive language of the liturgy and ways of addressing God in exclusively male terms have created new blessings that reflect their experience. The 'heart and soul and bones of Hebrew prayer' (Falk: xv) is the *berakha,* or blessing, which encompasses every aspect of Jewish life. Substituting inclusive images of divinity for the traditional, patriarchal formula—Blessed are You, Lord, King of the Universe—Falk has reached a whole range of Jews from the liberal denominations such as Conservative, Reform, and Reconstructionism to *chavurah* communities and unaffiliated Jews. Her *Book of Blessings* 'is for those immersed in Judaism, and for those standing at its gates, looking for ways in' (xxi). Recognizing that every alternative image for divinity is partial, she sought to create 'a process of ongoing naming' that would embrace diversity of experience (Falk: xvii). Her rewriting of the Blessing Before the Meal, for example, reads as follows: 'Let us bless the source of life that brings forth bread from the earth' (18). It is a communal formula that acknowledges unity in diversity.

Women's rituals such as *Rosh Chodesh,* honouring the New Moon and ushering in the beginning of the Jewish month, are proliferating. Other rituals, however, have been lost to women, as, for example, the ancient period of mourning by women of Jephthah's daughter's plight (Judges 11). This ritual occurred in the story of Jephthah, Israel's mighty warrior, who, in battle against the Ammonites, made a vow to God that should the Ammonites be delivered into his hand, he would offer up as a burnt sacrifice the first person to emerge from his house. This person is his daughter, who asks to be given two months to lament her virginity with her women friends. Thereafter 'there arose an Israelite custom that for four days every year the daughters of Israel would go out to lament the daughter of Jephthah the Gileadite' (verses 39b–40). Norma Baumel Joseph in the Canadian Film *Half the Kingdom* states '[H]ere's our biblical authority . . . here's our legitimacy. It was lost to us; let's bring it back . . . There's a time once a year . . . this is women's day . . . women celebrating women, mourning women'.

Judith Plaskow would concur on the basis of the principle of rabbinic openness, 'on the rabbinic insistence that the Bible can be made to speak to the present day (1990: 54). *Midrash* was the vehicle for this type of interpretation in the past and continues to be today. These *midrashim* are based on women's experience today. Therefore women's experience is authoritative: the experience of marginalization, exclusion, Otherness.

The 1994 documentary *Half the Kingdom* was produced by the National Film Board of Canada and Studio D, the now-defunct studio that focused on women's issues. Directed by Francine Zuckerman with Roushell Goldstein, the film captures the diversity of Jewish women's lived experience. It begins with an old legend about a man, retold about a woman: 'an old, arthritic [woman] gnarled and planting a tree'.

> People walk by her and ask, 'Why are you planting this tree, old woman? You'll never eat from its fruit'" She answers: 'There were trees planted by others when I came into this world. My job is to plant this tree for those who come after me. Our lot in life is not to finish everything but merely to begin'.

In dialogue with her young daughter and her husband regarding the infamous prayer said by males in the synagogue every morning 'Thank God for not making me a woman,' Norma Joseph's partner concludes that it was no longer appropriate for him to say this prayer. An Orthodox female and a professor at

Concordia University in Montreal, Norma Joseph herself concludes: 'If there were things I couldn't accomplish, the next generation might' (*Half the Kingdom*).

Naomi Goldenberg, professor of Religious Studies at the University of Ottawa, states in this film:

I am a Jew, I'm an atheist, I'm a feminist: I would love to find a group of people with whom I could be all those things. . . . For me, Judaism is about freedom and dignity and human independence of thought in the face of lots of hardships and lots of sadness. I want my daughter to have a sense of that Jewish rebelliousness of spirit, a sense of that connection with vitality that Judaism has. I want her to have Judaism as a chisel to work on this mono-lithic Christian identity that's being handed out so much in western culture and I'd like Judaism to be something or to have a place where my daughter could be comfortable.

On the other hand, Norma Baumel Joseph argued passionately in Jerusalem at the first International Jewish Feminist Conference in 1988 as follows:

I am a Jew. I'm a believing and practising Jew and I choose to be an Orthodox Jew. I find challenge and conflict in my existence as a female Jew. Frequently I feel divided as though parts of myself are in opposition, antithetical, antag-onistic, clashing, hostile. I wish to live as part of a community. I am often alone. The road has been difficult in ways I never expected. I knew the *yeshiva* world would not like me. I even knew I would be too feminist for the Jewish world. But when the feminist world finds me too Jewish and when this Jewish feminist world finds me too religious . . . I find it too difficult. Always an out-sider, women have tried to redirect me or disempower me as frequently as men and I reject it and reject their patronizing concept of me as an Orthodox Jew. You don't know me because you can label me. You don't know my pol-itics nor my radical feminism and you cannot tell me I am not there yet.

In the State of Israel, Alice Shalvi, women's rights activist, professor, and principal of Pelach, a school for girls and one of the first in the last century, seeks to fuse a love of Judaism with general, secular studies. She seeks to inte-grate drama and theatre (in some Jewish traditions regarded as forms of lying and deception) into everyday Jewish life. In North America, Michele Landsberg, political activist and columnist for the *Toronto Star,* says: 'Politics is my halacha: it's my law of being . . . how to live. Our political beliefs in Democratic Socialism and a fairer, more just world . . . guides us in our daily life in the way that Jewish law guides the Orthodox' (*Half the Kingdom*). In the same film, Reform Rabbi Elyse Goldstein, currently director of Kolel, a centre for Jewish studies, states:

> I think what has been happening in the Jewish feminist community is very exciting in that women are having more of a voice—in everything. What makes me worried is a feeling that we might need permission to use that voice . . . We have permission—permission is given to us not by men, not by any human being but just by being who we are—by being alive and being God's creatures.

As for the future, Michele Landsberg maintains: 'If Judaism is too rigid and too formalized to accept this new stream of thought and experience that is coming from the women, then, I think, it will be simply amputating its living parts—and it will become a relic, a relic that can't go on being a creative and living force'. The film ends with a story by the biblical commentator Sporno, narrated by Elyse Goldstein:

> There are two kinds of trees: there is a tree that stands up straight against the wind and when a big gust of wind comes it refuses to bend—it's going to be straight. What is going to happen to that tree: eventually a gust of wind strong enough is going to knock it over. But then there is a reed in the water and the reed bends with the wind. When the wind comes the reed doesn't fight the wind—it goes with the wind. . . .

'That is what Jewish feminists really are . . . Many people would wish we were just a little breeze—oh, it's just a few crazy fringe Jewish women out there who want to change everything. No, we are that gust of wind and Judaism is either going to be that tree that's going to stand against us until it falls or it's going to be a reed in the water and bend with the changes and ultimately grow a great deal and become more beautiful and more blossoming as a result' (*Half the Kingdom*).

The last word on this documentary goes to Norma Joseph who articulates this sentiment at the very beginning:

> I love being a Jew: I want the community to survive; I want the tradition of Judaism to continue into the future and I want to have a part in being that future and I won't be silent.

NOTES

1.   Sepharad is the ancient name for Spain. Those Jews born there and their descendants are called Sephardim or Sephardi Jews.

2. The Yiddish language is a combination of Hebrew and German written in Hebrew characters and spoken by Ashkenazi Jews. The Yiddish word *tkhines* is based on the Hebrew term *tkhinna*, which means 'supplication'.

REFERENCES

Adler, Rachel. 1976. 'Tumah and Taharah: Ends and Beginnings'. *The Jewish Woman: New Perspectives*. Ed. Elizabeth Koltun. New York: Schocken Books: 63–71.

———. 1983. 'The Jew Who Wasn't There: *Halakhah* and the Jewish Woman'. *On Being a Jewish Feminist: A Reader*. Ed. Susannah Heschel. New York: Schocken Books: 12–18.

Aiken, Lisa. 1992. *To Be a Jewish Woman*. Northvale, New Jersey/London: Jason Aronson, Inc.

Adelman, Penina V. 1990, 1986. *Miriam's Well: Rituals for Jewish Women Around the Year*. New York: Biblio Press.

Alpert, Rebecca. 1997. *Like Bread on the Seder Plate: Jewish Lesbians and the Transformation of Tradition*. New York: Columbia University Press.

———. 2001. 'On Being a Rabbi at the Margins'. *Lesbian Rabbis: The First Generation*. Eds. Rebecca T. Alpert, Sue Levi Elwell, and Shirley Idelson. New Brunswick, New Jersey and London: Rutgers University Press: 173–180.

Baskin, Judith R. 1991. 'Jewish Women in the Middle Ages'. *Jewish Women in Historical Perspective*. Ed. Judith R. Baskin. Detroit: Wayne State University Press: 94–114.

Biale, Rachel. 1984. *Women and Jewish Law: An Exploration of Women's Issues in Halakhic Sources*. New York: Schocken Books.

Broner, E.M. 1982. 'Honor and Ceremony in Women's Rituals'. *The Politics of Women's Spirituality: Essays on the Rise of Spiritual Power Within the Feminist Movement*. Ed. Charlene Spretnak. Garden City, New York: Anchor Press/Doubleday: 234–44.

———. 1993. *The Telling: The Story of a Group of Jewish Women who Journey to Spirituality through Community and Ceremony*. New York: HarperSanFrancisco.

———. 1999. *Bringing Home the Light: A Jewish Woman's Handbook of Rituals*. San Francisco/Tulsa: Council Oak Books.

Brooten, Bernadette J. 1982. *Women Leaders in the Ancient Synagogue: Inscriptional Evidence and Background Issues*. (Brown Judaic Studies 36). Chico, California: Scholars Press.

Cantor, Aviva. 1983. 'The Lilith Question'. *On Being a Jewish Feminist: A Reader*. Ed. Susannah Heschel. New York: Schocken Books: 40–50.

———. 1995. *Jewish Women/Jewish Men: The Legacy of Patriarchy in Jewish Life*. New York: HarperCollins.

Falk, Marcia. 1996. *The Book of Blessings: New Jewish Prayers for Daily Life, the Sabbat and the New Moon Festival*. New York: HarperCollins.

Frankiel, Tamar. 1990. *The Voice of Sarah: Feminine Spirituality and Traditional Judaism*. New York: HarperCollins.

Freedman, Rabbi Dr. H., and Maurice Simon, trans., eds, commentators. 1961, 1939. *Midrash Rabbah, Genesis I*. London: The Soncino Press.

Ghatan, H.E. Yedidiah. 1986. *The Invaluable Pearl: The Unique Status of Women in Judaism*. New York: Bloch Publishing Company.

Gross, Rita M. 1983. 'Steps toward Feminine Imagery of Deity in Jewish Theology'. *On Being a Jewish Feminist: A Reader*. Ed. Susannah Heschel. New York: Schocken Books: 234–47.

Half the Kingdom. 1994. Dir. Francine Zuckerman with Roushell Goldstein. Documentary. National Film Board of Canada, Studio D.

Hauptman, Judith. 1974. 'Images of Women in the Talmud'. *Religion and Sexism: Images of Woman in the Jewish and Christian Traditions*. Ed. Rosemary Radford Ruether. New York: Simon and Schuster: 184–212.

Heschel, Susannah. 1983. 'Introduction'. *On Being a Jewish Feminist: A Reader*. Ed. Susannah Heschel. New York: Schocken Books: xiii–xxxvi.

———. 1990. 'Anti-Judaism and Christian Feminist Theology'. *Tikkun* May/June: 25–8, 95–7.

Kaufman, Michael. 1993. *The Woman in Jewish Law and Tradition*. Northvale, New Jersey/London: Jason Aronson, Inc.

Koltun, Elizabeth. 1976. *The Jewish Woman: New Perspectives*. New York: Schocken Books.

Kuikman, Jacoba. 2000. 'Christ as Cosmic Tree'. *Toronto Journal of Theology* 16/1: 141–54.

LaCocque, André.1990. *The Feminine Unconventional: Four Subversive Figures in Israel's Tradition*. Minneapolis: Fortress Press.

Meyers, Carol. 1988. *Discovering Eve: Ancient Israelite Women in Context*. New York and Oxford: Oxford University Press.

The New Revised Standard Version of the Bible. 1991. New York: Oxford University Press.

Niditch, Susan. 1989. 'Eroticism and Death in the Tale of Jael'. *Gender and Difference in Ancient Israel*. Ed. Peggy L. Day. Minneapolis: Fortress Press.

Olyan, Saul. 1988. *Asherah and the Cult of Yahweh in Israel*. Atlanta, GA: Scholars Press.

Ozick, Cynthia. 1983. 'Notes toward Finding the Right Question'. *On Being a Jewish Feminist: A Reader*. Ed. Susannah Heschel. New York: Schocken Books: 120–51.

Patai, Raphael. 1990. *The Hebrew Goddess*. Detroit: Wayne State University Press.

Plaskow, Judith. 1979. 'The Coming of Lilith: Toward a Feminist Theology'. *Womanspirit Rising: A Feminist Reader in Religion*. Eds. Carol P. Christ and Judith Plaskow. San Francisco: Harper and Row: 198–209.

———. 1983. 'The Right Question is Theological'. *On Being a Jewish Feminist: A Reader*. Ed. Susannah Heschel. New York: Schocken Books: 223–33.

———. 1990. *Standing Again at Sinai: Judaism from a Feminist Perspective*. New York: HarperCollins.

Romney Wegner, Judith. 1991. 'The Image and Status of Women in Classical Rabbinic Judaism'. *Jewish Women in Historical Perspective*. Ed. Judith R. Baskin. Detroit: Wayne State University Press: 68–114.

Starr Sered, Susan. 1992. *Women as Ritual Experts: The Religious Lives of Elderly Jewish Women in Jerusalem*. New York/Oxford: Oxford University Press.

Tanakh. 1985. A New Translation of The Holy Scriptures according to the Traditional Hebrew Text. Philadelphia/New York/Jerusalem: The Jewish Publication Society.

Torton Beck, Evelyn, ed. 1989, 1982. *Nice Jewish Girls: A Lesbian Anthology*. Boston: Beacon Press.

Umansky, Ellen M. 1991. 'Spiritual Expressions: Jewish Women's Religious Lives in the Twentieth-Century United States'. *Jewish Women in Historical Perspective*. Ed. Judith R. Baskin. Detroit: Wayne State University Press: 265–288.

Under the Domim Tree. 1994. Dir. Eli Cohen. From the novel by Gila Almagor. Hebrew with English subtitles.VHS. Wellspring.

Von Kellenbach, Katherina. 1994. *Anti-Judaism in Feminist Religious Writings*. Atlanta, Georgia: Scholars Press (The American Academy of Religion).

Weissler, Chava. 1991. 'Prayers in Yiddish and the Religious World of Ashkenazi Women'. *Jewish Women in Historical Perspective*. Ed. Judith R. Baskin. Detroit: Wayne State University Press: 159–81.

Wolfson, Elliot R. 1995. *Circle in the Square: Studies in the Use of Gender in Kabbalistic Symbolism*. Albany: State University of New York Press.

FURTHER READING

Adler, Rachel. *Engendering Judaism: An Inclusive Theology and Ethics*. Philadelphia/Jerusalem: The Jewish Publication Society, 1998.

Hyman, Paula E. *Gender and Assimilation in Modern Jewish History: The Roles and Representation of Women*. Seattle & London: University of Washington Press, 1995.

Peskowitz, Miriam, and Laura Levitt, eds. *Judaism Since Gender*. New York and London: Routledge, 1997.

Rudavsky, T.M., ed. *Gender and Judaism: The Transformation of Tradition*. New York and London: New York University Press, 1995.

CHAPTER 3

WOMEN IN THE BUDDHIST TRADITIONS

Eva K. Neumaier

INTRODUCTION AND OVERVIEW

Buddhism is a religion with a 2,500-year history; its sacred texts number in the tens of thousands and are preserved in numerous classical languages of Asia, ranging from Pāli and Sanskrit to Chinese, Tibetan, and less known languages such as Khotanese. Since the end of the nineteenth century, non-Asian people in Europe and North America have gradually adopted Buddhism, and in the West today, Buddhism is the fastest growing of all religions. In absolute numbers, however, it is still a minority religion. Buddhism has played a part in a vast array of societies, cultures, and historical periods, ranging from Iron Age India to contemporary California.

What follows is a modest attempt to lay a historical background, including the most important facts and documents pertinent to the status and roles of women during the early period of Buddhism in India (*c.* 400–200 BCE). The emphasis is on how various Buddhist traditions reacted to woman as a social being but also to woman as a symbol representing specific 'feminine' values and traits. We focus on how women were represented within the life story of the Buddha; analyze the poems left behind by the first Buddhist nuns; reflect on the rules specific to the nuns; and discuss how the earliest extant texts in Pāli represent the Buddhist laywoman, comparing the textual testimonies with contemporary inscriptions. While women were quite visible in the early historical documents of Buddhism, later (approximately from the second century BCE on) they seem to fade into the background. Around the fifth century CE, they vanish completely from the historical records. Though women in mainstream Buddhist traditions tend to be absent, there are a few documents emphasizing the presence of the Buddhist woman during the pre-modern era. This chapter provides readers with the historical and cultural information necessary to develop an informed opinion, and endeavours to engage readers in theoretical reflections permitting a critical assessment that recognizes the vast diversity characteristic of the Buddhist traditions.

THE ORIGIN OF BUDDHISM

The religious traditions that the modern world knows as Buddhism originated in India around the middle of the last millennium, prior to the inception of the Common Era. Buddhism thus arose at about the same time as thinkers in ancient Greece were trying to base their understanding of the world on reason rather than on myth, and as, in China, Confucius was teaching nobility as a moral value and not as a privilege of birth. The Buddhist movement began as an ascetic but also rebellious movement of members of the social elite. Its founder, a prince named Siddhartha Gautama, who later became known as Buddha, the Enlightened One, was born into a noble family that ruled over a small principality in an area that is now on the Indian-Nepalese border.

Although he was brought up in the luxury common to his class, Siddhartha nevertheless experienced a yearning for a state of mind beyond suffering and beyond death. At age 29 he left his family and noble surroundings in order to pursue the life of an ascetic wanderer in search of enlightenment. After several years of arduous striving under the guidance of different teachers who taught various systems of yoga, Siddhartha faced a personal crisis. With great vigour he had followed the time-honoured rules of asceticism, but to no avail. Close to death by starvation, he made one final attempt to seek that coveted spiritual breakthrough. The following night, meditating under a fig tree, he gained insight into the law of *karma* (that is, he realized that past activities determine the present situation and that this life is only one in an endless chain of re-embodiments). Furthermore, he realized the so-called four-fold noble truth: that life is inevitably saturated with suffering (birth, sickness, old age, and death); that desire and yearning is the cause of suffering; that the end of yearning implies the end of suffering, which is *nirvana*; and that there is a path toward realizing nirvana (consisting of wisdom, morality, and contemplation). Only through moral and mental discipline and a ruthless inquiry into the true nature of things would one gain nirvana; no gods or spirits, no magic could be of any help in this endeavour.

When the morning dawned, Siddhartha had reached the inner assurance that now suffering had come to an end and that nirvana, a state beyond any description or words, had been achieved. Siddhartha had become an Enlightened One, a Buddha. After some reluctance to share his insight with others, he wandered over the dusty roads of the eastern Ganges Valley for more than 40 years. He shared his experience and his insight with those who were eager to hear it. During these four decades a large and diverse following began to assemble around him. The teaching of the four-fold noble truth was complemented with the teaching of interdependent origination, illuminating how all phases of life are interconnected and depend on each other. He also taught an elaborate system of meditation that would lead to the realization of nirvana. Similar to his contemporaries in ancient Greece or China, Buddha criticized the belief in the potency of gods and demons; he emphasized that nobility means nobility of character, and that this can be achieved only through strenuous self-discipline, never by birthright. In the ascetic-spiritual view of the Buddha, there is no room for an omniscient and almighty god, male or female, or for a concept similar to the Christian concept of sin or hell. One's present deeds determine one's future according to the rule of karma, which cannot be altered, not by any god or Buddha. Based on textual studies, early modern scholars considered Buddhism a form of moral humanism rather than a religion. Later scholars argued that this approach that reduced a living faith to a moral philosophy disregarded the living expressions of practising Buddhists.

Soon after Buddha had realized enlightenment, fellow ascetics and yogis were drawn to him. Although he never encouraged anyone to follow him, or to abandon their families, a following of men and women began to form. Among them were aristocrats, wealthy guild masters, artisans, tradespeople, courtesans, and ordinary folks, as well as beggars and even criminals. They were drawn to the Buddha in the expectation that they too would be able to attain a state of being beyond suffering where they could see 'things as they are', a state described as *arhantship* as long as the person was alive, and as nirvana, once the person passed away. They would then be cleansed of the distorted vision of reality, of all forms of yearning and desire, as well as of all forms of rejection and hatred.

Judging from extant literary sources, it seems that at first Buddha's followers lived by simply imitating their master's way of life, a life of utmost simplicity. But when society took issue with some of the habits of this new community—such as former spouses wandering together through the countryside as fellow ascetics—the need for 'rules' emerged. Each of the monastic rules ascribed to Buddha (and there are several hundreds) is introduced by a story that recounts the circumstances that necessitated its proclamation. A number of these rules deal with how women should behave within this newly founded ascetic community and how they should interact with laypeople, male and female. Some rules regulate sexual and erotic activities. There are two sets of rules, one for monks and one for nuns. The monks' rules certainly predate the formulation of the nuns' rules and serve as the template for the latter. A thorough discussion of these rules provides insight into how women were seen by the early Buddhist community.

The place of women in Buddhism has to be seen against the background of general social organization in India at that time. Unlike ethnic religions such as Hinduism or Judaism, religions that originate with a historical founder, such as Confucianism or Islam, always present themselves in dialogue, and often in contrast to an existing socio-religious situation. This is the case with Buddhism. Many of its doctrines contested general views and beliefs held in high esteem by Indians at that time. The status and roles of women in early Buddhist communities are defined and circumscribed by the mainly non-Buddhist society of early India. Pre-Buddhist India recognized woman mainly for her reproductive capabilities, whereby the delivery of sons was of great economic and ritual significance. Not long before the rise of Buddhism, Indian society underwent a transition from being a mainly pastoral and semi-agricultural, village-based society to an urban one typified by labour diversification, a rise in mercantilism, and artistic accomplishments. This urban climate provided women of the upper classes with opportunities to unfold their intellectual and artistic talents. Thus, I.B. Horner wrote:

> The birth of girl-children was no longer met with open-eyed and loud-voiced despair, for girls had ceased to be despised and looked upon as encumbrances. They were now allowed a good deal of liberty. Matrimony was not held before them as the end and aim of their existence, and they were not regarded as shameful if they did not marry; but if they did, they were neither hastened off to an early child-marriage, nor bound to accept the man of their parents' selection. Princesses and ladies of high degree seem to have had some voice in the matter of choosing their husband. As wife a woman was no mere household drudge, but she had considerable authority in the home, ranked as her husband's helpmate, companion and guardian, and in matters both temporal and spiritual were regarded as his equal and worthy of respect. . . . Under Buddhism, more than ever before, she was an individual in command of her own life until the dissolution of the body, and less of a chattel to be only respected if she lived through and on a man. (Horner 1930: 3)

Despite a general improvement of women's status, the early Buddhist community certainly challenged the social mores of Indian society when it began to accept women as wandering ascetics side-by-side with men. This novelty must have stirred some emotions among the general Indian populace. Many of the rules specific to the nuns' order were obviously designed to minimize society's discomfort with independent women, exempt from the reproductive routine and male supervision and outside the range of domestic duties, roaming the country. While women of the elite certainly enjoyed not only the privileges of their class but also a modest participation in such male-dominated fields as philosophical debating and governance (only in the absence of a male heir), it was unheard of that they would join migratory ascetic groups in pursuit of mystical experiences. Given the circumstances of its beginning, the

Buddhist traditions had the opportunity to include women more than did any other religious group emerging at that time.

WOMEN'S OFFICIAL AND UNOFFICIAL ROLES AND BACKLASH

Throughout history Buddhist women participated in the practice of their faith. However, when reflecting on past periods we can judge women's roles only on the basis of historical evidence, which are either inscriptions on stone or copper tables or textual evidence. Thus, the picture we gain based on these sources is necessarily incomplete as it treats unrecorded events with silence. We gain some information about women by examining the female characters in Buddha's life story and by studying the records of Buddhist nuns.

Women in Buddha's Life Story

Women figure in the Buddhist literature from early on. However, the historic accuracy of these accounts remains in most cases questionable. A major crux is that 'the word of the Buddha', which makes up the core of the Buddhist scriptures, was not put to writing before the last or second-last century BCE, 200 to 300 years after the founder's death.

First, let us examine how women were represented in Buddha's own life stories. In a text from the first century CE, Buddha's conception and birth are praised in the flowery language of court poetry:

> This ruler of men, with his queen, enjoyed, as it were, the sovereign of Vaiśravaṇa. Then without defilement she received the fruit of the womb, just as knowledge united with mental concentration bears fruit.
>
> Before she conceived, she saw in her sleep a white lord of elephant entering her body, yet she felt thereby no pain.
>
> Māyā, the queen of that god-like king, bore in her womb the glory of her race and, being in her purity free from weariness, sorrow and illusion, she set her mind on the sin-free forest.
>
> ....
>
> Then as soon as Puṣya became propitious, from the side of the queen, who was hallowed by her vows, a son was born for the weal of the world, without her suffering either pain or illness. (Aśvaghoṣa tr. by Johnston: 2–3)

While these verses hardly render a historical account, they speak articulately of the devotion that faithful Buddhists must have felt regarding Buddha's birth. As in similar accounts of a religion's founder, Māyā, Buddha's mother, is praised for her purity, and the conception happens 'without defilement'. The birth itself is miraculous as the future Buddha enters the world through an opening in his mother's waist. Needless to say, the child is precocious. Idyllic as these accounts are, they nevertheless cannot conceal the impression that the woman here is seen only as a means to the end—that is, to glorify the founder's birth as a unique event. Buddha's mother is said to have died soon after his birth, and her sister, Prajāpatī, became his wet nurse and nanny. She will be reintroduced in several texts as the first woman that Buddha formally ordained as a nun. In accord with the custom of his time and class, while still at home the adolescent Buddha got married and lived a life of luxury and splendour, surrounded by numerous concubines and female entertainers. Buddha's wife, Yaśodharā, a maiden and 'of widespread renown, virtuous and endowed with beauty, modesty and gentle bearing' (Johnston 1978: 25), is introduced as the mother of his only son, whom he called aptly Rahula, which means 'fetter'. Seeing as abject his wife as well as the numerous courtesans and female servants surrounding him, Prince Siddhartha left his palace in search of enlightenment. Later monk authors used this episode to indulge in rhetoric that vilifies women as seductresses and as beings of low morality, disinclined to philosophical inquiries. But there is also a text (see the section Marginal Voices) that speaks with a very different voice and that tries to affirm Yaśodharā's role in his achieving enlightenment

During the years in which Siddhartha travelled with groups of male ascetics and yogis, no encounter with a woman is recorded. However, when he was near death due to extreme fasting, Siddhartha met a woman who offered him a savoury rice dish. Desperate to experience a breakthrough in his spiritual search, he accepted the dish and regained his strength. And in fact, Siddhartha experienced in the following night a cataclysmic mystical ecstasy, his enlightenment. In this episode, the woman who offered him food is an embodiment of female compassion and exhibits the traditional virtue of generosity vis-à-vis mendicant yogis. Once Siddhartha was recognized as Buddha and when a following had gathered around him, he again encountered women eager to become his followers, some as laypeople, others as ascetics or nuns (bhikṣunī). Buddha addressed women affected by typical 'female' worries and sufferings, such as the premature death of a beloved husband or the death of a child, with empathy and compassion, but his interaction with them was not noticeably different from his interaction with men regarding their worries and sufferings. While one cannot observe expressions of distinct misogyny in Buddha's life story, there is also no affirmation of women as persons of intellectual and spiritual potency equal to that of men.

In contrast to the rather ancillary roles of women in Buddha's life story, numerous men are mentioned who exercised decisive influence on the prince's life: his father, his teachers of yoga and Upanishadic philosophy, his fellow ascetics, and finally his fellow monks. Among the monks, his cousin Ānanda stands out as Buddha's loyal attendant who never left his side; Śāriputra, Maudgalyāyana, and Kāśyapa are depicted as pillars of the early community; and kings, noble men, and wealthy merchants and artisans are described as his patrons. Among the nuns, only Prajāpatī, Siddhartha's former nanny, occupies a special position as she is credited with convincing Ānanda, who in turn persuades Buddha, that the creation of a nuns' order is desirable. Among the laywomen, Ambapāli, a wealthy courtesan, is mentioned as a devoted lay patron.

Nuns in the Early Sangha

We have no historical documents concerning those laywomen who are mentioned in Buddha's life story, but we have a collection of 73 poems ascribed to some of the nuns who were among Buddha's personal disciples; some of them are mentioned in utterances attributed to the Buddha. This collection is known as *Therīgātha*, the Songs of the Elder [Nuns] (Norman 1983: 75–7). It is questionable whether all the poems in this collection date back to the time of the Buddha. Some poems seem to have been composed later and retroactively assigned to some famous names. However, scholars agree that some of the poems may very well contain phrases and expressions of the early nuns. Some of the nuns refer to themselves as 'daughter(s) of the Buddha, born from his mouth' (Horner 1930: 171). The same phrase is used by the early monks, contemporary with the nuns discussed here, who also left behind a collection of poems expressing their religious experiences. This phrase means that its author sees him or herself as being reborn from the teaching of the Buddha (that is, through his mouth) and therefore, rightly his son or daughter. The gender difference is erased here in the light of the spiritual experience. An even stronger statement to this effect is attributed to the nun Somā:

> What should the woman's nature signify
> When consciousness is tense and firmly set,
> When knowledge rolleth ever on, when she
> By insight rightly comprehends the Norm? (Samyutta Nikāya V, para 2)

Reading the Songs of the Elder Nuns one cannot help but have the impression that, at the beginning of the Buddhist traditions, Buddhist nuns saw themselves to a large degree as equal to the monks. While the biological difference in sex could not be erased, the culturally determined gender difference became for them negligible in the light of their firm ascetic commitment and their spiritual achievements. What mattered for the early Buddhists was obviously the individual's progress on the path toward enlightenment and not the individual's gender. Enlightenment was available to both genders.

In their poems, the nuns state as reasons for entering the monastic life their desire for freedom from the burden of lay life, but also the yearning to transgress the endless cycle of rebirth and to attain arhantship. Others tried to find ways to cope with what seemed arbitrary torment inflicted on them, such as the loss of a child.

The Buddhist monastic order was open to people from all walks of life. However, the majority of nuns mentioned in the Songs belonged to the upper castes (royalty and nobility, wealthy merchants, prominent Brahmins). Only two nuns were reported to have come from poor Brahmin castes, and four were courtesans. In the Songs, some nuns are identified by their outstanding talents or achievements, including great wisdom (Khemā, former consort of King Bimbisāra), articulation in preaching the Buddhist religion (Dhammadinnā, from a wealthy merchant family), expertise in the monastic rules and regulations (Paṭācārā, also from a wealthy merchant family), paranormal insight (Bhaddā Kuṇḍalakesā, a convert from Jainism), memories of her former lives (Bhaddā, from the Kāpila Brahmin caste), and so on. The latter was also known as very articulate and fluent in religious discourses, while others were renowned speakers and excelled in religious debates with followers of other religious traditions (Horner 1930: 168–72). The early nuns were full members of the monastic order and were recognized for their extraordinary intellectual and spiritual talents and accomplishments. They were thus not much different from the monks. Even a few centuries later we read in some inscriptions—stone or copper tablets attached to ancient Buddhist buildings and which record the donor's name and often the purpose of the donation—of nuns who carried the title 'expert in the *Tripitaka*' (the three collections of early Buddhist scriptures). However, soon after that period this title became the exclusive domain of monks (Schopen 1997: 31).

Married as well as unmarried women entered the order, but among the authors of the Songs, the unmarried nuns outnumbered the ones who had been married or widowed. This fact permits the conclusion that, at the time of the Buddha, marriage was not mandatory for women as it had been in earlier and again in later times. As was the case for the monks, women who wanted to enter the order had to obtain their parents' consent and be free of debt and social bondage. In a few cases, women wanting to join the Order asked their husbands for approval, which in most cases was given without hesitation. Thus, one may conclude that at the time it was seen as within the boundaries of normalcy for a woman to leave family and household life to join the mendicant Order of the Buddha. On occasion, husband and wife decided to join the Order together. Some women are recorded as joining the Order not because of spiritual motivation but because relatives and friends had done so.

Entering the Order did not imply that the Buddhist woman had to be either a virgin or denounce the experiences of her previous life in the world.

To the contrary, nuns often maintained some contact with their families. Despite restrictive contacts with men, the rules permitted nuns to care for their own male children up to the time of puberty (Hüsken 1997: 470) Donative inscriptions dating from the first centuries of Buddhist history substantiate this claim that nuns maintained on occasion close contacts with their families. Some nuns are recorded to have made significant donations to an existing monastery (for instance, an elaborate masonry gate or wall) for the benefit of their deceased parents. Such inscriptions document first, that nuns maintained emotional and economic ties with their families; second, that there was a belief that making donations would positively affect the fate of deceased parents; and third, that these nuns had control over substantial material wealth (Schopen, 1997: 30–43, 56–67).

The Monastic Order and Its Rules

The Buddhist monastic order, or *Sangha,* is a self-governing body based on consensual decisions of the local monastic community. Men and women form independent communities and monasteries. Each local community that has its base in a monastery elects its own leader (Pāli: *thera*; Sanskrit: *sthavira*—both meaning 'elder') for a certain period of time. Textual and epigraphic evidence suggest that during the first 200 years of Buddhism the difference between the nuns' and monks' Orders was insignificant. Local communities were independent, as there was no countrywide or even global hierarchy overseeing them. In the twentieth century Western scholars predicted the demise of Buddhism due to this lack of a hierarchical structure, but history has proven them wrong on this point. Thus to speak of a 'Buddhist pope', whether with regard to the past or present, is wrong.

These egalitarian and democratically organized communities of monks and nuns were subject to subsequent and irreversible changes that altered the situation of the Buddhist nuns forever. In contradiction to the original rule that members of the Sangha had to keep distant from the ruler and the court system, a few centuries after Buddha's death (usually dated 480 BCE), the political system and its functionaries took, to some extent, control of the monastic system and used it often to their own advantages. Thus the independent and egalitarian nature of the Buddhist monastic system was undermined when kings and emperors meddled in monastic affairs. They tried to prevent dissent among its members or they called upon some monks to serve as advisors or court officials. For instance, in India, Emperor Ashoka (ruled 269–232 BCE), a devout Buddhist monarch who transformed the local Buddhist movement into a world religion, convened a council to resolve a schism within the Buddhist Sangha. To this council, he called only monks. In China, some T'ang emperors appointed Buddhist monks as advisors and bestowed on them ranks including that of court official. In Tibet, King Ral-pa-can (ruled 815–36) appointed not only a monk as minister of religious affairs but also put the monks' Sangha in charge of overseeing the Lower Assembly (Dargyay 1991: 124 ff.). In these and many more cases, only monks were called to the court, and this situation pushed the Buddhist nuns more and more into the background. While some of the monks' monasteries gained political influence, status, and significant wealth, nuns' monasteries remained dependent on the laity's voluntary contributions. This decreased their status in the light of the growing prestige associated with the monks.

The reasons for this dramatic change in the position of the Buddhist nuns vis-à-vis the Buddhist monks has to be seen in the gender preferences and restrictions governing the court culture of the time. Women were permitted at the court as mothers, wives, and concubines of the ruler, or as musicians and dancers (who were also available to the ruler for sexual enjoyment). The court protocol left no room for independent and celibate women—that is, nuns. They were left out of the political process and were excluded from those monastic institutions that garnered the most economic support and that enjoyed the most significant political power. Even today, the Tibetan monastery of Labrang Tashikyil, located in Gansu Province, China, which housed in 1995 about 1,600 monks, enjoys government patronage by being designated as a national heritage site. It is the destination of large tour groups and receives significant public funds. Its spiritual leader has his residence in the provincial capital of Lanchou and enjoys the privileges of a government official. However, three small nunneries next to the famous Labrang monastery exist in abhorrent poverty and deprivation. They receive no support from the government or from the rich monks' monastery.

When monks became advisors to emperors and kings, the construction of monasteries on palace lands and under the jurisdiction of the court was a frequent result (for example, Tendai temple in Japan; rNam-rgyal monastery as well as Sera, Drepung, and Gaden monasteries in Tibet). The senior monks of these monasteries often enjoyed royal privileges and luxury as well as significant political influence. Yet their control over other monasteries was at best limited, if not altogether absent. Being part of the power structure, these monastic institutions and their members became in all regularity defenders of the status quo and obstructed change and innovation. Two examples may suffice. The first illustrates the general resistance to modernization put up by politically entrenched monastic institutions; the second exemplifies the resistance to improving the nuns' status mounted by influential monks of some traditions.

First, in the aftermath of the British invasion of Tibet in 1904, some secular cabinet ministers urged a general modernization of the Tibetan socio-political system. The Three Monastic Seats of the state-funded large monasteries,

Sera, Ganden, and Drepung, all with enormous political influence, objected vigorously to any plans that would alter their privileged status. M. Goldstein summarizes the situation: '[The] Three monastic Seats . . . believed that they represented the fundamental interests of Buddhism and were obligated to preserve the religious values of the state. Thus, monasteries worked in the government to prevent modernization, which they believed to be detrimental to both the economic base of monasticism and the "value" monopoly of Tibetan Buddhism' (Goldstein 1989: 816).

Second, when in the late 1980s nuns from several Buddhist traditions (especially the *Theravāda* and Tibetan traditions) pushed for a reinstatement of full ordination for nuns, powerful monks of these traditions delayed the process indefinitely by insisting on a strict literal interpretation of the pertinent monastic rules (Tsomo 1988: 236–57). The issue of full ordination for Buddhist nuns and its absence in many traditions will be discussed in more detail later on under Social Change in the Wake of Colonialism.

The vast majority of the hundreds of monastic rules are the same for monks and nuns. Theirs is a life of simplicity and renunciation whose sole objective is to cultivate conditions leading toward enlightenment, or so is the ideal. Monks and nuns have their heads shaved and wear in most cases similar robes. Thus, outwardly there are almost no differences. However, tradition has it that the Buddha was reluctant to create a nuns' order parallel to the monks' order. He agreed to do so only if the nuns were willing to accept the eight chief rules: (1) every nun, regardless of her seniority, is junior to even the youngest monk; (2) nuns cannot spend the rainy season in a place where no monk is available (in order to instruct them in the monastic discipline); (3) nuns ought to ask the monks for setting the day of the confession ceremony and providing exhortations to them; (4) after the rainy season, the nun has to inquire before the monks' and the nuns' Sangha whether any fault can be laid to her charges; (5) a nun found guilty of serious offence has to undergo discipline before both Sanghas; (6) a woman who has completed the two years novitiate must ask the monks' Sangha for full initiation; (7) a nun must never revile or abuse a monk; (8) nuns cannot reprimand monks for violation of monastic rules and proper conduct, but monks can reprimand nuns. In practice these rules were modified so that the interactions and contacts between nuns and monks were closely regulated and minimized. However, every nun, even the most senior and respected one, had to consider every monk as senior regardless of how junior a rank in the Sangha he held. This rule can be observed today in every Buddhist country where in the streets nuns bow to passing monks and make room for them while the monks do not return these gestures of courtesy and reverence. Another aspect of the eight rules having an impact on the nuns' lives and resulting from the eight weighty rules is that the nuns' Sangha is under the jurisdiction of the local monks' Sangha, and that implies that nuns' ordination requires the presence not only of fully ordained nuns but also of fully ordained monks.

Despite some rhetoric to the opposite effect, in reality Buddhist men quite often seem to be unaware of Buddhist nuns living within their neighbourhood or of the existence of significant nunneries. For instance, a recent article describing and discussing the monastic communities in a remote valley of the Himalayas does not mention one of the six or seven nunneries also in that valley (Crook and Shakya 1994: 559–600). This is all the more regrettable as one of the nunneries dates back to at least the twelfth century and houses artwork from that period. Another anthropologist observes the following with regard to an adjacent area: 'The villagers assume an ambivalent attitude towards nuns. On the one hand, devotion to religion is to be considered in a positive sense, but on the other hand, not one of the women I met, not even the older ones, aspired to entering a monastery. Children will sometimes use the word *nun* as an abusive word' (Reis 1983: 224). The author observes that the primary definition of womanhood is reproduction, a fact that makes a nun appear to be 'deficient'—very much like a barren woman or a widow, traditionally pitied and derided (Reis 1983: 228).

The subordinate and economically as well as politically deprived status of nuns resulted in the formation of alternative organizations in some countries, a fact that will be further discussed under Social Change.

The Buddhist Laywoman

The Buddhist laywoman stands in the shadow of the renunciant male, the monk. She provides him with food when he comes begging for alms to her door. She is praised for her generosity, patience, and self-effacing attitude as mother and wife. If she displays piety and devotion for the faith, society heaps praise on her.

I.B. Horner, a pioneering British scholar of the early twentieth century, gave a detailed discussion of the literary sources pertinent to women during the early centuries of Buddhism in her book *Women under Primitive Buddhism: Laywomen and Almswomen*, first published in 1930 and later many times reprinted. It is still a valid and indispensable source of information. Horner arranged the material in two sections, 'The Laywomen' and 'The Almswomen'. The part dealing with the sources pertinent to laywomen categorizes women according to their social position as mother, daughter, wife, widow, and woman worker. This procedure highlights Horner's approach as mainly descriptive and informative rather than theoretical and analytical. Horner rightly points to the fact that a woman's life in pre-Buddhist India was measured according to how useful and valuable it was to her father, brother, husband, or son. A woman independent from a male relative or husband had no place in society;

she was an abnormality. But once her vital ties with a male relative were affirmed, and if she fulfilled her obligations, such as deference to her mother-in-law, adoring her husband like a god, and, above all, bearing sons, she became an honoured and respected member of society. In contrast to this rather restricted situation, Horner points out, within the early Buddhist communities a woman gained acceptance and status in her own right despite some lingering tendencies to hold on to some pre-Buddhist ideas with regard to the proper place of women in society.

The improved status of women within Buddhist communities becomes apparent with regard to inheritance practices. For instance, Bhaddā Kāpilānī, although married, appears to have been the sole owner of her property: For it is said that when she renounced the world, 'she handed over her great wealth to her kinsfolk' (Horner 1930: 54 quoting the Pāli commentary on *Therīgātha:* 37). In another case, also reported in the commentary on the *Therīgātha*, a father upon entering the monastic order bestowed his entire inheritance on his daughter (Horner 1930: 54f.). Epigraphic documents from about the same period substantiate the impression received from the textual sources that women owned property and could decide how dispose of it. Inscriptions from the ancient Buddhist site of Bhārhut, which date from 120 to 80 BCE, illustrate this point by preserving 14 inscriptions identifying nuns as major donors in contrast to 24 inscriptions of monks (Schopen 1997: 30). Moreover, Horner draws our attention to the fact that with very few exceptions it was the usage of the time to speak of 'mother and father' (Pāli *mātāpitaro*) when mentioning one's parents (Horner 1930: 5f.). This widespread convention may be seen as reflecting the social status of women at that time, which finds further support in the contemporary custom that men identified themselves by their mother's clan name. For instance, Buddha's own mother belonged to the clan of Gotama and he was known accordingly as Siddhartha (his personal name) Gautama (the adjective form of his mother's clan name). Interestingly, in later Buddhist texts (roughly from the beginning of the Common Era on) Buddha is known as Śākyamuni, 'the wise of the Śākya,' whereby Śākya was his father's clan name, while the custom to name him according to his mother's clan name became obsolete. Does this change in naming convention signal a change in the social status of women? Possibly, if we consider, for instance, a passage found in the *Milindapañha*, a text probably dating from the second century BCE. Here, Nāgasena, a senior Buddhist monk, advises King Milinda (Pāli for the Greek Menandros) as follows:

> There are, O king, these ten sorts of individuals who are despised and contemned [sic] in the world, thought shameful, looked down upon, held blameworthy, treated with contumely, not loved. And what are the ten? A woman

without a husband, O King, and a weak creature, and one without friends or relatives . . . (Horner 1930: 26)

This passage follows the same line of thinking as *The Laws of Manu,* where the possibility of a woman living in independence was strictly ruled out. The widow, who had neither father, nor husband or son to rely on, was seen as a social outcaste and the carrier of ill fortune. There are about 200 years between the conception of the earliest Buddhist texts and the Milindapañha. Would socio-cultural changes during this period permit speculations about the causes leading to the change in women's social position? Due to the dearth of socio-historical sources in ancient India, we can only speculate what causes may have lead to these changes in women's status and position.

Even today, Buddhist laywomen are hardly visible within the hierarchy. Individual women, often educated in the West, have gained certain notoriety through publications and public speaking. However, the monastic institution, which is the main voice of Buddhism, often refuses to recognize these women. As in the past, the laywoman is seen mainly as a person who quietly affirms the main concepts of Buddhism (generosity, compassion, patience, humility), supports the monks with food donations, and creates within her family an atmosphere conducive to the practice of Buddhism. Certainly, Buddhist women practised their faith throughout history but they had, with very few exceptions, no public influence or visibility.

UNIQUE FEATURE:
THE DISAPPEARANCE OF BUDDHIST WOMEN

Scholars have taken opposite views as to when and under what traditions of Buddhism women were more integrated into the monastic hierarchy, and when they came to be seen in a more positive light. I.B. Horner (1930) has provided evidence that in the early days of Buddhism, women were integrated into the monastic system and advanced—like their male counterparts—to arhanthood, or sainthood. She advocates that Buddhism significantly improved the status of women:

> Thus, amid many currents, intricate but potent, the tide turned; and in its flow the position of women, as manifested in secular affairs, became one which was no longer intolerable and degraded; women were acknowledged at last to be capable of working as a constructive force in the society of the day. (Horner 1930: 2)

In contrast to Horner, Diana Paul (1979: 303) argues that the Mahāyāna movement provided women with a better chance to become recognized and valued as integral members of the Buddhist communities. She stresses that because of the Mahāyāna emphasis on generosity and compassion, this movement saw the Buddhist layperson as equal if not superior to the monk or nun. Furthermore, within the Mahāyāna tradition a plethora of female deities embody the major soteriological and ethical concepts of Buddhism, which, Paul insists, points toward a valorization of women in general.

Recently, M. Shaw tried to establish evidence that Vajrayāna, or tantric Buddhism, as the 'crowning cultural achievement of the Pāla period' (1994: 20), propelled the female practitioner to the forefront. While it is undeniable that women continued to be Buddhist practitioners throughout the centuries, the question that needs to be asked is this: Did Buddhist women, monastic as well as laywomen, have status and power equal to Buddhist men? The clear answer applying to all Buddhist countries and periods of Buddhism's long history is no. Further, it remains an enigma that among the vast Buddhist literature preserved in many of the major Asian languages, there is not one text (with the exception of some parts of the *Therīgātha*) that can be attributed with certainty to a female author. If tantric women were so learned, as Shaw believes, why did they leave no texts behind while their male partners did so? Why do all tantric lineages comprise men and have only male founders?

The only exception, which is usually referred to when one wants to make the case of women's presence in Buddhist traditions, is the role Ma-gcig Lab-sgron (b. 1055) played in the establishment of a particular tantric tradition in Tibet. Jérôme Edou says of her, 'She is woman and mother, but she is also *ḍākinī* and deity, legitimized as such by being an emanation of the "Great Mother of Wisdom", Yum Chenmo, as well as of Ārya Tārā, who transmitted to her teachings and initiations. In this way she becomes an equal of the greatest Tibetan masters of her time' (Edou 1996: 6). But he also admits that the only source containing information about her life is her biography, which 'is far from being a historical work in the modern sense. Like most Tibetan sacred biographies, Machig's life introduces us to the magico-spiritual universe where the marvelous occupies center stage and the historical facts often recede into the background' (Edou 1996: 3). It says a lot about the self-definition of contemporary Buddhist women in Tibet when the twentieth century reincarnation of Ma-gcig Lab-sgron, Rig-'dzin Chos-nyid bZang-mo (1852–1953), pledged to be reborn as a man. This is in line with a common Tibetan prayer that is practised in particular by laypeople. It addresses Buddha Amitābha in order to realize a rebirth in his Buddha realm *Sukhāvatī*. A key sentence says, 'may I not be reborn as a woman'.

To sum up, one can say that while Buddhist renunciant women were almost equal to their male peers during the first few centuries of Buddhist history, the status and power of Buddhist nuns, not to mention that of Buddhist laywomen, began to decline thereafter. The causes for this decline are only partially known. Not before the collapse of the colonial powers in Asia did the issue of the status and power of Buddhist renunciant women surface again.

FEMININE SYMBOLIZATION IN LATER BUDDHIST THOUGHT

The symbolization of woman, apparent in various goddesses and symbols of feminine nature and values, occurs within a broader framework of religious and philosophical theorizing. The status of women as well as the symbolization of the feminine were significantly influenced by the two major developments within Buddhism—that is, the rise of Mahāyāna, the Great Vehicle, and of Vajrayāna, tantric Buddhism.

Mahāyāna Philosophy

Around the beginning of the Common Era, a new thinking took hold of the Buddhist communities in India. It became known as Mahāyāna, the Great Vehicle, indicating its more inclusive nature than the preceding Vehicles, which became derogatorily named Hīnayāna, Lower Vehicles. The main ideas propagated by Mahāyāna can be summarized as follows: (1) The spiritual goal was redefined from arhantship to buddhahood. While the pre-Mahāyāna traditions emphasized that enlightenment consisted of the elimination of desire, aversion, and ignorance, the Mahāyāna claimed that enlightenment means buddhahood, that is, omniscience and limitless compassion in addition to the elimination of desire, aversion, and ignorance. (2) The path toward enlightenment was not so much anymore the eight-fold noble path, but ten stages that a Buddha-to-be, or *Bodhisattva*, had to master in the course of numerous lifetimes. The key elements were to develop consummate wisdom, which entailed a pledge not to realize nirvana until all sentient beings of the entire universe would also be able to do so, and to cultivate an empathy that would embrace every living creature in love and respect 'like one's own mother'. (3) The ideal of the solitary monk entranced in meditation while sitting under a tree was often mocked in favour of the ideal of the Bodhisattva who lived in the world and activated his or her compassion and love within it. The Bodhisattva was in most cases a layperson, and in a few cases female. Several Mahāyāna texts develop an image of the feminine and paint a picture of Buddhist women. Diana Paul extracts two conflicting ideas of the feminine from these texts:

> The first is the notion that the feminine is mysterious, sensual, destructive, elusive, and closer to nature. Association with this nether world may be polluting and deadly for the male and therefore must be suppressed, controlled,

and conquered by the male in the name of culture, society and religion. Female sexuality as a threat to culture and society provides religion with a rationale for relegating women to a marginal existence. (Paul 1985: xxiv)

A good example of this attitude is provided in the origin myths of the Tibetan people as it is told in Buddhist texts: A female Rock Demon was infatuated with a male monkey, who in reality was a Bodhisattva. When she tried to seduce him, the monkey referred to his religious vows of chastity and declined her invitations. In response the Rock Demon indicated that she was consumed by passion and lust and that if he was not willing to comply, a male Rock Demon would certainly do so; and this would result in populating the world with many little demons and create havoc. In the end, the male Bodhisattva monkey gives in 'for the benefit of all sentient beings'. In this narrative, the female is wild, cannibalistic, and destructive while the male is tame, celibate, pious, and compassionate (Stein 1972: 37–9). Paul presents the second ideal as follows:

> The second theme is the notion that the feminine is wise, maternal, creative, gentle, and compassionate. Association with this affective, emotional, transcendent realm is necessary for the male's fulfillment of his religious goals and for his release from suffering. Sexuality may be either controlled or denied in the feminine as sacred. (Paul 1985: xxv)

This second aspect, the feminine as sacred, finds its most salient manifestation in the ideal of the Perfection of Wisdom, symbolized as a female and called 'the mother of all Buddhas'. While this phrase received wide circulation and approval among Buddhist traditions in China, Japan, Vietnam, Tibet, and Mongolia, it is questionable whether it had any positive effect on the status and roles of women as members of society. Ursula King (1995: 16) observes that the 'symbolic ascendancy of the feminine often goes with a social denigration and low status of women in everyday life', and that one must distinguish 'between the place given to women in the world of religious imagination and that accorded to them in the actual world of religious life'.[1] King expresses here a fact that can be observed in various cultures and periods, from Confucian China with its cult of the Queen of Heaven to medieval Europe with its cult of Mary, mother of Jesus. The female that is feared by the male as a personal threat and as a threat to culture and religion is transformed into a symbol of sanctity and thereby neutralized. Thus prodigiously worshipping the feminine as sacred (as defined by males) permits control and subjugation of women as social beings. This flip-over mechanism is a way in which cultures deal with individuals or institutions that are experienced as threatening.

Therefore, it is a gross mistake to assume that women enjoyed status and prestige similar to men whenever the feminine was extolled as a supreme symbol of sanctity.

A few Mahāyāna texts, however, advocate that gender differences are as empty as all other distinctions. Some of these texts, such as the *Teachings of Vimalakīrti*, are humorous in that they make fun of the self-righteousness of monks and ordinary people (Paul 1985: 220–32). Did this and similar texts influence Buddhist societies so that they would rethink the position and status of women? No substantive evidence is available to support this.

Vajrayāna

After Mahāyāna took hold of the Buddhist communities in India, another wave of new ideas spilled over the Buddhist communities around the middle of the first millennium. This new tradition became known as Vajrayāna, the Diamond Vehicle, often referred to as tantric Buddhism. It adopted Mahāyāna philosophy but integrated it with an elaborate system of rituals and symbols. Unlike the preceding Buddhist traditions, Vajrayāna Buddhism viewed sexuality as an instrument to realize the enlightened state. However, the use of sexuality was highly circumscribed and regulated. Intercourse had to be carried out without seeking or experiencing desire or pleasure; the male had to prevent ejaculation by absorbing the semen into the spinal pathway. Women became essential participants in these sexual rites. D. Snellgrove argues that these female partners, as well as the tantric deities, were never more than handmaidens of the male masters and male deities (Snellgrove 1987: 150), while M. Shaw argues that '[t]he presence of women and women's teachings, as well as affirmations of female energy and spiritual capacities, are distinct features of tantric religiosity. When one considers the historical position of Tantra, an influx of feminine elements and insights is consistent with the social inclusiveness of the movement and its receptivity to symbols, practices, and insights from new quarters' (Shaw 1994: 205).

Perhaps the most significant difficulty in deciding this issue is the fact that Buddhist tantric texts rarely distinguish in an unmistakable way between earthly human beings and symbolizations of them. For instance, the concept of *ḍākinī* oscillates between real women (most of low castes or tribal background) and various degrees of abstract symbolizations. The Buddhist ḍākinī shares this grey space between reality and religious fantasy with witches and fairies and similar nocturnal creatures. Another issue aggravating any decision on this thorny question is the fact that pre-modern India did not keep records of historical and social situations and their changes over time. Tantric practice was always considered a secret activity that sought to avoid the daylight and public scrutiny. Its social influence remains therefore unknown.

Tibetan tradition is the sole Buddhist tradition that has embraced tantric Buddhism without reservations. Tibetan monks who have become experts in tantric practice emphatically insist that all texts describing sexual practices have to be understood as allegories and that they should never be enacted literally. Tibetan commentaries support this interpretation by, for instance, understanding the term for *semen* as a cipher for the enlightened mind, or the term for *vulva* as a cipher for wisdom. If the only tradition that practises tantric Buddhism insists on its pure symbolic allegory, how can Western scholars argue otherwise? However, none would deny that occasional misuse of symbolic meaning and a literal interpretation of texts to cover personal licentiousness has occurred. Could it be that while Westerners questioned their inherited dualistic mind–body concept, they projected a desired solution to this dilemma onto tantric Buddhism?

MARGINAL VOICES: TEXTS AND INTERPRETATIONS

Buddhism, like many other religions, was founded by a man; his main followers were men; men occupy the decision-making institutions and form the hierarchy; men have written the normative texts; and men speak publicly for the religion. Women never enjoyed equal status with men; however, in the early centuries Buddhist women were closer to equality than they were later on. Despite this situation, there are some textual testimonies that speak—from the margin—with what is now called 'a woman's voice'. These texts are not necessarily written by women but they express views that do not support the ubiquitous assumption that men are the primary human beings. A few selected texts document this situation.

A Sanskrit text found in the mountainous area of Gilgit describes the two key events of Buddha's life, his leaving of home and family and his enlightenment, in a way that strays significantly from the common narrative (Strong 1995: 9–18). The common narrative says that Buddha's father tried to prevent the fulfillment of the prophecy that his son would become either a universal ruler or a Buddha by surrounding his son with beautiful women and grand luxury and by confining him to the palace grounds. At an outing, the future Buddha became aware of the suffering inherent in sickness, old age, death, and birth. He reacted with disgust to the seductiveness and youthful beauty of the palace women. Seeing his wife and his newborn son as nothing but a fetter that would chain him to this life of suffering, he secretly left his wife, parents, and palace to become a mendicant ascetic. Thus, the common narrative does not indicate that the future Buddha felt any remorse for leaving his wife and newborn son or that he had any concern for their future life. Feminist scholars have pointed out that there is a systemic misogyny represented here.

However, this Sanskrit text found in Gilgit renders a different account, although it retains some elements of the common narrative, such as the father's intent to ensure that his son would not become an ascetic by immersing him in sensual pleasures. The night before his departure the future Buddha reminded himself of his filial duties to ensure the continuation of his lineage, and he had intercourse with Yaśodharā, his main wife, who became pregnant with their first and only son. But the future Buddha had dreams announcing his impending enlightenment, while Yaśodharā had dreams foreshadowing her husband's departure. When the future Buddha realized the sadness his wife felt, he attempted to convince her that these dreams were 'nothing but dreams'. When she begged him to take her along, he responded, 'So be it; where I am going, I will take you'. His quest for enlightenment by fasting finds a parallel in Yaśodharā's health. When he got thin, she lost weight, and when finally the Buddha realized enlightenment, her son was born. The text constructs this parallel by insisting that Yaśodharā's pregnancy lasted for six years due to her fasting. While the common story interprets the son's name, Rāhula, as 'fetter', this alternative story treats the name as deriving from Rāhu, the divinity of the lunar eclipse, thus pointing to the lunar eclipse that happened at the moment of the son's birth while at the same moment his father, Buddha, eclipsed the sun as the Enlightened One. This narrative seems to present the son as the fruit of enlightenment, who could only be born into this world when his father realized enlightenment. One may ask, what made this text marginal and the other account so common? In its denial of family bonds, we may assume, the common story affirmed ideas and sentiments harboured by many young men who were about to leave their families to join the Sangha. The rejection of family bonds and responsibilities integral to the Buddhist view of a spiritual life contained the possibility to denigrate women because of their seminal role in any concept of family (reproduction, food preparation, homemaker). This may have enticed some monks to fall into a misogynist attitude, which found its expression in the texts revised or composed by them. Thus, all Buddhist texts should be read with a sense of suspicion and not be taken as the literal 'word of the Buddha'.

Another text that challenges the common gender perception embedded in Buddhist texts is the *Teachings of Vimalakīrti* (Thurman 1976). Here, the highly respected monk Śāriputra meets a fairy in Vimalakīrti's house who engages him in a philosophical yet witty debate. Within the context of exploring the ineffable nature of reality, Śāriputra asks the fairy why she would not change her female sex—endorsing the common opinion that the female sex is less desirable than the male one. The fairy retorts as follows: 'I have been here 12 years and have looked for the innate characteristics of the female sex and haven't been able to find them. How can I change them? Just as a magician creates an illusion of a woman, if someone asks why don't you change your female sex, what is he asking?' (Paul 1985: 230). When the monk continues to pressure the fairy on the issue of innate characteristics, she transforms the monk into her own female body, and transforms her own body into that of the monk. Śāriputra is confounded by this transformation, while the fairy declares 'if you can change into a female form, then all women [in mental state] can also change. Just as you are not really a woman but appear to be female in form, all women also only appear to be female in form but are not really women. Therefore, the Buddha said all are not really men or women' (Paul 1985: 230). This text argues that sex and gender distinctions are as 'void of inherent existence' as all other phenomena. Thus, had this text affected the monastic system, one might argue, the inferior position of nuns would have been untenable.

Another group of texts is sometimes viewed as documenting the supposed important position of women within the Buddhist traditions. Most of these texts are so-called hagiographies, quasi-biographical accounts of saintly persons. The objective of these accounts is to glorify a particular person as a religious role model rather than to account for historical and social facts. Tsultrim Allione has collected six such stories, some of which were transmitted in writing while others were transmitted as oral accounts only. In her introduction she states: '[T]he feminine took on a profoundly more important role than it had in primitive Buddhism' (Allione 1984: 12). These stories tell us about the lives of women who gained some repute within the Tibetan Buddhist tradition. Male teachers instructed all these women, and they, in turn, had male disciples. The male hierarchy of various monastic institutions assessed the spiritual authenticity of these women. The photographs added by the author portray women in two roles only: as nuns in a group, or as wives of male practitioners. It is hard to see how this amounts to a 'profoundly more important role' in comparison to early Buddhism when nuns achieved the rank of Master of the *Tripiṭaka* and were in control of substantial material resources used for donations (Schopen 1997: 31). The six stories about women who are noticed by the Tibetan Buddhist traditions stand in stark contrast to the hundreds, if not thousands, of hagiographies glorifying Tibetan monks or pious male practitioners.

Kathryn Ann Tsai has translated biographies of eminent Chinese nuns (Tsai 1994), *Lives of the Nuns,* and notes rightly that the nuns' convents were subject not only to interference from the state, the emperor, and the aristocracy, but also from the monks' Sangha. Unlike the monks, nuns were prevented from setting up convents outside the boundaries of cities and other settlements, which would have provided a situation less prone to interference. The Chinese text preserves information of a total of 65 nuns from the fourth to the sixth centuries CE, while the contemporary *Kao seng Chuan (Lives of Eminent Monks)* 'consists of 257 major biographies and a number of sub-biographies' (Tsai 1994: 107). This testifies to the fact that there were significantly fewer nuns than monks who were found worthy of a biography. Although the collection *Lives of the Nuns* does indicate that a few nuns achieved fame and influence, the text was compiled by a monk using older sources. Why did no woman, nun or otherwise, edit the collection?

In summary we can say that while there are scattered testimonies of Buddhist nuns who gained some form of fame and influence during their time, they are a very slim minority in comparison to the number of famous and influential Buddhist monks. Despite the increasing disappearance of the Buddhist nuns from written historical records, however, women continued to be Buddhist practitioners. And we must ask this: Who shaped the prominent strands of Buddhist philosophy, who occupied the decision-making ranks within the monastic institution, who controlled the economic resources of the Buddhist institutions, who had access to its educational offerings and, finally, who composed the most common texts and for whom were they composed? By pondering the answers to these questions, one comes to understand the gender imbalance within all aspects of the Buddhist institutions and organizations. The voices from the margin, however, could prove seminal in fostering social change.

SOCIAL CHANGE IN THE WAKE OF COLONIALISM

The fate of the various Buddhist traditions and institutions in Asia was connected with the political and economic history of each country. In general, Buddhist monasticism was the sole voice for all followers of the faith and it was closely tied to the individual monarchies of these countries. The role of the Buddhist laity was mainly to provide the monks, and to a much lesser degree the nuns, with subsistence (robes, food, medicine, and shelter). In the course of time, monastic institutions received huge donations in the form of land and bonded labourers so that they often formed states within the state. The Chinese Imperial Court, for example, was continuously concerned with the independent state of Buddhist monasteries, and in Tibet the great monasteries absorbed much of the state's revenue and enjoyed extraordinary political power.

The interlocking of monarchy and Buddhist institutions came to an abrupt end with the incursion of European colonial powers. Local monarchs were deposed and, as a consequence, the Buddhist institutions lost not only their most affluent donors and sources of income, but also their basis of political influence and prestige. To the colonial powers, the Buddhist monks were often nothing more than soothsayers, steeped in superstition, who kept the population in ignorance and dependence. Missionary schools were set up to improve education but also to spread European and Christian ideas in Asian societies and make the Asians more inclined to accept the superiority of their colonial masters. Better education with improved social status led Buddhist women to strive to improve the situation of Buddhist nuns, for whom, by the nineteenth century, full ordination was unavailable in all of South and Southeast Asia as well as in Tibet, the Buddhist Himalayan kingdoms, and Mongolia. The transmission of full ordination for women had ceased in India around the fifth or sixth century and in Southeast Asia by not later than the tenth century, with the consequence that only the rank of novice was open to women who sought the life of a Buddhist renunciant. Destitute women, rather than women seeking enlightenment, turned to becoming nuns, and this situation further undermined the nuns' status in the eye of the public.

Two responses to this state of affairs can be distinguished: The first was an attempt to improve the behaviour and comportment of the novice nuns. They turned now to providing social services in health and education while reserving time for meditation and studies. In Sri Lanka this resulted in the movement of the *Dasasila Mata*, Mothers of the Ten Precepts. The Dasasila Mata now enjoys a better public reputation than that of the fully ordained monks because its members are not involved in politics and are not tainted by the largesse of government support (Barnes 1996: 262–7). The second strategy was to reinstate full ordination of nuns. However, this proved to be a thorny issue. Traditionalists point to the rules governing the ordination of nuns that say that the presence of five fully ordained monks and five fully ordained nuns is necessary to bestow full ordination upon a female novice. As there are no fully ordained nuns anymore, no female novice can be fully ordained, so they argue. Proponents of this view conveniently forget that their own traditions take the liberty of interpreting many of the rules in a more liberal way whenever it suits their interests. To complicate the situation further, the rules of ordination require that all monks and nuns bestowing full ordination belong to the same *Vinaya* tradition.[2] While the full ordination for nuns according to the pre-Mahāyāna tradition ceased throughout the world many centuries ago, it continued within the transmission of the Mahāyāna Vinaya. Thus, Theravāda and Tibetan nuns seeking full ordination have often received it in China or Vietnam under the Mahāyāna Vinaya transmission. But they encounter opposition of various intensities from their own (male) Sangha, which does not recognize legitimacy of this ordination.

Traditionalists of both camps claim that the issue of full ordination is one promoted by Western feminists and that it is, therefore, alien to the Asian context. For instance, at the 1993 conference of Sakyādhītā, the international organization of Buddhist nuns in Sri Lanka, the Ministry of Buddhist Affairs offered its support to the conference on the condition that the reintroduction of full ordination for nuns would not be a topic to be discussed (www.sakyad-hita.org/newsletters/5-2.htm#Report). Recent research by Wijayasundara and Malalsekara into the various lineages of the Buddhist Vinaya and the transmission of ordination resulted in their statement that according to the authoritative texts a reinstatement of the full ordination for women is possible and legitimate (Wurst 2001: 133 n.1). Proponents of reinstating the full ordination point also to the *Mahāparinibbāna sutta,* where the Buddha authorized the ordination of nuns through monks alone and, further, point to the fact that minor rules can be and often are suspended, and that this could be applied to this issue (Wurst 2001: 130–3).

During the colonial domination, most Buddhist Sanghas declined in vigour, education, and in the impact they exerted on society. Sporadic attempts to revive the Buddhist tradition focused now on strengthening the role of the laity. In Vietnam, educated Buddhist laypeople showed leadership in breaking down the barriers that kept the various sects apart. In Taiwan in the 1950s, Master Hsin Yun created Fo Kuan Shan, a movement that complemented traditional Buddhist contemplative training with social work. The organization provides seniors' homes, mobile health-care facilities, schools, and orphanages beside the traditional monasteries. There, monks and nuns live and practise together, and in the rituals and ceremonies, monks and nuns file into the main temple hall side-by-side. Nuns are the heads of many of the movement's North American temples. They teach and conduct meditation sessions and are the superiors of other ordained members of the movement. Despite strong patriarchal tendencies in Chinese culture, Buddhist nuns and nunneries in China seem to enjoy more respect and support than they do elsewhere in Asia. In general one can say that improving the nuns' education and status meets the strongest opposition within those traditions where monasticism and government are closely intertwined (such as Tibetan-speaking areas, Thailand, Sri Lanka). Nevertheless, within these traditions some open-minded monks are working to provide nuns with access to levels of Buddhist learning from which they were previously barred, that is, mainly the philosophical and theoretical study of Buddhism.

Buddhism became known as a religion in the West from the late-nineteenth century on, and soon people from Europe and North America began to practise Buddhism. At first, the revised or 'Protestant' Buddhism as propagated by the English-educated elite from Sri Lanka gained much attention. After the end of World War II, all forms of Buddhism produced shoots in the West. Soon Buddhism in its ancient Asian garb encountered the new intellectual movements of the West, among them feminism, Beatniks, and the gay-rights movement. In particular, American feminism began to challenge the ingrained gender bias obvious in so many Buddhist traditions. Women demanded access to the training as Zen priests and, eventually, succeeded after overcoming many obstacles (Boucher 1988: 133–44). Western women became Buddhist nuns and spearheaded the reintroduction of full ordination within traditions where it had ceased long ago. At Bodhgaya, India, in 1987, nuns formed the international association of Sakyādhītā, which organizes annual meetings to discuss the situation of Buddhist nuns around the world. The organization has as its objective to improve the education and the status of nuns, and foremost to bring back full ordination.

The Beat movement introduced Buddhism to American pop culture and the drug culture to Buddhism, often creating the misconception that the drug culture and Buddhism are synonymous. Beat poets such as Jack Kerouac wove Buddhist ideas into their novels and poetry articulating feelings and anxieties of a generation that protested against the Vietnam War. The artistic creations of the Beat generation functioned as a conduit that made Buddhism part of pop culture. The gay-rights movement confronted some Buddhist assumptions about the right use of sexuality. The rules of ordination for both monks' and nuns' orders prohibit ordination of gays or lesbians. A few years ago, the Dalai Lama affirmed this position at an interview in California. At a press conference in June 1997 he stated that from a Buddhist point of view lesbian and gay sex is generally considered sexual misconduct. However, this belief is not based on the partners being of the same gender, he asserts. In fact, in his book *Beyond Dogma*, he has written that 'homosexuality, whether it is between men or between women, is not improper in itself. What is improper is the use of organs already defined as inappropriate for sexual contact' (quoted from http://www.religioustolerance.org/hom_budd.htm). Similar to what happened in other religions, gays and lesbians formed their own groups within different Buddhist traditions. Very active groups exist in New York, Boston, and San Francisco, among other places, while Buddhist groups in Toronto welcome gays and lesbians; Buddhist groups for gays and lesbians exist also in Norway, Great Britain, and the Netherlands, and Chinese Buddhist gays and lesbians held a national conference in Hong Kong in 1996. Historically, male homosexuality was at least tolerated if not openly accepted within certain Sanghas (such as in Tibet), while some traditions, such as Shingon Buddhism in Japan, even considered male same-sex love as a means toward realizing enlightenment. Perhaps not surprisingly, female same-sex relations were harshly punished in India as well as in Tibet (which otherwise was very tolerant vis-à-vis sexual activities) and are hardly ever documented (with the exception of the *Kāmasūtra*).

Due to the demographic composition of the North American public, Buddhist communities are often divided into 'ethnic Buddhist' communities and those that are predominantly composed of non-ethnic converts. The latter groups are more open to cultural and social change than the ethnic groups, which are more concerned with preserving their cultural heritage by hedging against too much 'Western' influence.

SUMMARY

While the Buddhist doctrine insists that men and women have the same potential to achieve the spiritual goal of nirvana or enlightenment, Buddhist cultures throughout their long and diverse history often adopted strong gender biases. During the early centuries of Buddhist history, Buddhist nuns could achieve ranks, such as Master of the *Tripiṭaka,* which signified utmost competence in the Buddhist scriptures, and they controlled large financial or material resources. Given the emphasis Buddhism puts on monasticism and a life of renunciation, laypeople, men as well as women, were not visible in the literary tradition of Buddhism. Their main role was, and to a large degree still is, to support the monk population and their monasteries. A few centuries after Buddha's nirvana (480 BCE), Buddhist monasticism was co-opted by the political powers of the time, which eroded the position of Buddhist nuns. Later the status and socio-cultural impact of Buddhist nuns began to decline, until, in some areas, they had become nothing more than servants. Monks, not nuns, compiled or composed Buddhist scriptures and other authoritative texts, thus effectively excluding the experience and views of Buddhist women. This is true despite a few singular texts that seem to affirm women's experiences and that call the gender bias into question. The intrusion of colonial powers broke up the linkage between monasticism and monarchy, which resulted in a challenging of Buddhist institutions and eventually a process of renewal and innovation (Queen and King 1996). From the late-nineteenth century on, an increasing number of people who were not born into a Buddhist society have adopted this religion, resulting in a heightened awareness of the situation of Buddhist nuns, the lack of full ordination within some Sanghas, and the general gender imbalance. Buddhism in the West is adopting many of the cultural and social characteristics of the modern Western world (such as feminism, gay rights, social concerns for the deprived, democracy, individualism, concern for the environment), thus leading to a new form of Buddhism that eventually will claim its own position within the wide spectrum of Buddhisms shaped by individual cultures and societies (Queen 2000).

NOTES

1.   I owe this reference to Danielle Lefebre, graduate student of Religious Studies at the University of Alberta.

2.   There are two main *Vinaya* transmissions: one accepted by the *Sangha* of all Theravāda traditions and by the Tibetan and Mongolian *Sangha*, based on pre-Mahāyāna thinking and a second one accepted by some communities in China, Japan, and Vietnam, based on Mahāyāna thinking.

REFERENCES

Allione, Tsultrim. 1984. *Women of Wisdom*. London: Routledge & Kegan Paul.

Barnes, Nancy J. 1996. 'Buddhist Women and the Nuns' Order in Asia'. *Engaged Buddhism. Buddhist Liberation Movements in Asia*. Eds Christopher S. Queen and Sallie B. King. Albany, New York: State University of New York Press: 259–94.

Boucher, Sandy. 1988. *Turning the Wheel. American Women Creating the New Buddhism*. San Francisco: Harper & Row.

Crook, John and Tsering Shakya. 1994. 'Monastic Communities in Zangskar: Location, Function and Organisation'. *Himalayan Buddhist Villages. Environment, Resources, Society and Religious Life in Zangskar, Ladakh*. Eds. John Crook and Henry Osmaston. Delhi: Motilal Banarsidass: 559–600.

Dargyay, E.K., 1991. *Sangha and State in Imperial Tibet, Tibetan History and Language. Studies Dedicated to Uray Géza on his Seventieth Birthday* (Wiener Studien zur Tibetologie und Buddhismuskunde Heft 26). Ed. E. Steinkellner. Wien: Arbeitskreis für Tibetische und Buddhistitische Studies, Universität Wien: 111–27.

Edou, Jérôme. 1996. *Machig Labdrön and the Foundations of Chöd*. Ithaca, NY: Snow Lion Publications.

Goldstein, Melvyn C. 1993. *A History of Modern Tibet, 1913–1952. The Demise of the Lamaist State*. 1989. New Delhi: Munshiram Manoharlal Publishers.

Horner, I.B. 1990. *Women under Primitive Buddhism: Laywomen and Almswomen* (1930). Delhi: Motilal Banarsidass Publishers.

Hüsken, Ute. 1997. *Die Vorschriften für die Buddhistische Nonnengemeinde im Vinaya-Pitaka der Theravādin*. (Monographien zur indischen Archeologie, Kunst und Philologie. Ed. Marianne Yaldiz. vol. 11). Berlin: Dietrich Reimer Verlag.

Johnston, E.H., trans. 1972. *The Buddhacarita or Acts of the Buddha*. 1936. Delhi: Motilal Banarsidass.

King, Ursula, ed. 1995. *Religion and Gender*. Oxford: Blackwell.

Norman, K.R. 1983. *Pāli Literature Including the Canonical Literature in Prakrit and Sanskrit of all the Hīnayāna Schools of Buddhism* (*A History of Indian Literature*. Ed. Jan Gonda, vol. VII, 2). Wiesbaden: Otto Harrassowitz.

Paul, Diana Y. 1985. *Women in Buddhism. Images of the Feminine in Mahāyāna Tradition*. Berkeley: University of California Press.

Queen, Christopher S., ed. 2000. *Engaged Buddhism in the West*. Boston, Mass.: Wisdom Publications.

Queen, Christopher S., and Sallie B. King, eds. 1996. *Engaged Buddhism. Buddhist Liberation*

Movements in Asia. Albany, New York: State University of New York Press.

Reis, Ria. 1983. 'Reproduction or Retreat: The position of Buddhist Women in Ladakh'. *Recent Research on Ladakh. History, Culture, Sociology, Ecology (Schriftenreihe Internationales Asienforum).* Eds. D. Kantowsky and A. Graf von Waldenburg-Zeil. Munich: Weltforum Verlag: 217–29.

Schopen, Gregory. 1997. *Bones, Stones, and Buddhist Monks. Collected Papers on the Archeology, Epigraphy, and Texts of Monastic Buddhism in India.* Honolulu: University of Hawaii Press.

Stein, R.A. 1972. *Tibetan Civilization.* Trans. J.E. Stapleton Driver. London: Faber and Faber.

Strong, John S. 1995. *The Experience of Buddhism. Sources and Interpretations.* Belmont, California: Wadsworth Publishing Company.

Thurman, Robert A.F. 1976. *The Holy Teaching of Vimalakīrti.* University Park: Pennsylvania State University Press.

Tsai, Kathryn Ann. 1994. *Lives of the Nuns. Biographies of Chinese Buddhist Nuns from the Fourth to Sixth Centuries.* Honolulu: University of Hawaii Press.

Tsomo, Karma Lekshe. 1988. 'Prospects for an International Bhiksunī Sangha'. *Sakyādhītā Daughters of the Buddha.* Ed. Karma Lekshe Tsomo. Ithaca, New York: Snow Lion Publications: 236–57.

Wurst, Rotraut. 2001. *Identitätim Exil. Tibetisch-Buddhistische Nonnen und das Netzwerk S Sakyādhītā.* (Marburger Studien zur Afrika- und Asienkunde, Series C, vol. 6). Berlin: Dietrich Reimer Verlag.

FURTHER READING

Cabezón, José Ignacio, ed. *Buddhism, Sexuality, and Gender.* Albany, NY: State University of New York Press, 1992.

Gross, Rita M. *Buddhism after Patriarchy. A Feminist History, Analysis, and Reconstruction of Buddhism.* Albany, NY: State University of New York Press, 1993.

Horner, I.B. *Women under Primitive Buddhism: Laywomen and Almswomen* (1930). Delhi: Motilal Banarsidass Publishers, 1990.

Paul, Diana. *Women in Buddhism: Images of the Feminine in Mahāyāna Tradition.* Berkeley: University of California Press, 1979.

Queen, Christopher S. and Sallie B. King, eds. *Engaged Buddhism: Buddhist Liberation Movements in Asia.* Albany, NY: State University of New York Press, 1996.

Tsomo, Karma Lekshe, ed. *Sakyadhītā: Daughters of the Buddha.* Ithaca, NY: Snow Lion Publications, 1988.

❧

CHAPTER 4

WOMEN IN THE CHINESE TRADITIONS
Lee D. Rainey

INTRODUCTION AND OVERVIEW

Chinese culture has long been perceived in the West as exotic, and Chinese traditions as mystical. Early Western missionaries saw women as downtrodden and connected this to Confucianism and Buddhism. Twentieth-century Chinese reformers emphasized this image as part of their general critique of traditional China. Thus stereotypes of the oppressed, devoted Confucian woman persist and do so in tandem with the stereotype of the dragon lady—imperious, mysterious, and powerful, creating difficulties in clearly understanding Chinese traditions and women in China.

While it is clear that religious traditions have informed the status of women in China, throughout history, women have found ways to work within their traditions, reshaping the thought of some and incorporating the strictures of others. Women in both traditional and modern China have not simply been the passive recipients of whatever the traditions had to say about women.

Ancient China
The active role of women in Chinese religious traditions was never clearer than in very ancient times. There was a Mother Goddess in ancient China, and there were also a large number of female gods: Nu Gwa (also, Nu Wa; see Paper 1999: 51) was a deity who created human beings; Xi Wang Mu, the Queen Mother of the West, held the secrets of immortality; Tou Mu, the north star, controlled the books of life and death. The gods and the forces of nature were dealt with by *wu* (shamans), who were mostly women and who had a number of functions: they were matchmakers; they danced and prayed for fertility; they called back the *hun* (soul) of the sick; they dealt with the dead, spoke to the gods, performed divinations, exorcized building sites, forecast the weather, danced to end drought, and played important roles in government. Ancient texts record all of these activities and demonstrate that the shamans worked directly for the ruler, performing religious rituals and offering political advice.

Over time, both the shamans and female deities lost ground. One god, for example, the 'Millet Queen', the earliest ancestor of the Zhou Dynasty (*c.* 1040–256 BCE), was transformed into the 'Lord of Millet'. By 693 BCE, some states banned women from court entertainments, and characterizations of women as dangerous and the source of moral and political decline are found in texts dated from 692 and 509 BCE (*Guo Yu*, 'Chou Yu'; *Zuo Zhuan*, 'Duke Zhuang 692 BCE', 'Duke Chao, 509 BCE'; see Legge 1960).

CONFUCIANISM

By the time Confucius (551–479 BCE) came on the scene looking for some way to solve the problems of the continual civil war and social upheaval of the Warring States period (722–221 BCE), the status of women had declined. Confucius began by talking about ritual, which he understood not simply as religious ritual, but as moral and social actions that hold a society together. He believed that the social chaos of his time was due to a breakdown in proper relationships between people, the loss of mutual respect, and the loss of the idea of mutual responsibility. In its simplest form, the 'please' and 'thank you' of ritual conveys mutual respect and social trust and delineates relationships. An example is the social ritual of greeting where a greeting and response are exchanged acknowledging, respecting, and defining the status of those involved.

Morality is the essential requirement for the performance of these social-political-religious rituals. For Confucius, morality consisted of the exercise of a number of virtues: loyalty, sincerity, filial piety (see below), moral courage, honesty, and so on. A person with all these virtues would then have the attitude of *ren* (humanity). Confucius defined humanity as 'not doing to others what you would not have done to yourself' (*Analects* 4.15). He encouraged his followers to look first to themselves and then to act, through ritual, so as to treat others as they wished to be treated.

Ritual can truly be understood only by moral beings who are trained to examine their own consciences and then to act in society. Confucius called them *junzi* (gentlemen). The foundation of the Confucian gentleman's morality was filial piety: respect and service to one's parents. Gentlemen were to be well versed in the ancient classics, to offer moral and political advice to the ruler, and to be an example to the people. Government would be best served by gentlemen who began in filial piety, became educated, and took their rightful places as government ministers. Such a government, with a moral base, would ensure that the people internalized moral behaviour and became happy and prosperous. The ruler, himself a Confucian gentleman or at least advised by Confucian gentlemen, would rule properly and morally.

Confucius rarely had anything to say about women, and it is clear that his philosophy is addressed almost entirely to men. In a culture that was becoming increasingly patrilineal and patriarchal, filial piety addressed male actions toward fathers and grandfathers, as opposed to the earlier matrilineal inheritance and descent lines. Confucius affirmed this trend. Confucius and his followers understood women to be one of the major impediments to implementing their programme. In practical political terms, they abhorred the influence that wives, mistresses, and shamans had on rulers; in theoretical terms, they believed that they, educated Confucian gentlemen, should be the ones to offer political advice and carry out the rituals of state. In the next two centuries, Confucian political and theoretical views were in conflict with the political and social influence of upper-class women. The classic Confucian texts pointed out that the downfall of states was often the cause of meddling women.

Mencius (371–289 BCE), about two generations after Confucius, continues the same approach to ritual, but with Mencius, we see ritual gradually developing in two directions: first, there is an increase in specific regulations (how one should eat, for example); second, there is a stronger set of rules dealing with the separation of men and women. Separation included separate living quarters in the home, separate spheres of activity, and detailed regulations concerning the interaction of men and women. This separation seems to have been widely discussed among Confucians at this time and was the point of many debates. The significance of Confucian debates on the separation of the sexes has been compared to that of keeping the Sabbath in first-century Judaism (Fehl 1971: 96). As it developed, Confucian views on ritual dealt not just with royal courts, but also with the home and the rituals and relations of people in the family.

'PHILOSOPHICAL' DAOISM

Confucianism was not the only tradition that began in Warring States China. Daoism (sometimes referred to as 'philosophical' Daoism in contrast to Religious Daoism) also began at this time. This school was based on the Dao, the Way, the ultimate pattern of change in nature and the universe. Daoism was said to have begun with the shadowy figure of Laozi, roughly contemporary to Confucius. Human beings find their proper place, Daoists argue, only when we act in harmony with the Dao. The writings we have from this tradition, particularly the *Laozi*, also called the *Dao De Jing*, describe the ultimate, the Dao, using images of women. Some scholars have made much of this, seeing Daoism as a feminist tradition in opposition to a masculine Confucianism (Chen 1974: 51–64). However, the Dao is not feminine, as it encompasses all things, and the images of women in the text are given from a male point of view. The *Laozi* argues that aggressive, 'macho', actions run counter to the way the Dao works. These aggressive actions, whether those of a ruler or private individual, will always fail. The Dao, they say, is never aggressive; it performs all its actions without looking for praise or exalting itself. Because of this the Dao is described as passive and weak. And it is because of this correlation that the Dao is described as female. The reason that women are like the Dao, the *Laozi* says, is that they are passive, quiet, and meek. The Daoist critique of attributes usually associated with masculinity is in contrast to most of the thinking in the Warring States period; Daoists prefer what they see as feminine attributes. But this critique did not lead to a genuine argument for the equality of men and women. While Daoist texts at least address women, what they say is not necessarily positive.

BUDDHISM

Buddhism came to China in the first century CE, bringing with it already formed views of women and its own organizational structure. The ideas of religious professionals who were celibate and who lived in communities under strict rules were new notions in China. Chinese women were given, for the first time, an authorized option other than marriage and motherhood. Nuns were described as women who *qu jia* (left the family) and were seen as religious professionals. The Vinaya sutras set out the inferiority of nuns in relation to monks: monks always had precedence over nuns no matter how senior; nuns were not allowed to teach monks, and so on. Still, however low the status of nuns, the existence of the order of nuns gave Chinese women an option they had not had before.

The Buddhism that came to China, predominantly Mahāyāna Buddhism, had already come to the conclusion that women could not become enlightened while in a female body. Despite this, women became the major devotees of Buddhism in traditional China, and this remains the case today. In traditional China, women prayed at temples, set up altars in their homes, and went on pilgrimages. Lay Buddhists, men and women alike, took the Three Refuges and followed the Five Precepts (not to kill, steal, lie, be involved in illicit sexual relations, or drink alcohol); they were vegetarians; they might belong to a society that recited sutras. Women raised money for religious projects and organized festivals and pilgrimages. Devotion to Buddhism was seen as proof of virtue. As women's lives became more and more circumscribed, women were expected to stay in their quarters at home, except for religious activity. Nuns visited the women's quarters and often provided a basic education.

RELIGIOUS DAOISM

Religious Daoism began as a tradition of spiritual healing among ordinary people during the Han Dynasty (206 BCE–220 CE). Always eclectic, it also taught that immortality could be attained in this life, and, over time, grew to include a belief in almost all the popular deities. Religious Daoism thus covers a wide gamut of beliefs: the search for immortality, healing, meditation, good works, what we would call 'magic'; it continues to have temples and followers throughout China

In the early days of Religious Daoism, women acted as the chief priests of local communities of believers. Women could also become *Daoshi* (Daoist Masters) and are recorded as having achieved immortality by following a path just as rigorous as the men's. Although women were capable of becoming immortals, considerably fewer women than men are recorded as having done so. Religious Daoism includes the texts of philosophical Daoism, though it understands those texts as manuals in immortality. So, while the tradition uses early Daoist texts, like the *Laozi*, that do privilege the female over the male, it did not argue for the equality of women. This may be because, with the growth of the organization, Religious Daoism took in Confucian and Buddhist ideas as well. Early in its development, it began to talk about rituals, morality, and the proper harmony of families in the same way that Confucianism had. From Buddhism, Religious Daoism took the ideas of celibacy, karma, and samsara. Organizationally, it modelled itself on Buddhism, developing orders of monks and nuns—though, unlike Buddhism, it has an organizational head, the Celestial Master. Like Buddhism, it offered women an option for a religious life as a nun; like Buddhism, women were free to devote themselves to particular deities or attend temples for healing. Religious Daoism does not see itself as a radical alternative to Confucianism and Buddhism, but as a place where all these teachings meet.

POPULAR RELIGION

Popular religion in a variety of forms is pervasive in both traditional and modern China. Often taken into Religious Daoist practice, popular religiosity consists of everything from the worship of local gods to the ritual practices of celebrating the New Year. City gods, local gods, local religious traditions, and festivals were all central to the lives of most people. Confucian, Buddhist, and Religious Daoist ideas, deities, rituals, and practices were incorporated into the great fabric of everyday practice. A funeral, for example, is carried out according to Confucian ritual practice, while Buddhist monks recite sutras for the dead and Religious Daoist monks pray. This may all be happening at the same time and no contradiction is seen. In both traditional and modern China, people do not identify themselves in the sectarian way one finds in the West. While a few might identify themselves strictly as Confucian or Buddhist, most people practise all traditions. How one worships the gods depends on one's needs and intentions. At Chinese New Year, ancestral veneration (see below) is carried out in Confucian terms, but a Buddhist vegetarian meal is also part of many people's celebrations. In traditional China, as part of the celebration, people also visited Buddhist temples to pray to Guan Yin and local temples to pray to local deities as well. 'All the Buddhas teach the same dharma', it is said. What people mean by this is that there is little fundamental disagreement perceived among the teachings of all the 'great' traditions.

Mediums or shamans, often women, continued their work despite the disapproval of the elite and the eventual outlawing of mediumship in the thirteenth century. The rich, educated, and upper-class elite held much of popular religion in contempt, branding it as superstitious. Traditional Chinese governments feared popular religious sects because of their frequent involvement in rebellions against the throne.

TEXTS, INTERPRETATIONS, AND RITUALS

In the following sections we will examine some of the texts and rituals of Chinese religions, including Confucian Daoism and Buddhism as well as the rituals of ancestral veneration.

The Confucian Classics

The Confucian classics cover a wide range of topics and genres. There are books of poetry, history, ritual, and philosophy. They were considered the repository of the wisdom of the ancients. In traditional China, they were thought to have been either written or edited by Confucius, though modern scholarship has disproved this. The classics were not seen as the word of God or gods, and thus were not considered sacred.

In traditional China, men memorized and studied the classics so as to pass the civil service examinations and take their place in government. There were several levels of examinations and, if a man was successful, he gained the power and prestige of a government job. It was this that gave the Confucian classics their enduring, and widespread, authority. The classics were not considered revealed scripture, but, as the subject of these civil service examinations through the centuries, they were considered both the highest wisdom and the foundation of Chinese society. Given their importance to the elite, and their use in government, they were gradually considered authoritative by ordinary people as well.

One of the oldest of the classics is the *Shi Jing*, the Book of Poetry. It describes the differences in the status of sons and daughters by saying that while sons sleep on a couch and play with sceptres, daughters sleep on the ground, play with tiles, and 'it will be theirs neither to do right or wrong / They will think only about the spirits and food / And how to cause no sorrow to their parents' (Karlgren 1950: 189). As in other Confucian classics, like the *Book of History*, meddling women are blamed for the downfall of states: 'A clever man builds strong walls /A clever woman overthrows them / Beautiful is the clever wife / But her heart is cruel as the owl / Women with long tongues / forecast evil / Disasters are not sent down from heaven / They originate in wives' (Karlgren 1950: 264). Women, especially beautiful women, are dangerous: 'Where there is extreme beauty, there will surely be extreme wickedness' (*Zuo Zhuan*; cf. Legge 1960: 192). While women are not, like Eve, blamed for bringing evil into the world, they are seen as problematic. Ways to regulate these dangers are found in other Confucian classics.

The *Li Ji*, the Book of Rites, is a detailed description of how state and private rituals, from funerals to marriages, are to be carried out. The Book of Rites delineates a separation of the sexes: men and women are not to sit on the same mat; they are not to touch when handing one another something; women are to live in the inner quarters of the house, men in the outer. Women are to be modest and chaste.

Marriage is understood to be the union of families. The chapter entitled 'The Meaning of Marriage' in the Book of Rites begins by saying, 'The ritual of marriage is meant for the love between families of two surnames. For those above, the ancestors, it is to maintain services in the ancestral temple; for those below, descendants, it is to secure children to carry on the family line (*Li Ji*, 'Hun Yi'). In marriage, a wife's duties are discussed in terms of service and obedience; the roles of husband and wife were seen as separate but complementary. Women were to provide a harmonious household while men's sphere was outside the home.

The Book of Rites minutely describes funeral rituals as well. The manner in which such rituals were to be carried out depended on one's social status, determined by the outer world. The rituals of ancestral veneration required the service of both husband and wife, but were aimed at his ancestors. Birth and hearth rituals, which presumably existed as 'women's rituals', are not described in the ritual texts. The only one involving women that is described therein is a hair-pinning ritual to represent a woman's coming of age. In court rituals, women lost status as well, although they continued to be represented, carrying out the women's 'side' of the rituals. By the time of the Han Dynasty (206 BCE–220 CE), when Confucianism became the state orthodoxy, women's social and political roles had weakened; over the next centuries this view of women's status would percolate throughout Chinese society.

The Daoist Canon

In the second century CE, a man named Zhang Daoling received a series of revelations from Laozi, now a god, but originally the reputed author of the *Laozi*. These extensive revelations encompassed rituals for curing disease, praying to the gods, reciting the *Laozi*, and for the organization of Religious Daoism. These revelatory texts became the basis for the Daoist canon, which now includes 1,426 volumes. As the tradition progressed, it added texts on outer and inner alchemy. These were instructions on how to become immortal either through meditation or through the ingestion of special elixirs. Religious Daoism, as we have noted, also included Confucian notions of morality and Buddhist ideas such as karma. The Daoist texts record women becoming immortals, though we are told that a woman's path to immortality is different from a man's because of the difference in yin and yang (see below). The Religious Daoist priesthood, open to married people, originally gave the same status to husbands and wives who acted as priests. The Religious Daoist organization depended on female followers, who to this day make up the majority, and on local female leaders.

Buddhist Sutras

Buddhist *sutras* were already formed by the time Buddhism came to China. The sutras were mostly written by men and from a male point of view, but there is such a wide variety of sutras that it is not surprising to find a variety of views of women. Mahāyāna Buddhism was, and is now, the dominant form of Buddhism in China. Some Buddhists, following the thinking of the Mahāyāna school, Madhyamikā, argued that, given the insubstantial nature of the human body, gender does not matter in terms of enlightenment. The majority of sutras, however, held that gender *does* matter, because a woman, in a female body, is not capable of enlightenment. This is despite early sutras clearly setting out the names and roles of women who had become enlightened. Other sutras, such as the Pure Land sutras, argue that women have such a terrible time in life that they should look forward to a rebirth as men in the Pure Land. The majority of sutras assume that chaste women, nuns, are more holy than sexually active women; however, nuns, because of their gender, are far below the capacity and authority of monks. The Chinese also inherited sutras, especially the meditation sutras, that describe women as tempters, without virtue, and intellectually weak.

As a result, like Confucianism, Buddhism wanted to control female sexuality: in Buddhism, women were most virtuous when sexually inactive; in

Confucianism, women were most virtuous when chaste, whether married, single, or widowed. Chinese cultural notions of the necessity of submission from women fit in with many Buddhist notions of the lower status of women, even Buddhist nuns.

The Rituals of Ancestral Veneration

If one were forced to choose one basic ritual that underlies all religious practice in China, it would be ancestral veneration. The practice is an ancient one, predating Confucius perhaps by as much as a millennium. The dead of a family are understood as still very much connected to the family by the bonds of love and respect. The standard ritual form of veneration became the use of a wooden tablet, an ancestral plaque, with the name of the deceased inscribed on it. Food, drink, and incense were offered before these plaques; rituals included bowing and reporting family events. The ancestral plaques were set out in order of consanguinity.

One should be very clear that women were ancestors just as men were. The way in which women as ancestors differed from men as ancestors was in terms of family. As Chinese society became patrilineal, the ancestors a woman venerated were the ancestors of her father or her husband. When a woman became an ancestor, her plaque was linked to her husband's and she was venerated by their sons or by the male line of her husband's family.

SYMBOLS AND GENDER

The basic gender symbol, which permeates all the traditions of China, is the yin-yang symbol. Most Westerners are familiar with the circle that is divided into black (yin) and white (yang) intertwining halves with a small circle of black in the white half and a matching circle of white in the black half. This symbol, and its implications, were articulated most clearly by a Confucian. Dong Zhongshu (179?–104? BCE) and it is this understanding of the yin-yang theory that has lasted down to our time. Yang represents the heat of summer, the period of the most heat and light; yin represents winter, the period of deepest cold and dark. In the basic pattern of yin-yang, in the spring, yin is waning and yang is growing. Yang reaches its height in summer and wanes in the autumn as yin grows. Yin reaches its height in the winter, and, as it wanes and yang grows, spring comes again. The cycle repeats itself with each year. A similar pattern of yin and yang is found in the smaller cycle of night and day.

As a result, winter/summer and autumn/spring are not simply opposites: they are bound together in a cycle that balances the movements of yin and yang. Dong Zhongshu, and many other thinkers, used the yin-yang theory as the basis of a cosmological interpretation of how everything in the universe worked. They hoped to understand all things as part of the balance and harmony of yin and yang. If this balance could be achieved, whether in one's physical health or in government, human beings would be part of the harmony of the universe. The yin-yang theory of balance is still the basis of traditional Chinese medical thinking. As a result, Han Dynasty Confucians compiled enormous and complex lists of opposites and placed them in the categories of yin or yang. Some of the pairs of opposites (with the yang coming before the yin) are as follows: heaven/earth; ruler/subject; father/son; active/passive; outer/inner; sun/moon; birth/death; giving/receiving; ruler/subject; male/female.

The Confucians claimed that these pairs of opposites, and thousands of others, were opposites in the same way as yin and yang, and thus are complementary. It is clear, however, from even this brief overview of the pairs of opposites that this is incorrect. Preference is always shown for yang; the items under yang are things that society rewards or approves of (active, birth, ruler, and so on). Items under the yin category are seen in a more negative light (passive, death, subject). It is also clear that these pairs of opposites do not all relate to one another in the same way that yin and yang do: for example, fathers do not wax or wane in relation to a son. Finally, the most problematic part of the yin-yang theory is the assignment of gender: men are yang and birth; women are yin and death. The odd correlation of women with death and men with birth is part of the preference for yang. The ying-yang theory, which is accepted throughout Chinese culture and remains as popular as ever, has always acted as a metaphysical basis for male superiority: men and women are obviously different, it is argued, but complementary to one another just as are yin and yang. Men and women are different but equal. To go against this is to misunderstand the way the universe works.

The yin-yang theory worked well with Confucian ideas of the role of women as wives, mothers, and daughters. It worked just as well with Buddhist ideas of the secondary and inferior role of women, even as nuns. Thus the patrilineal and patriarchal nature of traditional Chinese culture found its theoretical base in the yin-yang theory.

SEXUALITY

The yin-yang theory and Confucian, Buddhist, and Religious Daoist thought all came together in traditional China to affirm both existing sexist attitudes and to provide theoretical rationales for them. All traditions agreed that sexuality, particularly female sexuality, had to be controlled. With the possible exception of Buddhism (an issue still being debated), none of the Chinese traditions saw sex as evil. Buddhist and Religious Daoist nuns and monks were expected to be celibate. Buddhist and Religious Daoist priests, on the other hand, could, and did, marry. Apart from the strictures concerning celibacy, it was generally assumed that the adult population would have, and indeed needed, sex. Sex was something all adults did; the issue for the traditions was how this was to be handled. Chinese culture has generally assumed, and still widely assumes today, that sex is a necessary part of life, that sex is not only enjoyable but also part of maintaining one's health, and that sex is part of marriage.

Confucian ritual texts, books that set out how rituals were to be performed, were used throughout society. The most influential was by the Neo-Confucian Zhu Xi (1130–1200 CE), whose ritual handbook, Family Rituals, set out the performance of marriages, funerals, ancestral veneration, and the private rituals of families. Zhu Xi also explained why rituals work the way they do, so that many people were exposed to standard Confucian thought about the status of women.

Like the Book of Rites, Zhu Xi's Family Rituals claims a complementary balance between male and female. He describes, for example, visits to the ancestral tablets to be carried out at New Year, the solstice, and the full moon:

> The participants, in full attire, from the presiding man on down, all enter the gate and take up their places. The presiding man faces north at the base of the ceremonial staircase. The presiding woman faces north at the base of the western steps. When the presiding man's mother is alive, she assumes a special place in front of the presiding woman. The wives of the presiding man's younger brothers and his younger sisters are slightly behind the wife, to her left. The wives of sons and grandsons, daughters, and female attendants are to the rear of the presiding woman in rows with the most senior at the eastern end. When everyone is in place, the presiding man washes his hands, dries them, goes up the stairs, and inserts his official plaque. He opens the tablet case, takes the spirit tablets of his ancestors, and puts them in front of the case. The presiding woman washes, dries, goes up the stairs, and takes the spirit tablets of the ancestresses and sets them to the east of the men's tablets. (Ebrey 1991: 14)

The man who presides over this ritual and his wife, the presiding woman, both handle the tablets. The other men and women, for this would be an extended family, stand in order of seniority. We should note, however, that the ancestors referred to here are the man's ancestors; the woman has married into the family. As well, only men address the ancestors, women do not; men initiate the ritual, women follow after. Throughout the rituals of ancestral veneration, and all the other family rituals, women have an essential place, but it is not an equal one. However, this is not the only interpretation of these rituals.

Other scholars understand these rituals as representing a balanced and reciprocal relationship between men and women (Paper 1999: 58).

Women took part in ancestral veneration, first as daughters in their natal home, venerating their father's ancestors, then in their husband's home as part of the rituals venerating his ancestors. As a woman's status increased in her husband's home, as she produced sons and grew older, she would assist her husband at these rituals, providing the food and handling the female ancestral tablets.

Neo-Confucian ritual handbooks return to the idea of complementariness between men and women when discussing funeral ritual. The presiding male mourner was the eldest son of the deceased; the presiding female mourner was the wife of the deceased. However, the son was thought to have a much closer relationship to his father and other male ancestors, because they shared in the same *qi* (life energy) (Ebrey 1991: 71, 105).

The ancestral tablets that were created for the dead of the clan were tablets for both men and women, provided that the woman was either the first wife of a male member of the clan or the mother of male heirs. Thus her status as an ancestor and the level of funeral ritual accorded to her depended on her relationship to her husband and his family. Before marriage, a woman would have taken part in the ancestral rituals of her natal family as a junior member who stood in place behind her grandmother, mother, and aunts. At her natal family's rituals she would not have acted, but was only present. As a married woman, she might eventually become the senior wife in the clan (if her husband was the eldest son) and she would serve by preparing and offering the food in the funeral or ancestral rituals. Thus, her status in these rituals depended on her marriage. Her status as an ancestor depended on her marriage as well: a woman who died was given an ancestral tablet if she was the first wife, though this was not displayed until the death of her husband. After the deaths of the couple their tablets were displayed together (Ebrey 1991: 52–3).

The degrees of mourning—that is, what clothes were worn, food eaten, and rituals carried out and for how long—depended on the patrilineal line. Once married, a woman mourned her husband's parents more than her own, though both husband and wife owed some degree of mourning ritual to her parents.

The ritual texts set out proper ritual that claims a complementary relationship between men and women. However, this complementariness did not apply to sexual behaviour. Confucians were deeply concerned with the chastity of women. A woman's virtue, they argued, consisted primarily of preserving her virginity before marriage, of modesty and sexual loyalty in marriage, and of continuing loyalty to the memory of her husband in widowhood. One of the primary ways of ensuring this was a strict separation of women in their own quarters in the household (practicable only for those who could afford such large households). If women did not meet men other than their husbands, or were properly chaperoned in mixed company, it would be easier to monitor women's chastity.

Marriage was never seen as a romantic tie: it was the bringing together of two families and its purpose was the production of children, particularly sons, to carry on the family and to carry on ancestral veneration. Families arranged marriages, and, ideally, the couple first saw each other on their wedding day. Parents were responsible for maintaining their daughter's virginity and her reputation as modest and chaste. Once married, the woman lived with the husband's extended family and was expected to be obedient, filial, modest, and to produce sons. Sexuality was considered a normal, indeed necessary, part of adult life. In some cases, before marriage, the couples were given 'pillow books' by their families so that they might explore many areas of sexual enjoyment. Sex was not seen as evil; it was part of the proper duty of all men and women and part of the order of nature. Sexuality was dangerous when it was outside the rules. The way to lessen that danger was to insist on women's chastity, not men's.

The separation of women and men extends from household to ritual. The Neo-Confucian Sima Guang said, 'In managing a family . . . what is most important is ritual. And the separation of males and females is the chief element in ritual'. He then described what this meant: men and women do not sit together or pass things directly to each other, men avoid their brother's wives, and so on (Ebrey 1984: 47–8).

Widowhood put women in an awkward position: they were supported by their husband's family, with whom they had no direct blood relationship except through their children. There were some families who wanted to get rid of the widow, but keep the dowry she had brought; she, on the other hand, might want to leave the family, either to remarry or to live alone, but wanted to take her bridal dowry with her. The complex economic, familial, and emotional issues that widowhood raised had to be addressed by the Confucians, who wanted to promote harmonious families. Zhu Xi and his Neo-Confucian school argued that widows were to remain loyal to the memory of their husbands and never remarry. However, widows who remained loyal might be starved by their husband's family, who saw no reason why they should support an outsider, or who wished to force the widow to turn over her dowry. When one Neo-Confucian was asked about this situation and whether the widow might remarry, given her extreme situation, he replied, 'This has come up just because people are afraid of dying of hunger and cold. Dying of hunger is a trivial matter; loss of virtue is extremely serious'. Widowers, however, were encouraged to remarry in order to continue the family line.

A man might divorce his wife for any of the 'seven conditions': disobedience to her husband's parents, barrenness, adultery, jealousy, incurable disease, talkativeness, or theft. The man was prohibited from divorce if she had mourned his parents, if he had become wealthy or received high honours during the marriage, or if her parents were dead. Wealthy and upper-class men did take concubines, particularly if the first wife was infertile; the first wife always remained the first wife, however, and was still in charge of the household.

The practice of foot-binding in traditional China was also connected to female sexuality. First mentioned in the Song Dynasty (970–1279 CE), the practice may be even older. The origin is not clear, though speculation links it to the taping of the feet of dancers in the Imperial Palace. It is clear that it began as an imperial practice and filtered down through the rest of society. Bound feet were considered sexually appealing—as much fantasy objects as breasts are in the West. It was also a sign of conspicuous consumption: a family that bound its women's feet did not need to have that woman go out to work. It soon became a sign of good breeding; girls with unbound feet would find it virtually impossible to marry. It was thought too that it decreased the possibility of female unfaithfulness because foot-binding made it difficult to walk. The proverb was, 'if you love your son, don't go easy on his study; if you love your daughter, don't go easy on her feet'. At about age four or five, girls' feet were wrapped with 2 metres (2 yards) of bandages, tightened to keep the foot from growing. The toes were bent under and into the sole of the foot, breaking the bones and bringing the toe and heel close together. The result was 8- to 13-centimetre (3- to 5-inch) feet, euphemistically called 'golden lotuses'. The practice could lead to gangrene, paralysis, or death.

Foot-binding was not a religious practice: no tradition is linked to its development. Confucians were of two minds about it. On the one hand, the only attacks came from some Confucian scholars who argued that it deformed the body given to us by our parents and thus was not a filial practice. Most Confucians, however, accepted the practice as a way of maintaining chastity.

Chastity was discussed solely in terms of heterosexual intercourse. Same-sex relationships were not generally seen as interfering with the proper duty of men and women to marry and have children. In traditional China, men and women were increasingly separated. Men's social life was carried out outside the home in restaurants and tea houses; women stayed home or visited each other. Mixed gatherings were rare except at theatres or temples. It is not surprising then that men's significant emotional relationships were to other men and women's were to other women. Often close friends would swear oaths of brotherhood or sisterhood, binding themselves to a lifelong friendship. It is not always clear to what extent sexuality was part of these relationships. The extravagant and loving language may well indicate gay or lesbian relationships, or it may be what we read into them. Traditional China, like many other cultures that divide male and female universes, clearly knew about same-sex relationships, but seems to have been troubled by them only when they interfered with family functioning. This attitude is in contrast with modern China, where Communist puritanism has made gay and lesbian behaviour illegal, and modern Chinese cultures where many Chinese people insist that only Westerners are gay or lesbian. The last decade has seen some loosening of attitudes, but in China and in overseas Chinese communities, it is still generally believed that sexuality is reserved for heterosexual marriage.

OFFICIAL AND UNOFFICIAL ROLES OF WOMEN

Much of what we have seen so far are the attitudes and proscriptions imposed on women. Yet Chinese women were never simply passive recipients of the traditions. As in other cultures, women understood their traditions and wove them into their lives in many different ways.

In the Confucian tradition, the underlying question for women was, and is, can a woman be a *junzi* (gentleman)? If so, in what ways? How does gender affect the way in which we understand 'gentleman'? Early Confucianism did not exclude women from the category, but did not explicitly include women either. One of the first women to respond to the problem was Ban Zhao (*c.* 45–120 CE), who had helped her brother to write an extensive history, the *Han Shu,* and then completed it after his death; she was court historian and a well-known scholar, tutor to the Empress and her advisor when the Empress became Regent. She also wrote *Nu Jie* (Women's Instructions) as a guide for her daughters, training them in moral behaviour. Ban Zhao advocated education for women because of their important role in the inner world, which is a foundation for the outer. When discussing women's qualities, she wrote, 'Women have four qualities, that is, womanly attainments, womanly speech, womanly appearance, womanly skills. As to attainments, a woman does not have to be extraordinarily intelligent; in speech she does not need to be clever; in appearance, she does not need to be beautiful; in skill, she does not need to be more than average. Being gentle and composed, quiet, chaste and orderly, careful in what she does, and to follow the rules—this is the real womanly attainment' (see Swann 1932: 86). The 'rules' Ban Zhao is referring to are the rules of proper behaviour set out in the Confucian classics. Women are to be thoughtful in dealing with others and are admonished to do all their work carefully. Ban Zhao argued that women should follow the instructions first of their fathers, then their husbands, and that they should not remarry if widowed. She did, however, also expect husbands to follow the rules in order for there to be a harmonious household: if a husband struck his wife that ruined the harmony of the household. Thus, not only was he acting immorally, but Ban Zhao advised the wife to leave. What we see in the *Nu Jie* is one of the first of many attempts by educated women both to follow the strictures of tradition and to become active moral agents by practising loyalty, filial piety, and chastity. Women were careful to guard their virginity and their reputations; there were countless instances of wives and widows remaining loyal to their husbands through many trials. When pushed to abandon these principles, some women committed suicide. Rather than rejecting the Confucian tradition, women often internalized it and saw themselves as ethical actors who worked very hard to succeed in becoming, in their own way, gentlemen.

This response to Confucianism is most often seen in upper-class women in traditional China who felt a responsibility to set an example. However, much of this attitude filtered down to ordinary people as well. One of the most remarkable glimpses into the attitudes of ordinary women can be found in the *nu shu* (women's hidden writings).

Women in a rural area in the southern part of Hunan province wrote songs, diaries, letters, histories, biographies, and poems in their own hidden form of writing. The symbols used in this writing are alphabetical, unlike Chinese characters. Women in the area were taught to read and write it, but very few men were. Women wrote to each other, recorded their lives, wrote out prayers, and presented these writings as gifts. These women swore oaths of sisterhood to one another in pairs or groups of 'sisters'. These relationships helped many women through their lives, allowing them to give each other advice as well as complaining about the families they had married into.

The elite of traditional China always described peasant women as 'superstitious' and 'ignorant', but when one reads their writings the women's religious attitudes are quite surprising. There are very few references to the Buddha, Confucius, and other common religious figures. They write about the Buddhist concepts of karma and samsara; they boast that they have 'done their duty' to their husband's family, according to the Confucian tradition. The women know the teachings, but there is remarkably little awe felt toward the 'great' traditions. The local, mostly female, deities were central to these women, as were festivals and pilgrimages in their honour. In the women's writing, prayers are offered to the gods for a number of purposes: wishes; a family reunion; good fortune; a good husband; children, particularly sons; and divine assistance. One prayer describes a woman's preparations:

> Seven days ago I fasted,
> Five days ago I burned incense,
> Three days ago I boiled fresh water,

And washed my clothes and myself.
Today I sit peacefully in an empty room,
To write an offering to the goddess Gu Po.
I offer it to ask Gu Po's blessing and protection,
To bring my husband safely home soon. (Rainey 1995: 145)

Prayers were written on paper or fans and then placed before statues in various temples.

These women believed in an afterlife and the presence of the spirits of the dead, but they were not afraid of them: they wrote poems to restless spirits. The spirits of the dead could, and would, these women believed, contact the living through dreams and through shamans. Despite the characterisation of peasant women as 'superstitious' and fearful, the women who wrote the hidden texts showed little fear of the dead and wished only to ensure that the spirits of the dead were content. As for ancestors and ancestral veneration, we very rarely find these rituals even mentioned in the hidden writings (Rainey 1995: 139).

Shamans or mediums, the inheritors of the office of *wu*, were extremely important for speaking with the dead. Official Confucian ritual rejected the idea of the possession of the living by the spirits of the dead, and by the time of the Ming Dynasty (1368–1644) it was illegal for the mediums that spoke to the dead to practise. However, mediums continued to speak to the dead on behalf of the living and continue to do so into modern times. The demand that underlies the continued existence of these mediums was mostly from women, and shows us that many women were dissatisfied with Confucian ritual where male ancestors were venerated. Women turned to mediums to satisfy a need to deal directly with the dead both from the family into which they had married and from their natal family. Mediums, frequently women, and their patrons, mostly women, continued their rituals for dealing with the dead despite official disapproval.

Most women in traditional China shared in one ritual: going on a pilgrimage. In the hidden writings we find that women often went on a pilgrimage together to mountain temples. Lay Buddhist pilgrims, looking for merit, participated in pilgrimages to sacred Buddhist sites.

We have a record of women pilgrims to Mount Tai in the 1600s. Women were the religious leaders for the pilgrimage and also made the financial and logistical arrangements. Women also led the organization that sponsored the pilgrimage. The purpose of the pilgrimage, one of the leaders says, was 'partly to build up good fortune, partly to enjoy the sites' (Dudbridge 1992: 41, 46). The ritual pilgrimage, then, did not have simply a religious motive: it allowed women to travel, to see new things, to enjoy each other's company, and, their critics claimed, to look for sexual adventures. The women held a three-day ceremony at a local temple dedicated to *San Guan Da Di*, the Three Agents, gods associated with heaven, earth, and water. Similarly, at the birthday of Guan Yin, the female leaders planned a three-day-and-night celebratory ceremony.

Women pilgrims are noted in most descriptions of pilgrimages, and of the religious rituals that women carried out, pilgrimages were one of the most common. Pilgrims journeyed to temples, and to sacred mountains and sites (such as Puto Island, sacred to Guan Yin). The religious aim of most of these pilgrimages was to venerate the gods and often to pray for sons. Pilgrimages were also one of the few sanctioned ways that women could move outside of the house.

The female organizations that set up pilgrimages also celebrated festivals, particularly those to do with their patron deities. Women in general celebrated the festivals of traditional China, either as part of the patrilineal family where women provided food and assisted in the ritual (as we have seen in ancestral veneration), or in festivals that were mainly celebrated by, and for, women.

In the first month of the lunar calendar New Year was celebrated. This included veneration of patrilineal ancestors, and, as well, the provision of new clothes, special foods, and other rituals. Family or home rituals were often organized and carried out by women. One female ritual of the New Year celebration was the veneration of the God of the Stove, or the Kitchen God, who reported the year's activities of the family to heaven: honey was smeared on his lips to ensure a good report.

The popular festival of Qing Ming falls in the third lunar month: the graves of the family were swept and cleaned; the fifth day of the fifth month is the time of the Dragon Boat Festival; Zhong Qiu, the mid-autumn or moon festival, is held on the fifteenth day of the eighth month, and so on. In the continual round of festivals, special foods were required, the patrilineal ancestors were venerated, and women were mostly responsible for the organization of the festival's rituals. The women's hidden writings record these festivals and many others, including a spring planting festival when, the night before the rice seedlings were set out, women returned to their natal home, especially women who had just married and those who had no children; they went back to their husband's homes when the rice was planted. The hidden writings tell us of many festivals that involved women meeting together in each other's homes and others where they returned to their natal homes. For example, beginning on the fifteenth day of the new year there were women's gatherings at which women read the hidden texts together. We can see then that women organized and carried out a number of religious activities not acknowledged by the elite traditions.

Women all over China, like the women who used the hidden writing, initiated their own pilgrimages, celebrated festivals, prayed to the gods, and fed the unhappy spirits of the dead. They wrote their own prayers and developed their own rituals of worship. In popular religiosity, women seemed to be much more free, though always within the strictures of the larger society.

Local deities, central to the women in southern Hunan, did occasionally become more nationally known, a phenomenon we see from about 800 to 1100 CE across China. One possible reason for the rise in popularity of certain deities may have been the invention of the printing press and dissemination of books and pamphlets. Contrary to Western mythology, the first printed book was the *Diamond Sutra*, printed in China in 868 CE. One of the deities that became nationally popular in this period was Guan Yin. Guan Yin is the Bodhisattva of compassion and mercy who began in the Mahāyāna Buddhist traditions of India as the Bodhisattva Avalokiteśvara. When Guan Yin appears in China, he is a male Bodhisattva (as he remains in Tibet), but, by around the tenth century CE, Guan Yin became female in China and remains so today. Scholars have debated the reason, and it is thought that one may be the association of local female deities and their histories with the figure of Guan Yin. Eventually, it is thought, these deities and their stories became so intermeshed that Guan Yin began to be portrayed as female. Stories about Guan Yin (all outside of the Buddhist sutras) are multiple; in them she is variously portrayed as a filial daughter, a nun, a chaste woman, or a teacher. However the change happened, Guan Yin was, and remains, the most popular deity in China. Images of Guan Yin are found not just in Buddhist temples, but also in homes, charms, and, nowadays, in taxis.

Guan Yin represented compassion, mercy, and, most importantly, she brought children. For women whose status in their husband's homes depended on producing an heir, this was a central concern. Life for many women was difficult, and women who felt powerless also turned to Guan Yin. Most women had a picture, statue, or altar to Guan Yin in their rooms. Like the Virgin Mary in the Christian tradition, Guan Yin is somewhat problematic for women: along with being a compassionate and merciful deity, she is an unmarried model of filial piety and chastity, and, like Mary, impossible to imitate completely. There are reports from sociologists that modern-day devotees envy and admire Guan Yin's freedom as a woman, for she is not locked into the social structure. A pilgrim song says, 'First, she does not suffer the ill-humour of in-laws; second, she does not eat food provided by a husband; third, she does not carry a son in her stomach or a grandson in her arms; fourth, she sits lightly on a lotus throne' (Levering 1994: 221).

Another deity that grew past her local roots is Ma Zu. She is like Guan Yin in that she too is merciful and compassionate. She saves people from danger, especially on the sea; she also gives and protects children. One of her titles is Holy Mother of Heaven. Ma Zu is said to have been a shy, religiously devout, young woman who died young saving her father and all but one of her brothers from drowning. She is still particularly popular in southern China and in Taiwan.

In general, women were looking for gods that dealt with their specific problems: childlessness, illness, family strife, and so on. In the hidden women's writings, we see women gathering to pray to local deities, calling them sociable names such as 'honoured aunt', and 'Niangniang', which means 'queen', or 'goddess', and is often added to the end of the god's name. Women prayed to these gods in their homes. Women also would join together to journey to the Niangniang's temple and there offer incense and gifts:

> I take up my pen to write these words
> To respectfully send them to Longyantang, Yuan township,
> Where the famous Gu Niangniang manifests her spiritual power.
> Every year in the second month we look forward to all the excitement.
> Households come with incense.
> Facing the altar that keeps out wind and rain,
> With the green mountains in the background, full of colours,
> And in front, the scenery is so beautiful.
> Gu Niangniang sends down blessings . . .
> Famous Gu Niangniang, heed us well,
> And never forget your concern.
> We yearly bring you incense and count on your will.
> Gu Niangniang is profoundly good,
> And her good name is known everywhere
> Famous Gu Niangniang send down blessings;
> Receive this fragrant incense and bless us all. (Rainey 1995: 151)

The writers of the hidden texts offered gifts that included fans, embroidery, and books with prayers written in the women's script. A woman who had given birth due to the intercession of Zisun Niangniang would return to Zisun Niangniang and leave shoes and red eggs (the celebratory gift given when a son is born). Other women who had no sons would take these gifts from the altars in order to carry home the good luck of others (Rainey 1995: 150).

Women served the gods and spirits at home as well: they were responsible for the spiritual welfare of the household. Thus they made proper offerings to the God of the Stove, the household gods in charge of the well or the doorway, hungry ghosts (the spirits of the dead who had no family and could cause trouble in the homes of others), and any other spirits who might cause mischief. Women offered incense, food, drink, and prayers to all of these spirits.

Women also prayed at local temples when someone was pregnant. At home, they hung pictures of tigers to encourage the birth of a son; they prayed to gods of children such as Guan Yin and Zisun Niangniang. During and just after childbirth, other prayers were offered to ensure the health and well-being of mother and child.

During illness, women would exorcize the room or house to try to get rid of the evil spirits. This was done by sweeping the room, hanging charms, reciting mantras or sutras, and offering the spirits food. At funerals as well, women performed rituals not mentioned in the official ritual texts, so as to drive off evil spirits and preserve the health and luck of the family.

In sum, in traditional China, women played active religious roles: they initiated and organized pilgrimages to sacred sites; they organized lay associations—Buddhist, Daoist, and local—that centred on a deity and that performed good works, such as famine relief; they continued to act as shamans or mediums. In the family setting, women performed a number of household rituals around birth, the home, and exorcism. The rituals of ancestral veneration were tied to inheritance and descent lines in the family and to official and accepted norms in the culture. In these rituals women had an essential role, but the role was always secondary and the ancestors were not hers.

It was in the organized settings—Buddhist and Religious Daoist monasteries and convent—that women took second place. Although Buddhist and Religious Daoist nuns were committed to their traditions and often noted for their holiness and advice, they could not shake the predetermined status that the tradition had set.

SOCIAL CHANGE

The culture of traditional China was a closed system: the political, religious, and social mores supported and reinforced one another. There were some criticisms of the world view that this culture implied. Li Ru-chen (1763–1800) wrote a parody of traditional culture in his book *Ching Hua Yuan* (Flowers in the Mirror), where men have their feet bound and their ears pierced, and where women sit for the Confucian civil service examinations. However, a serious examination of traditional culture and the status of women really began only when one of the bases of the culture, political stability, began to crack. By the 1800s it was becoming clear that the Qing Dynasty could not protect China against the encroachments of Western powers determined, as the German Kaiser Wilhelm said, to 'carve China like a melon'.

Kang Youwei (1858–1927), one of the best-known Confucians of the time, was part of the political reform movement that attempted to reform the Qing Dynasty government and make it a constitutional monarchy. He also established a 'natural foot' society in 1881 aimed at ending foot-binding. By then, Western missionaries had also begun campaigns against foot-binding and were joined by a number of the Chinese intelligentsia. Kang wrote about the Great Harmony, an ideal society in which men and women were equal. From the beginning, reform movements in China saw political and social reform as closely tied to the status of women. Critiques of traditional China throughout the twentieth century used the status of women as 'proof' of the inequity and cruelty of traditional society.

This is most clearly seen in the May Fourth movement, a loose conjunction of reformers that began in the 1920s and included novelists, poets, artists, journalists, and students. It was an intellectual and cultural crusade with the ideals of bringing science and democracy to a modern China. Across the wide range of reformers, Confucianism was blamed for being responsible for the decadent political situation, the backwardness of China, and the oppression of women. The slogan of the May Fourth movement was 'Down with Confucius and his shop'. The most popular play of the time was Ibsen's *Doll's House*. Nora's refusal to accept tradition as she slams the door on it was seen as a call for freedom from traditional culture and all that it implied toward women. Young men who wanted to criticize filial piety as blind loyalty and family responsibilities as suffocating, argued that women were enslaved in this system. They saw no way to reform traditional Chinese culture; they wanted the whole thing scrapped.

Buddhism and Religious Daoism were summarily dismissed as 'superstitious'. Buddhism had contributed to the backwardness of China, the reformers argued, because it encouraged 'otherworldliness' and excused social inequity as a result of karma. Religious Daoism was seen as corrupt and representative of the worst kind of superstition and non-scientific thinking. However, neither of these traditions was criticized for the views of women as much as was Confucianism.

Christianity played some role in the reform movement. Christian missionaries came to China beginning in the mid-1800s with a mindset of cultural and racial superiority. Missionaries, both Roman Catholic and Protestant, insisted that anyone converting to Christianity give up all participation in the rituals of ancestral veneration. This would cut converts off from most family activities. Most missionaries also confused Christianity with Western culture and tended to see conversion as conversion to Western thinking, Western ways, and Western dress. Missionaries were also tarred with the brush of imperialism. So, despite the large number of missionaries, and the money and energy spent, Christianity was not very successful in China. Missionaries did, however, object to foot-binding and to what they saw as the subservient status of women in China. They also opened schools for girls. They taught boys and girls their ideas about the roles of men and women and their ideas of democracy. As a result, many of the reformers of twentieth-century China—including Sun

Yatsen, considered the founder of modern China, and members of the May Fourth movement—had missionary school backgrounds. Whether Christian missions were a positive or negative influence in China is a subject still being debated, but in terms of reform, Christianity's influence cannot be ignored.

The attitudes of the May Fourth movement were echoed in the thinking of the Chinese Communist Party. More and more women, particularly young women, took active political and social roles, organizing demonstrations and boycotts, and, from the 1930s on, taking part in guerilla warfare against the Japanese and later the Guomindang. Women were active in the Communist Party, and when the Communists took over rural areas they organized women's unions; enacted laws that let women initiate divorce; forbade foot-binding, forced marriages, and domestic violence; and established education for women.

When the Communists came to power in 1949, equality was guaranteed in the 1950 Constitution. The Marriage Law of 1950 gave women the right to divorce and choose their own husbands. It outlawed polygamy, attempted to abolish the dowry system, raised the status of widows, and encouraged widows to remarry. As in many communist countries, it was assumed that communism, along with women in the workforce, would bring equality. The continuation of traditional attitudes from party cadres and the general population was ignored.

The communist view that religion is the opiate of the people, plus its international ties, meant that all religions were persecuted and suppressed. Christian missionaries were expelled. Religious leaders of all kinds, and some of their followers, were imprisoned, tortured, or killed. Religious buildings were closed and used for other purposes. Whatever was left of most religious practices went underground. However, to protect its image, the state set up some government-controlled religious bodies. Confucianism was attacked again during the Cultural Revolution (1966–76) as representative of a traditional culture that had to be destroyed (see Levering 1994).

Despite these attacks, traditions did not die. They remained vibrant outside of China in Taiwan, Hong Kong, and in the Chinese diaspora in Canada and elsewhere. In China, some religious practitioners went underground; some continued to believe but did not practise. With economic reforms, which began in the late 1970s, some loosening of restrictions occurred. In 1982, the Chinese government announced a new policy toward religions, which were to be tolerated except when criminal, counter-revolutionary, or leading to foreign 'infiltration'. There are now Buddhist temples in all provinces, as well as Buddhist publishers, seminaries, training centres, and lay groups. With the exception of Tibetan Buddhism, the Buddhist tradition in China seems to be making a comeback. This is particularly true in the south of China, due to influence, and money, from Taiwan. Religious Daoism has been slower to recover, though now one can find a priesthood, temples, and the performance of traditional rituals such as exorcism. A training programme for nuns has also begun, and men and women recite scriptures in Daoist centres (Levering 1994: 203). Even Protestant and Roman Catholic Christianity has grown in modern China, with its own churches, seminaries, and publishing companies. The most amazing resurgence has been in popular religiosity with the return of some traditional funeral rituals, ancestral veneration, and a large number of texts now available across China. It is now possible for women in China to practise their traditions, whether popular, Buddhist, Daoist, or Christian, as either a layperson or a religious professional. However, religious practice is still not completely tolerated. The recent persecution of Falun Gong, a new version of popular religiosity mixing traditional beliefs with the practice of meditation and *qigong* (a series of physical exercises), shows the government's fear of large and organized religious groups. Both male and female Falun Gong followers have been imprisoned, tortured, or killed.

The loosening of attitudes in China and the changes in Chinese societies outside the mainland has led to some attempts to re-evaluate traditions and their attitudes toward women. Outside of China, especially in Hong Kong and Taiwan, scholars began to argue that Confucianism can indeed encourage science and democracy. They believe that the Confucianism that was practised in traditional China was not the real Confucianism: arbitrary power, authoritarianism, and the low status of women actually run counter to real Confucianism. The 'New Confucians', led by scholars such as Tu Wei-ming, maintain that Chinese culture cannot function without Confucianism, for it is Confucianism that provides the moral base for Chinese society. It is in this context that women have also begun to investigate the Confucian tradition, asking the perennial question, Can a woman be a Confucian gentleman? Some have argued that Confucianism can and does include women: women can be equal partners in a family, for example, that practises mutual deference, mutual authority, and mutual respect. It is argued that if one returns to the Confucian classics and takes from them the notions of respect and mutual responsibility, one can overturn the authoritarian interpretation. The senior partner in relationships, a husband or father, is not permitted to act cruelly or immorally, and it is the right of partners in relationships to speak about injustice. When looking at Confucianism in this way, one scholar argues, 'Confucianism cherishes at its heart, equality in education and the *li* [principle] of change. These two principles, an equal opportunity to learning and an attitude of openness and flexibility, do not contradict feminism' (Woo 1999: 137). For some scholars, a 'real' Confucianism can be recovered.

Critiques of Confucianism continue, however. Lu Xiulian, a contemporary Taiwanese thinker, began a feminist critique of Confucianism. She argues that

Confucianism speaks only to men, equates maleness and being human, and sees women as second-class human beings (Lu 1974; Reed 1994: 227). In mainland China, the 1988 television documentary *River Elegy* argued that Chinese civilization is dead and stifling and that much of this is due to Confucianism. In practical terms, it can be argued that the vast majority of people agree. Family strictures, especially as they affect women, have begun to loosen, if slowly. Ancestral veneration has often been abandoned; it may be practised only for form's sake; or, in some cases, women have transformed it. There is growing anecdotal evidence that women are beginning to perform ancestral veneration rituals for their own parents and to follow matrilineal descent lines when doing so. In Taiwan, I have seen women, and their husbands, venerating the ancestral plaques of her parents. This was explained as being due to the social dislocation of the civil war and the move from China to Taiwan, but the fact that it happened at all is dramatic.

In Taiwan, Hong Kong, Singapore, Vancouver, and Toronto, wherever the Chinese community spread, it brought along the practices and views of traditional China. In Toronto or Vancouver one can find dozens of Daoist temples, and scores of Buddhist ones. These traditions have been exposed to Western culture and ideas, and the impact has been especially strong among the young. Even in Taiwan, where traditional Chinese thought has dominated, changes are found. In 1989, Taiwan legalized the practice of shamans and there is now an association of shamans, the vast majority of whom are women.

When one looks at religiosity in Chinese communities outside of China, one can see that many new ideas from the surrounding cultures are being brought into traditional thinking and practice A small, but telling, example is the wearing of a white bridal dress. White has always been the traditional colour of mourning, worn at funerals. Yet, in most Canadian Chinese weddings, one sees a white bridal dress at the ceremony and then the bride changes into red, the traditional wedding colour, for the reception. This practice is found in Taiwan and Hong Kong as well. But while younger Chinese people often do not practise ancestral veneration, or do so only to please their parents, many people still pray to the gods; restaurants and homes have traditional altars; statues of Guan Yin adorn dashboards.

As new social structures and ways of thinking transform traditional practice, Chinese women find themselves in an odd situation. Much of traditional thinking has been associated with Confucianism. The difficulty is in how one can change Confucianism. This is a tradition that has no priesthood, no organization, no central body or head. If one wants to change the Roman Catholic Church, for example, one tries to work with priests, theologians, cardinals, and the Pope. When there is no organization to approach, there is a real difficulty in effecting change. Scholars such as the New Confucians may reread the

Confucian classics, but this will not necessarily change traditional thinking. The only way to reform Confucian ritual is through changing everyday practice and the ideal of family based on the patrilineal line; this would require a very strong initiative from a large number of women. Modern Chinese women have taken one of three routes their mothers and grandmothers took: they go along with tradition; they abandon the tradition altogether; or they privately change the tradition to suit themselves. It is important to note that Confucianism cannot just be ignored. Dealing with Confucianism is a pressing issue in that Confucian notions permeate thought about gender, law, society, and religiosity.

Changing Buddhism is both easier and harder than changing Confucianism. Because there are Buddhist sutras that show women as enlightened beings, women as teachers, preachers, and missionaries, there is then a ground for arguing against the later Buddhist idea that women cannot become enlightened. But Buddhism too has no central authority. As a result, women must either change the thinking of the particular school or temple to which they belong, or simply develop their own.

The foremost example of women taking their own paths is Dharma Master Cheng Yen, a Buddhist nun in Taiwan who founded the 'Buddhist Compassion, Belief, Love, and Mercy Foundation'. In the early 1960s, she became convinced that women could take on the same religious responsibilities as men and sought out a Dharma Master who agreed with her and would ordain her. In 1966 she set up her own foundation, which has grown to a membership of four million people. They provide medical, financial, or spiritual aid to anyone in need: in the 1999 Taiwan earthquake, they were the first on the scene, just as they were after an earthquake in Mexico. The foundation has offered medical services and distributed food from Haiti to Thailand. It runs free hospitals, seniors homes, medical training colleges, and schools. Cheng Yen rejects many of the traditional rituals and beliefs of Buddhism and has, in essence, founded a new school of Buddhism that is socially active and that sees itself as returning to the basics of Buddhism. Her followers say that she is a reincarnation of the Buddha.

Like Dharma Master Cheng Yen, some Buddhist and Religious Daoist nuns and laypeople have struck out on their own, arguing that women can become enlightened, can be teachers and leaders. The Chinese traditions are unique in that, in most cases, the traditions are not centrally organized, and this can allow women to forge their own path. This can work against women as well, because there may not be a central body to legislate the changes women want. Buddhist monks may continue to reject Cheng Yen's views; the neighbours may look askance at women who venerate their natal family's ancestors.

Fundamentalism, as we understand it in the West, does not, strictly speaking, exist in Chinese culture. Fundamentalism, associated with the exclusivist belief in the literal truth of a text, the Bible or Qurán for example, is not found in traditions such as Confucianism or Buddhism, which do not see their texts as sacred. There is, though, a broader use of the term fundamentalism to mean an unswerving belief in a tradition, a demand for purity of practice, and, often, nostalgia for the past. One can find some of this, especially in more conservative Chinese communities such as Taiwan. In Taiwan, all-male Confucian groups still understand Confucianism in traditional terms and blame the problems of modern society on those who would change or abandon Confucianism as they see it. Similarly, there are Buddhist monks and laypeople who reject any change in tradition. Ordinary people too may worry that radical changes in tradition will lead to a loss of the essentials of Chinese culture.

For 50 years the Communist government in China attempted to stamp out religiosity and it was spectacularly unsuccessful. Since restrictions were lifted, popular practice, Buddhism, Religious Daoism, and Christianity have sprung back to life, fed in part by the continuing traditions outside of the mainland. But the experience of the twentieth century has changed these traditions irrevocably. Exposure to other cultures, rethinking of the traditions, and a reassessment of the roles of women has seeped through Chinese culture. The traditions are changing, even if only slowly and bit by bit. This is a trend that can only continue.

REFERENCES

Andors, Phyllis. 1983. *The Unfinished Liberation of Chinese Women 1949–1980*. Bloomington: Indiana University Press.

Black, Allison H. 1986. 'Gender and Cosmology in Chinese Correlative Thinking'. *Gender and Religion*. Eds. Caroline Walker Bynum et al. Boston: Beacon Press:166–95.

Chen, Ellen M. 1974. 'Tao as the Great Mother and the Influence of Motherly Love in the Shaping of Chinese Philosophy'. *History of Religions* 14: 51–64.

Chen, Kenneth S. 1973. *The Chinese Transformation of Buddhism*. Princeton: Princeton University Press.

Dudbridge, Glen. 1992. 'Women Pilgrims to T'ai Shan: Some Pages from a Seventeenth Century Novel'. *Pilgrims and Sacred Sites in China*. Eds Susan Naquin and Chun-fang Yu. Berkeley: University of California Press: 39–64.

Ebrey, Patricia Buckley. 1984. *Family and Property in Sung China: Yuan Ts'ai's Precepts for Social Life*. Princeton: Princeton University Press.

———. 1991. *Chu Hsi's Family Rituals*. Princeton: Princeton University Press.

———. 1993. *The Inner Quarters: Marriage and Lives of Chinese Women in the Sung Period*. Berkeley: University of California Press.

Fehl, Noah E. 1971. *Li, Rites and Propriety in Literature and Life: A Perspective for a Cultural History of Ancient China*. Hong Kong: Chinese University Press.

Gilmartin, Christina K. et al., eds. 1994. *Engendering China: Women, Culture and the State*. Cambridge: Harvard University Press.

Goonatilake, Hema. 1988. 'Nuns of China: Part I: The Mainland'. *Sakyadhita: Daughters of the Buddha*. Ed. K.L. Tsomo. Ithaca: Snow Lion.

Guisso, Richard. 1981. 'Thunder Over the Lake: The Five Classics and the Perception of Women in Early China'. *Women in China*. Eds Richard Guisso and Stanley Johannesen. New York: Philo: 47–63.

Legge, James. 1960. *The Ch'un Ts'ew with the Tso Chuan*. Hong Kong: University of Hong Kong Press.

————. 1967. *Li Chi: The Book of Rites*. New York: University Books.

Levering, Miriam. 1994. 'Women, the State, and Religion Today in the People's Republic of China'. *Today's Woman in World Religions*. Ed. Arvind Sharma. Albany: SUNY Press: 171–225.

Li Yu-ning, ed. 1981. *Chinese Women: Through Chinese Eyes*. New York: East Gate Books.

Mann, Susan. 1991. 'Grooming a Daughter for Marriage'. *Marriage and Inequality in Chinese Society*. Eds Rubie S. Watson and Patricia Buckley. Berkeley: University of California Press: 204–30.

Murray, Julia. 1990. 'Didactic Art for Women: The Ladies' Classic of Filial Piety'. *Flowering in the Shadows: Women in the History of Chinese and Japanese Painting*. Ed. Marsha Weidner. Honolulu: University of Hawaii Press: 27–53.

Paper, Jordan. 1995. *The Spirits Are Drunk: Comparative Approaches in Chinese Religion*. Albany: SUNY Press.

————. 1999. *Through the Earth Darkly: Female Spirituality in Comparative Perspective*. New York: Continuum.

Rainey, Lee. 1995. 'The Secret Writing of Chinese Women: Religious Practice and Beliefs'. *The Annual Review of Women and World Religions*. Eds Katherine Young and Arvind Sharma. Albany: SUNY Press: 130–64.

————. 1996. 'Woven as Close as Threads on a Spindle: Sisterhoods in the Hidden Writing of Chinese Women'. *Asian Profile* 24.4: 67–113.

Reed, Barbara. 1994. 'Women and Chinese Religion in Contemporary Taiwan'. *Today's Woman in World Religions*. Ed. Arvind Sharma. Albany: SUNY Press: 225–45.

Sangren, Steven P. 1983. 'Female Gender in Chinese Religious Symbols: Kuan Yin, Ma Tsu, and the "Eternal Mother"'. *Signs* 14: 4–25.

Schuster, Nancy. 1985. 'Striking a Balance: Women and Images of Women in Early Chinese Buddhism'. *Women, Religion, and Social Change*. Eds Yvonne Haddad et al. Albany: SUNY Press: 87–112.

Schwarz, Vera. 1986. *The Chinese Enlightenment: Intellectuals and the May Fourth Movement of 1919*. Berkeley: University of California Press.

Sharma, Arvind, ed. 1994. *Today's Woman in World Religions*. Albany: SUNY Press.

Swann, Nancy L. 1932. *Pan Chao: Foremost Woman Scholar of China*. New York: Russell and Russell.

Tseng Pao-sun. 1992. 'The Chinese Woman Past and Present'. *Chinese Women: Through Chinese Eyes*. Ed. Li Yu-ning. New York: East Gate Books: 72–86.

Wolfe, Margery, and Roxanne Witke, eds. 1975. *Women in Chinese Society*. Stanford: Stanford University Press.

Woo, Terry. 1999. 'Confucianism and Feminism'. *Feminism and World Religions*. Eds. Arvind Sharma and Katherine Young. Albany: SUNY Press: 110–48.

Yao, Esther S. Lee. 1967. *Chinese Women Past and Present*. Berkeley: University of California Press.

FURTHER READING

Andors, Phyllis. *The Unfinished Liberation of Chinese Women 1949–1980*. Bloomington: Indiana University Press, 1983.

Ebrey, Patricia Buckley. *The Inner Quarters: Marriage and Lives of Chinese Women in the Sung Period*. Berkeley: University of California Press, 1993.

Gilmartin, Christina K. et al., eds. *Engendering China: Women, Culture and the State*. Cambridge: Harvard University Press, 1994.

Li Yu-ning, ed. *Chinese Women: Through Chinese Eyes*. New York: East Gate Books, 1981.

Yao, Esther S. Lee. *Chinese Women Past and Present*. Berkeley: University of California Press, 1967.

⚛

CHAPTER 5

WOMEN IN INDIGENOUS TRADITIONS

Dawn Martin-Hill

A Nation is not defeated until the hearts of its women are on the ground.
—Cheyenne proverb (St. Pierre and Long Soldier 1995)

INTRODUCTION AND OVERVIEW

Indigenous women's spirituality, which can be explored in a variety of ways, will be examined in this chapter in terms of the need to reclaim, restore, and revitalize contemporary Indigenous spirituality through a discussion of Indigenous feminine cosmological constructions. Historically in Canada, under the Indian Act of 1884, many Native ceremonies were made illegal. At this time, laws were also passed that banned Natives from wearing traditional clothing or dancing (Steckley and Cummins 2001: 172). The Act that condoned the active suppression of Indigenous spirituality through legal means in 1914 was finally repealed in 1951. However, Elders today feel that the persecution of Indigenous spirituality, by governments and missionaries alike, continues, and that the stigma attached to these beliefs remains. As a result, a primary issue in many Indigenous communities is the need to empower Indigenous women, and to restore their dignity and integrity and their traditional spiritual practices.

The holistic world view of Indigenous peoples requires some discussion as a means of positioning spiritual knowledge as interrelated with all spheres of life. To illustrate, this chapter articulates an Indigenous framework by way of a review of Indigenous women's literature and the testimonies of Indigenous women. The construction of representations of Indigenous women's spirituality is as complex and diverse as the many Indigenous cultures discussed in the literature. Since spirituality is thought of as a way of life, rather than as a rigid, organized institution, it is manifested in the values, beliefs, and world views that are expressed in everyday actions rather than in periodic ritual.

The objective of this chapter is to identify the symbols, cosmologies, and epistemologies of Indigenous people that demonstrate the diversity of Indigenous women's spirituality while linking the underlying, collective assumptions about the feminine nature of the earth and the universe. The Indigenous knowledge framework developed by Indigenous scholars identifies spirituality as a foundation rather than as a separate discipline of inquiry. The related issue of cultural survival through women is critical to the role of Indigenous women, who are the *cultural transmitters*. Anthropologist Wade Davis and Cree Grandmother Freda Ahenekew affirm that every time a mother does not sing Cree lullabies to her babies, a culture begins to die. Women play an instrumental role in preserving Indigenous cultures and spirituality in the ever-threatening climate of globalization. This is not a matter of returning to the past, but of transforming the present context to honour traditional wisdoms. Indigenous theory is thus concerned with the human condition of Indigenous women, including the emotional, spiritual, psychological, and physical realms of their ways of life. Therefore spirituality is part of the intellectual process of Indigenous societies, not a process of intellectualism.

The role of gender within colonialism develops as a critical issue in the pursuit of decolonization. Métis author Kim Anderson demonstrates the significant role that colonial subjugation played in the loss of status and power experienced by Indigenous women, which in turn crippled or fragmented our societal structures, including those affecting Indigenous women and their spiritual responsibilities. She states:

> It may seem incredible that this territory we now know as Canada once hosted societies that afforded significant political power to those currently most marginalized: older women. . . . For the first time in our history, our women found themselves on the margins, in ghettos of evolving culture. The exclusion of our women from decision-making in important political and community matters not only dis-empowered the women, it also dis-empowered Indigenous cultures. . . . As the church replaced Native spirituality and became a powerful agent in the structure of Indigenous communities, Native women's loss of both political and spiritual authority was achieved. . . . Through colonization and the work of missionaries, women were excluded and handed a marginal role. (Anderson 2000: 71–8)

Through the process of intellectual and spiritual decolonization we refrain from recreating the colonial categories that bind us to an ordering of the universe that has historically oppressed Indigenous woman, often representing her in a degraded manner (Green 1998: 182). The results of adapting Western ideologies and practices is best summed up by examining current statistics on Indigenous women in Canada

In Canada, the role of Indigenous women has been transformed through missionization and government-forced assimilation policies, resulting in a shift from respecting the authority of women to seeing them as subordinates. The representation of Indigenous women in Western literature is laden with patriarchal and sexist ideologies. To address these issues, the framework that contemporary Indigenous women authors have adopted is holistic and acknowledges how history has ignored the massive losses that the Indigenous women have experienced, resulting in 'historical trauma' (Braveheart 1998: 287–305). Indigenous women desire to participate in the development of a discourse based on their unique experience, identity, diversity, and aspirations. Drawn from many cultures and a variety of academic disciplines, such a discourse would remain steeped in their own spiritual traditions and knowledge.

UNIQUE FEATURES OF WOMEN IN INDIGENOUS TRADITIONS: INDIGENOUS KNOWLEDGE

Over the years Euro-Canadian historians and anthropologists have represented Indigenous women as 'victims' and passive recipients of colonial domination (Van Kirk 1980). Today, literature written by Indigenous women outlines issues such as their spirituality and ways they apply their traditional teachings to improve their quality of life, from both an individual and a collective perspective. This is in contrast to Western feminism, which sought to deconstruct traditional Eurocentric views of women as a means of empowerment. Unlike Western feminists, many Indigenous women traditionally had power within their community, but it was actively suppressed by missionaries and governments who believed such authority for women was ridiculous (Anderson 2000; Gunn Allen 1998) and even primitive. The father of social science, Emile Durkheim, argues for the evolution of civilization in this way:

> The further we look into the past, the smaller becomes this difference between man and woman. The woman of past days was not at all the weak creature that she has become with progress of morality. . . . These anatomical resemblances are accompanied by functional resemblances. In the same societies, female functions are not very clearly distinguished from the male. Rather, the two sexes lead almost the same existence. There are even now a very great number of savage people where the woman mingles in political life. That has been observed especially in the Indian tribes of America, such as the Iroquois, the Natchez; in Hawaii she participates in myriad ways in men's lives, as she does in New Zealand and in Samoa. (Durkheim 1933: 58)

The Eurocentric representation of Indigenous women followed patterns of abhorring the savagery of Indigenous women while promoting assimilation policies that were doctrines of subordination to patriarchy and Christianity. Therefore one cannot examine Indigenous women's spirituality without examining colonialism.

Indigenous women's discourse establishes the rich diversity of Indigenous women's knowledge as a systematic and valid way of knowing, rooted in the consciousness of Indigenous peoples and encompassing the spiritual foundations of our respective cultures. In developing an Indigenous knowledge framework, it is important to outline our holistic approach, which underscores the interdependence of all things in the universe; therefore, spirituality is entrenched in all aspects of our way of life. Indigenous epistemology incorporates 'mind, body, and spirit' as entities of being that seek balance. Indigenous knowledge is a form of spiritual and intellectual enlightenment and consciousness. For example, the relationship of Indigenous peoples with the earth is understood as spiritual; all living things embody spirit and they make offerings to these spirits based on physical, spiritual, or emotional needs. At the same time it is important to understand intellectually how natural laws demand co-existence with nature as essential for human survival. Indigenous people have relationships with the land and a dialogue exists between the people and the land. They speak to her and she answers.

This approach contrasts with Western epistemology, which discerns science or knowledge as objective and autonomous from spirituality, emotions, values, or beliefs. In fact, emotion is conceptualized as irrational or subjective and therefore having no place in science (Deloria 1999). The Indigenous holistic approach acknowledges this and understands that no human being's knowledge is capable of 'objectivity or neutrality'. We are all culturally influenced by the very land we live on and the language we speak.

Indigenous epistemologies portray a circular motion of both time and space in contrast to the linear view of the West. The Indigenous sense of time is not constructed according to Christianity. Also, Indigenous spiritual beliefs inform all human activity. Economic and social systems, as well as political culture all have a spiritual base. The key point here is that spirituality is interwoven with all aspects of human activity and therefore cannot be discussed as a separate category or discipline.

Mohawk scholar Marlene Brant Castellano exemplifies how Indigenous knowledge is a spiritual and intellectual process. Castellano identifies three approaches commonly used for acquiring Indigenous knowledge: spiritual revelations, empirical observation over time, and oral histories and teachings passed down through the generations (Dei, Hall, and Rosenberg 2000: 23). These multiple sources of Indigenous knowledge do not work well within Western social scientific inquiry, which is why an alternative paradigm is needed. Another key insight for understanding the complexity of Indigenous knowledge is related to the geographic location of any given Indigenous group. Indigenous peoples are rooted in and evolve from their landscapes and often those landscapes are integral to their spirituality. For example, the Navajo spiritual beliefs include the sacredness of corn pollen and the sand. Healing rituals include intricate sand paintings of specific Holy Ones (deities). The offering of corn pollen to the Holy Ones for healings, blessing, or guidance is customary. This ritual and belief system is *of* the landscape and of the culture rooted there for millennia. The ability of the Navajo and Hopi to grow corn in the southwest desert is a miracle and is treated as such. So much of the Navajo spiritual tradition emerges from the land that it would be impossible to 'transplant their belief systems' to other geographies. Another key aspect of any Indigenous spiritual tradition is the absence of 'conversion' in the teachings. There is no concept of proselytizing in Indigenous spiritual traditions; you simply are a Navajo, a Haudenosaunne, or Lakota.

The diversity of cultures, rituals, histories, symbolic orders, and 'world views' are not a set of identical experiences that formulate 'an Indigenous Women's Spirituality'. Rather, Indigenous women possess a set of assumptions about social reality that are immersed in spiritual relationships with the natural world. This is a tradition of ideas that when brought together form a coherent whole that is congruent with the Creator's natural law (Alfred 1999: 4; Hill 1992: 63).

The concepts developed by pre-contact Iroquoian society demonstrate the consciousness that existed prior to the arrival of Europeans. They also illustrate how the philosophy of the Peacemaker promoted participatory democracy based upon peace and the rule of women as authority figures (Wright 1993: 223–38; Lyons and Mohawk 1992: 1–13). The Iroquois operated their society on intellectually developed principles. Emile Durkheim missed that point. It is only recently, however, that scholars of the West have examined the First Americans as interdependent societies with autonomous political, social, and economic structures. Even more recent scholarship considers the historical authority and power of Haudenosaunne women.

Indigenous women contend with issues of racism and sexism within the context of colonialism, setting their agenda apart from most 'feminist' literatures. Representation of Indigenous people has been at best biased. Most often they are merely used as ideological vehicles to prove or disprove Western theories (Berkhofer 1979). Indigenous women have been almost non-existent in any literature, or media, until only a short time ago. Stereotypical images of Indigenous women do exist, however, thanks to the thousands of western films and fictional books that have been consumed by millions of North Americans for several generations (Churchill 1994; Green 1998). These genres dehumanized Indigenous women so completely that they rarely spoke or showed emotion. Frequently they were depicted as nearer to animals. Disney's *Pocahontas* portrays her as slithering along rocks like a snake in heat pining for the great John Smith. The 'almost animal' depictions of Indigenous women throughout history set them apart from 'human women'. And even sexism and racism do not quite capture the essence of the problems with the construction of 'Indian women' as North America created her and has come to both dread and fear her. The dehumanization of Indigenous women is compounded by the depiction that she is a beast of burden or slave-like creature to her owner, her husband. Today, Indigenous women are trying not only to overcome the stigma of generations of degrading North American representations in 'family entertainment', but also to heal from it (Green 1998).

The agenda of Indigenous women is to rebuild traditional structures within their communities and re-negotiate positions of authority that were stripped from them through legal frameworks such as the Indian Act. Accordingly, they are not always aligned with feminism that does not take into account colonialism and racism. While North American feminists are working to dismantle 'traditional' patriarchal structures, Indigenous women are trying to rebuild traditional structures based on tribal egalitarism and matriarchal lineages (Green 1998; Monture-Angus 1999; Anderson 2000).

Symbols, Rituals, and Interpretations

The bond among Indigenous women not only rests in their *collective* colonial experience but also is rooted in a spiritually based belief system. The conceptualization of power among Indigenous women differs from Western notions of power. By extension, so too do notions of powerlessness. For example, it would be erroneous for Indigenous people to define *power* in terms of material possessions. To be powerless is to be without the knowledge of *'who you are'*. To be weak is to display disrespect and ignorance (Gunn Allen 1998; Deloria 1997; Lyons and Mohawk 1992).

The variety of ways in which Indigenous women practise their spirituality and healing is not nearly as significant as the teachings within the journey itself. Clearly, the foundation of Indigenous ideology is located within ceremony and ritual expressions. Ideas and beliefs emerge from divine sources and are further reinforced through participation in ritual. The interaction between the physical and spiritual realms includes the bringing together of clans or kinships, and sometimes whole communities; this gathering of people is critical to the collective bonding within the ceremonial circle. The underlying assumptions of relationships to this world and the cosmos, and the consequences for ignoring our responsibilities are the same. A holistic approach to Indigenous thought offers the paradigm of a circle, within the heart of which is the spirituality and natural law provided to the people by the Creator. While each

Nation may approach this differently, it would appear that each holds the same philosophy about natural laws.

The strength of Indigenous 'power' via ceremonies and celebrations is illustrated by the repeated efforts of the colonists to wipe out such practices. The experiential nature of Indigenous spiritual knowledge fosters a rich and total sense of understanding *process*. The subjective, human nature of inquiry is defined by several truths and the individual must be prepared to engage in acquiring knowledge that is spiritual and emotional; the heart works in conjunction with the mind. Our ancestors understood that the physical, spiritual, and metaphysical are realities that coexist within a holistic framework—a framework firmly embedded in spiritual laws, not human-made laws—and their practices exemplified this understanding.

For example, within Iroquoian cosmology, a pregnant Sky Woman developed the earth. She fell to earth and landed on a turtle's back. Dirt was brought up from the ocean floor and placed on the turtle's back for her. Through the Creation story the energy of the universe is explained, the sun being male, and the earth and moon being female; things of water are female, and things of fire are male. The Creation story defines the world in both gender and kinship terms. The Creation story defines the cosmos and the relationships, roles, and responsibilities therein. The same can be said for the Lakota, Cree, and many other Indigenous groups, each holding their unique Creation story, each providing an explanation of the world and their relationships and place in it (Deloria 1992).

Another significant historical event of the Haudenosaunne, or Iroquoian, people is the arrival of the Peacemaker and his message of the Great Law. All five Iroquoian Nations—the Onondaga, Oneida, Seneca, Mohawk, and Cayuga—were embroiled in terrible warfare against one another. A divine spiritual messenger known as the Peacemaker came to the people. He appointed a speaker, known as Hiawatha, to help him establish peace among the Nations. He and Hiawatha helped establish the Great Law of Peace, which consisted of over 100 articles within the constitution known as the Great Law of Peace. He also appointed the first Clanmother, Jikonsahseh, known to have a neutral home in the time of these wars. The Peacemaker appointed Jikonsahseh as female leader and acknowledged the important role women play in decision making. Within the Great Law, women have authority within their clans (social systems). The term *Clanmother* is a socio-political title that values certain characteristics in women, peace being the primary one. The Great Law endows women with the power of appointing their clan Sachem, the male leader. The Clanmother best knew which of the children in her Longhouse has the attributes of kindness, peace, generosity, and other valued characteristics that a male leader should possess. She could (and still can) impeach her appointed Sachem if he displays unbecoming or immoral conduct (Barreiro 1992; Fenton 1998). A testimony given to the Royal Commission on women, from an unnamed source, states:

> The historical relationship and responsibilities of women in Iroquois/Mohawk society are quite significant, particularly within traditional political culture. During the formation of the Five Nations Confederacy, a woman was the first person to accept the Peacemaker's message of peace and unity. The woman was given a name Jikonsahseh, the 'Mother of Nation', by the Peacemaker, who explained that all women would have an important role in this peace. (Government of Canada 1996: 8)

The establishment of the five warring nations as a united Confederacy Council created the oldest continuing democracy in the Western Hemisphere, one after which the constitution of the United States is modelled (Barreiro 1992; Lyons and Mohawk 1992). Critical differences between the US constitution and the Great Law are located in the notion of women having rights to leadership and the recognition of peace as the formulating principle. Secondly, the Great Law incorporates ritual and ceremony wherein men being 'stood up' as Sachems must undergo spiritual healing so that they may have 'good minds and good hearts' (Martin-Hill 1992).

SOCIAL CHANGE

The Literature
Several scholars, including Patricia Monture-Angus, Linda Smith, Kim Anderson, and Paula Gunn Allen, outline the crucial role that colonialism played in displacing Indigenous women from once-esteemed positions. These women also identify cultural constructs as they relate to the identities of Indigenous women and reveal the problems with a Eurocentric knowledge base that has displaced Indigenous women to inferior positions. Indigenous women's ongoing resistance to the dominant hegemony and constructions of them as 'Other' is found both in artistic and literary expressions. Their work is primarily concerned with, and stands as a response to, both legal and social policies implemented through Christian missionizing and colonialism.

Paula Gunn Allen explores 'feminine' theory as a context to examine Indigenous women. She looks at the adoption of Christian values and ideologies through colonization that subordinated the authority of Native women in ways that transformed traditional female cosmologies into male patriarchal epistemologies. The spiritual powers a woman possessed were directly related to her social status and decision-making authority. Colonial policy legislated by the Canadian government is the tool that controls all aspects of Indigenous peoples' lives, including their religious beliefs.

Women suffered enormous losses through the imposition of the Indian Act, including losing the rights over raising their own children. A Lakota Elder, Cecelia Looking Horse, frames this experience as 'the stealing of our bundles of power' (Looking Horse: 1998). The emotional devastation of Indigenous parents watching their children being forcibly carted off to residential schools is still felt in many communities today. Many of the stories are shared in recent literature by Native women, such as *Stolen from Our Embrace* (1997). Another text, *Women of the First Nations: Power, Wisdom, and Strength* (Miller et al. 1996), is a compilation of essays by Native, Métis, and non-Native women contextualizing women in a feminist discourse. Their histories demonstrate the roles and responsibilities they had in food production and distribution of wealth, as well as how colonialism marginalized their power and roles. Through these stories it is obvious that spiritual power was and continues to be connected to their roles as mothers and grandmothers who nurture the continuation of a way of life. Stories of women's spiritual beliefs are also chronicled in texts such as *Walking in the Sacred Manner: Healers, Dreamers, and Pipe Carriers— Medicine Women of the Plains Indians* (St. Pierre and Long Soldier 1995). This latter author provides accounts of her own research and first-person interviews with Elders, healers, and medicine women, and shares the Plains spiritual philosophy of women's roles.

Contemporary accounts of Indigenous women's spirituality are part and parcel of the agenda to rebuild spiritual knowledge as a tool of decolonization. Through the reviving of ancient knowledge, Indigenous women are bringing back the teachings that value their roles in society.

From Theory to Practice

For the Lakota, there is the story of the White Buffalo Calf Woman who brought the Sacred Pipe to the people 19 generations ago. The story, as told by Black Elk in Joseph Epes Brown's *The Sacred Pipe* (1953), elucidates the sacred duties of women. According to the oral history recorded by Brown, two scouts were sent out by their camp to look for buffalo. The scouts saw a beautiful woman coming toward them carrying a bundle. One scout wanted to take her for a wife, but the other warned him that she was a spirit woman. She reduced the ill-minded scout to bones and informed the other to prepare his camp for her arrival. The next day she appeared singing a song that is still sung today. She gave the Pipe to Chief Standing Hollow Horn and explained the Sacred Rites. Upon her departure she said that she would return one day as a White Buffalo. She then walked away, turning into a White Buffalo as she went (Brown 1953: 8–9). The teachings of the story of the Sacred Pipe exemplify the power that women carry and give to the people. The notion of the female as sacred is celebrated by the fact that two of the Lakota's Seven Sacred Rites are for women: *Ishna Ta awi cha lowan* (Preparing a girl for womanhood ceremony) and *Tapa Wanka Yap* (Throwing of the ball ceremony). Both ceremonies celebrate womanhood and the powers of female energy. The story of Tapa Wanka Yap reveals a great deal about Lakota rituals and female energy. Holy man Black Elk tells the story:

> Moves Walking then picked up the painted ball and handed it to the young girl, telling her to stand and to hold it in her left hand and raise her right hand up to the heavens. Moves Walking then began to pray, holding the pipe in his left hand, and holding his right hand up to the heavens.
> 'O Grandfather, Wakan Tanka, Father, Wakan Tanka, behold Rattling Hail Woman, who stands here holding the universe in her hand . . . She sees her generations to come and the tree of life at the center. She sees the sacred path.' (Brown 1953: 133)

The notion of woman as central energy in the universe is both profound and simplistic. It is women who have the ability to give life. The Lakota Star knowledge reiterates the inter-connection between earth and the universe and the life-force energy that women hold. In fact, the Lakota Star knowledge that is embedded in their creation story traces their ancestry from the 'star nation' to the earth. The journey from the Stars was their beginning. Initially the Lakota lived under the earth, located in what is referred to as 'Pa Ha Sapa', the 'heart of everything that is', or what Americans call the Black Hills. A Spider tricked them into following her onto earth, and the Buffalo became the central icon in their identity. A physicist would not have a hard time understanding how human beings are actually of the same organic matter as the stars or the earth—it is something Lakota people have understood since the beginning of time; hence the term *Mitakuye Oyasin*. We are all related.

SEXUALITY

Views of Indigenous women's sexuality are often closely connected to child bearing and child rearing.

Our Sacred Bundles We Carry

> Through all the centuries of war and death and cultural and psychic destruc-tion we have endured, the women who raise the children and tend the fires, who pass along tales and traditions, who weep and bury the dead, and who never forget . . . We survive war and conquest; we survive colonization,

acculturation, assimilation; we survive beatings, rape, starvation, mutilation, sterilization, abandonment, neglect, death of our children, our loved ones, destruction of our land, our homes, our past and our future. We survive, and we do more than survive. We bond, we care, we fight, we teach, we nurse, we bear, we feed, we earn, we laugh, we love, we hang in there, no matter what. (Gunn Allen 1986: 50)

Indigenous Women are tied to their grandmothers, who act as spiritual guides, teachers, mentors, and healers. A grandmother's power is different from a grandfather's, especially when it comes to birthing and welcoming children into this world. Birthing is a spiritual experience, one that is sacred in many traditional Indigenous cultures. Women are spiritually connected to their unborn and often connect with their unborn spirit through dream and vision. The behaviours and actions of both the mother and father influence the child's well-being in many ways. The act of birthing is sacred and traditionally there is careful ritual surrounding the birth, umbilical cord, afterbirth, and veil (a sign that meant the child is an old soul returning and would be a seer or healer). While the Mayan, Navajo, Iroquois, Lakota, and Cree may perform the ritual, interpretations of the various moments of birthing may differ; however, all would agree on the premise of its sacredness and spiritual significance (Sakokwenonkwas 1989; Meili 1991; St. Pierre and Long Soldier 1995). It is from the womb, uterus, and ovaries that women's 'power' flows—it is no wonder that there is such a predisposition in Western medicine to remove, stigmatize, or control these sacred female body parts.

The ability to give life endows a woman with the experience of carrying another human being *inside* her body and knowing two hearts beating as one. The spiritual relationship that a woman shares with her unborn child weaves a powerful connection into her and her children's cosmological tapestry. A symbol for Cree people is the medicine powers of a female bear. She will protect her cubs at all costs and is willing to fight and die for her cubs—just as we, as human beings, want our children to live and will ensure that at all costs. The 'stealing of our bundles' (their babies) would have not only devastated women on an emotional level but also brings into question the strength of their spirituality and their own sense of power. The psychological trauma would have made women more vulnerable to missionaries manipulating them by reminding them of their savage state at every opportunity. Notions of shame, powerlessness, and guilt were introduced and contributed to the fragmenting of Indigenous women's traditional spiritual convictions.

For a woman considered 'two-spirited', or gay, there is no threat to her power if she chooses to not have children. All women have the spiritual connection by virtue of being. In fact, two-spirited people are considered twice gifted; often they have talents, insights, and spiritual powers that one-spirited people do not. Cree Chief Ernest Sundown explains:

> Two spirited people are sacred, we never put them down. They were often powerful. Often they were the best artist, singers or medicine people, it was only with Christianity that it became an issue, or stigmatised. (Sundown 2000)

Historically, two-spirited people would have been fully integrated into the collective fabric of their tribe based on their kinship systems. There was little sense of marginalization based on their sexual orientation. For example, children belong to a kinship system that creates a collective parenting group. Often uncles and aunties shared in the childrearing, and in this sense no one is 'childless'—and therefore 'powerless'. The family kinship structures ensured women and men, whether heterosexual or homosexual, security and acceptance based on social constructions and not sexual. Today, however, the adoption of Christian values and norms by many Indigenous peoples and their views of sexual orientation do not reflect traditionally held views.

OFFICIAL AND UNOFFICIAL ROLES OF WOMEN

Indigenous women play a host of important spiritual roles. Some of these were eroded under colonialism but are now being rediscovered and revalued.

Indigenous Women's Historical Status as Medicine Women, Healers, and Spiritual Guides

The appropriation of culture has had impacts on Indigenous tradition as we currently understand it. And the question of 'tradition' and the role of women has become a significant debate within Indigenous discourse. Brant Castellano refers to testimonials given by Métis women for the Royal Commission on Aboriginal Peoples. She writes:

> In briefs and oral presentations to the royal commission, aboriginal women in particular cautioned against accepting at face value claims to authority asserted on the basis of tradition. Examples:
> 'Tradition' is invoked by most politicians in defense of certain choices. Women must always ask—Whose tradition? Is 'tradition' beyond critique? How often is tradition cited to advance or deny our women's positions? (Dei, Hall, and Rosenberg 1993: 25, 27)

The impact of missionaries, residential schools, the Indian Act, and internalized colonialism upon several generations of women is severe. It has been far-reaching in erosion of social, political, economic, and spiritual systems. The spiritual authority and once-esteemed positions that Indigenous women held in their societies have been severely eroded and undermined through colonialism. However, Indigenous women are involved in addressing ways to repair and rebuild their families' lives and their traditional positions (Alfred 1999; Anderson 2000; Gunn Allen 1986).

In fact, Indigenous women share a host of experiences and processes that Indigenous men do not (Acoose 1995; Green 1998; Gunn Allen 1990; Monture-Angus 1995). The loss of Indigenous women's spirituality through residential schools and other colonial agents has placed Indigenous women in vulnerable circumstances including domestic violence. According to McGillvray and Comaskey's book, *Black Eyes All the Time* (1999), eight out of ten Indigenous women experience intimate violence. The contemporary reality of Indigenous women today is a direct result of assimilation policies that the government developed to civilize the 'savages'. The need for healing from decades of unjust policies and treatment has brought forth a resurgence of traditional healing and spiritual recovery. Dorothy Rosenberg has this to say:

> In traditional matriarchal cultures, healing was associated with the life giving capacities of women. . . . For most of human history holistic healing was practiced largely by women. . . . For many women, knowledge of herbal preparations was as common as knowledge of cooking today. . . .
>
> In addition, Indigenous healing practices maintained by laywomen for thousands of years remain among the most important healing practices in most rural parts of the world. According to WHO [World Health Organization], these practices provide 95 per cent of the world's needs. (Rosenberg 2000: 147)

Through the Eurocentric representation of Indigenous people, Indigenous spirituality, ritual, and ceremony was framed either as mythology and 'quackery' or through the present New Age movement as ultra-mystical and secretive. The truth is far less glamorous than some 'experts' suggest and more in line with Rosenberg's analysis. Again, spirituality is within our actions and interactions as a way of everyday life; this point cannot be overstated. As one Lakota Sundancer and Grandmother pointed out:

> A Sun dance is a powerful ceremony, a sacrifice for the people, unfortunately what people do not understand is life is a Sundance, it's what you do in between these ceremonies that counts as much as the ceremony itself. (Looking Horse 1998)

In *Medicine that Walks,* Maureen Lux (2001) cites numerous examples of historical records and archives documenting the traditional medicinal knowledge that women practised in Plains cultures. She quotes the account, given in the 1890s by Native American documentation enthusiast Walter McClintock, of a Blackfoot ceremony:

> Ekitowaki began to brew herbs from her medicine pouch, and while purifying herself with incense, beseeched the bison spirit to help her find the source of the disease. . . . Her fingers danced over Stuyimi's body until she announced the illness was in his chest . . . she danced in imitation of the bison. (Lux 2001: 76)

Lux discusses the spiritual nature of healing in Plains culture and how one Blackfoot woman, Last Calf, contracted tuberculosis and dreamed of a cure. She was instructed to boil pitch of the lodgepole pine and drink the brew. She was recorded as vomiting profusely until her chest was cleared. Last Calf's remedy was widely used for tubercular cough. Lux also elaborates on the high social standing of Plains midwives and how they performed not only prenatal but postnatal care for months for the woman and her child.

Sarah Carter's article 'First Nations Women in Prairie Canada' (1996) elaborates on the traditional medicinal knowledge of Indigenous people of the plains. Historical documentation by local doctors and writers suggests that medical doctors' use of traditional midwives and healers was common practice. She cites a number of examples of Indigenous women assisting medical doctors with births of Native and non-Native alike, and administering brew for jaundice and other ailments (Carter 1996: 62). Carter cites a passage from the archives dated 1880 that brings to life Indigenous women's historical role in healing:

> The Indian woman took in the situation at a glance. She pushed aside the terrified mother and picked up the ailing child. By signs she indicated hot water from the kettle on the stove. Into it she put a pinch of herbs from the pouch slung around her waist. Soon the gasping subsided, and a sweat broke to cool the fevered skin. She cooled the brew and and forced some of it between the blue lips of the infant. The baby relaxed into a peaceful sleep. Cradled in the arms of the crooning Indian woman . . . That mother to her dying day remained grateful. (Carter 1996: 64)

Sarah Carter also notes that Indigenous women were marginalized both formally and informally through legal, social, and economic intrusion. Neither historians nor anthropologists have specifically addressed colonialism's impact on Indigenous women's role in practising traditional medicine and ceremonial ritual (Smith 1999; Anderson 2000; Gunn Allen 1986; Rosenberg 2000). Elder and healer Rose Auger sums up the current reality that Indigenous women face today:

> Part of this waking up means replacing women to their rightful place in society. It's been less than one hundred years that men lost touch with reality. There's no power or medicine that has all the force unless it's balanced. The women must be there also, but she has been left out! When we still had our culture, we had balance. The women made ceremonies, and she was recognized as being united with the moon, the earth, and all forces on it. Men have taken over. Most feel threatened by holy women. They must stop and remember the loving power of their grandmothers. (Auger in Meili 1991: 25)

Today, a sensitive debate is taking place across the continent about women's roles in ceremonies. There are many Elders, healers, and spiritualists who do not allow women in healing ceremonies, pipe ceremonies, or any other spiritual activity. Indigenous women question when these traditions began to exclude women (Government of Canada 1996). The literature by Indigenous women examines 'modern tradition' in light of how Christian values may have transformed 'tradition' into a patriarchal system that positions Indigenous women as servants and not as the spiritual leaders they once were (Anderson and Lawrence 2003).

BACKLASH

In recent years, some non-Indigenous 'New Agers' have found financial reward in appropriating Indigenous women's spirituality by turning traditional ceremonies and healing practices into businesses targeting non-Indigenous consumers who have the funds to indulge in it.

The New Age Movement and Indigenous Women's Spirituality

Unemployment in many Indigenous communities reaches as high as 95 per cent. One reservation, Pine Ridge of South Dakota, is considered one of the poorest communities in the United States. The poverty experienced by many Indigenous families leaves esteemed Elders and spiritual leaders vulnerable to economic exploitation of their culture and tradition. Today's New Age movement is a multimillion-dollar industry that has displaced and exploited Indigenous spirituality (Battiste and Henderson 2000), but without benefitting the people and cultures from which it is taken. Thus, ironically, the revitalization of spirituality and healing practices and their newly acquired freedom

to be practised 'openly' presents new challenges for Indigenous cultural survival and Indigenous women's spirituality specifically. This appropriation of
spiritual knowledge can be referred to as the Last Frontier (Martin-Hill 1992).

A number of articles discuss the influence of Western culture and the commercialization of ceremonies and rituals that are attached to traditional medicinal practices. Lisa Aldred states, '[F]etishization of Native American spirituality
not only masks the social oppression of real Indian people but also perpetuates
it' (Aldred 2000: 329). Indigenous women are at the bottom of North America's
socio-economic ladder, and now their ability to remain the heirs to their own
spiritual identity and authority is in serious jeopardy. Mohawk author
Christopher Jock elaborates on this point:

> This issue of appropriation and intrusion by academics and the 'New Age'
> enthusiasts is . . . of the deepest concern to Native traditionalists these days
> . . . continuing economic and cultural invasion of Native communities,
> causing erosion of self-sufficiency and the decay of integrity in ceremonial
> work. (Irwin 2001: 73)

While the Indian Act served as a tool to legally control Indigenous people's
lives, academics have served officially to represent Indigenous people's culture
and spiritual practices. Academia's intellectual appropriation of Indigenous
Elders' knowledge has a long history (Deloria 1997). More recently, however,
New Agers have appeared who have the financial resources to promote and
consume Indigenous practices, thus compounding the problem: the lack of
authority Indigenous peoples have over their own culture. This erosion of
Indigenous participation in their own spiritual practices is of grave concern to
Elders and spiritual leaders. Compounding the seriousness of this appropriation is the reality that Indigenous women are displaced in their own spiritual
practices by New Agers and by Indigenous spiritual leaders who need the
financial support the New Agers are providing. Many Indigenous women were
shipped off to mission-run boarding schools, where they were taught that their
traditional ways were evil, and thus they suffered 'spiritual trauma'. These
women are the ones most in need of spiritual healing, and yet they are alienated from the very ceremonies that might provide that healing. As one Elder
confided to me, 'I shook the first time I saw the pipe, every fibre of me believed
it was evil, I had been told this from the time I can remember. I cried, there
stood those White people smoking the very pipe I could not behold'
(Gathering, Ottawa 1995).

While conducting research on Indigenous knowledge, I travelled through
North America from 1992 to 1996, interviewing Elders. I was made painfully
aware at Indigenous gatherings, healing circles, ceremonies, and Sundances

that many of the participants were White people, mainly women, many of whom owned pipes and bundles and who were at podiums speaking, praying, and conducting ceremonies. They often funded the Indigenous events, and were quickly beginning to displace Indigenous women from their own culture, gatherings, and sacred spaces (Hill in Anderson and Lawrence 2003).

Re-victimization
Cynthia Kasee substantiates the imperialism of the ruling colonial population's exploiting Native spirituality. She denounces the ongoing marginalization of Indigenous women in Native American religious beliefs due to the appropriation by the dominant culture (Kasee 1995).

As discussed, Indigenous women have been affected adversely by colonial policies resulting in overrepresentation of Indigenous women in recent statistical data on social issues such as domestic violence, imprisonment, suicide, and general poor health (Government of Canada 1996). Indigenous women need now, more than ever, to heal the wounds inflicted by residential schools, forced removal of their children, and loss of land and culture. However, Kasee points out that Indigenous women are re-victimized when their lack of knowledge of tradition and marginal social status prevents them from gaining access to their own traditional healing and ceremonies. The traditional spiritual leaders and healers are caught between needing to provide for their families by 'selling' their healing to non-Indigenous seekers, and continuing traditional ceremonial work, which often prevents them from participating in the labour force. The consequence of the traditional practitioners' need for money and the New Ager's ability to pay, leads us to a new wave of imperialist activity—the mining of Indigenous knowledge and spirituality—within which context Indigenous women are simply re-marginalized. The result: they enjoy privileges in neither culture. Colonialism severely eroded the spiritual integrity Indigenous women once enjoyed, and now the New Age movement threatens to further displace them. The current struggle to re-establish Indigenous women's spirituality is tied to both past colonial policies and women's present marginalization within their own culture.

SUMMARY

Historically Indigenous women were constructed as powerful. Traditional Indigenous religions viewed the world as gender-based with women having key roles within the dynamics of the universe. All things were female and male; the goal within the cosmological constructions of the universe was balance. Women's power flowed from her spiritual knowledge, which gave women authority to make decisions regarding the good of the people. While colonialism has had a negative impact on Indigenous women, they have resisted oppression and continue to use spirituality as a major source of strength, courage, and wisdom. For in spite of all the obstacles and challenges, Indigenous women are in fact rebuilding and revitalizing their spirituality. The current movement by many women, as seen through their writing and work, is to reclaim their traditional knowledge and restore the dignity and integrity stripped away by residential schools, missionaries, and the Indian Act. The current spirituality of many Indigenous women is concerned with healing: healing trauma, healing families, healing communities, and the return to sacred sites to heal through the land. It is this spirituality that forms an integral part of the intellectual and political pursuits of Indigenous women who want to achieve a higher quality of well-being for themselves and their children. This is the spirit of our ancestors' knowledge. The reconstruction of traditional roles and responsibilities that were once endowed with authority, wellness, and respect is the path to true intellectual and emotional recovery, liberation, self-determination, and decolonization. The overwhelming theme that emerges from the oral stories and the literature reviewed is that the strengthening of Indigenous women will strengthen the Nation.

Going Home
by Ulali
I'm going home, goin' home
North Carolina is crying in my soul
Creator I'm reaching out to you
Tell them on the other side
That they are alive within my soul
Return their prayers that run through my veins
Return the land and heal her pain
The hidden truth
Tell the world
The blues where it comes from
I'm going home, goin' home
North Carolina is crying in my soul
Well the Noose River runs through the land
Where my great grandmother sleeps,
under the earth the Tuscarora nation was freed
I hear Nigerian chains
That say they are buried real deep
Tobacco fields
Trail of tears,
Stolen people on stolen land

I'm going home, goin' home
North Carolina is crying in my soul
Creator I'm reaching out to you
Tell them on the other side
That they are alive within my soul
Return their prayers that run through my veins
Return the land and heal her pain
The hidden truth
Tell the world
The blues where it comes from
I'm going home, goin' home
North Carolina is crying in my soul
Creator I am reaching out to you
Tell them I know

(Ulali, *Mahk Jchi*: 1994)

REFERENCES

Acoose, Janice/Misko-Kisikawihkwe (Red Sky Woman). 1995. *ISKWEWAK—Kah' Ki Yaw Ni Wahkomakanak: Neither Indian Princesses nor Easy Squaws*. Toronto: Women's Press.

Ahenakew, Freda, and H.C. Wolfart, eds. 1992. *Our Grandmother's Lives as Told in Their Own Words*. Saskatoon: Fifth House Publishers.

Aldred, Lisa. 2000. 'Plastic Shamans and Astroturf Sun Dances: New Age Commercialization of Native American Spirituality'. *American Indian Quarterly* 24: 329–52.

Alfred, Taiaike. 1999. *Peace, Power, Righteousness—An Indigenous Manifesto*. Toronto: Oxford University Press.

Anderson, Kim. 2000. *A Recognition of Being: Reconstructing Native Womanhood*. Toronto: Second Story Press.

Anderson, Kim, and Bonita Lawrence. 2003. *Strong Women Stories: Native Vision and Community Survival*. Toronto: Sumach Press.

Armstrong, Jeanette. 1992. 'The Disempowerment of First North American Peoples and Empowerment Through Their Writing'. *An Anthology of Canadian Native Literature in English*. Eds Daniel David Moses and Terry Goldie. Toronto: Oxford University Press.

Barreiro, Jose, ed. 1992. *Indian Roots of American Democracy*. Ithaca: Akwe:kon Press.

Battiste, Marie and James (Sa'ke'j) Youngblood Henderson. 2000. *Protecting Indigenous Knowledge and Heritage: A Global Challenge*. Saskatoon: Purich.

Berger, Thomas R. 1991. *A Long and Terrible Shadow: White Values, Native Rights in the Americas 1492–1992*. Toronto: Douglas & McIntyre.

Berkhofer, Robert. 1979. *The White Man's Indian*. New York: Vintage Books.

Braveheart, Maria. 1998. 'The Return to the Sacred Path: Healing the Historical Trauma Response Among the Lakota'. *Smith College Studies in Social Work* 68 (3): 287–305.

Briggs, Jean, ed. 2000. *Interviewing Inuit Elders: Volume 3 Childrearing Practices*. Iqaluit, Nunavut: Language and Culture Program of Nunavut Arctic College.

Brown, Joseph. 1953. *The Sacred Pipe, Black Elk's Account of the Seven Sacred Rites of the Oglala Sioux*. Ed. Joseph Epes Brown. Norman: University of Oklahoma Press.

Carter, Sarah. 1996. 'First Nations Women in Prairie Canada'. *Women of the First Nations: Power, Wisdom, and Strength*. Eds Miller et al. Winnipeg: The University of Manitoba Press.

Churchill, Ward. 1994. *Indians Are Us? Culture and Genocide in Native North America*. Toronto: Between the Lines.

Dei, George J. Sefa, Budd L. Hall, and Dorothy Goldin Rosenberg. 2000. *Indigenous Knowledges in Global Contexts: Multiple Readings of Our World*. Toronto: University of Toronto Press.

Deloria, Vine. 1992. *God Is Red: A Native View of Religion*. Golden, Colorado: Fulcrum Publishing.

Dickason, Olive Patricia. 1992. *Canada's First Nations: A History of Founding Peoples from Earliest Times*. Toronto: McClelland & Stewart.

Durkheim, Emile. 1933. *The Division of Labour in Society*. New York: The Free Press.

Dyck, Noel. 1986. 'Negotiating the Indian "Problem"'. *Culture* 6: 31–41.

Fenton, William N., ed. 1984. *Iroquois Indians: A Documentary History of the Diplomacy of the Six Nations and their League*. Woodbridge, CT: D'arcy McNickle Center.

———. 1998. *The Great Law and the Longhouse*. Norman: University of Oklahoma Press.

Frideres, James S. 1993. *Native Peoples in Canada: Contemporary Conflicts*. 4th edn. Scarborough: Prentice Hall Canada.

———. 1997. *Native Peoples in Canada: Contemporary Conflicts*. 5th edn. Scarborough: Prentice Hall Canada.

Fouillard, Camille, ed. 1995. *The Davis Inlet People's Inquiry: Gathering Voices Finding Strength to Help Our Children*. Vancouver/Toronto: Douglas & McIntyre.

Fournier, Suzanne and Crey, Ernie. 1997. *Stolen From Our Embrace: The Abduction of First Nations Children and the Restoration of Aboriginal Communites*. Vancover/Toronto: Douglas & McIntyre.

Government of Canada. 1996. *Report of The Royal Commission on Aboriginal Peoples: Volume Four: Perspectives and Realities*. Ottawa: Canada Communication Group Publishing.

The Grassroots Women's Collective, eds. 1999. *Voicing Our Stories / Remaking our Lives: Women Speak Out*. Toronto: Second Story Press.

Green, Rayna. 1998. 'The Pocahontas Perplex: The Image of Indian Women in American Culture'. *Native American Voices: A Reader*. Eds Susan Lobo and Steven Talbot. New York: Longman.

Gunn Allen, Paula. 1986. *The Sacred Hoop*. Boston: Beacon Press.

———, ed. 1990. *Spider Woman's Granddaughters: Traditional Tales and Contemporary Writing by Native American Women*. New York: Ballantine Books.

———. 1998. *Off the Reservation: Reflections on Boundary-Busting, Border-Crossing, Loose Canons*. Boston: Beacon Press.

Harcourt, Wendy. 1994. *Negotiating Positions in the Sustainable Development Debate: Situating the Feminist Perspective*. London: Zed Books.

———, ed. 1994. *Feminist Perspectives on Sustainable Development*. London: Zed Books.

Hull, Jeremy. 2000. *Aboriginal Single Mothers in Canada, 1996: An Invisible Minority*. Winnipeg: Prologica Research Inc.

Irwin, Lee. 2000. *Native American Spirituality: A Critical Reader*. Lincoln: University of Nebraska Press.

Jaimes, Annette. 1993. *Turtle Quarterly*. Johnson R. Native American Centre for The Living Arts.

Jaimes, M. Annette, ed. 1992. *The State of Native America: Genocide, Colonization and Resistance*. Boston: South End Press.

Jamieson, Kathleen. 1987. *Indian Women and The Law in Canada: Citizens Minus*. The Advisory Council on the Status of Women: Indian Rights for Indian Women. Ottawa: Minister of Supply and Services Canada.

Kasee, Cynthia. 1995. 'Identity, Recovery, and Religious Imperialism: Native American Women and the New Age'. *Women's Spirituality, Women's Lives*. Eds Judith Ochshorn and Ellen Cole. New York: Haworth Press: 83–93.

Kehoe, Alice Beck. 1981. *North American Indians: A Comprehensive Account*. New Jersey: Prentice Hall.

Kingsley, Cherry, and Melanie Mark. 2000. *Sacred Lives: Canadian Aboriginal Children and Youth Speak Out about Sexual Exploitation*. Ottawa: Save the Children.

Kirby, Sandra and Kate McKenna. 1989. *Experience Research Social Change, Methods from the Margins*. Toronto: Garamond Press.

Lux, Maureen K. 2001. *Medicine that Walks: Disease, Medicine, and Canadian Plains Native People, 1880–1940*. Toronto: University of Toronto Press.

Lyon, S. William. 1996. *Encyclopedia of Native American Healing*. New York: W.W. Norton & Company.

Lyons, Oren, and John Mohawk. 1992. *Exiled in the Land of the Free, Democracy, Indian Nations, and the U.S. Constitution*. Santa Fe: Clear Light Publishers.

Martin, Joel. 2001. *The Land Looks After Us: A History of Native American Religion*. Oxford and New York: Oxford University Press.

Martin-Hill, Dawn. 1992. *As Snow before the Summer Sun*. Brantford, ON: Woodland Cultural Centre.

———. 1995. *Lubicon Lake Nation: Spirit of Resistance*. Ph.D. Thesis. Hamilton: McMaster University.

———. 1998. *Cecelia Looking Horse*. Notes: South Dakota.

———. 2000. *Indigenous Knowledge and Power and the Lubicon Lake Nation*. Hamilton: McMaster University.

McGillivray, Anne, and Brenda Comaskey. 1999. *Black Eyes All of the Time: Intimate Violence, Aboriginal Women, and the Justice System*. Toronto: University of Toronto Press.

Meili, Dianne. 1991. *Those Who Know: Profiles of Alberta's Elders*. Edmonton: NeWest Press.

Miller, Christine, and Patricia Chuchryk, eds, with Marie Smallface Marule, Brenda Manyfingers, and Cheryl Deering. 1996. *Women of the First Nations: Power, Wisdom, and Strength*. Winnipeg: The University of Manitoba Press.

Monture-Angus, Patricia. 1995. *Thunder in My Soul: A Mohawk Woman Speaks*. Halifax: Fernwood Publishing.

———. 1999. *Journeying Forward: Dreaming First Nations Independence*. Halifax: Fernwood Publishing.

Nene, Sibongile. 1993. *Development Policies and Women*. Johannesburg: Institute for African Alternatives.

Quinlan, Don, ed. 1999. *Aboriginal Peoples: Building for the Future*. Toronto: Oxford University Press.

Rosenberg, Dorothy Goldin. 2000. 'Toward Indigenous Wholeness: Feminist Praxis in Transformative Learning on Health and the Environment'. *Indigenous Knowledges in Global Contexts: Multiple Readings of Our World*. Eds George J. Sefa Dei, Budd L. Hall, and Dorothy Goldin Rosenberg. Toronto: University of Toronto Press: 23, 25, 27.

Ross. A.C. 1989. *Mitakuye Oyasin 'We Are All Related'*. Denver: Bear.

Saskokwenonkwas. 1989. 'Pregnancies and Mohawk Tradition'. *Canadian Women Studies* vol. 10, no. 2 & 3. Inanna Pub. & Education Inc.: 13.

Shiva, Vandana. 1997. *Bioethics: A Third World Issue*. New Delhi: Research Institute for Science, Technology and Ecology.

Smith Tuhiwai, Linda. 1999. *Decolonizing Methodologies. Research and Indigenous Peoples*. New York: Zed Books.

St Pierre, Mark, and Tilda Long Soldier. 1995. *Walking in the Sacred Manner: Healers, Dreamers, and Pipe Carriers—Medicine Women of the Plains Indians*. New York: Touchstone.

Steckley, John, and Bryan Cummins. 2001. *Full Circle. Canada's First Nations*. Toronto: Prentice Hall.

Sundown, Ernest. 2000. Field notes (taken by Dawn Martin-Hill). Joseph Bighead Reserve, Saskatchewan.

Thomas, Jake. 1994. *Teachings of the Longhouse*. Toronto: Stoddart Publishing Co., Limited.

Van Kirk, Sylvia. 1980. *Many Tender Ties: Women in Fur-Trade Society, 1670–1870*. Norman: University of Oklahoma Press.

Ulali. 1994. *Mahk Jchi*. CD. Prod. Sheldon Steiger. USA.

FURTHER READING

Anderson, Kim, and Bonita Lawrence. *Strong Women Stories; Native Vision and Community Survival*. Toronto: Sumach Press, 2003.

Carter, Sarah. 'First Nations Women in Prairie Canada'. *Women of the First Nations: Power, Wisdom, and Strength*. Eds Miller et al. Winnipeg: The University of Manitoba Press, 1996.

Fournier, Suzanne, and Ernie Crey. *Stolen from Our Embrace: The Abduction of First Nations Children and the Restoration of Aboriginal Communities*. Vancouver/Toronto: Douglas & McIntyre, 1997.

Gunn Allen, Paula, ed. *Spider Woman's Granddaughters: Traditional Tales and Contemporary Writing by Native American Women.* New York: Ballantine Books, 1990.

Irwin, Lee. *Native American Spirituality: A Critical Reader.* Lincoln: University of Nebraska Press, 2000.

CHAPTER 6

WOMEN IN CHRISTIANITY

Pamela Dickey Young

INTRODUCTION AND OVERVIEW

Christianity is a religious tradition that arose around Jesus, whom early followers began to call 'the Christ', which means the Messiah, the one sent and
anointed by God. Jesus was born around 4 BCE. He was Jewish, as were most
of his early followers, those he seems to have attracted through his charisma.
After Jesus' death, the followers continued to recount stories about him and his
effect on them, and they tried to convert others to follow Jesus as well. The
existing sources about him and his life are mostly from the Christian New
Testament, which means that they are texts composed by followers who testify
to his effect on them rather than recount historical facts. The gospels are not
eyewitness accounts and they are not history books. Traditions about Jesus circulated orally and in snippets of writing before they were finally compiled in
their current forms as the gospels of Matthew, Mark, Luke, and John. Each
gospel has its own particular emphasis.

The New Testament is a collection of books, including the four gospels,
which appeared in written form between about 50 to 100 CE. Much of the rest
of the New Testament consists of letters from early converts to Christianity,
especially Paul, who wrote to various churches. The Christian churches also
count the Hebrew Bible (which they rename the Old Testament) as sacred
scripture.

Jesus' followers were men and women who gave up virtually everything,
including their families to go with him. The stories about Jesus are many,
several of which tell us about the interaction between Jesus and women.
Remarkably enough, given the patriarchal times in which the stories were told
and written down, none portrays Jesus as re-inscribing the view that women
are lesser beings than men.

Christianity was, from early on, a missionary religion, seeking not only
to win formerly Jewish followers, but also to extend itself throughout the

known world. Over the centuries, Christianity has taken a wide variety of historical and cultural forms, and some of these forms are the results of major splits within the church. In the first five centuries of Christianity much effort was expended to define orthodoxy or right belief. Many of the traditional Christian ideas or doctrines date from this era.

In 1054 the first major split in Christianity occurred when the churches in the East (now called 'Orthodox' churches) separated from the churches of the West (the Roman Catholic Church), mostly over disagreements about the Holy Spirit. Then, in the sixteenth century, another major division took place in the churches of the West when a number of 'reformers' such as Martin Luther and John Calvin tried to reform what they saw as the excesses of the church. Both Luther and Calvin found themselves excommunicated as a result. Since the beginnings of this Protestant Reformation there have been many different splits resulting in the formation of many different Christian denominations too numerous to detail here.

One of the main differences between Roman Catholicism and Protestantism is the official locus of authority. For Roman Catholicism, authority is, finally, vested in the Pope and the Bishops. For Protestantism, the supreme locus of authority is usually seen to be scripture. Governance is generally carried out by the people, but the degree to which this is the case is tempered by the type of Protestantism.

Christianity is not monolithic. There is never one single 'Christian' way to believe or act. Christianity takes a wide variety of social, historical, geographic, and cultural forms. Thus, when feminists study 'Christianity' it is always helpful to remember that they are studying particular forms of Christianity, not a single unified and univocal religious tradition. All conclusions about, for example, whether Christianity is liberating to or oppressive for women, have to recognize the particular context in which that judgement is situated.

To urge caution here does not, for a minute, suggest one overlook the fact that much in the history of Christianity has been oppressive to women. Historically within Christian thought, when the topic of women arose, it was mostly men talking about women: about women's nature and purpose, about whether or not women were in the image of God, about whether women could be saved, about what sorts of leadership roles women could and could not play.

Thus, for example, Tertullian, a second-century 'father' of the church, called women 'the Devil's gateway' (Tertullian 1869: 1.1.2). Augustine, a famous and influential fourth- and fifth-century thinker, believed that males alone were the full image of God and that women could only be in the image of God when joined to males as helpers (Ruether 1974: 156). For Augustine, women were equated with the body and men with the mind. This made women sexually dangerous to men. According to Augustine, women are more carnal than men and therefore more subject to temptation and to sin. Women, however, can only overcome such temptation and be rational instead of carnal if they renounce sexuality completely.

> That woman has a rational mind equivalent to man's is never entirely denied, and indeed is assumed by the view that allows her to lead the monastic life. But since she is somehow made peculiarly the symbol of 'body' in relation to the male (i.e., in a male visual perspective), and is associated with all the sensual and depraved characteristics of mind through this peculiar 'corpo-reality' her salvation must be seen not as an affirmation of her nature but a negation of her nature, both physically and mentally and a transformation into a possibility beyond her natural capacities. (Ruether 1974: 161)

For Augustine, before sin entered the world through the fall (that is, before Eve ate the forbidden fruit and gave it to Adam), sexuality was dispassionate, for procreative purposes only. After sin, sinful carnality overcame rationality in the form of human sexual arousal. For Augustine, the male erection becomes the 'essence of sin [and] woman, as its source, became peculiarly the cause, object and extension of it' (Ruether 1974: 163). Thus, sin is transmitted throughout the human race by the sexual act, and woman as both original and continuing sexual temptress is primarily to blame.

TEXTS, INTERPRETATIONS, AND RITUALS

The central texts of the Christian tradition are those of the Bible. The biblical texts include the texts of the Jewish Bible (usually referred to as the Old Testament by Christians) and the New Testament texts. The New Testament was written over a period from about 50 CE to the early second century by a variety of different authors who, as far as we know, were all male. Oral traditions preceded the writing down of the gospel texts. It took several centuries before the Christian church decided more-or-less definitively on which texts were to be seen as authoritative. (This is known as the process of canonization.) There were other texts that could have been included in the New Testament canon but which were not, such as the gospel of Thomas or the various Gnostic gospels.

The biblical texts are human documents, written for particular purposes in specific times and places. The New Testament texts themselves are already interpretations of the event and importance of Jesus and testimonies to the growth of a community of followers around him. Thus, texts are already interpretations, and, subsequent to their being written, the biblical texts have histories of interpretation that can give a particular focus to the way they are read today. For example, the common reading of Eve in Christian tradition as the temptress and the source of all sin in the world is only one possible reading of the text of Genesis 3, read back through the eyes of Augustine's interpretation of original sin. The text itself mentions disobedience, but the notion that there is an inherited sinfulness for which Eve is primarily responsible is a Christian reading of the text that comes much later. The biblical texts, even when they mention women (sometimes named women, often unnamed women), present women or any particular woman in the male, patriarchal perspective. This is simply to say that women in the biblical texts are seen through men's eyes. The texts about Jesus are somewhat removed already from Jesus and show him as interpreted by those who told the stories and eventually wrote down the texts. Not all the texts view women in the same way.

Even though there is dispute among feminists about how to interpret New Testament texts, if one reads the texts with the question of women and their status and roles in mind, some insights are notable. For example, the interactions between Jesus and women are in all cases presented as remarkably open. Women listen to Jesus; they also teach Jesus (Mark 7:24–30; John 4:1–39). And they are commissioned to preach (John 20:17–18). The purity laws that affected women's qualifications for public action do not seem to have mattered to Jesus (Mark 5:25–34). Although no women are named in the list of the 12 central disciples, the actual listing of these names varies somewhat and the list is more dependent on the importance of the number '12' (after the 12 tribes of Israel) than on the specific names. But many people, including women, followed Jesus from place to place (Matthew 27:55–6), and this is one of the central understandings of what it means to be a disciple.

There are indications that women occupied many leadership roles in the early Christian community. Women are called 'deacon' and 'apostle' (Romans 16:1, 7). Women preach. They have churches in their houses, or are in other ways patrons of the new Christian community.

The early Christian movement was what is usually called a 'charismatic' movement, which means that it did not have set structures or rules for organization. In the early Christian movement the roles of women and men seem in large part interchangeable. The earliest Christians tended to think that the end of history was at hand and that the second coming of Jesus Christ would take place in their own lifetimes. As time went on and this did not happen, more formal structures were put in place that tended to exclude women (for example, I Timothy 3:2–13). Many of the passages most problematic for women are from this later period of New Testament composition (I and II Timothy and Titus, which, according to most scholars, are not written by Paul). In letters thought by most scholars to be by Paul, there are still some problematic passages where women are enjoined to silence in churches and seen in relation to the husband who is 'head' (see I Corinthians 11:2–16; Ephesians

5:22–33). There is no question that Paul was a person of his time who had a patriarchal understanding of the place of women. This is occasionally balanced by places where he seems to see the message of Jesus as abolishing traditional hierarchical distinctions (Galatians 3:27–9).

Christians have used the biblical texts in a variety of ways throughout history. Since the eighteenth century, biblical scholars have understood the texts to be historical texts written for particular purposes in particular times and places. Biblical scholarship does not regard the texts as given directly by God.

In the late nineteenth century, a group of female scholars led by Elizabeth Cady Stanton published a book entitled *The Woman's Bible,* in which they sought to comment on the texts that were of particular interest and importance to women. They commented, for instance, on the creation stories and on the stories of Sarah and Abraham. They commented when women were visible as actors and when they were treated as second-class citizens. They commented on women's leadership in Romans 16 and on the passages of the New Testament where women seemed to be subordinated (Stanton et al., 1974).

When, in the mid-twentieth century, feminists began interpreting the biblical texts, they did so using a variety of strategies and with a several purposes in mind. 'In the footsteps of Cady Stanton, women's biblical studies have developed a dualistic hermeneutical, or interpretive, strategy that is able to acknowledge two seemingly contradictory facts. On the one hand, the Bible is written in androcentric language, has its origin in the patriarchal cultures of antiquity, and has functioned throughout its history to inculcate androcentric and patriarchal values. On the other hand, the Bible has also served to inspire and authorize women and other nonpersons in their struggles against patriarchal oppression' (Fiorenza 1993a: 5). Thus, those who seek to be feminists within the Christian tradition generally do not deny the patriarchal nature of the biblical texts and contexts, but, for the most part, they see the texts as potentially valuable beyond their patriarchal context and content.

One feminist approach to reading biblical texts argues that the texts need to be read in light of their historical, patriarchal contexts. When we interpret these texts we must be willing to give them the most charitable interpretations possible. This approach tends to be taken by feminists in more conservative denominations, where the biblical texts are seen as divinely inspired.

A second approach argues that one can look to the texts for a liberating message or some support for a liberating movement, or some other liberatory features, but one cannot assume that such a message can always be found, nor that it exists everywhere in the biblical texts. Some texts according to this approach may not be redeemable. Such an approach looks perhaps to the example of Jesus, or to stories such as that of the Exodus, the liberation of the people of Israel from Egypt.

A third approach tends to read the biblical texts without regarding them as authoritative for the Christian tradition. The Bible here is not a set of normative texts, but 'a cacophony of interested historical voices and a field of rhetorical struggles in which questions of truth and meaning are being negotiated' (Fiorenza 1993a: 8). Because the whole process of canonization itself inscribed certain values and visions, the texts and the final canon must themselves be questioned.

Elisabeth Schüssler Fiorenza argues for a 'hermeneutics of suspicion' that approaches the biblical texts searching for patriarchy and looking for who benefits and who is injured. She also argues for a 'hermeneutics of re-vision' that looks at texts broadly for 'values and visions that can nurture those who live in subjection and authorize their struggles for liberation and transformation' (Fiorenza 1993a: 10).

After the earliest period of Christianity, when it seems that both men and women were ritual actors in roles that were defined as needs arose, it has been mostly men who have acted in official capacities in ritual. In most churches only the ordained can function as celebrants of the sacraments and as preachers, and since most of those ordained have been male, little has changed until recently, when more women have begun to be ordained in various Protestant denominations. Thus, for most of the church's history, sacraments and preaching have been mainly a male preserve. When women have been ritual actors, it has mostly been in small groups of women who met for prayer or teaching on their own, but rarely has there been official sanction.

SYMBOLS AND GENDER

A symbol is a picture, word, thing, act, or concept that bears particular meanings for a particular group. Christianity employs a variety of symbols to convey its tradition and message. One central symbol for Christianity is the word and concept 'God'. Another is the concept of Jesus as Christ or saviour, which captures meaning and importance beyond simply seeing Jesus as a historical person who lived in a particular place and time. Mary, the mother of Jesus, is also a symbol as well as a character in the biblical texts. Actions such as the performing of the Christian sacraments of baptism and eucharist are symbolic actions. The cross too is a typically Christian symbol.

This section focuses on two of the central symbols of Christian tradition: God, and Jesus as the Christ or saviour.

Although some scholars would argue that all religious symbols are projections of human needs and desires rather than symbols that point to a transcendent reality, adherents of the Christian tradition usually agree that *God* points to some reality beyond the mere word. No single view of God is held by all

Christians. That said, it is also generally agreed that whatever God is, God does not have biological sex of the sort that human beings have. Yet most Christian language for God has been male language and male pronouns, and thus it evokes stereotypical male images.

Feminists have long raised questions about what it means to use primarily or solely male language and imagery for God. Religious symbols function both as symbols *of* reality as well as symbols *for* reality. That is, they claim to portray reality as it is as well as to act as prototypes for how reality ought to be (see Geertz 1966; Christ 1979: 274–5). Thus, presenting the symbol of God only in male language and images might give the impression that the 'reality' of God is that God is male. In turn, the apparent maleness of God might also reinforce a social system that connects maleness to godliness. Mary Daly argues that 'if God is male, then the male is God' (Daly 1973: 19). What she means is that male language for God associates God more closely with males than with females. It gives the impression that maleness is more like godliness than femaleness, hence males have the right to exercise godlike power.

If language about God were simply a matter of convenience and convention for most Christians, there would be no problem in changing the language about God to a language that uses female images or pronouns instead of or alongside male ones. Many Christians have found the idea of 'God-she' problematic, which then raises for feminists questions about how language for God has an impact on our views of the status of women vis-à-vis men. Thus, some scholars, like Daly, have argued that the Christian God is so inherently male that no change of language can or will alter the Christian tradition about God.

There are, in fact, some biblical images for God that portray God in female terms. For example, God is portrayed as a midwife (Isaiah 66:9; Psalm 22:9–10); as a woman giving birth (Isaiah 4:14; Deuteronomy 32:18); and as a mother hen (Matthew 23:27) (see Mollenkott 1985). Most feminist Christians have argued that one needs to augment male language for God with female language for God, and that neither is superior to the other. This argument also often goes hand in hand with recognition that, because Christians speak of a personal relationship with God, language about God needs, at least in part, to be personal. Thus, depersonalizing all language about God is not an option for most Christian feminists. Further, depersonalizing all language about God might well mean that the assumptions about the appropriateness of male language about God will never be directly or fully challenged.

Elizabeth Johnson, for example, has developed a wide-ranging rethinking of the Christian God in terms of the biblical image of 'Sophia' (wisdom). In the biblical tradition (both Hebrew Bible and New Testament), Sophia is one possible name for or aspect of God who is always personified as female. Johnson suggests that one can rename the Christian Trinity as Mother-Sophia,

Jesus-Sophia, Spirit-Sophia, where female language can rightly be used for all three traditional persons of the Christian Trinity (Johnson 1992). Feminist Christians also caution against using only 'mothering' language as a way to provide female images of God because that may simply re-inscribe rather than challenge stereotypical views of parenting (Ruether 1983: 69–70).

Jesus, a historically male figure, is central to the Christian tradition as the one who is claimed as Christ or Messiah, Saviour, Lord, and so on. Christian feminists examine what it means to have a male figure at the centre of a tradition. They ask: Can a male saviour save women? (Ruether 1983: 116). Is Jesus' maleness essential to his role as saviour? Here the question of the overlap between Jesus' historical maleness and his symbolic function of salvation come to the fore.

As there is no single Christian view of God, so there is no single Christian view of Jesus and how he 'saves' humans. Early on, Christians came to the agreement that salvation was offered to women as well as to men (Ruether 1998). Thus, women were welcomed as members of the Christian church. That said, however, the maleness of Jesus has had serious implications for women. For one thing, the maleness of Jesus reinforces and extends the notion of the maleness of God. If, as Christians claim, Jesus is the incarnation of God, and if Jesus is male, then maleness is even more like godliness than it is in a tradition such as Judaism where male language is the chief problem.

Also under discussion is the idea that God 'chose' a male human being in which to become incarnate rather than a female human being. Thus, God's choice of maleness must indicate something of the importance of maleness, or the normativity of maleness instead of femaleness.

There is a long history in Christianity of debating what exactly incarnation—that is, God's coming in human flesh—means. Although many Christians read the idea of incarnation as a straight equation that somehow Jesus is the same as God, there is a whole history of nuanced discussion on this matter that looks at exactly what incarnation could reasonably mean. The maleness of Jesus is also used in Roman Catholicism as one of the justifications for an all-male priesthood (Paul VI 1977). When a priest celebrates the mass he is said to represent Jesus to the people. Jesus was male, therefore priests must be male, for only maleness can represent Jesus.

Thus, the maleness of Jesus has been used in ways that subordinate women. And any feminist response must take these long-standing problems seriously.

SEXUALITY

Christianity has historically been far more ambivalent about sexuality than has Judaism. There is no evidence that Jesus was married, although that would have been unusual for a Jewish man of his time. The earliest Christians thought that the second coming of Christ would occur during their lifetimes. Also, one became a Christian by conversion, not by being born into a Christian family. Thus, the value placed on procreation was less than in Judaism.

Christianity arose under the influence of both Jewish apocalypticism and classical Neoplatonism (Ruether 1979). Around the time of Jesus, Judaism developed an apocalyptic pattern of thinking that looked less and less toward God's fulfillment of human hopes within history and more and more to an otherworldly fulfillment after a cataclysmic destruction of the present world. In Neoplatonism, the intellect/soul longs to be separated from the body, which drags it down from its true spiritual home with God. The upshot of such influences was a Christian tradition that associated maleness with mind and soul as superior, and femaleness with body as inferior. Although it had other strands recognizing the goodness of creation, Christian tradition tended to be fearful of the body and all its appetites. Rosemary Ruether sees these 'dualisms' (as she calls them) to be at the root of traditional Christian attitudes both toward women and toward sexuality.

Virginity came to be seen as the preferred Christian calling, although it was clear that this was not everyone's calling. Today we tend to read the notion of virginity as a choice for women that devalues sexuality, especially in light of the interpretations of fourth- and fifth-century Christian men such as Augustine, Ambrose, or Jerome. However, there is also a countercultural possibility of reading women's early choices of virginity as renouncing the authority of a man over them (Malone 2002: 146–9). A woman who chose virginity and a life of holiness could, if she was a hermit, avoid the control of men entirely. Or, if she lived in a monastic community of women under the official authority of bishops or priests, she could live in such a way that her day-to-day life was not determined by men.

Still, by the fourth century, sexuality, especially women's sexuality, had become an object of fear and revulsion at the hands of 'fathers' of the church who clearly felt their own sexuality out of control but blamed women. Augustine, for instance, thought that lust was a result of the sin of Adam and Eve. He believed that through the weakness of human will, rooted in lust, the original sin of Adam and Eve was passed on to each new generation. Augustine's works give us insight into the fact that he himself was troubled that he could not control his own sexual urges. Scholars know that, before his conversion to Christianity, he had a concubine and a son. But after his conversion he renounced sexuality and, insofar as possible, the company of women. The Virgin Mary, who was understood to have had no lust, became the model of Christian living. She was the asexual woman whose body was simply a vessel for the birth of Jesus and who remained ever a virgin.

Thus, even though celibacy was not absolutely required of male clergy until the Middle Ages, the life of virginity was officially established as the preferable life by about the fifth century. Consequently, although all women were viewed as temptresses because women were more associated with the body and men with the spirit, those women who chose virginity were seen, at least to a certain extent, to be more like men. In the face of the lauding of virginity and the equation of women with unruly sexuality, Christian churches have found it difficult to retrieve a notion of the goodness of sexuality.

In the Protestant Reformation (sixteenth century), Luther was an exponent of the positive value of marriage. But historic Christian views of marriage considered women the property of their husbands, so it was not until recently, when a view of marriage as a relationship between equals emerged, that a central emphasis began to be placed on the quality of a marriage relationship. The result has been a revaluation of the goodness of marriage, and with it, sexuality.

In more contemporary times, different churches hold very different official views of sexuality. From the 1950s onward, many North American Protestant churches began to laud birth control for married couples as a means to prevent unwanted pregnancy and thus eliminate undue strain on marriages. As the women's movement in North America developed, churches began to recognize the importance of allowing women to control their lives. One way of accomplishing this was ensuring that they had access to birth control.

In the 1970s and 1980s churches had to struggle with premarital sex. The focus of most Protestant writing on sexuality changed from one on marriage to one on the quality of human relationships. In most Protestant churches in North America today, official opinions on sexuality are based less on traditional 'rules' about sexuality than they are on discussions of the human relationship that should underlie and support sexual activity.

Worries about sexuality in most Protestant churches in North America have changed to concentration on gay and lesbian sexuality. At the time of writing, there is a spectrum of official opinions concerning gay and lesbian sexuality in North American Protestantism. The Metropolitan Community Church was founded to welcome and minister with gay men and lesbians. Churches such as the United Church of Canada and the United Church of Christ have extended their views on sexuality as relationship to include gay and lesbian sexuality and have stopped speaking of heterosexuality as normative. Presbyterians, Anglicans, and United Methodists have positions that separate the person from the sexual activity, arguing that it is no sin to be gay or lesbian, but that 'acting on' gay or lesbian sexuality is sinful.

In this progression we can see that, in North American Protestantism, discussions about sexuality have been coincident with those in the broader culture of which these churches are a part. Roman Catholicism is a different matter. Whereas it appeared to many in the 1960s that the Roman Catholic Church was going to embrace artificial means of birth control, all inclination to do so changed with Paul VI's encyclical *Humanae Vitae* in 1968, which directly forbade any means of birth control except the rhythm method. Although *Humanae Vitae* names unitivity (for the couple) as one of the goods (virtues) of marriage, procreation is still seen as the primary good of marriage and goal of sexual relationship. Sexual activity, in Roman Catholicism, does not have a place outside marriage. Divorce is still prohibited insofar as divorced Catholics may not remarry within the Roman Catholic Church. Gay and lesbian sexuality is reduced to sexual activity and identified as sinful. Thus, a rules-based approach to sexuality is still in place in official Roman Catholicism.

Lesbian sexuality has never been as central to Churches' worries as has the sexuality of gay men. In the Hebrew Bible no mention is made of women being sexual with women. In the New Testament, the only mention of what might be seen as same-sex activity between women is in Romans 1:26 in the context of a discussion of those who worship idols instead of the true God: 'For this reason God gave them up to degrading passions. Their women exchanged natural intercourse for unnatural, and in the same way also the men, giving up natural intercourse with women, were consumed with passion for one another. Men committed shameless acts with men and received their own persons the due penalty for their error'.

Historically, most churches have extrapolated from what they see as scriptural condemnations of male same-sex activity to female same-sex activity. Such positions usually rely on a relatively literalist interpretation of texts such as Leviticus 18:22; Leviticus 20:13; Romans 1:26–27; I Corinthians 6:9ff.; and I Timothy I: 8:10. Churches that are opposed to same-sex activity often try to differentiate between the activity, which they see as sinful, and persons who might have a homosexual orientation but not act on it—that is, they say they condemn the sin, not the person.

Churches that are reinterpreting gay and lesbian sexuality in a positive light (as are, for example, the Metropolitan Community Church, the United Church of Canada, and the United Church of Christ [in the US]) first of all do not treat the texts (which are, in any event, very few in number) as rules to be followed. They argue that there are biblical principles (for example, that Jesus teaches us to love one another as God loves us) that are more central to understanding Christianity than establishing certain texts (whose principle of selection is not always immediately obvious) as rules. Secondly, they note that there are disputes about what sorts of activity are actually in question in these texts. Is it all same-sex activity, or only certain sorts of such activity (some, for example, have suggested that relationships of older persons with younger persons is what is at issue in the Romans texts). Third, they argue (with Foucault) that 'homosexuality' as a category is a relatively recent invention, as is the notion that one has a sexual orientation. Most inclusive churches also argue that sexual orientation is a given and thus that gay men and lesbians cannot be, and ought not to be, expected to change. At the same time, they ought not be told that any sexual relationship is out of the question. So, most such churches embrace gay and lesbian sexuality under the heading of sexuality in general and talk about the importance of the quality of the relationship between two people (same sex or opposite sex) as central to determining what is morally acceptable.

Even the inclusive views of homosexuality held by some churches depend in large part on views that sexual orientation is a given (even a given-by-God) and that it cannot be changed. Thus, churches have not yet even begun to deal with the view that sexuality is socially constructed, whether it be male–female or gay–lesbian.

SOCIAL CHANGE

Many people today view organized religion as a force that strengthens rather than challenges the status quo. Thus, it is often assumed that Christianity cannot be a means to improve the status of women. The following are two examples of ways in which Christianity has been part of a social change for the better in the roles of women.

In the late-twelfth century in Europe there arose a movement of women who were pious and dedicated to good works but who did not want the restrictive life of the cloister. These women, called beguines, sometimes lived in houses with other such women and lived solitary lives. They did not follow any particular accepted religious rule and were not directly subject to a bishop or male abbot, although sometimes they made alliances with local Franciscan or Dominican male orders. Beguine houses often included women of mixed class origins, unlike cloistered women who were often upper-class and who could not work outside the cloister and thus had to support themselves by bringing dowries with them.

Beguines earned their livings in a variety of ways, including teaching, preaching, nursing, and engaging in commerce, as well as sometimes begging. Because these women lived lives of poverty and did not demand as much as their counterparts in the market in return for their labour, their entry into commerce and manufacture, such as weaving, spinning, and so on, often ran these women afoul of men in the labour market.

As one might imagine, the question of whose authority should be exercised over these women was an important one. The Second Council of Lyons in 1274 declared that any religious orders founded without papal approval must be dissolved. In a 1298 Papal Bull, Boniface VIII decreed that all religious women had to live cloistered lives. There followed countless edicts by bishops and councils designed to wipe out uncontrolled women such as these. Often beguines were persecuted and killed. Some were among the targets of the witch craze.

Some beguines left writings, or had 'lives' written of them, among them Mary of Oignes (1177/78–1213), Marguerite Porete (d. 1310), Hadewijch, and Mechthild of Magdeberg (1210?–1294?). In her book *The Flowing Light of the Godhead*, Mechthild of Magdeberg criticized the corruption of the church and the clergy of her day, and, as a consequence, she had to flee from Magdeberg to a convent at Helfta. Marguerite Porete's book *The Mirror of Simple Souls* was read throughout the late Middle Ages despite her condemnation for heresy. In the book she argues that the institutional Church itself is not the final word on what is holy or loving (Porete 1993: 122). Marguerite refused to obey an ecclesiastical order not to distribute her book; she also refused to answer to the Inquisition. She was burned as a heretic in 1310. These women often endured persecution and death as the price of the freedoms they sought. They also provide excellent examples of those who challenged the status quo and attained a certain degree of social change for women in their time.

Nellie McClung (1873–1951) was a first-wave feminist and an activist for social reform and women's rights in Canada. She was an advocate for women's suffrage and served as a Liberal Member of Parliament in the Alberta Legislative Assembly from 1921 to 1926. She was one of the 'Famous Five' women who in 1929 argued to the Canadian government that women, like men, were 'persons'. She was a member of the Women's International League for Peace and Freedom, and Canadian delegate to the League of Nations in 1930. She was a Methodist and an advocate for the ordination of women. She was a temperance worker. She believed that women and men were equal and needed to be treated equally by state and church alike. 'Man long ago decided that woman's sphere was anything he did not wish to do himself, and as he did not particularly care for the straight and narrow way, he felt free to recommend it to women in general' (McClung 1972: 70). She was a prolific writer who published books, novels, stories, speeches, and newspaper columns.

What is most important to note for purposes here is that the main motivation in all her activities was her understanding of the Christian message (Warne 1993: 186). Although she was certainly aware that churches were not living up to her understanding of the essential Christian message, she took her inspiration from that message. 'Christ was a true democrat. He made no discrimination between men and women . . . . He applied to men and women the same rule of conduct' (McClung 1972: 68). She thought that Christianity had a particular obligation to be concerned about those who were oppressed in society, and she advocated that Christian women had a specific responsibility for the conditions of society: 'When Christian women ask to vote, it is in the hope that they may be able with their ballots to protect the weak and innocent, and make the world a safer place for the young feet' (McClung 1972: 77).

McClung advocated theological ideas that have only recently been 'rediscovered'. For instance, she was an advocate of using female as well as male imagery for God. 'I believe the Protestant religion has lost much when it lost the idea of the motherhood of God' (McClung 1972: 79).

McClung uses the biblical story of Martha and Mary (Luke 10:38–42) to argue that women are called to 'thinking', not just to serving. 'The question of whether or not women should think was settled long ago. We must think because we were given something to think with, ages ago, at the time of our creation. If God had not intended us to think, he would not have given us our intelligence. It would be a shabby trick, too, to give women brains to think, with no hope for results, for thinking is just aggravation if nothing comes out of it' (McClung 1972: 32).

McClung was a liberal feminist and a product of her times, but she does give us insight into the fact that Christian beliefs can be the source and sustainer of social reform, particularly reform for women.

OFFICIAL AND UNOFFICIAL ROLES OF WOMEN

As mentioned above, women took on leadership roles in the biblical Christian communities. As time went on, those roles that were associated with power and liturgical leadership came officially to be given to men. But that does not mean that women did not have an important place in the Church.

In the Priscilla Catacombs in Rome there is a fresco dated at least to the early third century, but probably earlier. In this fresco we see seven women at a table where bread and wine and fish are visible. The woman on the far left of the table has her hands raised in a gesture of eucharistic celebration. Here is pictorial evidence that women were in liturgical leadership. Although some have tried to argue that these figures are men, the body shapes, hairstyles, jewellery, lack of beards, and length of skirts indicate females (see Houts 1999 and Irwin 1980).

Women were among those persecuted by the Roman Empire in the second and third centuries and revered by the Church for their martyrdom. By the end of the fourth century Christianity had become the official religion of the Roman Empire, and persecution of Christians had ceased.

From the second century onward, women gave themselves to lives of chastity and asceticism. They were given titles such as deaconess, widow, and virgin. *The Apostolic Constitutions*, a fourth-century document, contains a service for the ordination of a deaconess. Deaconesses seem to have been entrusted with the pastoral care of married women as well as with ministering to the poor and the infirm. But by the fifth century the role of deaconess seems virtually to have disappeared in the Western churches, and bishops were revising history, arguing that there had never been deaconesses at all (Malone 2000: 126–8).

Sometimes in these first few centuries of Christianity women lived ascetic lives in the desert alongside men who did the same, since the desert was seen as a place to escape the temptations of the flesh. Sometimes ascetic women lived in cities where this life was an option mostly for well-to-do, educated females. Some of these women became founders of communities of women. Although the ascetic movement in Christianity does tend to denigrate the body and sexuality, it also provided women a spiritual equality with men and a certain amount of freedom from the direct control of men.

Women also began to cluster together in Christian communities. Marcella was the leader of a group of Christian women in fourth-century Rome. 'Under her guidance, the women learned to pray, to dispose of their possessions wisely, to live in utter simplicity, and to learn the art of governing their own lives' (Malone 2000: 139). Such were among the benefits that the calling to Christian communities offered women and, over the next centuries, women flocked to such communities, which quickly became formalized as religious orders. Women in such orders, although they were ultimately responsible to bishops and dependent on male priests for the sacraments, developed a fair amount of independence in their communal lives. The religious life for women was an alternative avenue to marriage and the male dominance that came with it. In addition, religious life often offered the possibility of education to women, and it has remained such an alternative for Roman Catholic women ever since.

There also developed a tradition (in about the seventh century) of double monasteries (one of men, one of women) headed by an abbess. One such famous abbess is Hilda (d. 680 CE) of the monastery in Whitby, England. Hilda was a scholar and developed an enormous library at Whitby that became an important gathering place for theologians and a teaching centre.

The Protestant Reformation (sixteenth century), which disavowed the calling of celibacy and tried to reclaim the positive value of sexuality within marriage, eliminated the calling to the religious life for women, eliminating an option that allowed women to live outside of direct male control. In the Reformation churches until the late nineteenth century, one of the main leadership callings of an active Protestant woman was as a minister's wife. Protestant women in general were expected to live out the Christian callings of wife and mother.

In nineteenth- and twentieth-century North America, women's roles in churches changed, sometimes propelling, sometimes following societal changes. In Methodism, founded by John Wesley in the late-eighteenth century, there was an emphasis on the gifts of the Holy Sprit, and consequently women who felt a calling to pray and testify to their conversions as well as to preach began to do so.

In the nineteenth century, Protestant women's groups began to do various kinds of charity work at home and abroad. This work was aimed at education, social reform, taking care of the poor, and mission. A whole class of women church workers known as 'deaconesses' materialized. These deaconesses worked primarily for the underprivileged in cities, in the fields of social work and evangelism, but they were not considered to be members of the ordained clergy. This changed in the mid-nineteenth century with the movement for women's ordination. The first woman ordained in modern times was Antoinette Brown, in 1853 in the Congregationalist Church in East Butler, New York. In Congregationalism, early ordinations were possible because local churches were able to make individual decisions about who could and could not be ordained. Some groups of Methodists also ordained a few women in the late-nineteenth century. The first woman to be ordained in the United Church of Canada was Lydia Gruchy, in 1936.

It was not until the 1960s and 1970s that most mainline Protestant churches in the United States and Canada either began to ordain women or to accord them equal status to ordained men. It was not until the 1980s and 1990s that the numbers of women in Protestant theological schools became equal to and then exceeded the numbers of men.

The Roman Catholic Church does not ordain women. The argument against the ordination of women, stated in detail by Pope Paul VI in 1976 and reaffirmed in recent years by Pope John Paul II, makes three main points. First, tradition, assumed to have been dictated by God, has always affirmed that men only be priests. Second, Jesus had an open attitude toward women and could have chosen women to be part of the 12 disciples but he did not. This decision applies to all times and places. Third, when the priest celebrates the mass he is called to represent Jesus Christ to the people. This representation requires a 'natural resemblance' between the priest and Jesus Christ, and this natural resemblance must be the resemblance of maleness.

Many people, including many Roman Catholics, have refuted all three arguments. Briefly, these arguments take the following forms. First, the church has changed in a variety of ways over time. Why not in this way, too? Second, the lists of the 12 disciples or apostles are not uniform in the biblical sources (compare Mark 3:14–19 and Acts 1:12–13). Further, many other people, including women, followed Jesus from place to place. Twelve is a significant number because of the 12 tribes of Israel, but there is no indication that these 12 individuals alone are important in Jesus' life and ministry. As well, one cannot simply make an equation between the choosing of followers and ordination. Jesus does not seem to have been cognizant of founding an institution that would remain in existence in perpetuity. How can one move so quickly from a charismatic movement to a notion that this movement determines the structures of the institutional church for all time? Third, why is it the 'natural resemblance' of maleness that is all-important? Jesus was Jewish; he probably had brown eyes; he probably had dark skin. Why is genitalia more important than these characteristics in establishing 'natural resemblance'?

These refutations of the official arguments against the ordination of women, however, are not likely to sway the current Pope or his bishops. A different decision on the matter of the ordination of women will have to wait for another Pope who is more open to change within the Church. The fact that fewer and fewer men are choosing the calling of celibate priesthood, especially in North America and Northern Europe, will probably eventually have an impact on this matter as well as on others.

BACKLASH

As defined by Letty Russell, backlash is 'a powerful counterassault on the rights of women of all colors, men of color, gay, lesbian and bisexual persons, working-class persons, poor persons and other less powerful groups both in the US and abroad' (Russell 1996: 477). In other words, backlash is a strategy for the traditionally powerful and privileged to retain power and privilege against arguments for full inclusion of others in the church and in society. Backlash is the enemy of diversity and of those who are marginalized. In North America, backlash against women is often supported by Christians who, theologically or politically, are opposed to changes in the status and roles of women and to theologies that support such changes.

One common form that backlash takes is to blame societal woes on the breakdown of 'traditional' families. The idea is that before women worked outside the home, before so much divorce, before single parenting was considered socially acceptable, before there was so much recognition of gay and lesbian relationships, families were more stable, children were better raised, and everyone knew his or her place in the social structure. One problem with this argument is that it is not historically supportable. In fact, 'Backlash rewrites history' (Hunt 1996: 50). The whole notion of separate private spheres for women away from the public, and especially away from economic production, is largely a product of the Industrial Revolution when families ceased to be the economic unit and men became wage earners. Further, this separation of spheres only worked for upper-class women. Poor women, especially poor 'women of colour', have always had to work outside the 'private sphere'. When private and public are separate spheres, women become the guardians of the private, including the guardians of family piety (Rudy 1997: 26).

Supporting this ideology of the family through Christian argumentation also has its serious limitations. The New Testament does not teach or uphold anything like the modern notion of family. People lived in extended kinship groupings. Jesus called people to leave their families and follow him. And Paul thought that singleness was a better state than marriage.

Yet the idealized non-historical view of family has had a powerful impact on Church and politics, precisely because it allows those who have traditionally held power and privilege to retain it. In the United States, the Christian right has been strongly allied with the Republican Party, and successive Republican presidents and candidates since Ronald Reagan have enlisted Christian preachers and 'biblical' arguments to bolster their appeal. In Canada, where the population as a whole is less susceptible to arguments of religious authority, only the Alliance Party makes any overt use of the 'Christian values' argument. Even the Alliance Party position on this matter is subdued given that there is Alliance support beyond those who are Christian and that Canadians expect their politicians at least to pay lip service to cultural diversity.

Often when religious institutions seek to put forward or defend positions that are against advances in the status and roles of women, they use female spokespersons to assure listeners that there are women who do not want gains such as ordination; access to safe, legal abortions; more social funding for women raising children alone; and so on. This strategy is supposed to make one think that only 'radicals' or those 'far to the left' want such changes. It is a strategy devised to pit women against each other. It is also deceptive in that it shifts the focus from the question of whether something is merely for the marginalized to the question of whether 'all women' want it.

Positions that would restrict women's roles in Church and society are often bolstered by a sprinkling of particular biblical passages and theological interpretations sometimes called 'fundamentalist'. Fundamentalism, however, is hard to define. The notion of fundamentalism grows out of the American Christian context of the early twentieth century, when a series of pamphlets called The Fundamentals was published. But more recently fundamentalism has been used to describe particular movements within many world religions, which, among other things, are opposed to Enlightenment values of critical and rational inquiry and depend on a highly structured and authoritarian view of the particular religious tradition. All the major leadership roles in Christian fundamentalisms are taken by males with a central charismatic male leader (Lawrence 1989; Marty and Appleby 1991–5).

Christian fundamentalists take a view that the Bible is the literal and inerrant Word of God. Statements on women from I Corinthians, Ephesians,

Timothy, and Titus are often used to substantiate such views. One hallmark of such use is that the passages are not read in the historical contexts discussed above, but read as if they were literal words of God that one could simply take from the first century and apply in the twentieth century. What is deceptive here, though, is that not all biblical passages are used equally. In fact, as noted above, the views of women and family that inform the selection and interpretation of particular passages are themselves relatively recent and from a particular historical and cultural point of view. Conservative Christians, whether or not they would call themselves fundamentalists, usually hold the view that male language for God is the language that God 'himself' wants used.

UNIQUE CHARACTERISTICS

Some symbols, movements, and themes are unique to Christianity, or take specifically Christian forms. In the following pages a few of these are explored.

Mary
Mary the mother of Jesus has been an ambiguous figure for Christian feminists. She is one of the few biblical women whose name is known and about whom we have more than just a few words of text. She has not figured as prominently for Protestants as the early Protestant Reformers thought that veneration of Mary was too easily confused with worship of her. The traditional image of her as fostered by the church, especially the Roman Catholic Church, has been one of the obedient woman who was chosen precisely because she was demure and passive and who acted as the vessel for God's plan. Mary, the obedient one, is often contrasted to Eve, the disobedient one. Women are instructed to model their lives on this passive, obedient Mary who served her son and his interests. The Roman Catholic doctrines of the Immaculate Conception of Mary (Mary herself was conceived without sin), of Mary's perpetual virginity, and of her bodily Assumption into heaven were set in place to protect Jesus' sinlessness and his intimate relationship to God. But they also serve to create an idealized woman: the unattainable virgin-mother. Thus, Mary, unlike all other women, is the woman untainted by sexuality.

Yet Mary has not been confined to such a role in the church. In the devotion of Catholic women worldwide, Mary has also been a strong and powerful figure who has supported them in standing up for their rights. Often such views of Mary quote the Magnificat (Luke 1:46–55), where Mary says that God has 'brought down the powerful from their thrones, and lifted up the lowly'; and has 'filled the hungry with good things and sent the rich away empty'. Mary is the one who understands their plights even when God and Jesus seem far away. Not only that, but because the line between devotion to Mary and worship of Mary does get blurred, Mary at times seems very much like God, only nearer and more accessible. And so we do have a female figure who functions goddess-like in the devotion of many Roman Catholic women (see Daly 1973: 90–2).

Women as Missionaries
In the nineteenth century women became heavily involved in the missionary enterprises of extending the Church, both Catholic and Protestant, to all parts of the world. At first, Protestant women were involved in organizing funding and support for the missionary effort without themselves becoming missionaries. Throughout the nineteenth century, however, Women's Missionary organizations grew in both the US and Canada. Such missionary organizations were among the first organized women's activities in the Church. They focused on educating their own members and raising money for the missionary efforts. Initially many women spent their lives doing 'good works' in the 'mission field' as missionaries' wives. Finally churches realized that male missionaries were not always allowed contact with the women of the peoples among whom they were supposed to work, and so, by the mid-nineteenth century, Protestant churches began to send single women as missionaries. Indeed, many single women who were professionally trained, such as the early female doctors, often found that they were more accepted in the mission field than back at home (MacHaffie 1986: 93–106; Grant 1972: 57–8).

Roman Catholic nuns also entered into mission work in the nineteenth century. Pope Pius XI ordered that all congregations of nuns should have missionary communities to convert non-Westerners to Christianity, and some new religious orders were founded specifically as missionary orders (McNamara 1996).

Development of Feminist Theologies
As the women's movement developed in North America in the 1960s and 1970s, women within the churches began to articulate feminist critiques of both the institutional churches and the patriarchal theologies that supported them. Further, they began to propose new ways of thinking about theology (see Young 1995).

In 1960, Valerie Saiving wrote what is usually considered the first article in contemporary feminist theology, 'The Human Situation: A Feminine View', where she raises the question of experience that becomes central to feminist theology. She opines that women do not experience the world in the same way men do and thus that traditional theological definitions of sin and salvation do not apply to women in the same way they apply to men (Saiving 1979). In

1968, Mary Daly wrote *The Church and the Second Sex,* raising questions about the status and roles of women in the history of the Church. And from these roots, and other books and articles like them that began to appear, a whole set of questions emerged. There were questions about the biblical texts and interpretations. There were historical questions. Where were the women in the Bible and in church history? Could their stories be recovered? What is the importance of noticing that the biblical texts and the history of the Church are told from a male/patriarchal point of view? And there were theological questions. Why is God always portrayed as male? Why are women seen to be primarily responsible for sin?

Feminists who wanted to stay within the church began to write biblical commentaries, histories, and theologies that took women's experiences within the church seriously and that took with utmost seriousness the full humanity of women. Thus, feminist theology quickly moved beyond critique to the construction of new ways of thinking about history and theology. Feminist theologies arose from both Roman Catholic and Protestant women who did not accept that the patriarchal institutional church was the only or best interpreter of Christianity. Although some feminist theologians like Mary Daly (1973, 1975) and Daphne Hampson (1990, 1996) have left the Christian Church behind as irretrievably patriarchal, many other feminist theologians have decided that within Christianity there are liberating strands that can be woven together into a non-patriarchal whole (Young 1990).

The work of feminist historian and theologian Rosemary Radford Ruether has spanned more than three decades. It was she who brought attention to the construction of Christianity in hierarchical dualisms such as mind/soul over body and humans over nature (Ruether 1975). She wrote one of the first books of constructive theology where, going beyond criticism of the patriarchal theologies, she formulated a theology from a feminist starting point (Ruether 1983). Letty Russell, whose work was parallel to Ruether's, developed ideas of partnership to overcome hierarchical thinking (Russell 1974, 1979, 1993).

Today feminist theologies are many, varied, and diverse, arising from new contexts to speak to new experiences.

Christian feminism has a variety of global and cultural forms. Early Christian feminist theologies were rightly criticized for speaking from basically one stance, that of white, educated, heterosexual, and relatively privileged women, yet using the term *woman* as a generic. Women of colour, women from geographic locations outside North America and Europe, and lesbian women began to raise questions about the assumptions of these early theologies that all women's experiences were alike. They raised new questions. They explored new outlooks. Lesbian women began questioning the construction of sexuality as focused on heterosexual pairs (Heyward 1989). Within North America there are womanist theologies (from an African-American perspective), and *mujerista* theologies (from a Hispanic perspective). There are also *mujerista* theologies from Central and South America, African feminist theologies, and Asian feminist theologies (Russell et al. 1988; Fabella and Oduyoye 1988; Fabella and Park 1989; Chung 1990; Aquino 1993; Oduyoye 1995; Isasi-Díaz 1996). Each of these theologies tries to take its own cultural context and its own particular version of patriarchy into consideration. For example, Maria Pilar Aquino, writing of Latin America, specifically addresses issues within the Roman Catholic Church, the dominant church in Latin America. Issues of colonialism and capitalism affect women in Latin America. She also examines the cultural specificity of *machismo*.

> *Machismo* does not derive or have its origin in capitalism, although it converges and combines with it in mutual reinforcement. But it can also combine with socialist structures in which unequal relationships persist between men and women, if there is insufficient criticism of women's double workload, the sexual division of labor, and inequalities between the sexes in general. (Aquino 1993: 23)

Aquino suggests many contributions that a specifically feminist Latin American theology can make to theological understanding. One such contribution is to portray God as a God of life:

> The starting point for this new experience of faith is the general context of suffering and oppression of the Latin American masses. In the light of faith this situation is *unnatural*, and God is not indifferent to it. On the contrary, realizing that this immense suffering is against God's plan for fullness of life for humanity has led to the discovery of God in the suffering faces of the oppressed. . . . This encounter with God in the faces of the poor, of women, and all the oppressed has given faith a new meaning. . . . [P]recisely because life is preeminent to women, they feel called by God—like the biblical prophets—to denounce every threat to it. (Aquino 1993: 132–3)

Chung Hyun Kyung is a Korean feminist theologian who has sought to integrate traditional Korean women's shamanistic practices and beliefs and other expressions of women's popular religion in Asia into her feminist Christianity. Indeed, when she invoked the spirits of her ancestors in the context of a speech to the World Council of Churches in 1991, she was denounced by many of the more conservative church persons present as a syncretist (one who indiscriminately combines or collapses two or more religions into one) (see Chung 1988 and 1990).

We Asian women theologians must move away from our imposed fear of losing Christian identity, in the opinion of the mainline theological circles, and instead risk that we might be transformed by the religious wisdom of our own people. We may find that to the extent that we are willing to lose our old identity, we will be transformed into truly *Asian* Christians. . . . Who *owns* Christianity? (Chung 1990: 113)

Chung notes that because most shamans in Korea have been women, Korean women relate best to Jesus in the image of a woman. To make her point, she quotes from the poem 'One Day I Shall Be Like a Banyan Tree', by Indian theologian Gabriele Dietrich:

> I am a woman
> and the blood
> of my sacrifices
> cries out to the sky
> which you call heaven.
> I am sick of you priests
> who have never bled
> and yet say:
> This is my body
> given up for you
> and my blood
> shed for you
> drink it.
> Whose blood
> has been shed
> for life
> since eternity?

(Quoted in Chung 1990: 69 from
Gabriele Dietrich [1985])

Christian Feminist Anti-Semitism

One of the temptations of Christian feminist theology is to portray Christianity as superior to Judaism on the matter of the status of women. When Christian women began express concern about the patriarchy endemic to the Christian tradition they often began with Jesus' teachings and acts as recorded in the New Testament. Often, a contrast was too quickly drawn between 'Christianity' and its non-patriarchal roots and 'Judaism' as patriarchal. This characterization fails to recognize that Jesus was himself a Jew and that what became Christianity was in its beginnings a movement within Judaism. It also fails to take seriously the official Judaism of Jesus' time and place (centred on the temple and ritual practices by a priestly caste), which was no more a monolithic representation of all Judaism than the Christianity of any particular time and place is of all Christianity. In Jesus' time there was reaction against this official Judaism from a number of Jewish quarters (see Ruether 1998: 14–15). The aims of Christian feminism cannot be met if the route to 'rescuing' Christianity for women means denigrating another religious tradition. Christian feminists can draw on Jesus' acts and teachings without having to find them superior to all other religious movements of the period (see Fiorenza 1994: 67–73).

CONCLUSION

There is no singular way to talk about women in the history of Christianity. Women's roles have been varied and variable. Patriarchy has been a given and women have worked around that to discern roles. For many women, Christianity has offered more than its patriarchal forms would seem to suggest. There is also no singular way to talk about the prospects of reforming Christianity in a non-patriarchal manner. Like all other cultural forms, Christianity is closely related to the values of the cultures in which it finds itself. Sometimes forms of Christianity lag behind those values, sometimes they forge ahead, sometimes they simply keep pace.

The question of whether one can be Christian and feminist at the same time does not allow for an easy answer. One response is that there are lots of women in a variety of social and geographical contexts who name themselves this way. They see liberating potential within some forms of Christianity even as they recognize the patriarchy. They see the possibility of reform.

It will be crucial to examine how Christianity modifies as scholarship begins to take seriously the critiques of feminist theory on issues that once seemed simple and straightforward, such as whether 'women' is a category defined only or fully by biology or whether one might, regardless of one's biology, perform (or refuse to perform) the gender role 'women'. It is clear that ongoing feminist reflections will continue to be important and necessary to the academic study of Christianity.

REFERENCES

Aquino, Maria Pilar. 1993. *Our Cry for Life: Feminist Theology From Latin America*. Maryknoll, NY: Orbis.

Christ, Carol P. 1979. 'Why Women Need the Goddess: Phenomenological, Psychological and Political Reflections'. *Womanspirit Rising*. Eds Carol P. Christ and Judith Plaskow. San Francisco: Harper & Row: 273–87.

Chung, Hyun Kyung. 1988. 'Following Naked Dancing and Long Dreaming'. *Inheriting Our Mothers' Gardens: Feminist Theology in Third World Perspective.* Eds Letty Russell et al. Philadelphia: Westminster Press: 54–74.

———. 1990. *Struggle to be the Sun Again: Introducing Asian Women's Theology.* Maryknoll, NY: Orbis.

Daly, Mary. 1973. *Beyond God the Father: Toward a Philosophy of Women's Liberation.* Boston: Beacon.

———. 1975. *The Church and the Second Sex, with a New Feminist Postchristian Introduction by the Author.* New York: Harper Colophon.

Fabella, Virginia, and Mercy Amba Oduyoye, eds. 1988. *With Passion and Compassion: Third World Women Doing Theology: Reflections from the Women's Commission of the Ecumenical Association of Third World Theologians.* Maryknoll, NY: Orbis.

———, and Sun Ai Lee Park, eds. 1989. *We Dare to Dream: Doing Theology as Asian Women.* Hong Kong: Asian Women's Resource Centre for Culture and Theology.

Fiorenza, Elisabeth Schüssler, ed. 1973. *Searching the Scriptures: A Feminist Introduction.* vol. 1. New York: Crossroad.

———. 1993. 'Transforming the Legacy of *The Woman's Bible*'. *Searching the Scriptures: A Feminist Introduction.* vol. 1. Ed. Elisabeth Schüssler Fiorenza. New York: Crossroad: 1–24.

———. 1994. *Jesus Miriam's Child, Sophia's Prophet: Critical Issues in Feminist Christology.* New York: Continuum.

———, and M. Shawn Copeland, eds. 1996. *Feminist Theology in Different Context.* London: SCM.

Gebara, Ivone. 1999. *Longing for Running Water: Ecofeminism and Liberation.* Minneapolis: Fortress.

Geertz, Clifford. 1966. 'Religion as a Cultural System'. *Anthropological Approaches to the Study of Religion.* Ed. Michael Banton. London: Routledge: 1–42.

Grant, John Webster. 1972. *The Church in the Canadian Era: The First Century of Confederation.* Vol. 3 of a History of the Church in Canada. Toronto: McGraw-Hill Ryerson.

Hampson, Daphne. 1990. *Theology and Feminism.* Oxford: Basil Blackwell.

———. 1996. *After Christianity.* London: SCM.

Heyward, Carter. 1989. *Touching Our Strength: The Erotic as Power and the Love of God.* San Francisco: Harper & Row.

Houts, Margot G. 1999. 'The Visual Evidence of Women in Early Christian Leadership'. *Perspectives* 14: 7–11.

Hunt, Mary. 1996. '"Reimagining' Backlash'. *Feminist Theology in Different Context.* Eds Elisabeth Schüssler Fiorenza and M. Shawn Copeland. London: SCM: 45–52.

Irwin, Dorothy. 1980. 'The Ministry of Women in the Early Church: The Archaeological Evidence'. *The Duke Divinity School Review* 45: 76–86.

Isasi-Díaz, Ada María. 1996. *Mujerista Theology.* Maryknoll, NY: Orbis.

Johnson, Elizabeth. 1992. *She Who Is: The Mystery of God in Feminist Theological Discourse.* New York: Crossroad.

Lawrence, Bruce. 1989. *Defenders of God: The Fundamentalist Revolt Against the Modern Age*. San Francisco: Harper and Row.

MacHaffie, Barbara J. 1986. *Her Story: Women in Christian Tradition*. Philadelphia: Fortress.

Malone, Mary. 2000. *Women and Christianity, Volume 1: The First Thousand Years*. Ottawa: Novalis.

Marty, Martin, and Scott Appleby, eds. 1991–5.*The Fundamentalism Project*. 5 vols. Chicago: University of Chicago Press.

McClung, Nellie L. 1972. *In Times Like These*. Toronto: University of Toronto Press.

McNamara, Jo Ann Kay. 1996. *Sisters in Arms: Catholic Nuns through Two Millennia*. Cambridge, MA: Harvard University Press.

Mollenkott, Virginia Ramey. 1985. *The Divine Feminine: The Biblical Imagery of God as Female*. New York: Crossroad.

Oduyoye, Mercy Amba. 1995. *Daughters of Anowa: African Women and Patriarchy*. Maryknoll, NY: Orbis Books.

Paul VI, Pope. 1969. 'Humanae Vitae: On the Regulation of Birth'. *Journal of Church and State* 11: 16–32.

———. 1977. 'Vatican Declaration: Women in the Ministerial Priesthood, 1976'. *Origins* 6 #33: 517–24.

Porete, Marguerite. 1993. *The Mirror of Simple Souls*. Trans. Ellen L. Babinsky. New York: Paulist Press.

Ranft, Patricia. 1996. *Women and the Religious Life in Premodern Europe*. New York: St. Martin's Press.

Rudy, Kathy. 1997. *Sex and the Church: Gender, Homosexuality and the Transformation of Christian Ethics*. Boston: Beacon.

Ruether, Rosemary Radford. 1974. 'Mysogynism and Virginal Feminism in the Father of the Church'. *Religion and Sexism: Images of Women in the Jewish and Christian Traditions*. Ed. Rosemary Radford Ruether. New York: Simon and Schuster: 150–83.

———. 1975. *New Woman New Earth: Sexist Ideologies and Human Liberation*. New York: Seabury Press.

———. 1979. 'Motherearth and the Megamachine: A Theology of Liberation in a Feminine, Somatic and Ecological Perspective'. *Womanspirit Rising*. Eds Carol P. Christ and Judith Plaskow. San Francisco: Harper & Row: 43–52.

———. 1983. *Sexism and God-Talk: Toward a Feminist Theology*. Boston: Beacon.

———. 1998. *Women and Redemption: A Christological History*. Minneapolis: Fortress.

Russell, Letty. 1974. *Human Liberation in a Feminist Perspective: A Theology*. Philadelphia: Westminster Press.

———. 1979. *The Future of Partnership*. Philadelphia: Westminster Press.

———, Kwok Pui-Lan, Ada María Isasi- Díaz, and Katie Geneva Cannon, eds. 1988. *Inheriting Our Mothers' Gardens: Feminist Theology in Third World Perspective*. Philadelphia: Westminster Press.

———. 1993. *Church in the Round: Feminist Interpretation of the Church*. Louisville: Westminster/John Knox.

————. 1996. 'Practicing Hospitality in a Time of Backlash'. *Theology Today* 52: 476–84.

Saiving, Valerie. 1979. 'The Human Situation: A Feminine View'. *Womanspirit Rising*. Eds Carol P. Christ and Judith Plaskow. San Francisco: Harper & Row: 25–42.

Stanton, Elizabeth Cady et al. 1974. *The Woman's Bible*. Seattle: Coalition Task Force on Women and Religion.

Tertullian. 1869. 'On the Dress of Women'. *Ante-Nicene Christian Library*. vol. 11. Eds Alexander Roberts and James Donaldson. Edinburgh: T. & T. Clark: 304–9.

Warne, Randi R. 1993. *Literature as Pulpit: The Christian Social Activism of Nellie L. McClung*. Waterloo: Wilfrid Laurier University Press.

Warner, Marina. 1976. *Alone of All Her Sex: The Myth and Cult of the Virgin Mary*. London: Pan Books.

Young, Pamela Dickey. 1990. *Feminist Theology/Christian Theology: In Search of Method*. Philadelphia: Fortress.

————. 1995. 'Feminist Theology: From Past to Future'. *Gender, Genre and Religion: Feminist Reflections*. Eds Morny Joy and Eva K. Neumaier. Waterloo, ON: Wilfrid Laurier University Press and Calgary Institute for the Humanities: 71–82.

FURTHER READING

Clifford, Anne M. *Introducing Feminist Theology*. Maryknoll, NY: Orbis, 2001.

Fiorenza, Elisabeth Schüssler, ed. *Searching the Scriptures; Volume 1: A Feminist Introduction, Volume 2: A Feminist Commentary*. New York: Crossroad, 1993, 1994.

Malone, Mary. *Women and Christianity; Volume 1: The First Thousand Years; Volume 2: From 1000 to the Reformation*. Ottawa: Novalis, 2000, 2001.

Ruether, Rosemary Radford. *Sexism and God-Talk: Toward a Feminist Theology*. Boston: Beacon, 1983.

Russell, Letty and J. Shannon Clarkson, eds. *Dictionary of Feminist Theologies*. Louisville, KY: Westminster John Knox, 1996.

CHAPTER 7

≈

WOMEN IN ISLAM

L. Clarke

INTRODUCTION AND OVERVIEW

Islam arose in the Arabian peninsula, the area now largely occupied by the modern state of Saudi Arabia, in the early seventh century. The religion was founded by the Prophet Muhammad, who spurned the cult of idols in his native town of Makkah (also spelled 'Mecca', located on the west, Red Sea coast of the peninsula) and finally succeeded, after much struggle, in establishing the principle of worship of one God—known in Arabic as Allah, or *The* God. Following the death of Muhammad in 632 CE, his successors, the caliphs, succeeded in conquering the entire area of the Middle East, and then beyond. Islam continued to spread in the following centuries to areas as diverse as Africa, Spain, Eastern Europe, the Indian subcontinent, Central Asia, Indonesia, and eventually, through immigration and conversion, to Europe, Australia, and North and South America. Islam is currently reputed to be 'the fastest growing religion in the world'.

Muslims are linked together by basic beliefs, such as belief in a Day of Judgement and a continuous line of prophets, culminating in the last Prophet, Muhammad. They are united by the text of the Qurán,[1] believed to be the literal word of God as sent down to His Prophet through the angel Gabriel. The sense of being heir to a glorious history and rich culture, as well as a concern to see the place of Islam and Islamic nations recognized and secured in the modern world, also inspire in Muslims a sense of common cause.

Islam is, at the same time, a most diverse and dynamic tradition. The daily lives and customs of Muslims living in disparate parts of the world are naturally very different, so that their Islam is outwardly expressed in different ways. There is also a wide spectrum of Islamic thought aimed at doctrinal, societal, and political issues. Among the most intensely debated of these issues is, without doubt, that of the position of women.

There are, generally speaking, two streams of thought on gender in Islam. Many contemporary Muslims view the advent and subsequent development of their religion as having guaranteed women a position of respect and protection within an ideal system of gender relations. The task of the Muslim community, in the view of this group (which I will call 'conservative'), is therefore to pre- serve and restore that ideal; and since, moreover, correct gender relations are vital to the social fabric of Islam, their preservation will also serve to strengthen and defend Islam itself. Others believe—somewhat on the model of a femi- nist critique of patriarchal religion—that while the Qurán and the Prophet did attempt to secure the position of women, that spirit of reform was neglected and obscured by later generations, including the religious scholars. This group (which I will call 'liberal') contends that an extensive rereading of history and reinterpretation of the texts is needed, both to discover the original Islamic ideal and to bring that ideal forward into modern times.

OFFICIAL AND UNOFFICIAL ROLES OF WOMEN

Muslim women at the dawn of Islam were instrumental in the founding of their religion, and these have become role models for women today. As Islam then grew and flourished, women also exercised political power, reached the station of mystics and saints, and became scholars. It is true that women's activities and renown in these areas were much less than those of men. This circum- stance, however, is not peculiar to Islam. The basic position of women has always been on the margin; but they have nevertheless found openings through which they could creep toward the centre. It is useless to simply celebrate one or lament the other. The questions rather to be asked are: Where were the openings and how were they created? What were the limitations? And what does all this mean for Muslim women today?

Women and the Advent of Islam

The period before Islam in the Arabian peninsula is known as *Jáhilíyah*, the 'Time of Ignorance' or 'Time of Unrestraint'. Islam, by contrast, means literally 'Submission [to God]'. Most Muslims believe—although the data concerning women in the Jáhilíyah is somewhat mixed—that the coming of Islam freed women from corrupt and degrading practices, that women were given, as is often said, their 'dignity' and proper position.

Women certainly did play a significant role in establishing Islam. This picture is important because of the religious—indeed, the human—tendency to seek models for one's life in ideal figures of the past. The tendency is rein- forced in the case of Islam by the concept of *Sunnah*. Sunnah, meaning 'accepted custom', refers to the pattern of the life of Muhammad and the early community; emulation of this pattern is for believers a religious ideal as well as one of the sources of the Law.

The Prophet's first revelation came to him, according to tradition, in 610 CE when he was 40 years old. Muhammad's Biography tells of the important role of his wife Khadíjah in his life at this time. She was, according to the Biography, 'a woman of dignity and wealth . . . determined, noble, and intelligent', (Ibn Hishám: 82) who had charged Muhammad with carrying her goods abroad by caravan. She proposed marriage to him, and he accepted. She was later able to reassure him of the truth of his mission, even verifying that his inspiration came from an angel and not a satan, so that, as the Biography declares, 'She was the first to believe in God and His apostle, and in the truth of his message' (Ibn Hishám: 111). God is supposed to have reassured Muhammad after her death that she had been granted 'an abode in heaven' (Bukhárí, *Manáqib, Tazwíj Muhammad Khadíjah*).[2]

The Biography confirms that among those who were then attracted by the new religion, despite persecution by the wealthy merchants of Makkah, were 'both men and women' (Ibn Hishám: 117). They included, for instance, the sister of Umar, the second caliph, whose reading of the Qurán inspired his conversion; and Sumayyah, who died through being exposed to the heat of midday as she refused to recant her faith, so that she became the first martyr in Islam. A woman called Nusaybah was among those who came from Madínah to secretly pledge allegiance to Muhammad; she later fought against the tribes who rose up against Islam after the death of the Prophet, and returned 'having suffered', the Biography says, 'twelve wounds from spear or sword' (Ibn Hishám: 203, 212).

The prominence and participation of women in this first period is extolled by all Muslims, but to somewhat different purpose. The conservatives take the example of the first female Muslims to mean that women should be strong and active *within prescribed limits, in the cause of their religion*. They do not see the examples of the first Muslim women as meaning that women should occupy positions of authority or venture for their own purposes outside the family. The practice in early times of women going to war not only to lend support to the combatants but as combatants themselves tends to be viewed by this group as having occurred under exceptional circumstances. The liberals, on the other hand, see the first female believers as forerunners of the modern, independent Muslim woman who is both rooted in her religion and reaching toward the goal of fullest participation in society. The Iraqi scholar Haifaa Jawad remarks: 'Contrary to the traditional image of women being secluded and suppressed, women in early Islam participated in armed conflict either by organising food and water and taking care of the wounded, or through playing a crucial part in the actual fighting when it was needed'; and she takes this instance of 'political action', as well as the fact that Muhammad had women along with men pledge allegiance (bay'ah) to him and consulted them about community affairs, to indicate that the first Muslim women were 'pioneers' in 'radical social change that allowed more space and greater mobility for women in society' (Jawad 1998: 86, 88).

The Example of the Prophet's Family

The establishment of the Muslim community in Madínah in 622 CE following the Hijrah ('migration') from Makkah marked a change in the Prophet's family life. Following the loss of his beloved first wife, Khadíjah, some years before the Hijrah, Muhammad had married two other women, Sawdah and Á'ishah; and now in Madínah he contracted additional marriages. He is said to have had nine or twelve wives in all (the count differs in different sources), of whom his favourite was apparently Á'ishah, daughter of the first caliph of Islam, Abu Bakr. The wives came to him under a variety of circumstances. Sawdah was a widow of about 50 years of age. Muhammad married Á'ishah very young, at the age of nine or ten; she may have been the only virgin among the wives. Juwayríyah was captured when her tribe was defeated by the Muslims, and her marriage to the Prophet served to cement their allegiance to the cause of Islam. Safiyah was originally a Jewish captive, while Maryam, probably a concubine instead of a wife, was a Copt (Egyptian Christian). Some of the wives were beautiful, such as Juwayríah, and some, such as Sawdah, were reputedly not.

Muslims usually argue that Muhammad's marriages after Khadíjah were contracted not for pleasure, but in order to provide widows with protection and confirm alliances. The apparently logical argument that the marriages simply represent the common practice and mores of a different time, which it would be unreasonable to judge by present standards, does not seem to appeal to Muslims, probably because it runs up against the problem of the Muhammad's life being considered a timeless standard. Although the classical Islamic tradition takes a positive view of sexual pleasure and praises Muhammad for his love of women and virility, this reply has also not been popular. Muslims have not, in any case, been overly concerned with the Prophet's polygamy—which they view as a circumstance special to his station and not a model for themselves—except as the question has been raised by outside critics. What is important for them instead is the personalities of the wives and the Prophet's relations with them.

The wives of Muhammad, honoured with the epithet 'Mothers of the Believers' (after Qurán[3] 33:6: 'The Prophet is closer to the believers than their selves, and his wives are as their mothers'), are highly respected by Muslims. This respect is attributable largely to their closeness to the Prophet. The wives are also, however, credited with their own personal virtues. Á'ishah is reputed to have spent much time reading the Qurán, fasting, and praying, to have freed slaves (an important religious act), and to have generously given her income in charity. Zaynab bint Khuzaymah was so well known for her charity that she was called 'Mother of the Poor' (*Umm al-Makáskín*). The reverence in which the wives are consequently held may be gauged by the fact that the violent reaction in 1989 to Salman Rushdie's novel *The Satanic Verses* was stirred as much by the perception that he had insulted them as that he had insulted the Prophet himself.

Focus on Muhammad's relationships with his wives is useful for purposes of Sunnah, because it provides material that serves as a model and precedent for man–wife relationships. It is also much appreciated by Muslims, who discern in the tales of Muhammad and his family an image of tolerant kindness. The story of Muhammad's relationship with Á'ishah is certainly the best-known example. We hear how Á'ishah used to apply perfume to her husband and worry about his health, while Muhammad joined in her games when she was yet a child and took her to public amusements. As a husband, Muhammad is gentle, indulgent, and even a little put-upon by his large family. Some of the wives are supposed to have been very jealous; several hadíths tell how Á'ishah was vexed even by the affection Muhammad retained for his deceased first wife, Khadíjah.

More than any other wife, Á'ishah has her own prestige. Married, according to most sources, at the age of nine, she lived with Muhammad for nine years, being widowed at eighteen. Her fame in relation to the Prophet of Islam was nevertheless guaranteed by her long life thereafter (she died in her sixty-fifth year), during which she recounted—or, depending on one's opinion of the reliability of the hadíths, there were recounted in her name—many anecdotes of his words and actions. Thus Á'ishah, along with, to a lesser extent, her co-wife Umm Salamah, is a great source of hadíths, hadíth being the second Islamic scripture after the Qurán. Bukhárí preserves over two hundred texts he judges to be authentically from her, out of many more circulated in her name.

Á'ishah is pictured as actively enquiring about, even initially objecting to, the Prophet's pronouncements, so that it was said of her that 'She would never hear something she didn't understand without reviewing it until she did' (Bukhárí, *Ilm*). Several hadíths attributed to Á'ishah even have her deciding herself what the Prophet *would have ruled* had he spoken to a situation—as in the following statement concerning women going to the mosque: 'Were Muhammad to see what we see of women today, he would prohibit them from going to the mosque' (Bukhárí, *Adhán*). In a few hadíths, Á'ishah is presented as using her fund of knowledge to correct the perceptions of later generations regarding women. For instance, a man doubted that his wife could serve him during her menses; but he was answered with Á'ishah's insistence that she used to comb the hair of the Prophet while she was menstruating, even as he prepared to go to the mosque (Bukhárí, *Hayd*).

Á'ishah was finally unable, however, to extend the influence she acquired as a wife of the Prophet to include political power. Later in her life, she joined a movement opposing the fourth caliph, Alí ibn Abí Tálib, which culminated in 656 in a battle near the Iraqi town of Basrah. The incident is known as the Battle of the Camel, because Á'ishah, mounted on a camel, urged on the troops as the battle raged about her. She and her cohorts were defeated. Although she was then, as a mark of the respect due to her, escorted back to Madínah and allowed to continue her life there, her defeat was taken by tradition to indicate the inadvisability of women interfering in politics.

Fátimah is the other female figure that stands out in Muhammad's life. She was one of four daughters borne by Khadíjah, these being the Prophet's only offspring to survive. A well-known hadíth (sometimes connected to the Prophet's forbidding her husband, Alí ibn Abí Tálib, to take additional wives) has Muhammad say: 'Fátimah is a part of me; who angers her, angers me' (Bukhárí, *Manáqib*). We are told how Fátimah shielded the Prophet as she washed and ministered to him when he was wounded (Bukhárí, *Wudú*); and he is said to have declared her to be 'mistress of the women of Paradise' (Bukhárí, *Manáqib Fátimah*).

Fátimah is depicted by tradition as a tragic, suffering woman. Because of her marriage to Alí, Fátimah is particularly beloved by the Shiites, now the chief minority group in Islam after the majority Sunnites; it was reverence for Alí that first prompted the emergence of the Shiites. Tales of Fátimah's poverty, constant religious exercise, and charity become highly magnified in Shiite pietistic literature. Stories are told of her tragic visions of the future in which she foresaw the martyrdom of her sons Hasan and Husayn. Fátimah is linked in many legends to the supernatural. Her birth is accompanied by a light that illuminates the earth; she is spared menstruation; she receives the epithets 'Luminous' (*Zahrá*) and 'Virgin' (*Batúl*); and she plays a prominent role in the Final Judgement, crowned with jewels, surrounded by hosts of angels, demanding revenge for her murdered sons and granting intercession for the Shiites who were loyal to her descendants.

Among the Shiites, Zaynab, sister of Husayn, is also presented as a model for women. Zaynab was present at the great battle at Karbalá in Iraq in 680 in which Husayn was martyred, and stories are told of how she took up arms as the men were killed and of her proud defiance as she was marched as a captive to Damascus.

Liberal Muslims, of course, respect the wives of the Prophet, but they are more likely to focus on the initiative and prestige of the two most independent-minded, Á'ishah and Khadíjah, along with the exploits of the founding heroines. Conservative perceptions of the wives and of Fátimah, on the other hand, concentrate on womanly virtue and domesticity. The image might be one of strength; but it is particular kind of strength, centred on piety, modesty, service, and devotion to the Prophet. One liberal thinker who has attempted to overcome the difficulty of dwelling on 'womanly' virtues is Alí Shariatí, one of the forerunners of the Iranian Islamic revolution (Shariatí died in 1977, just two years before the revolution came to a head). Shariatí's famous tract, *Fátimah is Fátimah*, creates a Fátimah who does not allow herself to be defined solely as daughter or wife, but rather is engaged in a constant struggle to realize herself *as a person*: 'Fátimah must become Fátimah on her own. If she does not become Fátimah, she is lost'. This Fátimah, Shariatí thought, would be the model for the modern Muslim woman who 'wants to be herself, wants to build herself, wants to be reborn'.

Women and Political Power

Madínah continued as the centre of the expanding Islamic empire at least up to the founding of the Umayyad Dynasty in the later seventh century and consequent transfer of the capital to Damascus. With the overthrow of the Umayyads by the Abbásids in 750, the focus of the ever-expanding Islamic world then shifted to Baghdad. Abbásid rule survived in Baghdad until 1258, when the Mongols extirpated the caliphal line. But the banner of Islam had already been taken up by a host of other tribes and states—not only Arab, but Turkic, Iranian, Indian, and Berber. The caliphate, which had once symbolized the unity of Islam, was gone; Islam as an international creed and civilisation went on to win new peoples and territories.

Khayzurán, mother of two successive Abbásid caliphs, the short-lived al-Hádí and legendary Hárún al-Rashíd (reigned 786–809), is one early example of political influence in this 'classical age' of Islam. Khayzurán was a favourite concubine of the caliph al-Mahdí. Apart from her beauty, she was cultivated, as the most expensive slave girls were expected to be; she recited poetry and had some religious learning. She is suspected of having poisoned her son Hádí, since he had tried to limit her influence; with the succession of her other son, Hárún al-Rashíd, however, she was able to maintain a high position until her death. In the course of her climb, Khayzurán amassed great wealth and became noted for her charity, including restoration of sites around Makkah.

Themes in the story of Khayzurán—concubinage, manipulation, and good works—are repeated throughout the classical period, in various combinations. Some females, however, were able to come closer to independent power. In Yemen in the eleventh and first half of the twelfth century, the queens Asma and Arwa shared power with their husbands, members of a dynasty connected with the Ismá'ílí movement, an alternative branch of Shiism. Shajarat al-Durr (her name means 'Tree of Pearls') conspired with the Mamlúk army in Egypt to keep the death of her husband secret while she repulsed a besieging Crusader army. In 1250, the military placed Shajarat al-Durr herself on the throne to secure their position. She reigned for only a few months. As the Abbásid caliph refused to bestow legitimacy on a woman, she was deposed, and eventually murdered. A few women managed to rule directly rather than acting as associates—as, for instance al-Sayyidah al-Hurrah ('free lady', a title also held by other female rulers, including the Arwa mentioned above), who attained the position of governor of Tetouán, Morocco, for some decades in the sixteenth century and engaged in both piracy and diplomacy until she married the king of Morocco.

What can the influence and occasional rule of women mean? Nabia Abbot, a pioneer in the study of women in Islam, believes the role of women to have been even greater than admitted in the classical sources, since '[Muslim] historians tend to pass over unpalatable references to women's rule as briefly as possible, frequently ignoring it altogether' (1946: 55). Certainly, it is one of the difficulties of women's history that their part tends to be undervalued as records are drawn up; from that point of view, the recovery of these figures is a necessary corrective. Abbot also expresses the hope that highlighting the role of women in Muslim politics will provide an example and precedent for modern times.

From a strictly historical point of view, however, the influence or rule of women in the Islamic past is not so remarkable. Throughout the classical period, political power, or at least the symbol of it, was located in the court. Court rule often opens a path to power for women, both because command depends on shifting alliances within a relatively small family group, and because outside players may choose to use females connected to the court in their manipulations, as happened to Shajarat al-Durr.

The rule behind the exception is brought home in frequent misogynistic remarks about women's rule. Khayzurán was supposed to have been warned by her son, al-Hádí, not to 'overstep the essential limits of womanly modesty . . . [for] it is not dignified for a woman to enter upon affairs of state' (Abbott 1946: 89–90). The theme of disastrous women's rule even received scriptural authority as it made its way into several hadíths. One very well-known text, sometimes linked to Á'ishah's part in the Battle of the Camel and still quoted today, declares: 'A people who place women in charge of their affairs will never prosper' (Bukhárí, *Fitan*).

Nevertheless, a number of women have ruled Muslim states in modern times. The incidence of female rule is, in fact, more than that of Western nations: Benazir Bhutto of Pakistan, Tansu Çiller of Turkey, Khaleda Zia and Sheikh Hasina Wajed of Bangladesh, and Megawati Sukarnoputri of Indonesia have all served as president or prime minister. In all but the case of Çiller, however, these were the daughters of previous rulers. The election of women as heads of state, in other words, appears to be still an outcome of political dynamics akin to court or family rule, rather than preference for the candidates in their own right.

But there is another side to the story of women and political power in Islam, seen in a series of incremental developments that may herald real change. States in the Persian Gulf—for instance, Qatar and Bahrain—that had not given women the vote are now finally yielding to their demands, while many nations in which women have already had the vote for decades—among others, Egypt, Syria, Iraq, and Iran—count a number of women among their parliamentarians.

A most important step in women's gaining political power is to legitimate that power Islamically. Here we see two contrary trends. On one side, many opposition Islamist movements believe that it is not women's place to play an active role in government. The Saudi regime also seems to take the position that women should not hold any formal position of power; women have not, for instance, been included in the advisory Consultative Council first set up in the kingdom in 1991. On the other side, however, one hears the argument that women's participation in the political process is actually an Islamic standard. The respected, though controversial, Egyptian scholar and journalist Ahmad Khalaf Alláh has argued that women in the time of the Prophet enjoyed political rights specified in the Qurán itself (1977: 189–93), while the African-American Muslim feminist Amina Wadud argues that the Qurán (27:23ff.) depicts the Queen of Sheba's 'ability to govern wisely' in a special feminine way (Wadud 1999: 41–2).

The pro-politics opinion has actually become an important part of the self-view of many Muslims. I myself have heard my students (not necessarily a very liberal group) cite women's rule and other high achievement in the Muslim world as evidence of the superior rights granted women by Islam. It seems that thought concerning political participation, like gender thought in Islam in general and the social realities that inform it, is in a state of flux.

Woman Mystics

Women have actively participated in Islamic mysticism, called Sufism after the rough woollen (súf) cloaks worn by the early ascetics. It is often said that females are more easily admitted into mysticism than more conventional expressions of religion. This does appear to hold true, to an extent, for Islamic mysticism. It is surely unrealistic to say, as does Annemarie Schimmel, that in Sufism, 'woman enjoys full equal rights' (Schimmel 1997: 15). Women are still most often on the margin. Sufism, however, like mysticism in general, plots itself by a hidden realm, in which the structure and values of this world are altered or reversed. Sufism also focuses on individual charisma, the sources of which lie in that same mysterious world. This results in a certain flexibility of doctrine and authority, which has been exploited not only by women but by others on the social margin such as devotees of folk religion.

We hear of numerous female saints in Islam; although, as we have come to expect from women's history, many fewer than male saints. The most famous female saint of Islam is, without doubt, Rábi'ah al-Adawiyah of early eighth-century Basrah in Iraq. Her story as it has come down to us touches on several common themes of saints' lives: a humble beginning (she was said to have been a slave girl), sudden conversion (she repented of singing and entertaining) and self-denial. Rábi'ah appears in Sufi lore as an early exponent of love-mysticism, which was to eclipse the earlier ethic of asceticism. Perhaps the most famous anecdote of all of Sufism is told of her in this connection: She was seen running through the street with a torch in one hand and a bucket of water in the other. Asked what she was doing, she replied that she wished to put out the fires of Hell and destroy Paradise, so that God would be worshipped not out of fear but for His sake alone.

Rábi'ah's femaleness gives her legend a special colouring. Her physical characteristics are noted (she is supposed to have been beautiful), she refused offers of marriage, and there are numerous apocryphal stories in which she bests Hasan al-Basrí, an equally famous male mystic. This emphasis alerts us to the shadow of an ambivalence toward female sainthood. It is true that the esteem in which female saints were held was not inferior to that of males. This is a consequence of the very nature of sainthood, which involves mysterious qualities that cannot easily be ranked. We might, however, read Rábi'ah's story in another way. The basic mystical lesson Hasan al-Basrí must learn—the danger of creeping pride—is driven home by the fact that it is delivered by a mere female. Rábi'ah's legend in general intimates that her accomplishment is all the more remarkable and unexpected *because she is a woman*. She is doubly exceptional; we do not expect all people to be like that, but especially not many women.

Residual discomfort with female saints[4] is also seen in assertions that women had by their sainthood transcended their gender and become essentially men. Thus the twelfth-century Persian mystical poet Attár in his 'Memorials of the Saints' places Rábi'ah with the men, rather than the women, explaining that 'When a woman becomes a man in the path of God, she is a man and one cannot any more call her a woman' (Attar 1966: 40). The American scholar Valerie Hoffman reports that she sometimes received the 'compliment' during her fieldwork among Sufis in Egypt that she was not a woman but actually a 'brother', and that some female *shaykhas* (the feminine equivalent of *shaykh*, meaning 'esteemed authority') affected the behaviour of men in relations with their followers (Hoffman 1995: 45–6, 227, 249, 292).

Some Sufi theosophists, nevertheless, incorporated the feminine principle into their cosmological speculations. Consideration of the feminine emerges in a fascinating way in the work of the most influential theosophist of Islam, Muhyi al-Dín Ibn Arabí of thirteenth-century Andalusia. Ibn Arabí declares love for woman to be 'one of the perfections of the Gnostic . . . for this is a prophetic heritage [the Prophet having declared in a famous hadíth that the three things most dear to him were perfume, women, and prayer] and a divine love'. He proposes that God is seen most fully in woman, since she reflects His Beauty and gives birth to the perfect human form. Sachiko Murata in her *Tao of Islam* argues that Ibn Arabí expressly acknowledges the complementary roles of the male and female principles in the structuring of the universe (1992: 178ff.).

But does femininized theosophy have any impact on regard for real women in the real world? It seems that for Ibn Arabí, at least, reverence for the feminine as an ideal was actually joined with respect for women. He was profoundly influenced by his saintly woman teachers, conferred the patched mantle of Sufism mostly upon women, and even allowed that they could be members of the hierarchy of hidden arch-saints.

Positive attitudes and practices such as those of Ibn Arabí had always to compete, however, with a negative view of women stemming from the ascetic element of Sufism. According to the ascetic view, woman is a fleshly distraction from God and a frivolous being that draws man into material entanglements. The base ego-soul (*nafs*), Sufis have often noted, is grammatically feminine in gender, while the goal of the mystic is to tame and wear away that very soul so he can focus his attention constantly on God. Thus the attitude toward women of Sufism, like that of other mysticisms, is best described as ambivalent.

As for leadership in the formal structure of Sufism, women have led women's circles, as seen in the Darqawíyah order in Morocco in the mid-twentieth century and many other cases today. A few have then found their way into higher echelons, as in the case of Lala Zaynab, whose charisma allowed her to gain the upper hand over her nephew in the direction of an important section of the Rahmáníyah order in nineteenth-century Algeria. In Egypt, Hoffman encountered a shaykhah whose personal prestige had also caused her to overshadow the authority of her brother, the official head of the order. It does appear that women can in exceptional instances circumvent the ban on formal authority through the mysterious power of charisma.

TEXTS AND RITUALS

Much attention is paid to women in the Qurán and hadíths, the two scriptures of Islam. The primary reason for this focus seems to be that the new religion was determined to reorganize Arab tribal society on the basis of the family unit, and definition of the role of women and of male–female relations was central to this project. The Islamic scriptures are also, however, interested in women for their own sake, including their spirituality and welfare within marriage and the family. All these concerns are evident in citations throughout the essay.

The first part of this particular section focuses on women and texts from the point of view of their long-standing *participation* in those texts—that is, in the tradition of Islamic learning. We see that religious learning has afforded opportunities for women, but has also involved certain limitations—above all, limitation on the authority that might be gained through learning. The second part of the section follows the same theme of opportunities and limitations by looking at women's participation in rituals within the restraints of purity and space.

Religious Learning and the Question of Authority

The female learned pursuit *par excellence* in classical times was transmission of hadíths, a role initiated by women contemporary with Muhammad (Á'ishah being the most outstanding) who were credited with witnessing his all-important words and actions. It is not necessary to consider the doubts raised by Western scholars concerning the overall authenticity of the hadíths. What is significant is that the tradition accepted women as witnesses, confirming that they were held in high, perhaps equal regard. The proportion of woman Companions (as the members of the first generation of Islam are called) rated by hadíth scholars as trustworthy transmitters is not less than the proportion of men, suggesting that 'the reliability of hadíths was weighed without regard to the gender of their first transmitters' (Roded 1994: 65–6).

In later generations, the number of woman hadíth scholars dropped dramatically (Roded 1994: 45–6). This, however, may be explained by the very different natures of first-generation and later-generation transmission, rather than anti-female bias. The witness of members of the first generation was relatively passive. They were candidates simply by virtue of being there, and stood, moreover, close enough to the Prophet to catch his reflected prestige. Later transmission, by contrast, was a formal enterprise, requiring active participation in a (men's) world of scholarship. We know that women's endeavours tend to be depressed as platforms are formalized, so it is not surprising to see fewer transmitters in this setting.

Women nevertheless continued to participate and even excel in hadíth transmission. More than one-quarter of 130 trusted hadíth authorities acknowledged by the fifteenth-century scholar al-Suyútí are women—an outstanding example but not an exceptional one (Berkey 1991: 151). Women also went on to engage in other scholarship. They commonly obtained *ijázah*s, or 'licences', testifying to their expertise, and not only learned from, but also taught men.

Encouragement of and respect for women's learning were no doubt blunted by misogynistic evaluations of women's character and intelligence, some of which were themselves, ironically, enshrined in hadíths (though not in the Qurán, which is remarkably free of misogyny). The best-known phrases of this kind are 'Women are deficient in intellect and religion' and 'Most of the inhabitants of Hell are women' (Bukhárí, *Hayd*; the authenticity and interpretation of both have been questioned). Nonetheless, learning, since it focuses attention on the bearer's merits *as an individual*, has the potential of allowing him or her to dim prejudice and cross social boundaries; respect for learning was potent enough in Islam that it provided an opening not only for women, but for slaves, some of whom also became noted scholars.

The remarkable role of women in Islamic scholarship may also have been driven by class. Women who pursued learning were from scholarly and cultured merchant families—that is, from families with a tradition of learning already in place. Such women were educated or began their education with close relatives, such as the father. The author has noticed the same type of family education of daughters and wives in Arab countries and Iran among scholarly and mercantile-scholarly families, and has observed that religious learning adds to the prestige of a woman and her family (marriage still involving family alliance) when marriage is sought. Remembering that the female scholars mentioned in the biographies came from such family backgrounds, we might think of women's learning as contributing to the maintenance of the prestige of such family groups, and indeed of the whole class. To put it another way, for what we might call the Islamic medieval bourgeoisie, learning was social capital, valuable enough in itself and in the very important social transaction of marriage that it became advantageous to accumulate it also in females.

Once initially encouraged, such women might have actually enjoyed some advantage in learning. One advantage women of the higher classes have sometimes had over men in private intellectual pursuits is leisure. Widowhood, polygamy, and domestic slavery might also have favoured scholarship, since these help to free a woman from the demands of husband and household. When we add to this the fact that Muslim women could be financially independent (since Islamic Law gives them the right to own and control property), it is not surprising to find that some turned to pietistic pursuits, including the learning for which Islam provided a relatively favourable atmosphere.

There were, nevertheless, many fewer women than men engaged in learning significant enough to be noticed in biographies. An analysis of the twelfth-century *History of the City of Damascus* of Ibn Asákir shows about 4.5 per cent female scholars in the first century of Islam, and 2 per cent—13 women against

627 men—in the third (Abyad 1981: 183). Other works reveal similar numbers. The ratio might be adequately explained by the natural dynamics of male–female relationships in a patriarchal society, but there are two additional factors to be taken into account: seclusion and authority.

An Iranian religious scholar who used to give private lessons in theology and law once recounted to me how one of his heavily veiled female students remarked that she had before coming to the lesson carefully calculated the reward of learning against the necessity of sitting with a man. The merit of learning, apparently, won out. As the anecdote suggests, the ideal of 'seeking knowledge' might have to compete with the ideal of seclusion. Learning, however, could still prevail. As we have already seen, women not only learned from, but also taught men. They sometimes attended mixed lessons, for instance at a mosque in the company of a male relative; and a few even struck out on 'journeys in search of knowledge' (*rihlah fí talab al-ilm*) to acquire learning from more distant authorities. Nevertheless, seclusion must have been severely limiting—keeping in mind that in classical times, seclusion was not voluntary as in the example just given, but controlled by a responsible male.

Knowledge is authority. A woman who had acquired significant knowledge must have enjoyed some kind of informal authority, amounting at least to respect or deference, while knowledge itself was of such value in Islam that male scholars were willing to endorse that authority by taking instruction from her. This is rather different, however, from formal, coercive authority. By formal authority I mean the offices of *muftí* (one who issues legal responsa in accord with the heritage of one of the Sunnite schools of law), *mujtahid* (one who issues responsa according to his own reasoning, the activity called *ijtihád* presently characteristic of the Shiite school), and *qádí* (judge). According to majority Sunnite opinion—remembering that, in Islamic law, there are variant opinions on almost every question—a woman may be a muftí (so also a slave); but she cannot, according to the Shiites, be a mujtahid guiding others (though she may, if her learning qualifies her, be a mujtahid guiding herself only). Nor, it is agreed almost unanimously, can she be a judge. The logic of allowing a woman to be a muftí might be that a muftí is confined, at least in theory, to communicating the legal doctrine already laid down by one of the schools, and thus acts merely as a conduit for established tradition. Or the logic might be that the opinion of a muftí is merely advisory—this is essentially true—and thus the muftí's authority is not really coercive, and women may exercise it. The authority of the Shiite mujtahid, on the other hand, is certainly coercive. The Shiite believer is obliged to select one mujtahid and follow that one and no other in all his views of the Law, including in questions for which he has never himself asked for a response. The case of a judge is clear. The judge's authority is coercive, like that of the ruler, and therefore both must be male;

one of the qualifications Islamic political theory specifies for the ideal ruler is male gender.

The underlying principle seems to be that authority granted to women, no matter how well qualified, can only be informal, limited, inconspicuous, or— as we have seen in the case of Sufism—charismatic. Authority must be granted, above all, at the pleasure of men—that is, it must be non-coercive. As long as this rule is obeyed, low-level or sporadic episodes of female authority do not crucially challenge the all-important hierarchy of male over female. In considering this, however, we should remember that hierarchy and assumption of male authority are nearly universal human conditions. They are not original to classical Islamic society or law, but merely manifested in them.

Change and reform in modern Islamic nations have demolished much of the socio-legal structure that once sanctioned hierarchy. The actual authority of Muslim women in the workplace, government, and universities, which they have thoroughly penetrated in many Islamic nations, is well established and widely accepted. Women have also begun to claim religious authority, although this is typically done not by following the path of traditional learning and infiltrating the religious establishment, but through more general discussion of Islamic gender ideology, often in the form of journalism. In the meantime, the interdiction on women's *religious* judgeship (remembering that there are already woman judges and lawyers in the secular courts of many Muslim countries) as well as authoritative ijtihád is being questioned by a few members of the religious establishment itself.

Despite social progress and legal reform, however, the effects of a long tradition of hierarchy endure. The odour of male authority still hangs about the personal law, while gender hierarchy continues to colour social relations. Lingering assumption of male command is, of course, a hard fact of all societies with a patriarchal heritage (including our own); but religion in the Muslim world still has enough power that it can be effectively invoked to justify hierarchy. Rapid social change and Western dominance, in addition, prompt many Muslims to look to the past for clarity and strength, and there is nothing so simple, dramatic, and altogether comforting as assertion of male authority and the traditional structures that go with it. The apparent contrast with the West, where male authority has been somewhat reduced, makes this turn even more appealing.

Rituals, Purity, and Space

The basic rituals of the high tradition of Islam—the common, legislated rituals that must be performed by all Muslims—are daily prayer, fasting during the month of Ramadán, and pilgrimage to Makkah. (The other two of the five so-called Pillars of Islam are pronouncing of the *shahádah*, the 'witness' that 'there is no god but God and Muhammad is His Messenger', and payment of *zakát*, the poor-tax.) There is no legislated female ritual in Islam. Nor does female practice differ from that of males. This might be a legacy of the spiritual equality assumed between men and women in the time of the earliest community when the rituals were laid down; or it could simply be in keeping with the very spare character of ritual in Islam in general. Female practice does, however, diverge somewhat from that of males where considerations of purity and space intervene.

A woman is not to pray or fast while she is menstruating (though she should make up the days missed of the fast). If she begins to menstruate during the *hajj*, however, she is to complete her pilgrimage, with only slightly different ritual consequences. This facility for the pilgrimage is obviously necessary from a practical point of view; but it is also consistent with the not very severe attitude of Islam toward menstruation and parturition. The basic principle is that a woman's person during her menstrual time is not impure, so that she does not transfer impurity to things or persons she touches; though, of course, the menstrual blood itself, if spilled, does contaminate. The result is that, apart from the prohibition against intercourse in Qurán 2:222 (the only verse in which there is warning about menstruation), the menstruous woman continues to function fully in society, including in regions where ritual is being carried out.

There is nevertheless a tendency, often on the part of lesser authorities or of local tradition as in Africa and the Subcontinent, to elaborate menstruation rules—for instance, by forbidding the menstruous woman from entering the mosque, or having her undertake a purification at the end of her menses more complicated than simple washing. The high tradition, in the meantime, resists this tendency, beginning in the hadíths (as in the hadíth from Á'ishah cited earlier in this chapter), and continuing with *fatwá*s (opinions issued by religious authorities) into modern times.

A similar tension exists in the case of ritual and women's space. In the ritual prayer performed five times a day, women stand behind the men. (In Iran, one also sees men and women side by side, with a cloth or other division down the middle, but this may be a modern development.) The original purpose of the women's standing behind the men at the dawn of Islam could not, it seems to me, have been to separate the sexes, since the arrangement obviously does not accomplish that. Perhaps the women were behind the men because this was how the tribe migrated or went to war; the Qurán seems to link the careful lining up of those praying into straight ranks with the standing of soldiers shoulder to shoulder ready for battle (cf. Q. 61:4). Nevertheless, the reason very soon supplied by the tradition for the division was that it helped the participants, effectively the men, avoid distracting sexual thoughts.

Some hadíths and a body of opinion built upon them even asserted that women should not come to the mosque for prayer at all. Rather, they should pray in their houses (see for example, Abu Dáwúd, *Saláh*). The reason given for preventing women from attending the mosque is that they are likely to stir up sexual anarchy (*fitnah*); the theme of sexual distraction during prayer is here expanded and used to limit space absolutely. A contrary group of hadíths and opinions, in the meantime, continues to insist on the right of women to pray, presumably behind the men, in the mosque (for example, Bukhárí, *Adhán*). Still other statements attempt to harmonize the two judgements (or submerge the second) by allowing that a woman may attend, but only if absolutely unadorned and with the knowledge that her mosque-going is actually less meritorious than her staying home to pray.

Argument over the location of women's prayer is much sharper than dispute over menstruation, because there is much more at stake. Division of space has been the great exclusionary principle of the Islamic tradition. Mixing in the mosque, it appears, is a powerful symbolic blow at that principle. For this reason also we do not see, as in menstruation, more learned authorities consistently 'holding the line' by defending women's mosque-going against creeping exclusionism. (Here I assume permission—in fact, encouragement—for women to go to the mosque to be the basic and original position of the tradition; see Clarke 2003: 235–40.) The lines are formed up chiefly instead between modernists and some conservatives who wish to see women 'reclaim' their place in the mosque, and extreme traditionalists who regard unrestricted mosque-going as the thin edge of a lifting of other restrictions on space, leading ultimately to a wearing away of domesticity and all the further societal consequences that would entail.

This basic configuration of the dispute should not, however, obscure other cross-currents. Every well-organized social movement tries to control and harness the power of women. Thus it is not surprising to see many apparently conservative Islamic movements encourage co-optable woman's activism. That activism may be channelled, as far as space is concerned, into divided activities such as women's study circles or—a phenomenon familiar to us all—women's auxiliaries of various kinds. But it may also spill, at least a little, over gender-space boundaries, with or without the connivance of the father movement. Post-revolutionary Iran offers some examples. The Tehran Friday prayer is broadcast each week; women are strongly encouraged to attend along with the men, and the cameras never fail to pan them. The government facilitates female preachers, Qurán-reciters, and so on, and these may occasionally be heard over loudspeakers, in recordings, and even seen on television—all disturbing to traditionalists. In another example of women's religious activism spilling over gender boundaries, as Muslim religious consciousness is on the rise in North America, more women, along with men, are attending the mosque.

Ritual practised by Muslim women sometimes develops distinctive features. For instance, some Sufi and also Shiite pilgrimages have been colonized by women, who gather together for mutual support and appeal to the saint for their own special concerns. Women exclusively perform the exorcism rituals (zár) established in Upper Egypt and Sudan and loosely connected to popular Sufism. There has not, however, been any conscious movement in Islam, as in Judaism and some other traditions, to revive or create rituals to express the concerns of women. This is because the tradition lays great stress on correct practice as the manifestation of faith. 'Correct' means established by the Sunnah of the Prophet and early community; anything not legitimated in this way is liable to be viewed as 'innovation', bid'ah, the opposite of Sunnah.

Women's ritual is also hobbled by a long-standing traditional view, seen in classical literature and even the hadíth (though certainly not the Qurán), that unsupervised activity entails certain hazards arising from the female psyche. Women, it is thought, are naturally superstitious; they are prone because of both their nature and ignorance to engage in un-Islamic practices (Lutfi 1991). They should not visit graves, as that might become an outlet for frivolous dressing up and socializing. They should not attend funerals, as their lack of emotional control might spoil the dignity of the occasion; this has actually become a legal norm.

Can separate ritual space and feminized ritual be of any advantage to women? I happen to think that the ultimate route to power and equality is through capturing the centre, rather than building on the periphery. Separation should be at most a temporary strategy. In the meantime, however, we deal with present realities, and so it might be best to look at the advantages or disadvantages of individual cases. In one example, among the thirty million or so Muslims of China, the separate women's mosques (nusi) that first developed in the late-eighteenth century have not only afforded women a measure of collective strength and independence, but also served as centres of religious and health education, sometimes under the guidance of ordained female ritual experts (nu ahong) (Jaschok and Shui 2000).

WOMEN'S SEXUALITY: ISLAMIC LAW AND BEYOND THE LAW

This section begins with discussion of the rules of the Sharíah (Islamic law) relating to marriage and divorce. Marriage and divorce are central to the regulation of woman's sexuality, since intimate relationships must take place exclusively within that legal framework. The rules related here are those of the classical law, formulated in the first centuries of Islam and no longer entirely in place in any Muslim state. This is not, however, simply a study in the past. Since family law is regarded as the heart of God's plan for society, Muslims have been reluctant to see it openly cancelled, so that all governments, even avowedly secular ones—for instance Iraq under pre-war Baathist rule—have been obliged to approximately form or at least justify their codes in Islamic terms. The restoration of family law is also a central part of the platform of Islamist groups. Where these groups succeed in gaining influence or power, such as in Pakistan, Afghanistan, or Iran, classical Sharíah, or a certain understanding of it, suddenly becomes very relevant. Even among apolitical, liberal Muslims and Muslims living as minorities in the West, Sharíah is of great concern as they try to extract from it a religious ideal to guide them in their most personal relations, or to square it with what they already practise.

The basic norm or structural characteristic of the classical law of marriage and divorce is male hierarchy. This is already suggested in the Qurán (4:34), where it is stated that men are 'set over' (*qawwámún*) women, and also that husbands have the right to discipline their wives in various ways, 'unless they [again] obey you'. The hadíth and Law go on to stiffen this suggestion of the Qurán and give it legal force. A series of hadíths suggests that women who are disobedient or ungrateful to their husbands will go to hell (for example, Bukhárí, *Imán*), while 'obedience' (*tá'ah*) becomes for the wife a legal duty to the extent that she may, if she leaves the marital home without sufficient cause, lose her right to maintenance and dower. The rule of hierarchy in marriage is not, however, absolute. It is mitigated in the legal realm by the fact that the woman is regarded as an individual with her own standing before the law; and then also in the moral realm by constant exhortation, in both the Qurán and hadíths, to the husband to behave fairly and equitably.

The ultimate basis of a Muslim woman's legal rights in marriage is that a mature female, meaning one who has menstruated, is a full legal person. Thus a woman cannot be given away; any right to her person must be granted by herself, freely. This principle generates the rules that a woman must consent to her own marriage, that her family does not receive money for her (since she is not sold), and that she may be freed by a judge from the power of a tutor aiming to prevent a marriage that is to her advantage.

This basic principle has to vie, however, with the power of the 'guardian' (*walí*), usually the father or paternal grandfather, over the minor female. The walí may even contract a marriage for a minor without her consent; though she then has the right upon attaining puberty to repudiate that marriage. The tension between the legal standing of a Muslim female and supervision of her walí is seen in variant opinions about the extent of the walí's power. To mention only two such opinions, the Sunnite Hanafí school says that 'the option of puberty' to repudiate a marriage may be exercised only if the contract can be shown to be defective, while some Shiite jurists assert that a walí is not needed at all.

The legal rights of the woman in marriage are secured through contract, and the essence of a contract of any kind is exchange, based on fully specified terms. The basic exchange of the marriage contract is between the wife's granting her husband exclusive access to her reproductive capacity and to her body for the purpose of pleasure; and his delivering to her an appropriate amount of wealth (the dower, called *mahr*) and undertaking to maintain her as long as the marriage lasts.

On the husband's side, access is unlimited and unfettered, so that a man has a right to enjoyment of any part of his wife's body in any way he wishes, with the exception of contact forbidden by the law such as intercourse during menstruation. Thus she apparently cannot—this is a point that has become slightly controversial in modern times—refuse him sex. The notion that the husband has the right to control his wife's freedom of movement seems to have made its way into the law as a consequence of the right to exclusive sexual access, since that might be threatened if she were to go about without his permission. The notion then apparently grew, under the influence of the powerful idea of male authority, into a right of absolute supervision. We see it emerge in the law of some modern states in the rule that a woman needs the permission of her husband to obtain a passport and travel out of the country.

On the wife's side, the dower is due to her personally, since it is she, as owner of her own self, who is the contractor. Nor does her husband have any power of any kind over it; for the buyer, of course, cannot retain any interest in the sum he pays. The law, beginning with the Qurán (for example, 4:4), is very concerned with ensuring that the bride be given her proper dower and that she be properly maintained. There is a real interest here in fairness of the contract and recognition that the position of the woman is liable to be relatively weak.

As much as the Qurán, hadíths, and law are concerned with marriage, they are even more concerned with divorce. Moral condemnation of divorce—meaning divorce by men, since women are given almost no grounds for it—is very strong. The most famous of several hadíths on this subject says: 'Of all things permitted, divorce is in the eyes of God the most detested' (Abu Dáwúd, *Taláq*). Anxiety over divorce results from tension between the need to give women some protection and preserve the family unit on the one hand, and the reality of male prerogative on the other.

Desire on the part of the law to protect the weak and the legal principle of integrity of the contract could not, however, stand up to the overwhelming force of male authority. The basic governing principle of divorce thus became free action for the man. The Muslim husband is not required to cite any grounds for divorce whatsoever. This is inconsistent with the binding contract that underlies marriage, since, strictly speaking, such a contract can be terminated only for cause. (The inconsistency is actually recognized in some of the law books in the listing of divorce under the heading of *íqá'át,* or 'unilateral actions'.) The logic of the law seems here to break down.

The pattern of the law of divorce thus becomes one of a series of modest obstacles to the husband's power to repudiate his wife. One such obstacle is the rule that divorce remains retractable *(raj'í)* for a period of three menses (Q. 2:228), during which the woman remains, fully maintained, in the marital home. This rule serves not only to forestall hasty divorce, but also to guarantee paternity. The man's obligation to fully pay the dower upon divorce can also act as a restraint. The Qurán suggests arbitration (4:35), and some modern reform has made arbitration a compulsory prelude to divorce. And there is, finally, moral restraint. The man is urged to exercise his prerogative justly and kindly: 'either retain them with kindness, or dismiss them honourably' (Q. 65:2; also 2:231), 'compensate them, and dismiss them in a becoming manner' (33:48)—and other examples from both the Qurán and hadíths.

These are—it must again be emphasized—the norms of the classical law. Though their basic spirit and pattern still influence modern legislation and Muslim thought, they are no longer followed absolutely. Many features of the law of marriage and divorce have been the targets of legislative reform, a movement that has been underway since the nineteenth century. Polygamy is one example. Polygamy is not widely practised in the Muslim world; and most Muslims now adhere to the view, advanced by the famous Egyptian reformer Muhammad Abduh in the late-nineteenth century, that the Qurán actually disapproves of multiple wives except in very restricted circumstances, as it says: 'If you fear that you shall not be able to deal equally with [two, three, or four], then [take] one only' (4:3), and then also: 'You will never be a able to deal equally between women, no matter how much you wish to do so' (4:129). Nevertheless, the difficulty of forbidding what seems to be permitted by God has made banning polygamy outright problematic. Most countries have resorted instead to obstructive rules that make taking more than one wife very difficult. One common such rule is that the first wife must either give her consent, or be allowed to obtain a divorce; another is that the man must demonstrate before a court sufficient reason for taking a second wife, and sufficient means to maintain her. Where polygamy is more common and not legally restrained, such as in some Persian Gulf countries, it has become a live issue for women's groups, who tend to regard it as a social ill.

Women's slender grounds for divorce is another serious issue. Though grounds have been widened in most countries, to include, for instance, desertion and failure to maintain, the idea of free divorce for women has met with determined resistance. An argument often made against women's free divorce is that it would destabilize the family, since women are supposedly more emotional than men and might therefore rush to divorce without thinking. But the real problem, of course, is that it would undermine the authority of the husband, and thus ultimately the imperative of male authority so essential to the traditional view of gender.

It is not, however, legitimate exercise of Sharíah that causes women the most trouble. The Sharíah is, most naturally, fitted to a patriarchal society; but it is, after all, a system of law, concerned with the setting of limits and order and the functioning of society. And Islamic law is actually quite attentive, within the limits of patriarchy, to women and their concerns. It is when patriarchy overruns the limits of the law that the worst abuse occurs.

The quick divorce effected by three declarations uttered in one instant is one illustration of this overflow. Quick divorce (in contrast to the more religiously correct, retractable divorce described above) violates the explicit instruction of the Qurán to the husband (65:1) to observe a waiting period. But it nevertheless forced its way into the law—where it is still termed by the jurists the bid'ah, or reprehensively innovative divorce—through practice. That is, since men were instantaneously divorcing their wives regardless of the Islamic standard, the law was compelled to recognize that as effective. Shiite law, however, refused to admit instantaneous divorce, and a common reform measure in modern times has been to ban it.

Nonpayment of dower has also been a persistent problem. The Qurán (2:229) and the law allow that a woman may give some or all of her mahr in return for her freedom (the khul' divorce). This seems to be a facility provided for women. But instead, it has been widely used by men to force women to buy their way out of an unhappy marriage or gain custody of children. Dower is thus traded off as part of the negotiations of divorce, rather than remaining, as envisaged by the tradition, a fundamental right.

The Islamic right of a woman to approve her own marriage is frequently not respected. The Sharíah assumes a social background in which the family is the girl's advocate and protector. But where family solidarity breaks down or family members turn against a woman who has no resources or power of her own, she is left fully exposed to the unkindness of patriarchy and may be forced into an unsuitable marriage, or virtually sold. The state has not yet sufficiently stepped in to provide protection in such cases, and it is also sometimes prevented from applying laws that it does have on the books—for instance, against child marriage—by the power of family, clan, and tribe.

Here we enter the very extensive territory of the entire dissolution of law and legal norms. Forced marriage without even the formality of consent and threats against couples who marry against the wishes of their families are two such instances. Knowledgeable Muslims roundly condemn such things as un-Islamic; but where they are part of local practice, the population may imagine them to be sanctioned by religion. The claim often made by Muslim women that liberation starts in 'reclaiming our rights according to Islam' begins to seem quite credible.

The phenomenon of so-called 'honour' killings belongs to this tour. The practice seems to have some connection with tribal society; it is found, for instance, among such populations in Jordan and the North West Frontier Province of Pakistan. Honour killing may be used to cover up simple murder or rape. Honour violence must have been known among the pre-Islamic Arab tribes, as the Qurán itself attempts to block it. One measure: a formal accusation of illicit sexual relations (*zina*) must be made, for which the standard of proof is very high—four male witnesses are required, instead of the usual two, and these must have witnessed the act of penetration itself (Q. 4:15; 24:6–8). Others: false accusation (*qadhf*), here assumed to be directed against women, results in lashing of the accusers (24:4); and a husband is to bring an accusation of adultery against his wife merely by solemn oath, which she then refutes by her own swearing (24:6–9), followed by divorce.

There is real recognition here not only of the danger of random violence brought on by sexual defamation, but the likelihood of it falling upon women. The Quránic principle of constraint on honour violence was apparently strong enough that the jurists did not subsequently allow honour to make inroads into the Sharíah. The only concession they made was to permit the theoretical penalty for the most outrageous cases—that is, fornication of free (non-slave) offenders who had been married—to be raised, in accord with long-standing Semitic practice, to stoning. Stoning, of course, originally had in tribal society the symbolic function of allowing the group to reaffirm its collective honour. Thus, many argue, honour killing is at odds with Islamic legal norms. Yet in some nations with majority Muslim population, the crime is forgiven or the penalty is very low, and (male) judges tend to overlook it.

Light punishment for honour killing rests on the belief that cherished social values depend ultimately upon the good behaviour and therefore discipline of women. Women are caught in a similar predicament by the movement in some self-proclaimed Islamic states such as Pakistan and northern Nigeria to reinstitute Sharíah law. Governments set out to establish Sharíah because they wish to legitimate their rule. And Sharíah is effective as a legitimator not only because it is, in the minds of many, equivalent to Islam, but because it is felt that it will secure social order, including the sexual morality believed to be the bedrock of that order, expeditiously. The regime answers to the expectations it has raised by quickly imposing the set of corporal punishments known as 'limits' (*hudúd*), said to have been fixed by God Himself. Now women, as the bearers and symbols of morality, play a central role in the drama. Punishment for sexual crime is typically aimed almost exclusively at females—exactly the victimization the Qurán seeks to forestall! This is accomplished through the device of considering pregnancy or the woman's accusation of rape evidence of the crime of *ziná* (fornication)—while men, due to the high standard of proof mentioned above, are unlikely to be convicted. All this is difficult to justify in Sharíah terms (see Clarke, forthcoming). The point, in any case, is clearly not law, but pseudo-legal scapegoating. By putting sin upon the head of the victim, the authorities hope to give the impression that they are successfully purifying society.

CONSERVATISM/BACKLASH AND SOCIAL CHANGE

Law reform, along with relatively isolated but more sensational instances of Sharíah reaction, are important barometers of change in the Muslim world. The following will consider two other indications of the state of Muslim women today. One is the very extensive modern literature that attempts to establish the ideal position of women in Islam. The other is the lived reality and actions of Muslim women themselves.

Most modern literature on women in Islam is conservative or apologetic, common titles being 'Veiling and Unveiling' (*al-Sufúr wa-al-hijáb*) and 'The Rights of Women in Islam'. Conservative discourse is apt to dwell upon the wisdom of Sharíah as it is, highlighting favourable clauses such as a woman's right to own property and demonstrating the various ways in which the paternal system of the Law ideally provides for and protects her. Unfavourable clauses such as woman's lack of grounds for divorce are likely to be skirted, or their wisdom demonstrated in terms of the welfare of family and society.

The conservative approach may be illustrated by treatment of a verse of the Qurán (4:34) that has become famously problematic in modern times: 'Men are set over women (*al-rijál qawwámún `ala al-nisá*), because God has made one to excel over the other, and because [men] spend their wealth [to maintain] those for whom they are responsible'. Conservatives are likely to point out that the 'excelling' pertains not to spiritual potential, but rather to agnatic responsibility. In the conservative view, the verse thus confirms the divinely mandated social order in which men are both responsible for and supervise women.

Outright misogyny (as can be seen in the interpretation cited above) is not very evident in current conservative discourse, since the goal is to present Islam as the ideal system also for women. Lack of overtly woman-negative material is also likely due to the fact that contemporary writings on 'women in Islam' are now also meant, perhaps even primarily, to attract and convince women themselves. This reminds us that although being cast in a key symbolic role involves a burden, one can also extract from it a measure of power by manipulating that role. Mai Yamani has described a 'new breed of female fundamentalists' that emerged in Saudi Arabia in the 1990s. These women wear a full veil and enter into religious debates in a way that, according to Yamani, 'infuriates religious as well as liberal groups' (1996: 278–80). Some women attached to fundamentalist or liberationist groups have even joined in military action, as in the participation of heavily veiled Chechen women in the October 2002 hostage incident in a Moscow theatre.

Power gained in this way, however, ultimately has to conform to the terms of the system. And the basic terms are, if one relies on the classical version of the Sharíah and traditional understanding of the Qurán, male authority. Female Islamists of the literalist, scripturalist (sometimes called 'fundamentalist') type deal with this aspect by imagining, much as fundamentalists in general do when they speak of an Islamic state, a kind of utopia in which a fully realized Islamic system would ensure the good behaviour of citizens and perfect justice for all. Like the female student of mine who passionately declared, in reply to my statement that men in the classical law may divorce freely, that 'Islam does not allow men to divorce', these women appear to rely on the moral voice of Islam (which does indeed condemn divorce), rather than actual law. They seem to be certain that Muslim men or Muslim society would unfailingly hearken to that voice as they themselves hear it, so that, for instance, all women in an Islamic society would be fully provided for as they stayed home to raise their families, and polygamy, though allowed by the law, would become virtually extinct as wives also fulfilled their duties. In this case, there is no need for 'reform'. Reform only hinders the divinely ordained system from realising itself. The action in 1999 of the Egyptian journalist and Islamist Safinaz Kazem in walking off the set of an *al-Jazírah* television programme when her interlocutor, the first female parliamentarian of Jordan, Toujan Faisal, condemned polygamy—and thus, in Kazem's view, questioned the Qurán—exemplifies the spirit animating this utopian scripturalism.

Faisal's experience points to a basic stricture facing liberal discourse today. The liberals or those who are relatively liberal must demonstrate that their point of view is properly Islamic, and more particularly that it is not influenced by the West. Not to Islamically legitimate one's discourse means marginalization at best, and at worst, threats from extremists, as has in fact happened in the case of Faisal, the veteran Egyptian feminist Nawál al-Sadáwí, and others. Often raised in this context is the old accusation against women asking for change that they are advocating immorality.

Threat is evidently not, however, the prime reason Muslim women reach for an Islamic idiom. Many early feminists—such as Huda Sharáwí of the Egyptian Feminist Union in the early twentieth century—believed that the path to progress for Muslim women lay in following the example of their Western sisters, including casting off the veil. This idea is now outmoded. Most Muslim women along with the rest of the community believe instead that they have their own, distinctive values, such as centrality of the family, rearing of children, and male–female harmony. They want to find a path forward that is authentically Muslim and that preserves these Muslim standards.

This approach rules out, of course, the radical and secular theories of Western feminism. (Female Muslim activists are, in fact, reluctant to call themselves 'feminists' precisely because of such connotations.) It certainly rules out consideration of female homosexuality, which becomes, in these terms, irrelevant. The more modest and rather cautious project of the liberals is instead to promote understandings of Islamic scriptures and history that undermine the principle of male dominance and bring women into the public space.

The liberal argument with regard to scriptures relies on the premise that the spiritual equality clearly established by God in the Qurán (as evident, for instance, in the care He takes to specifically include female believers in statements about religious duties and rewards; for example, 33:35 and other places) also implies social equality. This, however, raises the question of the few problematic verses that just as clearly confer social privileges on men. The verses are explained in various ways—for instance, by asserting that they were meant to refer to male supervision in a male-dominated society that no longer exists, while the basic Quránic principle of equality was meant to endure. Using these kinds of approaches, the American scholar Amina Wadud comes to the conclusion that *qiwámah*, the 'setting over' referred to in the 'men are set over women' verse, actually signifies men's responsibility for, or 'attitudes and treatment' of, women, this being the counterpart of women's responsibility to bear children (1999: 73–4).

To demonstrate that women should share in public space, the liberals turn to history. Instances of women's participation in politics, free movement, and heroics in the early battles of Islam are used to argue that the original model of the Muslim woman was that of a free and active person. Muslim society, liberals insist, should return to and build upon that original model.

This vision, however, runs up against the question of the meaning and intent of *hijáb* (the veil). For while the veil was formerly regarded by many modernists as a symptom of oppression and its removal a sign of liberation, the current Islamic revival has caused it to take on many different meanings. Some liberal Muslims, it is true, would still argue that the verses of the Qurán usually taken to indicate that women should cover are aimed at nothing more than modesty, for both men and women, with no really specific mode of dress specified, as in the following verses:

Say to the believing men that they should lower their gaze and guard their modesty . . . and to the believing women [also]; and that they should not display their adornment . . . and [should] draw their veils over their bosoms (24:30–2).

Even this group, however, has shifted its focus to the issue of free choice. Muslim women, they say, should be able to choose not to veil, *just as they should also have the right, if they wish, to veil*. This change in focus is dictated by the fact that many young Muslim woman today choose to wear hijáb as a sign of their own personal devotion to Islam and proud announcement of their Muslim identity. Hijáb has also come to be understood by many or most Muslims as meaning exclusively clothing, rather than strict confinement to the home as in the traditional view, so that there is less reason in this case to oppose it. Some women even assert that hijáb has liberated them by giving them freedom to move, properly covered and respected, in any space.

The conservative position on hijáb, by contrast, asserts that the Qurán, through the verse cited above as well as several others, has made veiling compulsory. The meaning of the revelation, they say, is clear; and it is confirmed by the long-standing consensus (*ijmá*) of the community. Many conservatives also take hijáb in the sense indicated in the hadíths and classical discussions (and probably also the sense current in most pre-modern urban Muslim societies); that is, woman's confinement to her home, with permission to go out limited, as one famous hadíth suggests, to 'need' (Bukhárí, *Tafsír*). There is a great difference between hijáb as a freely chosen mode of dress and hijáb as domesticity and limitation of space, and it is necessary in listening to debate concerning the veil to understand which is being talked about. This is not always easy, as what is often meant is a varying mix between the two.

The focus, in any case, on hijáb and on preoccupation of the West with the supposed 'oppression' of Muslim women by their religion have tended to obscure the fact that the tendency in the Muslim world today is actually one of gradual but steady progress. This progress is led by the individual efforts and accomplishments of Muslim women themselves, and it is unlikely that fundamentalist reaction will be able to reverse it.

The first thing to notice is the real impact on women's position of incremental social change. These changes have come about as a result of increased urbanization; the national mobilization of the post-colonial era; family ambition, as it becomes clear that daughters are also able to gather wealth and prestige; and demographic shift toward a younger population. Increase in female literacy is one leading example of social change. In the first part of the twentieth century, literate Muslim women were a small minority. But according to

UNESCO figures of about a decade ago, literacy for women between the ages of 15 and 24 in Middle Eastern countries ranged from 36.2 per cent and 46 per cent (compared to 67 per cent and 71.4 per cent for men) in Afghanistan and Morocco, to 90.9 per cent and 96.5 per cent (compared to 99.7 per cent and 98.1 per cent for men) in Libya and Jordan (http://unstats.un.org/unsd/demographic/social/literacy.htm).[5]

Indications are that literacy rates have continued to rise—save, perhaps, in the exceptional case of Afghanistan, where the nationalist ideal of mobilization gave way for a time in the midst of anarchy to the fundamentalist utopianism of the Tálibán. One result of the steep rise in literacy and education is that women have been increasingly successful in earning degrees and entering the professions. In some settings—for instance, Iran and Saudi Arabia—they are said to make up half or more of the university population.

Muslim women also continue, as they have done throughout the twentieth century and before, to form philanthropic and activist organizations to aid their sisters and articulate women's concerns. The by now decades-old campaign for the vote in Kuwait; the anti-Tálibán Revolutionary Association of the Women of Afghanistan (www.rawa.org); the International Network for the Rights of Female Victims of Violence in Pakistan (www.inrfvvp.org); the Women's Aid Organisation of Malaysia (www.wao.org.my); and, in America, the association of Muslim woman lawyers for human rights known as Karámah or 'Dignity' (www.karamah.org) are but a few of hundreds such organizations around the globe. The vigorous activity of Muslim women on their own behalf is not often acknowledged in the West, where the preferred media image is that of the helpless victim in need of aid and rescue.

The task for the future, at least from a liberal point of view, is to have the tradition catch up with these realities. The facts of education, political participation, and state law reform are well ahead of religious thought—despite the efforts of a few innovative clerics such as Ayatollah Muhammad Husayn Fadlallah of Lebanon and Saïdzadeh of Iran. Nor do religious discussions of women place real and difficult issues such as violence against women as concerns to be systematically and forcefully addressed, since the focus is on picturing a kind of ideal harmony between husband and wife, and on the ideal in general. Men's prerogative in personal and social relations, the universal rule of patriarchy enshrined in the classical law, is rarely questioned.

None of these factors is, of course, unique to Islam. Most institutionalized religion is slow to respond to change; indeed, it resists it. In the West, however, women have been able to sidestep religion by developing a separate tradition of secular feminism, and then the religiously committed among them have taken feminist thought and the confidence and authority gained through it and projected it back onto religion. This is not possible to the same degree in the Muslim world today, where the only 'legitimate' thought is Islamic thought.

Thus women are obliged to work within the tradition. And that should not, in fact, be so very difficult, as Islam has many woman-positive resources on which to draw, beginning with the Qurán itself. There is great potential here; and one might argue that progress legitimated by religion will be more lasting and have wider popular appeal. The prime obstacle, of course—again, one not unique to Islam—is that women do not presently own religious authority, so that they are not able to effectively make their views heard and accepted. Islam, however, has the advantage of a long history of women's learning, as well as some permission for women to produce legal rulings. Women's religious learning at the higher levels has, sadly, declined in modern times, but rebuilding and enlarging this tradition could be the key to a new power.

NOTES

1. Terms have not been fully transliterated. Long vowels and glottal stops in Arabic words have been marked only where they might aid in pronunciation.
2. The quoted phrase is from a *hadíth*, one of the 'anecdotes' of the Prophet's sayings and doings that establishes the *Sunnah*. In the eyes of the majority Sunnite school of Islam, Bukhárí and Muslim are the soundest canonical collections of hadíth.
3. The first number refers to the Chapter, or '*Súrah*', of the Qurán; the second refers to the verse, or '*áyah*'.
4. If there was not similar discomfort with woman scholars (discussed below), that may be because the social rules of the game were more clear. Though woman scholars might be more learned than men and even teach them, their ultimate potential authority was, as I will explain, still lesser.
5. All websites in this chapter were accessed 18 September 2003.

REFERENCES

Abbott, Nabia. 1946. *Two Queens of Baghdad*. Chicago: University of Chicago Press.
———. 1973. *Aisha: The Beloved of Mohammad*. New York: Arno Press.
Abou El Fadl, Khaled. 2001. *Speaking in God's Name: Islamic Law, Authority and Women*. Oxford: Oneworld.
Abyad, Malakah. 1981. *Culture et éducation arabo-islamiques au Shám pendant les trois premiers siècles de l'islam*. Damascus: Institut français de Damas.
Ahmed, Leila. 1992. *Women and Gender in Islam*. New York: Yale University Press.
Ask, Karin, and Marit Tjomsland, eds. 1998. *Women and Islamization. Contemporary Dimensions of Discourse on Gender Relations*. New York: Oxford University Press.

Attar, Farid al-Din. 1966. *Muslim Saints and Mystics*. Trans. A.J. Arberry. Chicago: University of Chicago Press.

Awde, Nicholas, trans. and ed. 2000. *Women and Islam: An Anthology from the Quran and Hadiths*. Richmond, Surrey, UK: Curzon.

Berkey, Jonathan P. 1992. 'Women and Islamic Education in the Mamluk Period'. *Women in Middle Eastern History. Shifting Boundaries in Sex and Gender*. Eds Nikki R. Keddie and Beth Baron. New Haven and London: Yale University Press.

Clarke, L. 2003. 'Hijáb According to the Hadíth: Text and Interpretation'. *The Muslim Veil in North America: Issues and Debates*. Eds Sajida Sultana Alvi, Homa Hoodfar, and Sheila McDonough. Toronto: Women's Press: 214–86.

———. Forthcoming. 'Fornication and Stoning'.

Hoffman, Valerie J. 1995. *Sufism, Mystics, and Saints in Modern Egypt*. Columbia: University of South Carolina Press.

Ibn Hishám. 1955. *The Life of Muhammad*. Trans. A. Guillaume. Lahore: Oxford University Press.

Jaschok, Maria, and Jingjun Shui. 2000. *The History of Women's Mosques in Chinese Islam. A Mosque of Their Own*. Richmond, Surrey, UK: Curzon.

Jawad, Haifaa. 1998. *The Rights of Women in Islam*. New York: St Martin's Press.

Khalaf Allah, Ahmad. 1977. *Dirását fí al-nuzúm wa-al-tashrí'át al-islámíyah*. Cairo: Maktabat al-Anjlú al-Misríyah.

Lutfi, Huda. 1992. 'Manners and Customs of Fourteenth-Century Cairene Women: Female Anarchy versus Male Shar'i Order in Muslim Prescriptive Treatises'. *Women in Middle Eastern History. Shifting Boundaries in Sex and Gender*. Eds Nikki R. Keddie and Beth Baron. New Haven and London: Yale University Press.

Mernissi, Fatima. 1975. *Beyond the Veil. Male-Female Dynamics in a Modern Muslim Society*. Cambridge, MA: Schenkman.

———. 1993. *The Forgotten Queens of Islam*. Trans. Mary Jo Lakeland. Minneapolis: University of Minnesota Press.

Mir-Hosseini, Ziba. 1999. *Islam and Gender. The Religious Debate in Contemporary Iran*. Princeton, NJ: Princeton University Press.

Murata, Sachiko. 1992. *The Tao of Islam. A Sourcebook on Gender Relations in Islamic Thought*. Albany: State of University of Albany Press.

Musallam, Basim.1983. *Sex and Society in Islam. Birth Control Before the Nineteenth Century*. Cambridge: Cambridge University Press.

Roded, Ruth. 1994. *Women in Islamic Biographical Collections. From Ibn Sa'd to Who's Who*. Boulder, CO: Lynne Reinner.

El-Saadawi, Nawal. 1999. *A Daughter of Isis: The Autobiography of Nawal El-Saadawi*. Trans. Sherif Hetata. London, New York: Zed Books.

Schimmel, Annemarie. 1997. *My Soul is a Woman*. Trans. Susan H. Ray. New York: Continuum.

Shariati, Ali.1981. *Fatima is Fatima*. Trans. Laleh Bakhtiyar. Tehran: Shariati Foundation.

Smith, Margaret. 1994. *Rabi'a: The Life and Work of Rabi'a and Other Woman Mystics in Islam*. Oxford: Oneworld.

Spellberg, Denise A. 1994. *Politics, Gender, and the Islamic Past: The Legacy of Á'ishah bint Abí Bakr.* New York: Columbia University Press.

Stowasser, Barbara Freyer. 1993. 'Women's Issues in Modern Islamic Thought'. *Arab Women: Old Boundaries, New Frontiers.* Ed. Judith Tucker. Bloomington: Indiana University Press: 3–28.

———. 1994. *Women in the Qur'an, Traditions, and Interpretation.* New York: Oxford University Press.

Wadud, Amina. 1999. *Quran and Woman: Re-reading the Sacred Text from a Woman's Perspective.* New York: Oxford University Press.

Warnock Fernea, Elizabeth. 1998. *In Search of Islamic Feminism. One Woman's Global Journey.* New York: Doubleday.

Yamani, Mai. 1996. 'Some Observations on Women in Saudi Arabia'. *Feminism and Islam. Legal and Literary Perspectives.* Ed. Mai Yamani. New York: New York University Press: 263–81.

Yazbeck Haddad, Yvonne, and John L. Esposito.1998. *Islam, Gender, and Social Change.* New York: Oxford University Press.

FURTHER READING

Ahmed, Leila. *Women and Gender in Islam.* New York: Yale University Press, 1992.

Awde, Nicholas, trans. and ed. *Women and Islam: An Anthology from the Qurán and Hadiths.* Richmond, Surrey, England: Curzon, 2000.

Kimball, Michelle R. and Barbara R. von Schlegell. *Muslim Women throughout the World: A Bibliography.* Boulder, Colo: Lynne Rienner Publishers, 1997.

Roded, Ruth, ed. *Women in Islam and the Middle East: A Reader.* London; New York: I.B. Tauris, 1999.

Warnock Fernea, Elizabeth. *In Search of Islamic Feminism. One Woman's Global Journey.* New York: Doubleday, 1998.

~

CHAPTER 8

WOMEN IN NEW AGE TRADITIONS

Leona M. Anderson and Pamela Dickey Young

INTRODUCTION AND OVERVIEW

New Religious Movements are among the fastest growing of all religions, both in terms of the number of adherents and the number of distinct groups that can be identified under this rubric. New Age groups are a subtype of the New Religious Movement category and the primary focus here. In the context of New Age, this chapter focuses on neopagan movements including Wicca and Ecofeminism, with particular attention paid to those forms of Wicca that are explicitly feminist in their self-understanding. Wicca can be seen as a New Religion with its practice concentrated on empowering individual women and groups of women to create positive change. Ecofeminism is usually identified with the New Age moniker, and it is examined here insofar as it is feminist and it focuses on the state of the world. Included are some comments on the New Age practices of channelling and healing that are sometimes understood as woman-centred. All of the religions and practices included here envision women and their roles as central, but no two see women in exactly the same way. Thus, these traditions offer a variety of ways of thinking about women and, in contrast to many more traditional religions, none of them teach that women are evil or stupid.[1] First, then, some general comments on New Age.

There are several factors that make New Age difficult to come to grips with and these factors permeate the literature. For example, there is no one belief or set of beliefs shared by those who identify themselves as belonging to New Age movements. Although most New Age religions weave material from other religious traditions, as, for example, from Buddhism, Judaism, and so on, into their doctrines and practices, many New Age believers do not identify themselves explicitly with any 'traditional' religion. Nor do they necessarily associate themselves with any particular New Age group or movement, at least not exclusively. In fact, most New Age movements position themselves in opposition to 'traditional' religions.

A second factor to be considered here is that New Age is not organized in any traditional way: there is no single text that is authoritative, no one person or group of persons that is looked to exclusively for religious guidance; and no one set of rituals or practices that all New Age religions or practitioners subscribe to. In general, New Age movements privilege individual experience as the final authority, and this 'experience' can be extremely diverse, both from one movement to another and within individual movements. Further to this point, there is a tendency in New Age religions to use the term *spiritual* and *spirituality* as opposed to *religious* or *religion* to describe themselves and their movements. Implicit in the preference for the term *spiritual* is that it is understood as personal, unique, self-validating, authentic, and authoritative; while religion is thought to be institutional, bureaucratic, social, inflexible, authoritarian, and bound by history and hierarchy. Spirituality emphasizes individual experience over and above the institution, and religion is often associated, in a somewhat derogatory fashion, with the latter. In this context, the tendency of New Age movements to dissociate themselves from mainstream traditions and to situate themselves in opposition to these traditions is much in evidence.

KEY CHARACTERISTICS

New Age religions are so diverse, and the term is so poorly defined, that they are almost impossible to categorize. In its current usage, New Age is descriptive of a variety of traditions, beliefs, and practices. It includes neopaganism, Wicca, Goddess religion, transpersonal psychology, theosophy, and channelling; various healing practices including the use of crystals, astrological charts, herbs, tarot, and group work; and a number of philosophical and psychological movements. Given this multiplicity of practices and concerns, the following sections on channeling and healing are designed as examples of New Age practices and concerns. Not all New Age religions practice channelling; nor do all focus on healing.

Channelling

One of the most striking manifestations of New Age religion is a practice known as channelling. The term is fairly self-explanatory; it refers to the perceived ability of an individual to receive information from a source not accessible by ordinary consciousness. The information gleaned from the channelling experience is sometimes likened to more traditional notions of revelation, at least in many New Age circles. Generally the purpose of channelling is learning and guidance (for example, receiving information regarding the meaning and purpose of life, prediction of future events, and many other types of information that are believed to assist one in living a full and meaningful life). New

Age channellers receive information from a host of sources including angels, spirit-guides, extraterrestrials, masters, gods, goddesses, and animals. Sometimes the channelling experience is achieved in a state of trance and the source transmitting the message takes complete possession of the body of the channeller, sometimes taking the channeller by surprise and completely incapacitating her or him. However, this is not always the case, and, theoretically at least, anyone can act as a channel. In this context, several do-it-yourself publications are available to assist neophytes in developing their channelling abilities. Despite this, there are certain individuals that are considered either to have natural abilities that can be cultivated or to be more gifted than others.

A significant number of channellers are women. Notable and well-known examples include Jane Roberts, who received revelations from an entity known as Seth from 1963 to her death in 1984. Seth is believed to be a disembodied personality who dictated a number of books to Jane. This material, received from Seth and 'scribed' by Jane, is known as the Seth material (Roberts 1970: 11–12). The content of the Seth material can be summarized as follows:

> The range of subject matter in Seth's books is broad. From dreams and out of body travel to life after death. Biblical history, space travel, other dimensions, parallel and probable selves, and behaviour of subatomic particles are just a few of the topics covered. . . . Throughout Seth's work the main themes return again and again . . . 'You create your own reality', and 'You get what you concentrate upon'. (http://www.secretoflife.com/seth/whoseth.html)

Other examples of New Age channellers include J.Z. Knight, whose famous encounters with her entity, Ramtha, are well documented (Hanegraaff: 29–30) and Eva Pierrakos, who, from 1956 through to her death in 1979, received information from 'the Guide', and wrote a series of lectures that came to be known as the Guide Lectures or the Pathwork Lectures. 'Pathwork' is a registered US trademark and refers to the path of personal transformation and spiritual self-realization set out in the lectures of Pierrakos. Pathwork communities throughout the world, including in the US and Canada, seek to interpret these teachings, through individual and group work, as a means for spiritual healing and personal growth. Important to include here as well is *A Course in Miracles*, more generally known as 'the Course'. This text, 'scribed' by Dr Helen Schucman, is a collection of self-study spiritual materials that, through a process of inner dictation, she identified as coming from Jesus (http://www.acim.org/about_acim_section/intro_to_acim.html). The Course is said to have travelled by word of mouth and to have been transmitted by photocopy. In 1975 the Foundation for Inner Peace, a non-profit organization, was founded and published the Course. A workbook consisting of 365 exercises, one for each day of the year, and a brief manual for teachers supplements the main text of the Course. Its contents are summarized in the introduction to the text as follows:

> This is a course in miracles. It is a required course. Only the time you take it is voluntary. Free will does not mean that you can establish the curriculum. It means only that you can elect what you want to take at a given time. The course does not aim at teaching the meaning of love, for that is beyond what can be taught. It does aim, however, at removing the blocks to the awareness of love's presence, which is your natural inheritance. The opposite of love is fear, but what is all encompassing can have no opposite.
>
> This course can therefore be summed up very simply in this way:
> Nothing real can be threatened.
> Nothing unreal exists.
> Herein lies the peace of God.
> (http://www.acim.org/about_acim_section/intro_to_acim.html)

Clearly, women play an important role in the reception of channelled material, often through physical contact with a perceived entity that takes over the channeller's body. It has been argued elsewhere that women are considered to be more susceptible to experiences of possession than men because foreign objects commonly invade women's bodies and, unlike men, women are socialized to accept these intrusions (Sered: 189–90). This is simply to say that it is not a unique situation for a woman to be invaded by an alien organism that occupies a portion of her body. Sered, drawing on the work of Hilary Graham and Ross Kraemer, notes the obvious parallels between pregnancy and spirit possession in her discussion of the gendered dimension of possession rituals (189). Whatever the explanation, a high percentage of channellers represented in New Age traditions are women.

Healing

Health and healing are prominent concerns in many New Age movements. A distinctive feature of many of these movements is that they employ a variety of alternative therapies including the use of herbs, diet, crystals, shamanic diagnostics and cures, magnetic therapy, massage therapy, and various psychological counselling techniques. Traditionally, women have often been associated with healing, especially in the context of herbal remedies and midwifery. Women are often assigned with, or socialized to accept, the role of healer in the context of the family and given the task of maintaining the physical and mental well-being of their family, as, for example, in the notion of 'Dr Mom'. It is thus not particularly surprising that women play important roles in the development and administration of many New Age therapies.

In the context of New Age healing practices, most movements focus on holism and holistic health. Holism refers to the treatment of the whole person, rather than the treatment of any one particular ailment. Primary here is the interaction among physical, emotional, mental and spiritual aspects of the patient's experience, as well as the consideration of social factors and the impact of the wider environment on the well-being of the patient (Hanegraaff: 48–50). The role of the mind is of primary importance in the healing process as described in New Age literature. In this regard, New Age healing traditions contain an implicit critique of modern Western medicine. In particular, they reject the mind–body dichotomy and with it the distinction between physical and mental ailments. It is notable that New Age literature, especially feminist New Age literature, often designates Western medicine as a male-dominated and patriarchal tradition.

New Age healing practices commonly concentrate on personal growth and on questions of balance and harmony, sometimes employing techniques that diagnose imbalance and on cures that address these imbalances. Very often, too, these movements draw inspiration from traditional methods of healing including the use of herbs.

The religious dimension of health and healing, with its emphasis on meaning and the interpretation of various sorts of suffering, are common concerns in New Age literature. Starr Sered notes the following in the context of her study of religions dominated by women:

> I believe that illness is significant to female religious specialists not because they are ill more than other people, but because they themselves see their illnesses as meaningful to their religious roles. (225)

She notes also that 'women religious leaders tend to attribute greater significance to their illnesses' (222). In the context of New Age religions, 'holistic healing is concerned with more than simply "fixing" isolated problems, healing is regarded as promoting harmony in the world and therefore carries at least implicit salvational overtones' (Hanegraaff: 45).

NEOPAGANISM AND WICCA

Two important movements in the New Age tradition are neopaganism and, as one movement within neopaganism, Wicca. Paganism comes from the Latin *paganus* referring to a 'country dweller', but it is used today as a broad term that embraces a variety of religious/spiritual practices and beliefs. *Neopagan* means 'new pagan', a reference to looking back from the present day and recovering pre-Christian traditions of nature worship. Neopagan movements are eclectic and malleable but can be grouped together because of a common desire to see human beings regain their proper place within nature rather than over it, against it, or above it. Through ritual and action, neopagans seek to overcome human alienation from the rest of nature. Magic—or as many Wiccans spell it, 'magick' (to differentiate it from stage magic)—is often viewed as an important part of Wiccan practice. Magic is understood as a source of personal empowerment and evidence of a connection with the Goddess. Ecology is also a central concern. The basic idea is that we, in the modern world, have lost pagan wisdom about our relationship to the natural world, and that the recovery of this wisdom is both desirable and crucial to our well-being. Freedom from external religious authorities is an important feature of all of these movements and it gives scope for inventing and reinventing rituals and sacred texts.

Wicca exists in a significant number of manifestations. It is also known as 'the Craft' and it is probably the most visible of the neopagan movements embraced by women. Often those who consider themselves part of Wicca call themselves witches. While it is safe to say that all Wiccans are neopagans, not all neopagans are Wiccans. The distinctive components of the Wiccan tradition include an emphasis on ritual and magic, a common ethical view of the world, and a focus on the Goddess.

Feminist Wicca has been constructed in large part to meet the needs of feminists who have found the patriarchy of most traditional religious options too much to bear. The Goddess at the centre stands sometimes alongside a God, sometimes alone. In the former case, She is sometimes thought of as Mother Nature, who is in turn understood as encompassing both female and male forces. Together the God and the Goddess create balance. They represent the birth, death, and regeneration of the world, and these events are enacted during neopagan rituals throughout the year. In the latter case, the Goddess is often understood as primary, especially by feminists who are uncomfortable with a male deity.

Most forms of Wicca today are variations of Gardnerian Wicca, which originated in 1939 with Gerald Gardner, a retired British civil servant, and his disciple Doreen Valiente. Essentially this is a nature-based movement focusing on two figures, the Goddess of Fertility and the Horned God. Gardner claims to have been initiated by Dorothy Clutterbuck (or simply Old Dorothy), who practised an ancient form of witchcraft that somehow survived the persecutions of the Middle Ages. Despite these claims, it is clear that Gardner did not revive an old religion, he created a new one.

Among other forms of Wicca, there is Alexandrian Wicca, which began with Alex Sanders, the self-proclaimed king of the witches, and his wife

Maxine. Alexandrian Wicca is a modified version of the Gardnerian type. Alex Sanders is thought to have obtained a Gardnerian *Book of Shadows* and started his own coven from it. He initiated a large number of people, including Janet and Stewart Farrar. Dianic Wicca is essentially a women's movement promoting female spirituality. The members of Dianic covens worship the Goddess as the primary deity and constitute a clear rejection of patriarchal religion. Dianic Wicca emphasizes the Goddess as described by authors including Zsuzsanna Budapest. There are also other varieties of Wicca, including Odinism, which is a modern movement that draws heavily upon Norse and Celtic traditions and essentially seeks to revive pagan traditions of Northern Europe. Members of eclectic Wicca do not belong to one tradition or group; each individual creates her or his own traditions. Eclectic witches have their own beliefs and ideologies and, more often than not, practise alone and are called 'solitaire' Wiccans. They work with herbs, crystals and the like for the betterment of their family and community.

Some of these groups are all-women groups, some are mixed men and women. All-women groups tend to be non-hierarchical; mixed groups tend to have three ranks (Berger 1999: 13). Because in Wicca one is free to function as one's own religious authority, as many as 50 per cent of those who name themselves Wiccans are solo practitioners who might move in and out of covens over periods of time, but who would practise rituals on their own, maybe searching out groups for particular holiday celebrations (Berger 1999: 50).

HISTORY

Neopagans trace their roots to the pagans of pre-Christian Europe, who seem to have based their practice and beliefs on the cycles of the natural world. Pre-Christian pagan traditions are mostly lost to us historically, though some remnants of that tradition have been extrapolated from various pieces of archaeological evidence such as Stonehenge. As some neopagans would have it, pagans were persecuted and their traditions went underground, and were lost in the process. Margaret Murray contributed to this notion of a long history of persecution by suggesting the historical witch trials were attempts to eliminate adherents of an ancient religion (Berger 1999: 21). The *Burning Times* is a phrase found in Wiccan literature and the subject of the National Film Board of Canada film produced in 1990. The film argues that the witch hunts, which swept Europe from the fifteenth to the seventeenth century, contributed significantly to the destruction of pagan religion. For many Wiccans and many neopagans, these events evidence the results of misogyny, religious intolerance, and patriarchy, all of which Wiccans seek to overcome.

The notion of witchcraft as a continuing religion with a long history has been a powerful one for many neopagans, especially feminists, who want to think of the possibility not just of a contemporary religion without patriarchy, but of a pre-patriarchal religion to which one can return. Within Wicca itself and among religious studies scholars who are interested in Wicca there are active debates about whether the tradition is ancient or newly invented, or what parts of the tradition might be said to be ancient and what newly invented.

Those who argue for Wicca as an ancient religion usually draw on the evidence of prehistoric archaeology to point to times and places where the Great Goddess was central to human worship. The archaeological work of Marija Gimbutas in Central and Eastern Europe led her to use evidence from burial sites to theorize that in the Paleolithic (beginning 40,000 BCE) and Neolithic (8000–3000 BCE) periods, women and men were social equals and that society was peaceful and harmonious. Gimbutas and others also propose that the many female figures, especially figures with prominent breasts and genital markings, were goddess figures, pointing to the centrality of goddess worship as connected to social equality for women and men (Gimbutas 1982, 1989; Stone 1976).

There is also some evidence to support the existence of goddess worship of some form in other locations, as, for example, in the Indus Valley, which dates to approximately 2000–3000 BCE. The excavations at the ancient cities of this civilization, most notably at Mohenjo-daro and Harappa, have uncovered a large number of female figurines that have been interpreted as evidence of fertility worship. They have also been understood as confirmation that the worship of a Great Goddess, probably associated with Mother Earth, dominated the religious life of this civilization. The case for the worship of a female figure or figures in this location is complicated, though, by the absence of dominant female figures in the early Vedic tradition in the Indian subcontinent. At the village level in India, there is a proliferation of goddesses who have probably been worshipped since very ancient times. These goddesses are often associated with agriculture and are worshipped to ensure fertility of crops and the like. Male deities at this level tend to play a secondary role. Worship of goddesses gains significant momentum in the post-Vedic era. The numerous goddesses who emerge in mainstream, brahmanic Hinduism are sometimes interpreted as the resurgence of a goddess tradition that had been present since the Indus Valley civilization. Whatever the case, goddesses continue to flourish in India in modern times.

Goddesses in all locations tend to be complex and multifaceted, and there are many ways of understanding them. Sometimes they are presented as reflections of family dynamics, often using psychoanalytic method. In some of these studies, religion is treated as an epiphenomenon of childhood development.

Sometimes the goddesses are understood as parts or emanations of one Great Goddess. In his study of the Indian goddess Santoshi Mā, for example, Kurtz argues that she is simply a variant on the Great Goddess theme, in this case as the goddess Durgā with a makeover (14). There is also a tendency to present the goddesses as if they have (or should have) fixed personalities. Hence, Kālī is malevolent and Sītā is benevolent. While goddesses do have predominant character traits, and while some of the goddesses tend toward life affirmation and others tend toward life denial, all goddesses possess a range of emotions and character traits. Sorting the goddesses into artificial categories is hardly helpful.

All history is interpretation. Those who accept the idea of early societies that valued women and men equally and worshipped the goddess point out that there have been powerful patriarchal academic forces ranged against such opinion (Christ 1997). Other feminist scholars, however, think that the evidence used by Gimbutas and others, though interesting, is not sufficient to make the historical case that many want to make (Eller 2000). We cannot know, for example, how all those female figures were used. We do not know for sure if they were goddess figures or what role they played in societal life and story.

For many Wiccans, an equally important component of their tradition is not so much the recovery of lost history, but the power of goddess traditions in the present. Whether or not there was a religion of the Great Goddess in prehistoric times, there is one today. Whether or not women ever ruled in matriarchies, women are taking power today. Whether or not contemporary witchcraft has its roots in the Stone Age, its branches reach into the future (Starhawk 1982a: 415–16).

TEXTS, RITUALS, AND INTERPRETATIONS

Wicca is not a text-based religion. Ritual, rather than texts, are at its heart, although texts are used in the service of ritual. One of the striking features of Wicca is that there are no official sacred texts or official sacred rituals. Nor are there any universal rules regarding Wiccan behaviour, primarily because Wicca is not a legalistic or codified tradition. Indeed, the opposite is the case. Each group, or practitioner, decides on what is important for their practice. Texts and ritual can be drawn from almost anywhere, and many books are available to guide groups and solitary practitioners. In almost all Wiccan circles, creativity and inventiveness are considered desirable, and poetry and novels by women often provide textual sources for use in rituals. Individuals and groups have widely used textual material from Gardner and Gimbutas. In Wicca, women such as Merlin Stone, Zsuzsanna Budapest, Starhawk, and

Carol Christ have been recognized as leaders and have influenced the movement through their writing and speaking. Their works often function as central texts. There is some consistency between groups because material is shared at pagan festivals and through electronic media.

One of the most widely quoted texts is from Merlin Stone: 'In the beginning, people prayed to the Creatrix of Life, the Mistress of Heaven. At the dawn of religion, God was a woman. Do you remember?' (Stone 1976: 1). This quote is sometimes paired with one from Monique Wittig (1985):

> There was a time when you were not a slave, remember that. You walked alone, full of laughter, you bathed bare-bellied. You say you have lost all recognition of it, remember. . . . You say there are not words to describe it, you say it does not exist. But remember. Make an effort to remember. Or, failing that, invent.

Although Wiccan belief and practice is greatly varied, there are some ideas that keep recurring. One of these is the Wiccan rede: 'eight words the Wiccan rede fulfil-an' it harm none, do what ye will' (see, for example, Budapest: 214). *Rede* means advice or counsel.[2] This maxim is contrasted to the rules and regulations of organized religions, an important feature of Wicca as noted above. It is used as a general ethical guideline to indicate that personal freedom is restricted by the need to consider the well-being of everyone. Wiccans are cautious about their relationships with others and especially cognizant of their relationship with the earth. 'Harm none' applies equally to people, to animals, and to the earth. The Wiccan rede is easily comparable to the golden rule found in a variety of other traditions.

Another central idea is that what you do, either for good or ill, returns to you. Typically, this is expressed in the Rule of Three:

> Ever mind the Rule of Three
> Three times what thou givest returns to thee
> This lesson well, thou must learn
> Thee only gets what thou dost earn!
> (http://Wiccachile.tripod.com/moon/rule3.htm)

The Rule of Three basically cautions one to be careful what one wishes for, but also it is about the consequences of our actions and the relation of our actions and their results to the rest of the world. It thus focuses on the interconnectedness of the universe. The Rule of Three is about taking responsibility for one's actions, and it means that whatever you do, it will come back on you. In the end, though, the individual is the final authority, although individuals may have to temper that authority if they choose to belong to groups. Wiccan groups tend to be small (some say no more than 13 members per group) and formulate and reformulate over time as members enter and leave.

Wiccan rituals have several basic elements. Usually, a circle is cast, or marked out, to indicate the sacred space for the ritual. The powers or energies of all four quarters/directions are summoned. After the ritual, there is feasting and celebration, commonly called 'eating cakes and wine'. The circle that was marked out is 'unwound' at the end (Berger 1999: 16). In rituals, depending on the group and the purpose for which the ritual is being held, various powers and forces are called upon. Goddesses' names, for example, are often invoked to give energy, strength, and assistance to those who need it. Ritual expressions at Wiccan rituals include 'hail and welcome', 'hail and farewell', and 'merry meet and merry part, and merry meet again'. Rituals are used both to celebrate the sabbats and to 'raise energy' for magical workings. 'According to Gardner, Witches are able to project energy from their bodies, through dance, song, meditation, and directed thought that can be used to perform magical acts' (Berger 1999: 11).

Many Wiccan rituals involve a recitation from the 'Charge of the Goddess'. The 'Charge' is a poem attributed to Doreen Valiente, a student of Gerald Gardner. It was originally found in the Gardnerian *Book of Shadows,* a text written by Gerald Gardner outlining a sequence of rituals and Craft laws. It is revered by Wiccans as a statement of reverence of the Goddess and of nature (http://www.branwenscauldron.com/shadows_charge.html). More recently, the *Charge* has been reworked by Starhawk (http://www.reclaiming.org/about/charge.html).

Wiccans use various implements in their rituals. Almost every Wiccan coven has a ritual knife or sword (athame) and a cup (chalice). Some Wiccans have bells, candles, pentacles, brooms, wands, and a number of other tools. Ritual tools connect the practitioner with the elements and are used to direct her personal power. The *athame* is a ritual knife associated with the element of fire and used to direct energy, as, for example, in casting a ritual circle. The *wand* is a tool of communication associated with the element of air. The *chalice* holds the wine that is shared by the celebrants and is associated with the element of water, representing the womb of the Mother. The consumption of the beverage in the chalice symbolizes renewal and revitalization and connection to the Goddess. The *pentacle* is a disc on which the pentagram (a five-pointed star) is inscribed. It is linked to the element of earth, as it encompasses and protects everything within the circle. It is also a symbol of wisdom and is worn as an amulet of protection. The five points represent the elements: Earth, Air, Water, Fire, and Spirit. In rituals the pentacle symbolizes connection with the earth.

There are eight sabbats throughout the year that correspond to the ancient agricultural festivals. The celebration of these sabbats is designed to attune the practitioner to nature. The eight sabbats mark important moments in what many Wiccans refer to as the 'wheel of the year': the two solstices, the two equinoxes, and four other days.

Ostava, on 21 March, celebrates new beginnings and fertility. It signals the spring. On 1 May (Beltane) fertility and growth are celebrated. The summer solstice is recognized on 21 June, the longest day of the year. Lammas on 1 August celebrates first harvest. The Autumn equinox, on 21 September, acknowledges death. The recognition of seasonal change from summer to fall culminates in Samhaim on 31 October where the interface between the living and the dead is considered strongest. The 21 December marks the winter solstice, and Yule. This darkest day also marks the turning of the seasons and heralds the return of sun. On 2 February, Imbolc, or Candlemas, marks the end of winter. Wiccans also celebrate the cycles of the moon in rituals known as esbats.

Rituals are celebrated to mark rites of passage, birth and death, menarche, marriage (hand fasting), menopause, and various stages in relationships. They also are occasions for healing. For the people who celebrate them, the rituals are about self-identity and the capacity to change. They posit an ideal self to which the Wiccan aspires and offer her the power and support to create that ideal self. Rituals are about self-empowerment. In feminist Wicca, rituals are usually quite specific about creating strong, powerful women and, if men are part of the group, about helping get men in touch with their 'feminine' side. Rituals are said to raise 'energy' as a power for changing one's life. In any ritual the actual dancing, singing, or chanting is thought to bring about a group or communal will for change that is allied with the will of the goddesses and gods invoked (see Berger 1999: 31).

Wiccans embrace and understand the practice of magic in varying degrees. Magic usually refers to the ability to affect the outcomes of events through communal or individual thought and ritual action. Some practitioners think that there is a direct causative link between spells and events in the world. For others, the link is one where the participants' consciousness is affected by the ritual, thereby changing the outcome of events. Most Wiccans cast spells and practise magic, though these are not required. Other New Age practitioners also practise magic.

There is an ongoing debate in Religious Studies as to the distinction between magic and religion. In this debate, magic is usually contrasted with religion: magic is seen as a way of manipulating the universe by using specific spells, whereas religion does not see the universe as ultimately manipulable in this way, and, thus, seeks harmony with the universe rather than control over it. The use of magic in Wicca, however, tends to be less about manipulation than about tapping into the power of the Goddess and using that power to effect positive change in the world. The Wiccan world view has been identified as 'enchanted'. As Hanegraffe remarks:

> The defense of 'magick' by neopagans is very clearly based on a rejection of the 'cold world of cause and effect' in favour of an 'enchanted' world . . . . Neopagan magic indeed functions as a means of invoking and reaffirming mystery in a world which seems to have lost it. . . . (84)

SYMBOLS

Wiccans may invoke a variety of gods and goddesses from other mythologies, worship an independent figure known as the Goddess or worship the Goddess together with a figure known as the God. There are no definite rules. In those groups where the Goddess and the God are both invoked, they are conceived of as complementary, not oppositional. For some, the emphasis is on the Goddess, especially the goddess of the earth or the moon. For others, the Goddess/God are metaphorical ways to talk about qualities within oneself. For still others, the Goddess/God are convenient symbols to reference something that is completely beyond human understanding. In feminist Wicca, although a God is sometimes also invoked, the Goddess is the central divine figure. The Goddess of Wicca is understood to be the Creatrix, the Earth Mother, and the Queen of Heaven. Wiccans often refer to their beliefs as *thealogy*, in reference to the Greek word *thea*, meaning goddess, emphasizing the Goddess component in their belief system.

Some Wiccans talk about the Goddess and see her as one goddess having many and varied names from a variety of historical, cultural, and contemporary traditions. Others talk about goddesses in the plural without reference to one Great Goddess. Some think of the goddess(es) as existing beyond the consciousness of those who invoke them. Others see the goddess(es) existing only as symbolic of elements within the self. Often, in Wiccan ritual, women name themselves as goddesses. Many would say that all these ways of talking of the goddess(es) are appropriate and valid. Thus, often polytheism, monotheism, and pantheism exist side by side, and practitioners reject the need to choose only one way of seeing the world.

The sources for goddess names and images are eclectic and wide-ranging. Some Wicca covens invoke Greek and Roman goddesses such as Hecate and Isis, or the goddesses of Africa, Northern Europe, or the ancient Near East. Some invoke invented Goddesses, such as the goddess Asphalta, the goddess of parking spaces (Eller 1993). Sometimes the goddesses are invoked through their historical stories, sometimes only their names are recited.

The symbol of the goddess(es), however one thinks of their existence, is considered crucial for women who are exploring their own religious identities apart from traditional patriarchal religions. In her groundbreaking essay 'Why Women Need the Goddess: Phenomenological, Psychological and Political Reflections', Carol Christ argues that Goddess affirms 'female power, the female body, the female will, and women's bonds and heritage' (Christ 1979: 276) in ways that are not affirmed if divinity is male.

One popular way of speaking of and seeing the Goddess is in a threefold form of maiden, mother, and crone. As maiden, she is associated with the waxing moon. As mother, she is the goddess of fertility and growth and she is associated with the full moon. As crone, she is associated with the waning moon and the underworld, including death and decay. This affirmation of the Goddess also serves to affirm women's lives throughout the life cycle.

The Goddess is always associated with nature. She is Mother Earth. She is alive and exists in all things. She is closely attuned to the agricultural and fertility cycles of the year. Often in Wicca, it is assumed and celebrated that women are more aligned with their bodies, that they are more integrated with the rest of the natural world, than are men. Such arguments tend to give rise to a dichotomized view of maleness and femaleness that re-inscribes traditional views of women and valorizes these views. Thus, women are on the 'nature' side of the nature/culture split, and men are the culture-creators (see Ortner 1974). Some feminists argue that this simply replicates a patriarchal gender split with a romanticized view of women as somehow above the baser things created in male culture (such as war, for example). Others worry that this categorization assumes an essentialized view of both women and men that sees female nature and male nature as static, fixed, ahistorical entities.

When the God of Wicca is invoked, he is conceived of as the Horned God, and he functions as the consort of the Goddess. He is often associated with the goat-footed god, Pan. Wiccans worship him as the god of fertility and the god of the hunt. He is also the sacrificial victim whose death yields life. He is linked with Dionysius and Adonis as a god of the harvest. His death takes place at harvest and signals the gathering of the grain and his coming resurrection out of the womb of the Goddess. This deity is also aligned with Osiris as a god of fertility, death, and resurrection. The myth of Osiris describes his death and dismemberment and his resurrection at the hands of Isis, who gathers the pieces together and restores him to life again. Cyclical change is important to Wicca; death and rebirth are popular themes in Wiccan ritual. Thus, the Wiccan cycle of myths, as celebrated in the sabbats, are fairly common in Wiccan circles. In an ever-repeating cycle, the Goddess gives birth to the Horned God, they fall in love, he dies, and the Goddess descends into the realm of the dead.

Sometimes the Goddess is paired with the God in complementary fashion; but in feminist Wicca, the Goddess usually takes central place and the God is her consort—necessary for fertility, but not the main force to be reckoned with.

SEXUALITY

Wiccans see sexuality as essentially positive and there are several characteristics in Wicca that point toward an open attitude to sexuality. The explicit affirmation of the human body, especially the naked human body, is extended to an affirmation of sexuality as good. Sexuality is part of the sacred, not something separate from it, and sexuality is acknowledged as an aspect of Goddess. Motherhood is not separated from sexuality as it tends to be in Christianity, where the major symbol of motherhood is the Virgin Mother Mary. Nor is sexuality separated from the other things we do in our lives. We are sexual beings, erotic beings in all we do, not just in genital contact.

The celebration of Beltane (1 May) is an explicit celebration of sexuality as participants dance around the maypole. 'The dance symbolizes the sex act as men and women holding brightly colored ribbons weave in and out. The maypole is envisaged as a phallic symbol that is placed in a hole in the mother earth' (Berger 1999: 17).

In Wicca, there is a desire to negate the perceived rules and regulations of Christianity or Judaism in this context. Generally in traditional patriarchal societies, often bolstered by religious argument, women's sexuality is regulated because women are men's possessions, and ownership of them is passed from father to husband. Regulation of female sexuality also serves to guarantee paternity. Wiccans generally reject this sort of thinking and affirm women's sexual autonomy.

The maxim 'Do what you will and harm none' leaves quite a bit of latitude for sexual relationships and sexual practice, especially when we recognize that individuals are considered their own final arbiters of authority. Thus, there are no rules governing sexual practice in or outside of marriage except the rule of harming none. This has had interesting ramifications for bringing up a second generation within Wicca, as Helen Berger notes (1999: 92–6). Open affirmation of sexuality and a desire to teach children positive lessons about sexuality need to be combined with ensuring that children and teenagers are not exploited sexually.

Thus, responsible sexuality is important, and safe sex is expected. Although fertility is important, women's control over their own bodies is seen as more important, so there are no ethical questions surrounding the use of birth control. With regard to abortion, it is generally agreed that it is a serious matter, but not one that one individual can decide for another.

Gay and lesbian relationships are openly affirmed as good. Some Wiccan groups have only gay or lesbian or bisexual members. Such a stance is a far cry from the rejection or grudging acceptance of gay and lesbian sexuality in many religious traditions. This affirmation of gay and lesbian sexuality also means that there has had to be a certain amount of rethinking of the separate gender/sex roles and rethinking of the emphasis on literal as opposed to symbolic or metaphorical fertility.

> [S]exuality can be a powerful expression of our connection to others and to all beings in the web of life. Sexual energy can be an almost irresistible force drawing us to connect with ordinary selves, opening up our deepest feelings, connecting us to the soul as well as the body of another, expanding the limited boundaries of the ego. Sexuality can make us intensely aware of our immersion in the rhythms of the universe, our ties to the whole web of life. For us, sexuality can also become a mode of deep communication, a profound expression of intelligent embodied love. All sexual relationships, whether homosexual or heterosexual, monogamous or nonmonogamous, have this potential. But when we use our sexuality of [sic] dominate or violate, when we take our own pleasure without concern for the other, when we create children we cannot nurture, we rupture the web of life. (Christ 1997: 147)

SOCIAL CHANGE

Wiccans tend to be optimistic about their ability to connect with the immanent divine and to change their lives and the world. One of the common features of New Age spirituality generally, including the Wiccan tradition, is its emphasis on holism. Hanegraffe remarks in this respect, '. . . it is important to emphasize from the outset that the term "holism", in a New Age context, does not refer to any particular, clearly circumscribed theory or worldview' (Hanegraaff 1996: 119). This emphasis means a rejection of all types of dualistic thinking. Wicca is particularly critical of traditional systems for their dualistic way of conceiving of the world and of persons in the world. This includes a rejection of the split between body/mind and spirit/matter.

> The only thing which demonstrably unites the many expressions of 'holism' is their common opposition to what are perceived as non-holistic views, associated with the old culture which the New Age movement seeks to replace or transform. (Hanegraaff 1996: 119)

This quotation applies equally to Wicca.

Wicca is concerned with unity, interconnectedness, and inter-relatedness. Most Wiccans believe, to some degree or other, in the immanence of the deity in the natural world, especially in the cycle of the seasons, and in the individual self. They place great value on the earth, and tend to speak of an immanent deity and an enchanted creation as opposed to a transcendent divinity and a transcendent creation. There is here a sense of personal connection to the divine life source, which is open to contact through psychic power, mysticism, or natural magic.

One of the criticisms often made is that Wicca is a fairly homogeneous movement: white, upper-middle class, mostly well educated. Thus, individual fulfillment has often been privileged over social change. Many of the women studied by Eller (1993: 200–4) saw their spiritual and ritual practices as the main ways to effect social change, through asking the Goddess for intervention, through magic, and/or through changing themselves. Social change would be achieved in these ways, rather than through traditional political interventions.

The women Eller studied also were more likely to see the venues for cultural and social change as 'art, music, literature, language, mythology, folklore and, most importantly, of course, religion' (1993: 203) than to focus their attention on changing laws and political leadership. Wiccans do not expect or even hope for change to be achieved quickly. They recognize that political activists often suffer burnout if there is no community to sustain them in the long haul, and thus they privilege community and support networks.

At the same time, many women in this movement have tried to expand the Wiccan agenda along political lines. In *The Politics of Women's Spirituality*, Charlene Spretnak (1982) gathers a collection of articles that seek to show how spiritual power and political power are intimately intertwined.

Starhawk is one of the most famous devotees of the Goddess who is deeply involved in political activism. She is the author of many books, including the early and influential *The Spiral Dance: A Rebirth of the Ancient Religion of the Great Goddess* (1979) and has been a consistent voice for Goddess spirituality over a long period. She is a member of the Covenant of the Goddess, a league of covens that has been recognized as a Church in the US since 1975, and she has been active in social movements for more than three decades. She has also been involved in antinuclear protesting on several US sites. She has worked for sustainable development in El Salvador and Nicaragua. Recently she has been involved in the anti-globalization movement. Her website (www.starhawk.org) includes an activism page, which lists a number of alerts and reports on ongoing economic and ecological actions in which she and other pagans are involved. This page includes not only commentary on why she takes the positions she does, but also poetry, spells, and rituals designed to accompany the political actions.

On her Activism page she explains why she thinks it is important for those who follow the Goddess to be politically involved.

> Because I believe the earth is a living being, because we are all part of that life, because every human being embodies the Goddess, because I have a fierce, passionate love for redwoods and ravens, because clear running water is sacred, I'm an activist. And because the two hundred richest people in the world own as much wealth as the poorest forty percent, because every eco-system, traditional culture, old growth forest and life support system on the planet is under assault, and because the institutions perpetuating this un-just system are global, I'm kept very busy! (www.starhawk.org/activism/activism.html)

Ecological issues and issues involving the status and rights of women and gay/lesbian rights are important political concerns for Wiccans. Referring to a concept she derives from Anthony Giddens (1991), Berger speaks of the most important type of politics in Wicca as 'life politics', by which she means living in a way that is consistent with one's commitments. Within Wicca, living in a manner consistent with maintenance of the global ecosystem, supporting gender equality and the rights of others, are embedded components in the rituals, chants, and goals of the participants. Wicca is a moral system in the making, one which will never have the ultimate set of rules and regulations that typify the religious and moral systems that developed in earlier eras. It does, however, provide a form of political and moral life that helps to unify this com-munity (Berger 1999: 81).

WOMEN'S OFFICIAL AND UNOFFICIAL ROLES

Wicca is popular among feminists because it tends to be woman-friendly and earth based. Wicca worships the sacred as immanent in nature. Unlike some New Age movements that are led by charismatic men, Wicca has been self-con-sciously egalitarian in its leadership patterns. Women have always been leaders and participants in Goddess traditions, which embrace women's leadership rather than coming to it reluctantly, as most other religious traditions have done. Every member of a group is often referred to as a priestess. 'Having strug-gled to free themselves from traditional religion and from personal relationship in which men were granted automatic authority over them, spiritual feminists are suspicious of anyone telling them what to do' (Eller 1993: 90).

Most Wiccans begin their practice by attending festivals or other celebra-tions. Sometimes they form open groups called circles, which anyone can attend. Covens are more formal groups of like-minded Wiccans who meet and sometimes practise magic. New covens are traditionally created by a process called 'hiving', whereby one or more members of a group, led usually by a priestess, leaves one coven to form his or her own independent group. Covens also celebrate rituals and share both knowledge and companionship. Usually there is a High Priestess or Priest who leads the rituals and keeps the coven's *Book of Shadows*. The *Book of Shadows* is a customized reference book for Wiccans. It contains information on myth, liturgy, and one's own writings or records of dreams and magical workings. Many are available in print and online. However, not all Wiccans have such a book.

Forms and styles of leadership vary from group to group, but some groups model themselves on existing ones. Leadership responsibilities with a group often rotate from person to person (Eller 1993: 91). This means that each member usually has opportunity to prepare and lead the group's rituals and also to participate in other leadership tasks required by the group.

Some are recognized by others as leaders, especially those who were early participants in the Wiccan movement and those who have written widely, for example, Zsuzsanna Budapest, Starhawk, and Merlin Stone. And often a book by one of these early founder figures becomes the basis around which a group is organized.

There are generally three levels of training for a priestess or priest in the Wiccan tradition, though this varies from group to group. Most often these levels are referred to as degrees: hence, first degree, second degree, and third degree. These degrees are based both on knowledge and experience. Each is acknowledged by a formal initiation ceremony, sometimes involving an oath and the presentation of magical tools. In the first and third degree initiations, the initiate takes on a Craft name. Each ritual performance is concluded with food and drink. The priestess is generally not paid and her purpose is to act as a guide in rituals, and to teach and give advice.

Wicca privileges personal experience over any particular belief system. There is a marked tendency to allow for all sorts of personal experiences as spiritual. Wiccans have a healthy respect for diversity, and they are fairly tolerant of a wide range of beliefs, but personal experience is almost always the final authority. Wiccans tend to believe that all persons create their own paths and should be allowed to follow those paths as long as none is harmed. There is a tendency to speak of 'spirituality' and not 'religion'. Wiccans are suspicious of traditions that require sole allegiance to one way of being or believing: for Wicca, there is no monopoly on truth or revelation. Wicca is not a tradition that seeks converts, and they tend to be suspicious of any sort of evangelical tradition. The principle of gender equality is sometimes placed side by side with an essentialism that re-inscribes women as more connected to the body and nature than men are (Berger 1999: 45–6). And, like all social and religious movements, Wicca is connected to the wider society's roles and expectations of men and women.

BACKLASH

In a significant way, Wicca is a backlash tradition. A feature of this tradition, which most Wiccans share, is that it finds traditional religion unacceptable. Wiccans hold institutionalized Christianity responsible for the decline of paganism generally and for the negative image of Wiccans today. One of the features of Wicca is the conviction that Western conceptions of religions are narrow, confining, and given to patriarchy. As Vivianne Crowley remarks:

> Wicca does not believe, as do the patriarchal monotheisms, that there is only one correct version of God and that all other God forms are false: the Gods of Wicca are not jealous Gods. We therefore worship the personification of the male and female principle, the God and the Goddess, recognizing that all Gods are different aspects of the one God and all Goddesses are different aspects of the one Goddess, and that ultimately these two are reconciled in the one divine essence. There are many flowers in the garden of the divine and therein lies its beauty. (Vivianne Crowley 1989: 11–12 quoted in Hanegraaff: 185)

Another component of the backlash is that many Wiccans understand their legacy as one of persecution. It is important to remember that only in 1951 were laws against the practice of witchcraft repealed in England. Contemporary North Americans are generally content to see religion as an individual choice and so, by and large, there has not been a groundswell of negative reaction to New Age religious choices. We are not claiming that somehow Wicca has become 'mainstream' or that those who are practitioners do not need to be wary of others who might consider their beliefs and practices marginal. Today, however, freedom of religion in both the US and Canada, coupled with societal views of the priority of individual choice, means that New Age practitioners have basic protections for their religious preferences. The exception to this tolerance is, however, the reaction of some conservative Christian groups. Such groups tend to fear all forms of neopaganism as counter to the biblical witness. In particular, polytheism or worship of the Goddess rather than the 'one true' God, the embrace of sexuality without 'rules', and the use of the term *witch* are seen to be antithetical to the Christian scriptures. Wiccans are accused of being Satanists, devil worshippers, and practitioners of Black Magic. Neopaganism generally and Wicca in particular have thus been 'demonized' in some circles and tend to be viewed with suspicion. One source of the demonization is the

Wiccan worship of the Horned God, who is sometimes equated, especially among certain Christian groups, with Satan or the Devil. A common citation in this regard is Ephesians 6:12: 'for we wrestle not against flesh and blood, but against principalities, against powers, against the rulers of the darkness of this world, against spiritual wickedness in high places'. The Christian Broadcasting network led by Pat Robertson uses the terms *Wicca* and *Satanism* interchangeably. The Wiccan position is that they do not worship the devil, nor do they believe in hell.

A quick search of the Internet reveals many sites that recount the dangers of Wicca, paganism, witchcraft, and so on. In fact, most of these sites lump together as 'occult' many of the New Age religious views, and thus they often do not differentiate particular types of neopaganism. Typical of what is found on such sites is the following:

> I know that many in Wicca do state that they do not believe in Satan, and therefore cannot be Satanic. There are only two forces at work in this world, good and evil. Good is obedience to the words of Jesus Christ, the King of kings. Evil is disobedience to his word. Simply stated, if you do not serve Jesus Christ, you serve Satan. There is no in-between and it makes no difference what one claims. (www.thunderministries.com/cults/Wicca.html)

There are also numerous pagan and Wiccan sites that refute these Christian critiques. Thus, interreligious debate between followers of Wicca and followers of other religions is lively on the Internet.

UNIQUE FEATURES

A striking example of concepts that distinguish goddess religions from other religions examined in this book is the elastic concept of the goddess. She functions as an inclusive deity, infinitely adaptable, and affirming to the lives of women. A second distinctive feature is the loose organization of these religions and their lack of exclusivity. The final section looks at Ecofeminism, which is a central focus for many neopagans.

Concept of the Divine

The Wiccan conception of the divine is unique in that, generally, there is little interest in precise formulations about the Goddess. She is diverse. Ultimately, the authority is individual experience. As Starhawk remarks:

> This book is about the calling forth of power, a power based on a principle very different from power-over, from domination. For power-over is, ultimately, the power of the gun and the bomb, the power of annihilation that

backs up all the institutions of domination. Yet the power we sense in the seed, in the growth of a child, the power we feel writing, weaving, working, creating, making choices, has nothing to do with threats of annihilation. . . . It is the power that comes from within. There are many names for power-from-within, none of them entirely satisfying. It can be called spirit—but that name implies that it is separate from matter, and that false split, as we shall see, is the foundation of institutions of domination. It could be called God—but the God of patriarchal religions has been the ultimate source and repository of power-over. I have called it immanence, a term that is truthful but somewhat cold and intellectual. And I have called it Goddess, because the ancient images, symbols, and myths of the Goddess as birth-giver, weaver, earth and growing plant, wind and ocean, flame, web, moon and milk, all speak to me of the powers of connectedness, sustenance, healing, creating. (Starhawk 1982b: 3–4)

Conscious invention is a unique characteristic of neopagan groups, including Wicca. In Wicca, the process of invention and change of ritual, organization, and so on is expected and held in high esteem. Hence, whereas many religious traditions change slowly and sometimes virtually imperceptibly, change and destabilization is a central value in Wicca. If the ritual does not suit the group, change the ritual. If the group needs new customs to accommodate new exigencies, change the customs.

Organization

As mentioned above, in goddess-based spiritual practices there are no central authorities and there is not a lot of organization, especially bureaucratic organization. Each group makes its own rules regarding its leaders, rituals, forms, membership, and so on. But the quest for recognition means that more organization and more centralization might develop. When religious organizations desire tax-exempt status, or when they want to be able to perform legal marriages, standardization results. Thus, for example, Wicca was accepted as a legal religion in the United States in the mid-1980s and the Wiccan Church of Canada was formed as a non-profit religious organization in 1979 (see their website http://www.wcc.on.ca/). Also, homogenization of practice develops when groups desire a trained leadership, as is the case with some Wiccan groups.

Berger sees child rearing and career demands as also leading to routinization within Wicca. Passing rituals and stories on to children often leads to them becoming more set and less improvisational (Berger 1999: 86).

Neopagans make a great deal of use of the Internet, where individuality of expression is encouraged and where one can find information about lots of

Wiccan groups, on-line rituals, songs, Wiccan chat rooms, and so on. There is a huge variety of material available. Thus, unlike traditional religions that have relied on face-to-face contact as a way to include new people within the group, the Internet provides a whole new tool for the dissemination of information. And those who are curious can access the information anonymously. Given that many fear backlash, anonymity may be seen as desirable. Curiously, the Internet is itself, however, a standardizing force as various groups share information and practices rather than always inventing anew.

Ecofeminism

Many neopagans, including Wiccans, are part of a much larger and more diffuse Ecofeminist movement. Ecofeminism is a movement that explores the connections between the oppression of women and the oppression of nature. Ecofeminists notice that there is a traditional link between women and nature that aligns women more with nature and men more with culture (Ortner 1974). For some Ecofeminists, this link exists because women's 'nature' is different from men's 'nature', and they think women do have a different understanding of and empathy for the plight of the earth. For others, this relationship is more social, or constructed, than it is 'natural'. That is, because women have traditionally been placed on the 'nature' side of the nature/culture dichotomy, they are in a different place from which to analyze both their own oppression and the oppression of the earth. At different times in Western society, both nature and women have been seen as that which can be dominated and controlled rather than that which has autonomous identity and is good in its own right. Ecofeminists have differing views of what should be done about the plight of the earth, but all agree that we need to change our ways of thinking about both women and nature and our actions toward others—human and non-human. Ecofeminists tend to privilege an understanding of the universe as an interconnected whole, where all the parts are intimately related to one another; where nothing is unimportant or without value; and where bodies, including human bodies, are as important as, and inseparable from, human minds.

Particularly interesting to students of religion is that some Ecofeminists appeal to 'spirituality' as both a means of understanding woman and nature and as a way to change thinking and action.

> Earth-based spirituality influences Ecofeminism by informing its values. This does not mean that every Ecofeminist must worship the Goddess, perform rituals, or adopt any particular belief system . . . . What we are doing, however, is attempting to shift the values of our culture. We could describe that shift as one away from battle as our underlying cultural paradigm

and toward the cycle of birth, growth, death, and regeneration, to move away from a view of the world as made up of warring opposites toward a view that sees processes unfolding and continuously changing. (Starhawk 1989: 174)

For spiritual Ecofeminists, various spiritual or religious practices can realign our thought processes and, in turn, empower us to change our actions. 'If we believe, and experientially *know* through various practices such as meditation and holistic ritual that neither our sisters and brothers nor the rest of nature is "the other", we will not violate their being, nor our own. Ethics of mutual respect would not allow coercion or domination, such as forcing someone to give birth or to kill' (Spretnak 1982).

The earth is often symbolized as female: as Mother Earth or as Gaia (Ruether 1992). Earth in this view is a living whole. 'When this world is seen as the living body of the Goddess, there is no escape, nowhere else to go, no one to save us. This earth body itself is the terrain of our spiritual growth and development, which comes through our contact with the fullness of life inherent in the earth—with the reality of what's going on here' (Starhawk 1989: 178). Thus, we can see why there have been many interconnections between the Ecofeminist movement and various New Age groups.

For women who are seeking a spiritual/religious option that celebrates femaleness and that tries to go beyond traditional patriarchies, New Age traditions offer positive possibilities.

NOTES

1. See Starr Sered, who makes a similar comment with respect to the teachings of female dominated religions (210).
2 . There are two basic versions of the Wiccan rede. The first is a 26-couplet poem and the second is the last two lines of the first poem. The latter is the most common expression of the rede philosophy found today. See: http://www.draknetfree.com/sheathomas/concept.html for a fuller treatment of the history and usage of the rede.

REFERENCES

Anonymous. 1985. *A Course in Miracles*. 3 volumes in 1. Tiburon, CA: Foundation for Inner Peace.

Adler, Margot. 1986. *Drawing Down the Moon: Witches, Druids, Goddess-Worshippers and other Pagans in America Today*. 2nd edn. Boston: Beacon.

Berger, Helen A. 1999. *A Community of Witches: Contemporary Neo-Paganism and Witchcraft in the United States*. Columbia: University of South Carolina Press.

Budapest, Zsuzsanna. 1989. *The Holy Book of Women's Mysteries: Feminist Witchcraft, Goddess Rituals, Spellcasting, and Other Womanly Arts*. 1st Wingbow edn. Berkeley: Wingbow Press.

Burning Times. 1990. Dir. Donna Read. Canada: National Film Board.

Christ, Carol. 1979. 'Why Women Need the Goddess: Phenomenological, Psychological and Political Reflections'. *Womanspirit Rising*. Eds Carol P. Christ and Judith Plaskow. San Francisco: Harper and Row: 273–87.

———. 1997. *Rebirth of the Goddess: Finding Meaning in Feminist Spirituality*. Reading, MA: Addison-Wesley.

Eller, Cynthia. 1993. *Living in the Lap of the Goddess: The Feminist Spirituality Movement in America*. New York: Crossroad.

———. 2000. *The Myth of Matriarchal Prehistory: Why an Invented Past Won't Give Women a Future*. Boston: Beacon.

Farrar, Stewart. 1989. *What Witches Do: A Modern Coven Revealed*. 1983. Custer: Phoenix Publishing Inc.

Giddens, Anthony. 1991. *Modernity and Self-identity: Self and Society in the Later Modern Age*. Cambridge, UK: Polity Press.

Gimbutas, Maria. 1982. *The Goddesses and Gods of Old Europe, 6500–3500 BC: Myths and Cult Images*. London: Thames and Hudson.

———. 1989. *The Language of the Goddess: Unearthing the Hidden Symbols of Western Civilization*. San Francisco: Harper & Row.

Hanegraaff, Wouter J. 1996. *New Age Religion and Western Culture: Esotericism in the Mirror of Secular Thought*. Studies in the History of Religions. vol. 72. New York: E.J. Brill.

Knight, J.Z. 1987. *A State of Mind: My Story—Ramtha: The Adventure Begins*. New York: Warner Books.

Kurtz, Stanley. 1992. *All The Mothers Are One: Hindu India and the Cultural Reshaping of Psychoanalysis*. New York: Columbia University.

Ortner, Sherry. 1974. 'Is Female to Male as Nature Is to Culture?' *Woman, Culture and Society*. Eds M.Z. Rosaldo and L. Lamphere. Stanford: Stanford University Press: 67–87.

Pierrakos, Eve. 1990. *The Pathwork of Self-Transformation*. New York: Bantam Books.

Pike, Sarah M. 2001. *Earthly Bodies, Magical Selves: Contemporary Pagans and the Search for Community*. Berkeley: University of California Press.

Roberts, Jane. 1970. *The Seth Material*. Toronto: Bantam Books.

———. 1981. *The God of Jane: A Psychic Manifesto*. New York: Prentice Hall.

Ruether, Rosemary Radford. 1992. *Gaia and God: An Ecofeminist Theology of Earth Healing*. San Francisco: HarperSanFrancisco.

Savage, Candace. 2000. *Witch: The Wild Ride from Wicked to Wicca*. Vancouver: GreyStone Books.

Skutch, Robert. 1984. *Journey without Distance: The Story Behind* A Course in Miracles. Berkeley: Celestial Arts.

Spretnak, Charlene, ed. 1982. *The Politics of Women's Spirituality: Essays on the Rise of Spiritual Power within the Feminist Movement*. New York: Anchor.

———. 1991. *States of Grace: The Recovery of Meaning in the Postmodern Age*. San Francisco: HarperSanFrancisco.

Starhawk. 1979. *The Spiral Dance: A Rebirth of the Ancient Religion of the Great Goddess*. New York: Harper and Row.

———. 1982a. 'Ethics and Justice in Goddess Religion'. *The Politics of Women's Spirituality: Essays on the Rise of Spiritual Power within the Feminist Movement*. Ed. Charlene Spretnak. New York: Anchor: 415–22.

———. 1982b. *Dreaming the Dark: Magic, Sex & Politics*. Boston: Beacon.

———. 1989. 'Feminist Earth-based Spirituality and Ecofeminism'. *Healing the Wounds: The Promise of Ecofeminism*. Ed. Judith Plant. Philadelphia: New Society Publishers: 174–85.

Sered, Susan Starr. 1994. *Priestess Mother, Sacred Sister: Religions Dominated by Women*. New York: Oxford University Press.

Stone, Merlin. 1976. *When God Was a Woman*. New York: Harcourt Brace Jovanovich.

Wittig, Monique. 1985. *Les guerilleres*. Boston: Beacon.

FURTHER READING

Adler, Margot. *Drawing Down the Moon: Witches, Druids, Goddess-Worshippers and other Pagans in America Today*. 2nd edn. Boston: Beacon, 1986.

Christ, Carol. *Rebirth of the Goddess: Finding Meaning in Feminist Spirituality*. Reading, MA: Addison-Wesley, 1997.

Eller, Cynthia. *Living in the Lap of the Goddess: The Feminist Spirituality Movement in America*. New York: Crossroad, 1993.

Spretnak, Charlene, ed. *The Politics of Women's Spirituality: Essays on the Rise of Spiritual Power within the Feminist Movement*. New York: Anchor, 1982.

Starhawk. *The Spiral Dance: A Rebirth of the Ancient Religion of the Great Goddess*. New York: Harper and Row, 1979.

L'AUTRE PAROLE: A CHRISTIAN AND FEMINIST COLLECTIVE IN QUEBEC

Monique Dumais

One year after International Women's Year (1975), 5 years after the publication of the Women's *Manifeste* in Quebec and the first issue of *Québécoises Deboutte*[1] (1971), 7 years after the beginning of the Quebec Women's Liberation Front (1969), 10 years after women's admission to the study of theology in Quebec ecclesiastical schools such as Grand séminaire (1966), and 63 years after the foundation of the magazine *La Bonne Parole (The Good Word)*[2] (1913), the collective L'autre Parole was founded on 14 August 1976, in Rimouski.[3]

The L'autre Parole collective typifies Quebec religious transformation. This case study considers the social and religious context of the group's emergence, and examines its objectives and activities, its approach to theology, and its links with other feminist groups in Quebec and in other countries.

SOCIAL AND RELIGIOUS CONTEXT

Quebec society is marked by the Quiet Revolution which began around 1960. This sociopolitical phenomenon is characterized in these terms by Mason Wade (1971: 84): 'Quebec has rapidly changed from a rural agricultural society to an urban industrialized one', with accompanying integration into an educational and scientific modern world. Quebec sociologist, Guy Rocher, asserted that Quebec 'shifted very quickly from a mentality where change was perceived as an evil in itself or at least as an attack to order and harmony . . . to an attitude maybe excessively open to change'.[4]

It is recognized by all Quebec historians and sociologists that the Roman Catholic Church played a role of leadership in Quebec traditional society. This leadership was conservative and essentially male oriented, without a visible women's participation within the institution of the Church or in society itself. Women in the province of Quebec obtained the right to vote only in 1940, after more than 20 years of struggle. Bishops and priests sided with the Quebec elite and the premier, Duplessis, against this right (see Le Collectif Clio 1992). After this time, through the substantial modifications of Quebec social transformations and, in the 1960s, Vatican Council II, women's movements began to question the status quo, and to develop interventions intended to lead to new directions in the Church.

An important fact to consider in the Quebec religious domain is the very large number of nuns. Indeed, the province of Quebec was identified as holding the highest proportion of nuns in the Roman Catholic world during the decade 1940–50: 1 nun for 111 women (Denault and Levesque 1975: 45). Historian Marta Danylewycz has relevantly illustrated in *Taking the Veil: An Alternative to Marriage, Motherhood, Spinsterhood in Quebec: 1840–1920* (Danylewycz 1987) how, for women, religious life was an attractive alternative to a demanding motherhood and a not-valued spinsterhood. Nuns often had a fair amount of autonomy from the religious hierarchy and they were often innovators in such areas as education, making their own decisions about educational curriculum and methods of teaching, for example. They were, for instance, involved in developing advanced education programmes such as *le cours classique*—a humanities programme—which was offered to the girls by Les Dames de la Congrégation Notre-Dame for the first time in 1910 at Montreal. Note that a nun, Soeur Marie Laurent de Rome (Ghislaine Roquet), was the sole female member of the Royal Commission for Education in Quebec in the early 1960s (Dumais 1981).

Nevertheless, religious communities, female as well as male, are always under clerical jurisdiction: they must comply with Roman Catholic ecclesiastical or diocesan regulations. In fact, for each religious member the vow of obedience represents a real challenge for personal growth and social commitment: it implies an acceptance of submission to a person in authority and supervision by her or him. But Christians have always identified with the freedom of the resurrected Christ, which has always provided a model of liberated spontaneity and given Christians the freedom to achieve their individual and social missions even when the hierarchy of the Church might appear to desire something different (Sölle 1970; Radcliffe 2000). The Second Vatican Council (1962–5), in its recommendations, invited members to relate to others in a reciprocal fashion rather than in a hierarchical way—and religious communities in Quebec took this seriously and began to seek less hierarchical relationships among Church members, religious and clergy.

Members of religious orders and congregations and priests were historically involved in three major sectors (education, health, and social welfare). During the Quiet Revolution, those functions were recovered by the state. This new social context brought a rapid decline of memberships in active congregations and obliged these congregations to consider other avenues to express their specific missions (Belzile 2001). In terms of education, which was one of the traditional areas of work for women, for example, religious orders had to choose either to integrate with the public sector or to maintain private schools, the latter eventually proving effective principally in Quebec's major cities with large populations bases.

Over time, the number of nuns has declined and today is actually about 15,000 in Quebec, down from 40,000 in 1960, with the average age being about 74. Many of them are, however, still committed to social justice (Laurin 2002). Nicole Laurin, a sociologist who studied religious community life (1991), points out that 'the vocabulary of [women's religious] communities has changed and resembles in an astonishing way that of the left'. Indeed, religious communities realized an important socio-political turning point under the impulse of the Canadian Religious Conference[5] (*Le Devoir* 2 July 2002, B5).

L'autre Parole (The Other Word)

Women's groups mark a significant step for consciousness-raising in the Quebec Roman Catholic Church. They really allow women to establish their own territory: to discover their specific identity, to define their own task and mission, to concentrate their energies and their creativity. The development of women's groups was a way to maintain distance from patriarchal definitions of women's identity uniquely as mothers and to explore new ways of asserting their personalities as women. In 1976, four women who were deeply concerned about the study of Christian theology from a gender perspective met and began L'autre Parole (The Other Word) as a collective to provide a different way for women to experience the Word of God.

FOUNDATION

The incentive for L'autre Parole came from Monique Dumais, professor of theology and ethics at the Université du Québec à Rimouski (UQAR). She was just returning from her studies in the United States (at Harvard Divinity School and Union Theological Seminary in New York) where she had been in contact with some well-known women theologians such as Beverly W. Harrison, Rosemary Radford Ruether, Elisabeth Schüssler Fiorenza, and Letty M. Russell. In the fall 1975 semester, she agreed to teach a course on Women in Religions and Society. Drawing on her intensive experience gained in teaching the course, she discovered and decided that it was necessary to establish a network of communication among women in Quebec. She sent a letter to about 20 women in Quebec who were involved in teaching or studying theology, religious sciences, or catechetics and she very quickly received three enthusiastic answers. One of these respondents suggested a meeting, which was subsequently held on 14 August 1976, when she met with Louise Melançon, professor of theology at the Université de Sherbrooke; Bibianne Beauregard, studying theology at the same university; and Marie-Andrée Roy, studying theology at the Université de Montréal.

After one day of discussion, they decided to form a collective under the name L'autre Parole, inspired by Annie Leclerc's book, *Parole de femme* (1974). The group thought it very important that women express themselves in their own words—words that related to their own experiences. These women then established the following as an initial global objective: to integrate women's experiences into theological writings and also into the Church's activities. Principal aims were expressed in the first issue of their newsletter: 'at the research level, to rebuild theological discourses in taking into account women's experiences, and at the action level, to undertake steps in order to obtain a complete women's participation in the Church' (September 1976, 2).

Activities
During the year 1976/7, the co-founders easily recruited other women from Montréal, Sherbrooke, and Rimouski. And in the following years, women from Quebec City and recently some from Gatineau have joined the collective. Over the past 26 years, the membership of L'autre Parole has not been allowed to grow above 60. In fact, 'small is beautiful'—and also very effective. Reflections, analysis, writing, reactions to official Church documents, and contacts with other feminist groups have been the focus of their gatherings.

Reflection Groups
Solidarity is the basis of any feminist group, and for L'autre Parole it quickly became evident that women should combine forces and discover the dynamism of a collective search to question theological scientific discourses and ecclesiastical practices. Through the process of forming reflection groups L'autre Parole was able to draw on what is at the heart of women's lives and experiences as fertile material for their writings.

Seven reflection groups involving three to ten women each—in Gatineau, Montréal (three groups), Québec, Sherbrooke, and Rimouski—allow about 50 women to let new 'other' words emerge in feminist theologies and to undertake collective action (*L'autre Parole* no. 92, Winter 2002). A coordinating committee with representatives from each reflection group meets about four to five times a year to facilitate a network of thoughts and actions. The collective functions on a democratic basis, as its designation suggests, without any elected person as president or director.

A Magazine
L'autre Parole is also the name of the group's publication, which publishes quarterly, one issue for each season. It started in September 1976 as a modest

newsletter of only four pages (one folded 8-by-14-inch sheet), and then four pages were added to each issue until, by the 1980s, the full-fledged magazine boasted 28 pages. Now, regular issues have 44 pages and special ones offer more (no. 72, for the twentieth anniversary colloquium, *Une EKKLÈSIA manifeste,* was 88 pages; no. 92, for the twenty-fifth anniversary colloquium, was 64 pages). The appearance gradually improved; now with a coloured rigid cover, it is published in a computerized format, with relevant drawings, and, as a tribute to its handcrafted origin, a different colour of ink is used for each issue.

The magazine offers an interesting diversity of themes. One issue is devoted to the material produced during the annual colloquium; the one for the summer period gives reading suggestions, and discusses culture, including movies, art, gardening, and cooking. The two other issues feature changing themes, for instance: nuns (no. 14, March 1981); the Spirit (no. 15, June 1981); abortion (no. 17, April 1982 and no. 33, March 1987); women and power in the Church (no. 24, May 1984); women's ordination (no. 43, September 1989); thealogy—that is, female language for and images of God (no. 51, September 1991); Quebec women and the future of Quebec (no. 49, March 1991); feminist ecology (no. 74, Summer 1997); Christa—imaging the Christ as female (no. 76, Winter 1998); spiritualities and feminists in dialogue (no. 88, Winter 2001); the arts and women's spirituality (no. 89, Spring 2001).

It is clear that in *L'autre Parole* women are trying to reflect upon theological and Church issues as well as upon social ones. The members of the collective consider their participation in society to be linked to their expressions of faith.

Collective Actions

A major event each year is the organization of the colloquium, which is exclusively for members of L'autre Parole. (Other feminist religious groups are invited to special festivities, such as the twentieth anniversary, or for specific purposes such as the 2000 World March of Women.) The annual colloquium is an intense time for members to reflect together upon a specific topic using feminist readings of the Christian tradition. The theme of the first colloquium, held in August 1978 in Rimouski, was 'women's body and the Church'. It was an opportunity to explore the main obstacle to women in the Church—their bodies, which are perceived as impure sexual objects, keeping them out of any ecclesiastical order.

Other colloquia dealt with L'autre Parole's goals, a rewriting of the Beatitudes (see Study Questions), texts from Genesis, feminist spirituality, ecology, women-church (a church movement parallel to the official Church that takes women and their experiences seriously), Christa, and other relevant topics. For the 2002 colloquium, the chosen topic is a study of women prostitutes in order to discover and acknowledge solidarity and sisterhood with them. The 2003 colloquium focuses on the creation of new feminist rituals; the 2004 colloquium is oriented to women and Quebec politics.

L'autre Parole uses other means to reach public consciousness. For instance, the collective has published massive petitions in newspapers in reaction to significant events. This was the case when Theresa Kane, an American nun, following her request for the acknowledgement of equality for women and men in the Church, was simply blessed and dismissed by Pope John Paul II on his visit to the US in November 1979. At the prompting of L'autre Parole, 500 signatures were gathered and published in *Le Devoir* to support her act. In January 1996, the collective published an article to denounce the definitive refusal of women's ordination by Rome (*Le Devoir* 7 January 1996: A7). Another way to establish connection with a larger public has been to organize rituals. Often planned and presented before Christmas and during the Holy Week, these rituals are structured to highlight women's music and writings and they include use of new symbols meaningful for women. They also give participants the opportunity to experiment with innovative prayers, such as a Magnificat expressed through the five senses (Joubert 1989: 206–9). These rituals are usually held in churches to manifest that women are reappropriating their space.The World March of Women in 2000 offered an excellent opportunity for L'autre Parole to show its openness to many spiritualities. That year the group was in contact with women of many different religions (Baha'i, Buddhism, Judaism, Christianity, Wicca, Voodoo, Hinduism, Indigenous religions, Islam). The colloquium that year was a magnificent celebration that highlighted diverse religious rites. In October 2000 a larger event focusing on women's diverse spiritualities drew an audience of about 250.

Publication of books by some members of the collective, for example, *Souffles de femmes* (Dumais and Roy 1989) and *Mémoires d'elles* (Roy and Lafortune 1999), are another means of communicating the work of the group.

Relationships with Other Women's Groups

The collective L'autre Parole is also determined to develop relationships and solidarity with other feminist groups in Quebec and in other parts of the world. The group Femmes et Ministères (Women and Ministries) emerged in 1982 as an autonomous network of women involved in Church structures such as diocesan offices; members of parish teams; and also women theologians teaching pastoral theologies. The group focuses on sharing their work and stories in order to bring about changes that seek to assert their autonomy in relationships with the Roman Catholic Church (*La Gazette des Femmes* July–August 1984: 14–18).

Femmes et Ministères is especially well known because of a sociological study the group initiated to provide a portrait of women involved in the Quebec Church. This work was published under the title *Les soutanes roses (The Pink Cassocks)* (Bélanger 1988). In 1995 the group produced *Voix de femmes, voies de passage* to analyze that research and to give some perspectives on how the Church is more diverse than the picture painted by the Roman Catholic hierarchy. They directly question some positions of the Roman Catholic hierarchy. They principally emphasize the concept of *reception,* or passing on the tradition, which originated with the first Christian churches and was reinstated by the Second Vatican Council. As a process of communion, reception entails the whole People of God—women as well as men—to receive, interpret, and proclaim the Good News.

Women in the Church in Quebec who are interested in joining with other women with similar concerns have had many options, both within the province and in the Canadian context. Le Réseau oecuménique des femmes du Québec/Quebec Women's Ecumenical Network is another group that was formed in the 1990s. Its purpose is to give women of various Christian denominations a forum to work together on the urgent issues facing them. Nuns also created in 1977 the Association des Religieuses pour la Promotion des Femmes at the incentive of the Canadian Religious Conference.

L'autre Parole is an autonomous group, but it is also well connected to other groups that are concerned with the status and roles of women in both Church and society. For example, L'autre Parole is a member of Fédération des femmes du Québec (FFQ). Two international groups with whom L'autre Parole is involved are Femmes et Hommes dans l'Église, based in Brussels, Belgium and Paris, France, and the Groupe Orsay, a group of Protestant women in Paris. These two groups focus on changes in religions and their goals are close to those of L'autre Parole. Some members of the collective travelling in France attended the Groupe Orsay conference and presented papers.

INNOVATION: REWRITING THROUGH WOMEN'S EXPERIENCE

The most interesting process that L'autre Parole has undertaken is to rewrite some biblical and Church texts. The process involves workshops of two to four women each, taking one of the texts and examining its original patriarchal context and trying to rewrite sections to incorporate women's experiences. Mary Daly describes this radical approach:

> The method of liberation, then involves a *castrating* of language and images that reflect and perpetuate the structures of a sexist world. It castrates precisely

in the sense of cutting away the phallocentric value system imposed by patriarchy, in its subtle as well as in its more manifest expressions. (Daly 1985: 9)

These workshops have produced texts that have found widespread positive response as something new and exciting. Work on the Beatitudes (Luke 6: 20–6), and on Genesis texts (Genesis, chapters 1 and 2), for instance, was especially successful. These texts are used and reproduced by other feminist groups in their documents.

Feminist rewriting is a process that uses and is grounded in women's experiences. In feminist theology women's experience acts as a source and norm (Young 1990: 49–69) that orients the whole enterprise of interpreting the Word of God. Then, concrete experiences are taken and reflected upon in order to perceive their meaning for women's condition and for the Christian tradition. The point is that the Word of God receives an interpretation liberated from its patriarchal context and open to all human experiences. In L'autre Parole, the collective rewriting allows women to discover a sense of freedom and dynamism as they work together. This process of rewriting involves 'a shift from an androcentric to a feminist paradigm' (Fiorenza 1983: xxi). Several American women theologians—Elisabeth Schüssler Fiorenza, Mary Daly, Rosemary Radford Ruether, Letty M. Russell—were important guides in these feminist critical hermeneutics. Some women theologians writing in French— for example, France Quéré and Elisabeth J. Lacelle, who were not part of the collective—inspired its feminist reflections.

CONCLUSION

The women of L'autre Parole face important challenges: first, reaching the institutional Church; second, reaching other feminists; finally, grappling with the ways in which they themselves have been changed by their collective work. Among Canadian bishops that the collective has tried to connect with, Quebec bishops have proven themselves to be the most open-minded. In March 1986 they organized a large conference, involving bishops and representatives of women's groups, to point out and analyze the main difficult issues concerning women and the Church. However, then as always, their necessary relationship with Rome obliged clerical members to maintain a conservative attitude.

As far as the collective reaching other feminist groups, the challenge is that to many feminists, any organization with a religious aspect is at first glance suspicious; they see Christianity as a major obstacle to women's autonomy and equality. Women of L'autre Parole have to convey the necessity of questioning Christian churches from inside.

Women of the collective continue to struggle to find ways to empower women within a Christian context. Their quest for a better world is not without suffering; the strength of resurrection in Christ (Phil. 3:10) becomes their main dynamic force.

STUDY QUESTIONS

1. What factors influence women's lives in the Roman Catholic Church in Quebec and how have these changed over the last 50 years?
2. What social circumstances led to the emergence of L'autre Parole?
3. What are the objectives of L'autre Parole and how are they realized?
4. Discuss some of the themes that L'autre Parole has explored.
5. How would you describe the process employed by L'autre Parole in rewriting biblical texts?
6. Which part of the following rewriting of Beatitudes strikes you as the most significant for a woman involved in the Christian Church? Why?

Beatitudes

Happy are those women whose heart is not hardened
because they listen to women and to God.
Alas for those men and women who establish
and perpetuate women's poverty, because they betray God
in not acknowledging social and economic value for domestic work,
in withholding priesthood in the Roman Catholic Church
from women on the account of their sex,
in keeping women out of places where values
that govern their lives are fabricated.

Happy are the soft and aggressive women inhabited
by a *will to live:*
you disarm your oppressors in the hope
of reconciliation.
Alas for those who sow death;
hate and violence you will reap.

Happy are those women who, in becoming aware of
their oppressions are liberating themselves in a word
of forgiveness.
Alas for those women for whom to forgive is to give up.

Happy are those women who are working
to knead the bread of autonomy,

of equality,
of solidarity,
together, they will feed the earth.
Alas for those who are easily satisfied
with crumbs falling from the sacred table.
They paralyse Church growth.

Happy are those women who scream, who shriek
and squall to tear away at the silence of death,
Alas for those men and women who snivel
and grumble without touching the centre
of their oppressions.

Happy are these women audaciously taken
by the Gospel of Jesus Christ who have
the courage to be faithful more than in thought
and in word, but truly in deeds.
Alas for those women who dissociate thoughts,
heart and acts, because they tarnish the light
from the Gospel.
Alas for those women who are staying quiet to be in peace
because they maintain oppression.

Happy are those victims of patriarchal power
who find in the violence they experience
strength to build up peace.

Happy are you women scoffed because
of your speech;
by your tenacity, you build your liberation.
Alas for you who will have been
seduced by a discourse that will dispossess you
from the meaning of your struggle.

     —Translation from French by Monique Dumais

NOTES

1. A feminist magazine. The title means: Quebec women standing up! *Debouttes* is an unusual feminization of an adverb *debout*.

2. *La Bonne Parole* is a 'feminine magazine', according to the first definition given by its women promoters; it was published from 1913 to 1958.

3.   Rimouski is a small town of about 35,000 inhabitants, 600 kilometres east of Montreal.
4.   Translations into English are the author's.
5.   The Canadian Religious Conference is an organization representing all Canadian Roman
     Catholic men and women in religious orders and congregations.

REFERENCES

Baroni, Lise, Yvonne Bergeron, Pierrette Daviau, and Micheline Laguë. 1995. *Voix de Femmes,
     Voies de Passage: Pratiques Pastorales et Enjeux Ecclésiaux.* Montreal: Paulines.
Bélanger, Sarah. 1988. *Les Soutanes Roses: Portrait du Personnel Pastoral Féminin au Québec.*
     Montreal: Bellarmin.
Belzile, Louis.1999. *La Route des Ferventes. Un livre-audio,* Radio-Canada—Fides. 2001.
Caron, Anita, Marie Gratton, Agathe Lafortune, and Marie-Andrée Roy in collaboration with
     Nadya Ladouceur and Patrick Snyder. *Les Rapports Homme-Femme dans l'Église Catholique:
     Perceptions, Constats, Alternatives.* Montreal: UQAM. Les Cahiers de l'IREF, no 4.
Collectif Clio, Le. 1992. *L'histoire des Femmes au Québec depuis Quatre Siècles.* Montreal: Le Jour;
     Montreal, *édition entièrement revue et mise à jour.*
Daly, Mary. 1985. *Beyond God the Father: Toward a Philosophy of Women's Liberation.* 1973. With
     an original introduction by the author. Boston: Beacon.
Danylewycz, Marta. 1987. *Taking the Veil: An Alternative to Marriage, Motherhood, Spinsterhood
     in Quebec: 1840–1920.* Toronto: McClelland & Stewart.
Daviau, Pierrette, in collaboration with Jacynthe Fortin. 2000. *Projets de Femmes: Église en Projet.
     Jalons d'analyse Sociopastorale.* Montreal: Paulines.
Denault, Bernard, and Benoît Lévesque. 1975. *Éléments pour une Sociologie des Communautés
     Religieuses au Québec.* Montreal: Les Presses de l'Université de Montréal et de l'Université de
     Sherbrooke.
Dumais, Monique. 1979. 'La théologie peut-elle être du genre feminin?' *La Femme et la Religion
     au Canada Français: un Fait Socio-culturel.* Ed. Élisabeth Lacelle. Montreal: Bellarmin:
     111–26.
———. 1981. 'Les Religieuses, Leur Contribution à la Société Québécoise'. *Canadian Women's
     Studies/Les Cahiers de la Femme* 3: 18–20.
———. 1989. '*Témoignage d'un Groupe de Femmes: de l'émergence d'une Autre Parole Chez les
     Femmes Chrétiennes et Féministes*'. Ed. Isabelle Lasvergnas. *A/encrages féministes* Montreal:
     Université du Québec à Montréal. Montreal. GIERF, Cahiers de recherche: 145–52.
———, and Marie-Andrée Roy, eds. 1989. *Souffles de Femmes: Lectures Féministes de la Religion.*
     Montreal: Éditions Paulines.
Fiorenza, Elisabeth Schüssler. 1983. *In Memory of Her: A Feminist Theological Reconstruction of
     Christian Origins.* New York: Crossroad.
Joubert, Denyse. 1989. 'Mon âme exalte le Seigneur'. *Souffles de femmes: Lectures féministes de la
     religion.* Eds Monique Dumais and Marie-Andrée Roy. Montréal: Éditions Paulines: 206–9.

Lacelle, Élisabeth J., ed. 1979. *La Femme et la Religion au Canada Français: Un Fait Socio-culturel.* Montreal: Bellarmin.

———, ed. 1983. *La Femme, Son Corps et la Religion: Approches Pluridisciplinaires.* Montreal: Bellarmin.

Laurin, Nicole, Danielle Juteau, and Lorraine Duchesne. 1991. *À la Recherche d'un Monde Oublié: Les Communautés Religieuses de Femmes au Québec de 1900 à 1970.* Montreal: Le Jour.

———. 2002. 'Quel Avenir pour les Religieuses du Québec?' *Relations* 677: 30–4.

L'autre Parole. September 1976 to Present (quarterly). Address: C.P. 393, Succursale C, Montréal H2L 4K3.

Leclerc, Annie. 1974. *Parole de femme.* Paris: Grasset.

Quéré, France. 1982. *Les Femmes de l'Évangile.* Paris: Seuil.

Radcliffe, Timothy, o.p. 2000. *Je Vous Appelle Amis.* Paris: La Croix—Cerf: 117–147.

Rocher, Guy. *Le Québec en Mutation.* Montreal: HMH/Hurtubise.

Roy, Marie-Andrée, and Agathe Lafortune, eds. 1999. *Mémoires d'elles: Fragments de Vies et Spiritualités de Femmes.* Montreal: Médiaspaul.

———. 2001. 'Les Femmes, le Féminisme et la religion'. *L'étude de la Religion au Québec: Bilan et Prospective.* Eds Jean-Marc Larouche, and Guy Ménard. Quebec: Les Presses de l'Université Laval; Quebec, Corporation Canadienne des Sciences Religieuses/Canadian Corporation for Studies in Religion: 343–59.

Ruether, Rosemary Radford. 1974. *Religion and Sexism: Images of Woman in the Jewish and Christian Traditions.* New York: Simon and Schuster.

Sölle, Dorothee. 1970. *Beyond Mere Obedience.* Minneapolis: Augsburg.

Veillette, Denise, ed. 1995. *Femmes et Religions. Quebec:* Les Presses de l'Université Laval; Quebec, Corporation Canadienne des Sciences Religieuses/Canadian Corporation for Studies in Religion.

Wade, Mason. 1964. *The French-Canadian Outlook.* 1971. Toronto: McClelland and Stewart Ltd.

Young, Pamela Dickey. 1990. *Feminist Theology/Christian Theology: In Search of Method.* Minneapolis: Fortress.

FURTHER READING

Dumais, Monique, and Marie-Andrée Roy, eds. *Souffles de Femmes: Lectures Féministes de la Religion.* Montréal: Éditions Paulines, 1989.

Lacelle, Élisabeth J., ed. *La Femme et la Religion au Canada Français: Un Fait Socio-culturel.* Montréal: Bellarmin, 1979.

Roy, Marie-Andrée. *Les ouvrières de Dieu.* Montréal, Médiaspaul, 1996.

Veillette, Denise, ed. *Femmes et Religions.* Québec: Les Presses de l'Université Laval; Québec, Corporation Canadienne des Sciences Religieuses/Canadian Corporation for Studies in Religion, 1995.

≈⁀

TWO MUSLIM WOMEN IN NORTH AMERICA

L. Clarke

AISHA H.L. ADAWIYA

Muslims made up an unknown percentage of Africans enslaved in the New World. African-American Islam was subsequently reborn in the early twentieth century through the race-conscious, heterodox movements of the Moorish Science Temple and Nation of Islam. In the past few decades, however, most African-American Muslims have been integrated into orthodox Islam. Gender relations have always been a focus of African-American Islam, since the movement has sought to mend social disruption by strengthening the family unit.

Aisha H.L. Adawiya is coordinator of Islamic input for the Preservation of the Black Religious Heritage Documentation Project at the Schomburg Center for Research in Black Culture, located in Harlem in New York City. The grand-mother of two is also founding director of Women in Islam (www.womenin-islam.org), an advocacy and education organization focused on 'human rights and social justice'. Dressed in a long robe and with a voluminous white scarf draped around her head and shoulders, she speaks with the emphasis and con-fidence of a long-time community activist.

Aisha is a convert who presents her life as the story of her journey to Islam. Like many Black converts of the turbulent 1950s and 1960s, she remembers an early discontent with Christianity and a yearning for something more mean-ingful. Why, she would ask herself, were many of those who inflicted 'gross injustices' on African-Americans regarded as 'upstanding citizens and good Christians in the community'? 'I was,' she says, 'in search of something spiri-tual, but I didn't know what'. In 1961, Aisha left the small Alabama town of her childhood for New York City. Malcolm X was on the scene. 'I was fasci-nated by the social critique of Malcolm X and very much attracted to the teach-ings on a political level. People were looking for alternative ways to live their lives, and I was part of that.' She immediately gravitated toward the emerging health-food movement and began to explore various spiritual paths, including New Age spirituality, Buddhism, and Sufism. And then she found her first Qurán, 'on the bottom shelf in an occult store in Greenwich Village'.

By the time Aisha walked into the Islamic Center of New York one day in 1971 with the intention of uttering the profession of faith (shahádah), 'I was already Muslim; that was just a formality'. One of the things she remembers as having attracted her to Islam was 'the position of women'. The other was 'the right to self-defence' (an echo, apparently, of the early, nationalist stage of the African-American Islamic movement which asserted that it was legitimate to respond to direct assaults on the community).

She now took a new, non-slave name, an experience she describes as 'empowering and liberating'. 'Who', she asked herself, 'do I want to be like?' She chose 'Aisha', after the wife of the Prophet, and 'al-Adawiya', the tribal name of Rábi'ah, the famous female mystic of early Islam. 'These were examples for me of two powerful women within the Muslim tradition. Aisha was a scholar and stateswoman, and Rábi'ah was a powerful spiritual force in her own right. No one said to them, "You can't do that, it's not a woman's place."'

It was nevertheless difficult, Aisha says, to find books about the contributions of women to Islam, 'and we still need to foster more Muslim woman writers on these issues'. Muslim women, in her view, are engaged in a struggle to reclaim the rightful place they once owned, for which 'the blueprint is the example of the Prophet [Muhammad] and the early community around him'. Stereotypes about women coming from 'negative texts' should be 'dismantled, using the Qurán, hadíth, and other scholarly works'. The laws of marriage and divorce 'need to be revisited, and women must have input to redress abuses that proliferate due to ignorance and un-Islamic cultural practices'.

The key to restoring woman to her rightful place and promoting social justice is, in Aisha's view, education. 'Women have to understand what their rights and responsibilities in marriage are. In fact, both women and men have to be educated. Women raise up nations, both girls and boys, and once they are empowered with knowledge of Islam, they will make different choices for themselves and their families. Boys and girls will understand. We won't have tyrannical husbands and fathers'.

Though she sees great hope in members of the younger generation who are educating themselves about their religion, Aisha is vexed by woman-negative practices in the Muslim community. She reports that women are forbidden to enter some mosques, even in New York City, or that when they enter they become 'non-people'. 'Suddenly you are met with this barrier. In a town meeting at the largest mosque in New York City addressing the backlash after 11 September 2001, two woman photographers were not allowed to approach the front of the mosque to photograph the event until the women in the mosque protested. This is retrogressive! It is Islamic to insist that you will enter the *masjid* (mosque). Don't take no for an answer. Just go in.'

Aisha sees restoration of the rightful position of women as central to the success of Islam, or indeed of any civilization: 'Women are really the primary transmitters of ideology and culture in nations, and the power resides in the woman to develop the nation. Abuse and neglect of women lead to the destruction of nations.' Islam, in Aisha's view, originally and exceptionally recognized this truth. 'Allah gave us the unique experience of childbirth and mothering, and therein lies the power, and Islam creates an environment that can best foster that process of nation building. Although we are presently suffering from the abuse of men and women in Muslim society, we are beginning to understand how women around the Prophet were supported in their special roles'.

Aisha herself often negotiates in her statements between liberal and more conservative views. The original impetus in 1992 for her founding Women in Islam was the issue of rape camps in Bosnia. She reports some friction with 'feminists' at that time, some of whom thought 'Islam would have no use for women who were victims of rape and no longer virgins'. Abortion on demand was also an important issue for the feminist movement at that time. They did not realize, Aisha says, that from the Islamic perspective, rape victims are unwilling participants and are therefore innocent, and that abortion is allowed by Islam if there is a threat to the woman's life. But Aisha also points out that Black women who were raped during slavery did not abort their children, 'so there may be another option—to let them grow up to defend their mothers, families, and nation'.

Asked about fundamentalism, Aisha retorts, 'I do not use the word *fundamentalist*; I use the term *fanatic*'. She mentions 'gross abuses' against women in the Muslim world, including so-called honour killings. 'These are patently against Islam. It is outrageous to say them in the same breath'. She does not, however, condemn recent attempts to restore *Sharíah* law in some parts of Nigeria, only noting the injustice of trying crimes committed before Sharíah law was put in place. At the time of this writing in November 2002, the Miss World pageant had to be moved from Nigeria to London when some of the contestants left because a local woman was condemned by the Sharíah court to be stoned for fornication, and then riots ensued after a Nigerian journalist suggested that the Prophet might have chosen Miss World as one of his wives. While disapproving of these actions, Aisha is also critical of 'the insistence of the West on imposing the most decadent aspects of its culture on other people'. Does the Miss World pageant, she asks, 'elevate anyone in a spiritual way?'

Polygyny is described by Aisha as 'a valid institution, permissible under certain conditions'. 'It has nothing to do with men's sexual desires', she believes. Rather, if we look at the personal life of the Prophet Muhammad, we see that 'most of his wives were older women, demonstrating that polygyny is solely for the protection of women, as it is women's right to have a family, caring, and maintenance'.

As a Muslim African-American, Aisha is actively involved in building coalitions with other faiths and social justice movements. Especially after September 11th, she says, 'stereotypes and negative images abound', but this is also a 'wonderful time to be having conversations about the responsibility of faiths to promote social justice'. Referring to the war against Iraq, she adds: 'Women are the ones who have the children who go to war. And therefore women have the first right to protest against war'.

SHAHNÁZ

Another influence that has flowed into North American Islam is the experience of the immigrants. Muslims from the Middle East and Europe began to arrive in the United States and Canada as early as the mid-1800s, but most of the immigrant population dates from the last half of the twentieth century. This second wave is much more diverse than the first, hailing from, among other areas, the Subcontinent, Malaysia, Iran, and North Africa. Muslim immigrants—like the convert population, including African-Americans—must negotiate between their own religious values and those of the host society. The most sensitive issue by far is that of the position of women. How does one fit Islamic gender ideals into North American society?

'Shahnáz' (a pseudonym) is a businesswoman in her early fifties and a resident of Montreal, Quebec. She is an active member of the Canadian Council for Muslim Women, a long-standing national organization dedicated to the articulation of a liberal Islam and the active role of women within it.

Shahnáz immigrated to Canada with her husband in the 1970s from Pakistan, just as that country was plunged into the civil war that resulted in the birth of Bangladesh. The family was forced to flee; but Shahnáz still remembers the life of her upper-class family as somewhat idyllic. She attended a coeducational, English-language school, which included not only Sunnites and Shiites, but also Ismailis, Christians, and Hindus. There was, she recalls, 'no friction'; 'only when I came [to Canada] did I notice that this and that person is Muslim'.

Nor was it felt that the position of women was a problem requiring discussion. There was no feeling that women should be segregated or cover their hair, or indeed any consciousness that this was an issue at all, though cultural norms did require that each drape a diaphanous scarf over her head in religious gatherings. There was, Shahnáz says, 'no talk of women and their rights; we already *had* our rights'. The families of the community would gather in the local sports club, where the women also enjoyed sports of various kinds. The sports tradition continues in the family; one of Shahnáz's daughters is quarterback of the first women's football team in the province of Québec.

Shahnáz remembers her mother as somewhat reserved. Her father was the stronger figure; he was, she says, 'open', a community activist who taught her that 'you don't adapt to Islam, Islam adapts to you'. He nevertheless believed in marriage at a young age. This had the advantage, he thought, of allowing the wife to 'adjust to conjugal duties' and the couple to 'grow up together'. ('He was', Shahnáz remarks half-jokingly, 'wrong'.) She was married at the age of seventeen to a member of her set, someone she had met in the club. The proposal was initiated by the man's parents, at his request.

Shahnáz was brought up in an observant household, but this appears to have involved a natural religiosity quite different from the highly conscious, emphatic style of Islam she would encounter in Canada. It is difficult to say whether the religious awareness of the North American Muslim community had been sharpened by the experience of living as a minority, or was merely part of the late- twentieth-century revival of Islam worldwide. Whatever the case, it deeply affected Shahnáz. Her experience was not so much one of fitting Islamic ideals into North America as of consciously forming, for the first time, her identity as a Muslim woman.

She began to purposefully construct for herself, and is still constructing, a religious world view. Before emigrating, she used to read the Arabic words of the Qurán, as a good number of Muslims in the world do, without understanding, as a kind of incantation; 'I did not understand one word; but in Canada, I read the Qurán for the first time with meaning'. She embarked on a programme of reading in English. Her reading material included items such as the liberal-leaning translation of the Qurán by the famous Jewish convert Muhammad Asad; writings of the conservative Indo-Pakistani thinker Mawláná Mawdúdí; and the multi-ethnic, liberationist Muslim women's magazine *Azizah*, published in Atlanta, Georgia (www.azizahmagazine.com).

Remembering that in her vanished life in former East Pakistan, '*hijáb* was not even considered a part of faith', she adds, somewhat hesitantly, 'but maybe we were wrong'. Having always dressed 'modestly and conservatively', she made the pilgrimage to Makkah in 1997, and thereafter began herself to veil. Her *hijáb* consists of modest, rather chic, Western dress—long sleeves, skirt to the ankle—with matching scarves. Shahnáz attributes her veiling partly to the influence of 'young people around me', especially her beloved niece (also active in the CCMW), whom she describes as 'courageous' in her commitment to religion. She nevertheless believes that while the standard of dress demanded by the Qurán is 'modesty' only, it is up to each believer to interpret that standard as she wishes, 'according to her strength'.

Like Aisha, Shahnáz appears to negotiate between liberal views and more conservative standards she believes to be dictated by Islam and the Qurán. Man and woman, she says, are equal; 'the Qurán tells us that they are created equal, one for the other'. But males are 'given a bit more responsibility, some extra duties' (an apparent acknowledgement of the famous statement in Qurán 4:34 that men are 'set over' women since they are required to support them). In Shahnáz's view, however, this male responsibility is conditional: 'The man must provide for the woman [only] if she cannot provide for herself'. A woman can be a head of state if she is qualified, but 'she already has enough burden [since] her most important duty is to bring up children to be good citizens'. As for polygamy, Shahnáz finds that men are 'naturally polygamous'. The Qurán, she thinks, steps in to regulate and minimize this tendency.

Divorce in Islam has, according to Shahnáz, been 'misinterpreted'. For example, the man's pronouncing the formula of divorce three times in quick succession does not, in her view, actually lead to valid dissolution. *Sharíah*, she insists, requires that divorce finally take place only after three declarations, each separated by a 'waiting period' of three menstrual cycles. This for Shahnáz is yet another indication that Islam is 'a logical religion', since the waiting period allows anger to cool. Inspired, apparently, by the *hadíth* statement that 'God hates divorce', Shahnáz states that men do need some grounds for divorce. Women, she thinks, also have the right to divorce; when pressed on this question, she describes the *khul'* divorce—the divorce in which the man agrees to release the woman in return for her giving up her dower.

Like many Muslims, including probably most Muslims in the West, Shahnáz's views on the problematic issue of divorce reflect reformist ideas and reformed law more than they do the standards of the classic law. (That the triple divorce is not effective, for instance, is a reformist view, which has been passed into law by many Muslim states.) She is apparently unaware of the extent to which male prerogative actually rules the law and of the continuing struggle in the Muslim world to attenuate that prerogative—probably because among the people she knows now in Canada and those she once knew in East Pakistan, social standards did not allow that prerogative free rein.

Shahnáz points to the dower as evidence of Islam's care for women. She recounts that her husband had promised her a large sum when he married her overseas, which grew even larger when they came to Canada, due to the rule that dower is payable in local currency. He did well enough in his shipping business (in which Shahnáz is a working partner) that he was finally able to settle the debt by giving her the very substantial house in which they now live. 'It is her house,' jokes her husband. 'She could throw me out if she wanted!'

Both Shahnáz and her husband are perplexed by the fundamentalism on the rise in the Muslim world today. They seem hurt by the media's focus on a version of Islam they themselves find strange, and they are anxious to dispel that image. They are especially insistent that Islam gives freedom and respect to women, and angry against groups such as the Táliban they consider to have betrayed Islamic ideals. 'One should not', cautions Shahnáz, 'judge religion by the acts of its followers'.

STUDY QUESTIONS

1. What similarities and differences do you see between Aisha's and Shahnáz's views of Islam?
2. What did you learn about their views of fundamentalism, and how does this relate to other things you have learned or read?
3. What issues do Aisha and Shahnáz bring up concerning Sharíah (Islamic law), and how do they deal with those issues?
4. How do Aisha's and Shahnáz's views differ, or how are they similar, to those of other Muslim women you have met, including your classmates?

FURTHER READING

Aswad, Barbara C., and Barbara Bilgé. *Family and Gender among American Muslims: Issues Facing Middle Eastern Immigrants and their Descendants.* Philadelphia: Temple University Press, 1996.

Bakhtiyar, Laleh. *Sufi Women of America: Angels in the Making.* Chicago: Institute for Traditional Psychoethics and Guidance/KAZI, 1996.

Hollick, Julian Crandall, prod. *Islam in America: Black Muslims: The Other Face of Eve,* cassette 6. Audiocassette. Littleton, MA: Independent Broadcasting Associates, 1984.

Khan, Shanaz. *Aversion and Desire: Negotiating Muslim Female Identity in the Diaspora.* Toronto: Women's Press, 2002.

McCloud, Beverly. 'A Method for the Study of Islam in America through the Narratives of African American Muslim Women'. PhD dissertation, Temple University, 1993.

Tate, Sonsyrea. *Little X: Growing Up in the Nation of Islam.* San Francisco: HarperSanFrancisco, 1997.

Under One Sky: Arab Women in North America Talk about the Hijab. Dir. Jennifer Kawaya. 40 min. VHS. Montreal, PQ: National Film Board of Canada, 1999.

Waugh, Earle, Sharon McIrvin Abu-Laban, and Regula Burckhardt Qureshi, eds. *Muslim Families in North America.* Edmonton, Canada: University of Alberta Press, 1991.

Webb, Gisela, ed. *Windows of Faith: Muslim Women Scholar-Activists in North America.* Syracuse, NY: Syracuse University Press, 2000.

INDEX